COLLINS FIELD GUIDE

INSECTS

OF BRITAIN & NORTHERN EUROPE

COLLINS FIELD GUIDE

INSECTS

OF BRITAIN & NORTHERN EUROPE

3rd Edition

MICHAEL CHINERY

Illustrated by

Gordon Riley
Denys Ovenden
Brian Hargreaves

Collins

HarperCollins*Publishers*
77–85 Fulham Palace Road
London W6 8JB

First Edition 1972
Second Edition 1976
Third Edition 1993

16 18 20 19 17 15

15 14 13 12 11

ISBN-13 978 0 00 219918 6
ISBN-10 0 00 219918 1

1006616409

Printed & bound in China

Contents

Preface to the Third Edition

The extensive changes that have taken place in the taxonomy and nomenclature of insects during the twenty years since this Field Guide first appeared have necessitated major revision of most of the sections, and while carrying out such revision I have taken the opportunity to include much new ecological and behavioural material resulting from my insect-watching adventures in many parts of Europe.

I have drawn information from a great many sources during the preparation of this guide and have much pleasure in thanking all those friends and acquaintances, notably many past and present staff at the Natural History Museum in London, who have made helpful comments and suggestions and who have pointed me towards the many publications and collections that I have consulted during the original writing and the various revisions of the book. I am particularly grateful to my three colleagues – Brian Hargreaves, Denys Ovenden and Gordon Riley – for the meticulous way in which they have drawn and painted the insects, and I would like to re-iterate my thanks to my long-standing friend Denys Ovenden for his enthusiasm and encouragement right from the start of the project over a quarter of a century ago! Frederick Warne & Co. kindly allowed me to base my key to the families of Heteroptera on that which appears in *Land and Water Bugs of the British Isles* by Southwood and Leston. I am also indebted to the Royal Entomological Society of London for permission to use and adapt the key to the families of stoneflies that appears in *Handbooks for the Identification of British Insects Vol. I Part 6* and the key to the Caraboidea that appears in *Handbooks for the Identification of British Insects Vol. IV Part 1*. Dr Ian McLean gave me much valuable help with the key to the families of Diptera.

I hope that the book will continue to be of value to anyone with an interest in insects and that readers will continue to send in their comments and suggestions for improving the book and keeping it up-to-date.

Michael Chinery
Hundon, Suffolk, 1993

How to Use this Book

The **text** provides a general introduction to entomology and the classification of insects, and this is followed, on pages 38–44, by a key to the orders of insects occurring in Europe. By following the instructions at the beginning of the key, it should be possible to place almost any adult insect in its correct order.

Each order is then described, and further keys are provided for the identification of the families within most of the orders, although the Lepidoptera, Hymenoptera, and Coleoptera contain so many families that these orders are keyed only as far as their super-families.

Many insects can be identified simply from the **colour plates**. The first four (un-numbered) plates illustrate insects characteristic of each of the European orders, all approximately life-size or slightly larger apart from those enclosed in blue circles, which are highly magnified. Select the illustration most like the specimen you want to identify and turn to the plate(s) or page indicated.

The rest of the plates illustrate all the major insect families, the species being chosen to show the typical features of each family.

The **caption pages** facing the plates give the names of the species illustrated, together with brief notes on the families and orders and how they may be distinguished. Where necessary, diagnostic features are shown in enlarged diagrams on the captions pages. The small ▲ for a species and Δ for a family indicate that it does not normally occur in the British Isles. Most of the insects shown on the plates are enlarged and the degree of enlargement is given by each name. Where no figure is given it may be assumed that the insect is shown at more or less its natural size. The sexes are distinguished only where they are significantly different.

Introduction

Throughout recorded history insects have been both the delight and despair of mankind. No other group of living creatures has such variety of form, colour, function, and habitat and, although the insects are often persecuted as pests or simply dismissed as commonplace 'creepy-crawlies', many people love them. Not least among these is the 'bug-hunter', and it is hoped that this book will be of some service to him or her, be he or she amateur or professional.

It is impossible to give a simple definition of insects beyond the fact that most of them have six legs at some time in their lives. There are so many kinds of insects – 30 million different species according to one estimate, although the real total is likely to be between one million and ten million species – that no simple definition could possibly take in all the variations. The best that can be done is to list those features of insects that distinguish them from other animals.

Insects belong to the large animal phylum called the Arthropoda – a name that refers to the jointed limbs and body. The arthropod body is covered by a tough shell or skeleton, and flexible joints between the skeletal plates allow the animal to move. As well as the insects, the arthropods include the crustaceans (crabs, shrimps, woodlice, etc), the myriapods (centipedes and millipedes), and the arachnids (spiders, scorpions, mites, etc). It is with these groups that the insects – especially the wingless ones – are most likely to be confused and the figures below show the main features by which each group can be distinguished.

An insect's body is divided into three regions – head, thorax, and abdomen. The head bears one pair of antennae and the thorax usually carries three pairs of legs – hence the alternative name Hexapoda (= six feet) for the insects. Wings are usually present on the thorax. All winged arthropods – in fact, all winged invertebrates – are insects, but this does not mean that all insects have wings. You will see many wingless creatures in the pages of this book, but they are just as much insects as the more familiar butterflies and moths. The three body regions and the three pairs of legs prove their identity.

Insect: 3 pairs of legs: 3 body divisions: usually winged

Arachnid: 4 pairs of legs: no antennae, though palps may resemble antennae: no wings

Crustacean: several pairs of legs: 2 pairs of antennae: no wings

Myriapod (centipede): many pairs of legs: no wings

Using the information given so far, the beginner should have no difficulty in deciding whether an adult specimen is an insect or some other arthropod. But what about the young stages? Many young insects resemble their parents in all but size and the lack of wings, but there are many more in which the young are completely different from the adults. To take but two examples, there is virtually no similarity between a caterpillar and an adult butterfly or between a maggot and a bluebottle, yet the caterpillar develops into the butterfly and the maggot becomes the bluebottle. According to our chart, the adults are clearly insects, but the caterpillar might be classified as a myriapod while the legless maggot would not appear to be an arthropod at all. It is these great differences between adults and young that make it impossible to give a definition that will cover all insects at all stages of their lives.

The bug-hunter is often regarded as a crank, but there is a great deal to be gained from studying insects. By studying, I do not simply mean chasing them with a net and popping them into a killing bottle – this teaches nothing except that insects can be very elusive. I mean searching for insects, watching them, and getting to know their habits and life histories. To get to know insects properly necessitates killing a few here and there, but the aim should be to discover how they live and not to have cabinet drawers full of dead ones – there are millions of specimens in museums to be looked at if one is merely interested in shapes and colours. There is probably little left to learn about insect anatomy, but a great deal remains to be discovered about the habits of insects and there is plenty to interest anyone wishing to investigate them.

But insects are more than just interesting. There are more than a million known species – about 80 per cent of all known animals – and many of these exist in enormous numbers: just think of the numbers of ants that you see in a disturbed nest or the numbers of gnats swarming over a small pond. Insects clearly play a major role in the economy of nature – as predators, parasites, and scavengers and also as prey for larger animals. Few fields of natural history can be pursued very far without coming into contact with insects, and human activities are not without insect interference. Who would have thought that insects could hold up the building of a canal? But mosquitoes did just that. Thousands of labourers working on the Panama Canal died from mosquito-borne malaria and yellow fever, and work had to stop for several years until the diseases could be controlled. A great many other diseases of man and his crops and animals are carried by insects. Ten or even 15 per cent of the world's food production is destroyed annually by insects, either in the fields or in store after harvesting, and huge sums of money are spent in combatting the ravages of wood-boring beetles. Neverthless, relatively few insect species are actually harmful: some are extremely useful. Bees and many other insects help to pollinate our crops and ensure fruit and seed production. Ladybirds and others destroy pests, while more tangible benefits from insects include honey and silk.

Whether you meet insects in the course of your job – as a farmer or botanist, for example – or are simply interested in insects, you will want to know the names of those you meet, or at least to know the groups to which they belong. There are more than 20,000 species in the British Isles alone, and probably 100,000 species in Europe, and it would be quite impossible to describe them all in a single book. There are many specialist books dealing with individual orders or even families of insects (see Bibliography on p. 300) and going into the detail necessary to identify individual species, but a certain amount of specialised knowledge is needed to be able to use these books, and in many cases the non-specialist does not know the group to which a specimen belongs. This book has been designed to help with just this kind of problem – to facilitate the placing of an insect in its correct group and to provide the basic knowledge necessary for tackling the more detailed works. It is hoped that the specialist may also find the book useful in dealing with those orders with which he or she is less familiar.

The Biology of Insects

The insects have often been described as the most successful animals on earth, and if success is judged on the numbers of species and the range of habitats that they occupy there can be no arguing with such a description. Over a million insect species have already been discovered and described and, although many species are probably being lost every day through the destruction of the world's rain forests, it is thought that there may still be another three or four million awaiting discovery. Many factors have contributed to the outstanding success of the insects, but the following five features are generally given the credit for the insects' numerical superiority: 1) the tough, horny skeleton, 2) small size, 3) adaptability, 4) ability to fly, and 5) metamorphosis during life.

1. The Skeleton In common with other arthropods, the insects have a tough outer skeleton composed largely of horny chitin (see p. 13). This protects the body very efficiently but above all, by restricting water loss, it has allowed the insects – and some other arthropods – to leave the damp surroundings to which their unprotected, worm-like ancestors must have been confined. Freed from the necessity to remain in damp places, the insects were able to spread into new habitats and in this they have been aided by the following three features.

2. Size All insects are relatively small creatures, ranging from under 0.25mm to about 30cm in length and from about 0.5mm to about 30cm across the wings. Europe can claim some of the smallest species, but the largest insects all live in tropical areas. Although some stick insects reach 30cm in length and some moths have wingspans of 30cm, their bodies are all rather slender: very few are more than about 1cm in diameter and rarely is any point more than about 5mm from the surface. The main reason for this small size lies in the insects' breathing mechanism. Vertebrates and most groups of invertebrate animals have special breathing organs – lungs or gills – in one part of the body and a transport system – the blood – which carries oxygen from the breathing organs to all other parts of the body. But the insects use a different system. The body is permeated by a system of fine canals called tracheae which open on to the body surface at the spiracles. Air enters through the spiracles and the tissues absorb its oxygen in the finer branches of the tracheae. Although some of the larger and more active insects, including some wasps and hover-flies, can pump air along their tracheae by muscular action (see p. 22), most insects rely on simple diffusion to carry oxygen from the spiracles to the tissues. But diffusion is a very slow process and is effective only over short distances, and having once started along the path of tracheal respiration, the insects were inevitably restricted in size thereafter.

Small size, however, conveys a definite advantage when it comes to finding somewhere to live, for it enables the insects to colonise tiny places and to fill ecological niches totally denied to larger creatures. Individuals need only small amounts of food and large numbers can therefore exist in restricted places. To take an extreme example, it is quite common for a single oak leaf to support over 100 spangle galls

(Pl. 51). Each gall contains a tiny insect grub feeding on the nutritious tissues, so a single oak leaf can support more than 100 insects for several months, although not all of the insects may reach maturity.

3. Adaptability The adaptability of insects appears almost unlimited. There are very few places on earth without insects – mountain tops, hot deserts, lakes and rivers, and even hot springs have their insects inhabitants. Only the sea remains unconquered by the insects for, although there are many shore-living species, only a handful of species actually live in or on the sea.

The limbs of insects have been adapted to suit various modes of life and some of the most important adaptations have been in conjunction with feeding habits. The jaws, which are actually modified limbs, have been adapted to cope with a very wide range of both solid and liquid foods and few organic materials – living or dead – are immune from insect attack. Every plant, except perhaps the marine seaweeds, plays host to one or more insect species. Even such (to us) poisonous plants as the deathcap fungus are readily consumed by certain insects. Other insects feed on animal matter, consuming smaller creatures or sucking the blood of larger ones. Furniture beetles, carpet beetles, flour beetles, clothes moths, booklice, hide beetles, dung-flies, cigarette beetles – these names indicate just a few of the unlikely materials that support insect life and show that the insects are not short of ideas when it comes to finding food.

4. Flight The insects are the only invertebrates that can really fly. Spiders and other small creatures can drift in the wind, but they have no wings and they cannot direct their travels. The ability to fly has been a major factor in the success of insects. It enables them to escape from their enemies more effectively, to find mates more easily, and to reach new feeding grounds in which to leave their offspring.

5. Metamorphosis during Life Although less obviously than the preceding features perhaps, the metamorphosis undergone by many insects plays a large part in their abundance. When two stages, such as the leaf-eating caterpillar and the nectar-sipping butterfly, feed on different foods a given area can clearly support more insects than it could if the insects fed on one type of food throughout their lives. It is significant in this context that the most abundant and successful insect groups are those with complete metamorphoses, involving larvae which are totally different in appearance from the adults. Larvae and adults generally feed on totally different foods, although this is not true of many beetles which, in terms of numbers of species, might be said to be the most successful of all insects.

Add to these five main features the rapid and prolific breeding habits of many insects and you have the answer to their success and the reason why more than 80 per cent of all known animals are insects.

The Structure of Insects

This book is no place for a detailed account of insect anatomy, but the classification of insects depends on structural features and a general description of external anatomy is necessary here to explain the terms used in the identification keys. The glossary on pp 287–298 will give further help in this direction. Only the briefest account of internal anatomy is attempted here for, with the exception of the genitalia, it is of no value in the identification of the insects.

Adult insects typically have three parts to the body – head, thorax, and abdomen. The head carries one pair of antennae and the thorax usually carries three pairs of

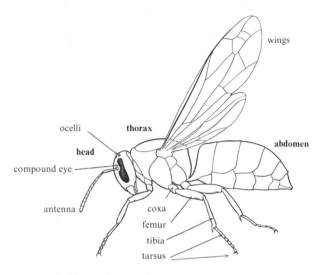

A typical insect showing the major components of the insect body

legs. One or two pairs of wings are also usually present on the thorax. The adult abdomen has no legs, although it may carry a number of cerci or other outgrowths at the hind end.

Like all arthropods, the insect has a segmented body composed of a number of fundamentally similar rings or segments. There are basically 20 segments in the insect body – six in the head, three in the thorax, and eleven in the abdomen – but some are fused together and it is not possible to count them all.

The body wall consists largely of the cuticle, which is a complex non-cellular layer secreted mainly by the cells of the underlying epidermis. The major component of the cuticle is the nitrogenous polysaccharide known as chitin, which forms up to 60 per cent of the cuticle's dry weight. It is bound up with various proteins. In most segments the cuticle becomes hardened to form the tough plates called sclerites. This is brought about by a process of tanning, in which neighbouring protein chains become linked together. Between the segments the cuticle remains soft and flexible, forming the joints which enable the body to move. One of the most interesting materials in the cuticle is a rubber-like protein called resilin. It occurs mainly in the thorax, where its almost perfect elastic recovery after distortion makes it the ideal material for the wing-hinges.

The Head The six segments of the head are intimately welded together to form a rather tough capsule. This carries many grooves or sutures but these do not necessarily correspond with the original segments and sclerites of which the head is formed. The figure shows the basic head structure of a cockroach, which is regarded as a rather primitive and generalised insect. The regions shown can be distinguished in most other insects but the pattern is often complicated by the fusion and/or sub-division of various sclerites.

Insects have no internal jaws like our own and the limbs of the head segments have been modified to assist in the capture and eating of food. All cutting and chew-

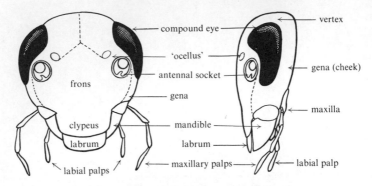

Front and side views of a cockroach head - a typical hypognathous head with the mouth-parts below the eyes. The ocelli of the cockroach are actually very poorly developed and are usually represented by little more than two pale patches near the antennae

ing is performed by these external mouth-parts before the food is passed into the mouth. Again, the cockroach reveals the basic structure. Its simple, biting mouth-parts, unspecialised and suited to a wide variety of food materials, are believed to be similar to those of the earliest insects.

The paired mandibles are the cutting parts of the feeding apparatus and are usually simply called the jaws. They are hard and heavily sclerotised and commonly toothed, and they are often provided with powerful muscles. Many of our larger insects can give the handler a painful nip: the Wart-biter, a bush-cricket rare in the British Isles, gets its name from the old Swedish custom of encouraging this insect to bite off warts. Arising on the underside of the head, the mandibles are not normally conspicuous, but in a number of insects they have taken on new functions and have developed accordingly. The male Stag Beetle (Pl.19) has enormous antler-like mandibles, sometimes as long as the rest of the body, but they are of sexual significance only and are not nearly as powerful as one might imagine. The soldier castes of some ant and termite species, however, have muscles worthy of their large mandibles. Large-jawed ants have long been used to stitch wounds in parts of Africa: the ants

The mouth-parts of the cockroach, dissected out to show their structure

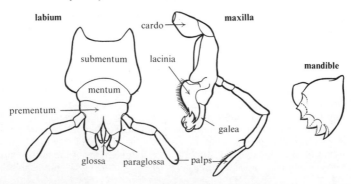

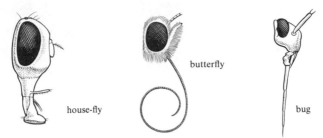

house-fly

butterfly

bug

Three entirely different modifications of the mouth-parts for taking liquid food

are made to bite into the skin across a cut and are then beheaded, the jaws staying firmly closed and being left in position until the wound has healed.

Behind the mandibles there is a pair of maxillae or secondary jaws. In the cockroach these help to hold the food while the mandibles cut it. The palps of the maxillae, resembling short antennae, are well supplied with sense organs and they are concerned with finding food and determining its acceptability. The labium or lower lip is formed by the fusion of two maxilla-like appendages and it performs functions similar to those of the maxillae themselves.

Lying in the middle of the underside of the head, just behind the mouth, is the hypopharynx. It is not one of the paired head appendages and is associated with the ducts of the salivary glands. In the cockroach and most other insects it is a small, tongue-like structure but it is well developed in flies – especially the blood-sucking forms. The mouth-parts are completed by the labrum, a single structure formed from a single plate at the very front of the head. It forms a roof over the region in which the mandibles cut up the food and is aptly called the upper lip. Its lower surface sometimes bears a small lobe called the epipharynx.

Biting mouth-parts similar to those just described are found in most of the lower orders of insects – cockroaches, grasshoppers, dragonflies, and so on – as well as in the more advanced beetles and wasps. Sucking mouth-parts, adapted for liquid food, are found among the butterflies and moths, true bugs, flies, fleas, and a few other insects. There is a great variety among these sucking mouths – witness the difference between the slender proboscis of a butterfly, the needle-like stylets of a bug, and the 'mop' of a house-fly. Nevertheless, they all seem to have evolved from the primitive biting type of mouth-parts by differential development – especially of the maxillae and labium.

The antennae are concerned largely with the senses of smell and touch. They are composed of a number of segments, ranging from one in a few beetles to over 100 in cockroaches, bush-crickets, and some other insects. Among the lower orders of insects the antennae are slender and thread-like, with all segments more or less alike but there is a great deal of variation in the higher orders. The first segment, which is often much longer than the others, is called the scape. This is followed by the pedicel, which is usually a short segment, and the rest of the antenna forms the flagellum. The latter may consist of several separate segments, or else the component segments are fused together. When the scape is particularly long and the rest of the antenna hinges on it the antenna is said to be geniculate or elbowed.

The antennae of certain male moths, including the Emperor Moth (Pl.40), are extremely large and are used to locate their mates. The female moths emit specific

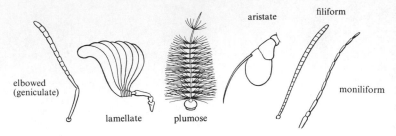

Some types of insect antennae

scents which the males can pick up more than a mile away. The concentration of scent particles at such distances is very low, but the feathery development of the male antennae makes up for this by presenting the largest possible area of receptive cells to detect the scent. As soon as a male picks up the slightest trace of the appropriate scent it turns to fly upwind, and thus eventually reaches the source of the scent.

Insects have two main types of visual receptors – the compound eye and the simple ocellus. A great many species have both types, but one or the other – or both – may be missing. The compound eye is the larger of the two and is quite conspicuous in many insects, but this kind of eye is never found in larvae.

Compound eyes are composed of a number of separate visual units called ommatidia. These are cone-shaped and each has its own lens or facet at the surface of the eye. This arrangement is responsible for the reticulated appearance of the insect eye when seen under a lens. Each ommatidium makes its own image and sends its own signal to the brain, so the insect sees a mosaic image made up of many small pieces. The picture is not sharp but this arrangement of the eye is well suited to detect movement, for any movement in the surroundings results in the stimulation of different ommatidia. The greater the number of ommatidia in the eye, the sharper the picture and the smaller the movements that can be detected. Dragonflies, which capture their food on the wing, have up to 30,000 ommatidia and extremely good sight.

The compound eye, showing how its surface is composed of numerous lenses or facets. Each lens is at the end of a conical body called an ommatidium, shown greatly enlarged on the right. Each ommatidium is insulated from its neighbours by pigmented collars, and light passes straight down to the nerve fibres at the base. Only light rays coming perpendicularly through the lens can reach the nerves, so each ommatidium has a very limited field of view

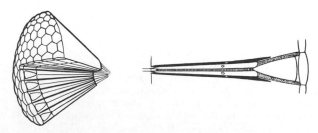

Their eyes are so large that they appear to take up almost the whole of the head. Associated with their almost complete dependence on sight, the dragonflies have very small, bristle-like antennae.

The simple ocelli, when present, are usually three in number and they form a triangle on the top of the head. They are quite small and inconspicuous in most insects, although quite easily seen in bees and wasps and some of the other large hymenopterans. The ocelli have no focusing mechanism but they are very sensitive to changes in light intensity and are thought to control the working of the compound eyes in some way. Larval ocelli are placed on the sides of the head and probably give a vague indication of the nature of the surroundings, sufficient at least for the insect to distinguish between exposed and shaded regions.

The Thorax The three thoracic segments are named, from front to back, the prothorax, mesothorax, and metathorax. Each segment carries a pair of legs and the wings, if present, are carried on the mesothorax and metathorax. Wings are never found on the prothorax, which is often small and insignificant. The meso- and metathoracic segments are usually fused together, forming the pterothorax, and the two component segments are not always easy to distinguish. The forewings, carried on the mesothorax, are normally larger than the hind wings and in consequence the mesothorax is usually larger than the metathorax. In the Diptera, whose hind wings are reduced to pin-like halteres, the mesothorax makes up almost the whole thoracic region, the prothorax and metathorax being reduced to small rings fore and aft. Among the beetles, whose forewings are modified as protective elytra, the mesothorax is quite small.

The sclerites of the thoracic segments are usually divided into numerous smaller plates and there is an elaborate system for naming them, but only the major divisions are of interest here. The primary sclerites of the dorsal surface – the nota – are each divided transversely into three regions known as the prescutum, scutum, and scutellum, but the divisions of the pronotum and metanotum are usually obscured. Unless otherwise stated, the terms scutum and scutellum refer to the mesothorax.

The pleural sclerites on the sides of the thorax consist basically of an episternum and an epimeron in each segment. The episternum is the anterior of the two and separated from the epimeron by the pleural suture. There are many sub-divisions of these pleural sclerites but they are of no concern here. The ventral sclerites or sterna

A typical insect leg (ground beetle), together with some modifications for specialised functions

mole cricket (digging)

bush-cricket (jumping)

tibia

coxa
femur
trochanter   tarsus

ground beetle

water scorpion (grasping)

are each divided into three main regions corresponding to the divisions of the nota and known as the presternum, basisternum, and sternellum.

Six legs are present in almost all adult insects. Their primary use is obviously for walking or running and their typical structure is best seen in the cockroach and in some of the ground beetles. The basal segment of the leg is the coxa, which articulates with the thorax. The trochanter is always a small segment, movable on the coxa but rigidly fixed to the femur. The latter is usually the largest segment of the leg, although the tibia is often longer. The tibia often carries a number of spines and these are particularly well developed near the distal end, where they form the tibial spurs. These are often important aids to classification and identification. The tarsus consists of between one and five segments plus a pretarsus, the latter usually consisting of one or two claws and a small pad called the arolium.

This basic structure is common to all insects but there are many variations associated with the habits of the insects. Notable variations include the enlargement of the hind femur in grasshoppers and some other jumping insects and the enlargement of the front legs in the Mole Cricket and some other burrowing insects. Many aquatic species have rather broad legs, often fringed with hairs, which make swimming more efficient. True flies have extra pads under the claws.

The Wings The classification of winged insects depends to a great extent on the nature of the wings. Most of the insect orders have names ending in -ptera, derived from the Greek *pteron* meaning a wing. Thus we get Lepidoptera (scale wings), Diptera, (two wings), and so on.

There are usually two pairs of wings, carried on the meso- and metathoracic segments. The typical wing is a membranous outgrowth of the insect's outer coat or integument, supported and strengthened by a framework of veins. The two pairs of wings usually have similar textures, but they are sometimes quite different – as in the beetles and many of the bugs, in which the forewings are tough and serve to protect the membranous hind wings.

Among the wingless insects there are two distinct groups – the Apterygota (see p. 45), whose thoracic structures indicate that they have never had wings during their existence, and the secondarily wingless insects. The thoracic structures of this latter group, which includes the lice and fleas, indicate that the insects have passed through a winged stage during their evolution. The loss of wings in the lice and fleas is clearly associated with their parasitic habits, for any tendency towards reduction or loss of wings would be an advantage to an insect spending its adult life crawling through fur or feathers: such tendencies have been favoured by natural selection and the once-winged parasites gradually evolved into wingless forms.

*Some insect wing-coupling mechanisms: **a**. a row of microscopic hooks on the front edge of the hind wing (Hymenoptera, p. 253); **b**. overlapping bristles (Mecoptera, p. 163); **c**. frenulum (some Lepidoptera, p. 217); **d**. jugum (swift moths and some other Lepidoptera, p. 216)*

Wings of a damselfly (left) and a chalcid wasp, showing two extremes of wing venation

Dragonflies and a few other insects move their two pairs of wings independently during flight and the early winged insects are believed to have done the same. It cannot be said that such an arrangement is inefficient, for the dragonflies are among the most aerobatic and manouevrable of all insects, but during insect evolution there has been a tendency for the two pairs of wings to develop a coupling apparatus and to act as a single pair. The coupling apparatus varies from a simple overlap, as in many butterflies and moths, to elaborate systems of hooks. Associated with the coupling, there has been a general reduction in the size of the hind wing, especially among the fast flying bees and wasps and some of the moths. In the true flies (Diptera) the hind wings have been reduced to tiny, pin-like halteres which are concerned with balance and play no part in propulsion.

Within the winged orders, especially those with membranous forewings, the arrangement of the veins is of great importance in classification and identification. You have only to look at the wings of a dragonfly and a chalcid wasp to realise the tremendous range of variation in venation. Between these extremes comes every possible stage of complexity, yet the veins are not arranged haphazardly and it is possible to detect a basic pattern. Much of the credit for uncovering this pattern goes to Comstock and Needham who put forward a hypothetical wing venation from which all other venations can be, and presumably have been evolved. Their ideas were originally put forward around the end of the 19th century and have been modified in the light of later work, but the essence of their scheme is still generally accepted.

The costal vein or costa (C) does not branch and it normally forms the anterior border of the wing. Behind it is the sub-costa (Sc), normally a rather thin vein that forks rarely and meets the edge of the wing somewhere along the costal margin. The

The hypothetical venation pattern of an ancestral winged insect, showing the major veins and cross-veins. No living insect possesses all the veins, but the main ones can be recognised in most winged species. C = costa; Sc = sub-costa; R = radius; Rs = radial sector; M = media; MA = anterior branch of media; MP = posterior branch of media; Cu = cubitus; A = anal veins; m-cu = cross-vein from media to cubitus (posterior cross-vein); r-m = cross-vein from radius to media (anterior cross-vein).

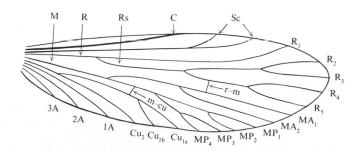

radius (R) is generally quite prominent in the anterior section of the wing. It gives off a branch called the radial sector (Rs) which divides into four – making five branches of the radius in all. These are numbered R_1 to R_5 in the order in which they reach the wing margin. Running more or less through the centre of the wing is the median vein or media (M), which divides into anterior (MA) and posterior (MP) branches. MA is absent in most living insects and MP (usually abbreviated to M) sends four branches to the wing margin. These are numbered M_1 to M_4. Prominent in the posterior section of the wing is the cubitus (Cu) which divides into two main branches, of which Cu_1 may divide again into Cu_{1a} and Cu_{1b}. The three anal veins are usually unbranched. The diagram also shows the two principle cross-veins – r-m which is often called the anterior cross-vein, and m-cu which is often called the posterior cross-vein.

The membranous areas between the veins are called cells. If completely surrounded by veins they are called closed cells and if they reach the wing margin they are called open cells. The cells are named according to the vein forming the anterior margin, so we get costal cell, radial cell, and so on.

Variations on the basic pattern include additional cross-veins and extra branches of the main veins, but in no known insect is there any increase in the number of primary veins arising from the base of the wing. The commonest variations involve the loss of some of the veins, by degeneration or by the fusion of neighbouring veins. It is then often difficult to decide what veins remain, but many wings do carry some clues. Among the lower orders the wings usually bear a number of shallow ridges and furrows. Some veins follow the ridges and some follow the furrows, and a given vein always keeps to its own station. The radius is always on a ridge and thus prominent on the upper surface of the wing. Veins Cu_{1a} and 1A are also convex (on ridges), while the radial sector and median veins are concave (in furrows) and less prominent on the upper surface. By looking for the convex and concave veins it is possible to work out which veins are which in many of the lower insects, but the pattern is usually obscured in the more advanced insects.

Before leaving this section on wing venation, it must be said that the Comstock-Needham system is not the only one in use for naming veins and cells, and that the cubitus of one system does not necessarily correspond with the cubitus of another system. Lepidopterists and dipterists, many of whose subjects exhibit a reduced venation, frequently employ a system of numbering the veins as they reach the wing margin (see p. 174).

The Abdomen The insect abdomen is basically 11-segmented but the 11th segment is always small and it is absent in the higher insects. The first segment is also small. Fusion of segments, particularly at each end of the abdomen, may make the abdomen appear to have fewer segments than are actually present.

Young proturans (see p. 48) have only eight abdominal segments plus a tail or telson, but segments 9, 10, and 11 are added in front of the telson during development. This form of growth is not found in other insects, although it is common in many other arthropods, and it is evidence of the primitive nature of these insects: in fact, many zoologists do not now consider the proturans to be insects at all (see p. 45). The same goes for the springtails of the order Collembola, which never have more than six abdominal segments at any stage of their lives.

Each abdominal segment has a dorsal tergum and a ventral sternum, but there are no pleural (side) sclerites. Appendages are present on some or all of the abdominal segments in the apterygote insects – again indicating their primitive nature. Abdominal appendages occur in the embryos of other insects and in many larvae, but they are confined to the hind end of the abdomen in the adults of the pterygote insects. The appendages of segments 8 and 9 are modified to form the genitalia, concerned with mating and egg-laying. The structure of these organs is often important in separating closely related species. They are usually small and concealed in the body, but some female insects – notably the bush-crickets and some ichneumons – have very conspicuous ovipositors which enable them to lay their eggs deep in the soil or inside plant stems or other insects. Among the bees and wasps the ovipositor has lost its egg-laying function and has become modified as a sting, used for defence and for paralysing prey.

Apart from the conspicuous ovipositors just mentioned, the most obvious abdominal appendages are the cerci which spring from the last abdominal segment. They may be long and slender as in the mayflies, but they are more often short and stubby. They are modified to form the defensive pincers in the earwigs, and in some bush-crickets, grasshoppers, and neuropterans the male cerci form prominent claspers which grip the females during mating. Cerci are absent from most of the higher insects. The dorsal sclerite of the 11th abdominal segment extends backwards to form the epiproct in some insects. In the thysanurans and some mayflies it is long and slender and forms the third 'tail' between the two cerci (fig. p. 45).

Internal Anatomy

This book is intended primarily for the identification of insects and little need be said on internal structure, but the following brief summary, although not covering all the organ systems, will provide the basic classroom information needed by the elementary student.

The digestive canal is a relatively simple tube running from the mouth to the anus and bearing a greater or lesser number of pouches. It is rarely much more than the length of the body, although in some insects there is much coiling and therefore a much greater length. In general, and somewhat surprisingly, the liquid-feeders have longer canals than the insects taking solid food. The first part of the canal is the fairly slender oesophagus, often with a muscular pharynx at its upper end – especially in sucking insects. The oesophagus leads into a very variable, thin-walled region called the crop, which is a food-storing area. Then comes the muscular gizzard where the food is broken up, although it is well developed only in those insects eating solid food – cockroaches, grasshoppers, beetles, and others. The gizzard is hardly differentiated in the flies, which take only liquid food.

Up to this point, the whole canal is lined with cuticle and is known as the fore-gut. Beyond the gizzard lies the mid-gut, which has no cuticular lining although there is a special membrane lining it and keeping the food out of direct contact with the cells of the gut wall. Digestive enzymes are produced in the mid-gut and some absorption takes place there. The effective surface area of the region is often increased by the development of pouches or caeca. In a number of liquid-feeding larvae, whose food contains little indigestible matter, there is no exit from the mid-gut and what residue there is accumulates there until it is connected with the hind-gut in the adult. The larvae of lacewings and of bees and wasps usually exhibit this condition. The hind-gut is lined with cuticle and its surface is often thrown into folds. Food absorption is completed here and water is re-absorbed in the rather globular chamber at the hind end.

Excretion is performed mainly by the malpighian tubules, which are narrow, blind tubes attached to the digestive canal close to the junction of the mid-gut and hind-gut. Uric acid is the principal substance excreted, passing along the malpighian tubules and into the hind gut to be eliminated with the faeces. In some young insects, including certain lacewing larvae, some of the malpighian tubules have become converted to silk-producing organs.

The insect blood system, in common with that of other arthropods, has relatively few blood vessels. The blood exists mainly in large cavities and freely bathes all the internal organs. The cavities collectively form the haemocoel. The blood itself, which may account for 75 per cent of an insect's weight, consists of plasma and cells. The latter may number 100,000/cu.mm and their main function is to clear the blood of bacteria and particles resulting from the breakdown of old cells. A good deal of waste carbon dioxide is carried in the blood, but the blood plays almost no part in oxygen transport and haemoglobin, so important in vertebrate blood, is found in only a relatively small number of insects. Circulation is at low pressure, brought about partly by general body movements and partly by the pumping of a simple heart in the dorsal region of the body.

Respiration takes place through a system of air tubes called tracheae which penetrate all parts of the body and open to the outside at the spiracles (fig. p. 218). There are basically ten pairs of these openings – eight pairs on the abdomen and two pairs on the thorax – but this number is often reduced. In all of the higher insects the spiracles can be opened and closed as required. The tracheae are really ingrowths of the body wall and they are lined with cuticle, which forms spiral ridges around the insides of the tubes to strengthen them. Some bristle-tails and other primitive insects have a separate tracheal system for each spiracle but the higher insects have a single system, with all the spiracles leading into one maze of tubes.

When the spiracles are open oxygen diffuses along the tracheae and it has been shown that this diffusion, although slow, is quite sufficient for the needs of small or inactive insects. Larger insects can increase their oxygen supplies through the development of air-sacs and breathing movements. The air-sacs are thin-walled expansions of the tracheae which become filled with air. Pumping movements of the body squeeze the air out of these sacs and then, when they relax, fresh air rushes into them. Such pumping movements can easily be seen in resting wasps and hover-flies.

Each trachea ends in a tiny star-shaped cell, the branches of which are minute tubes, under 1μ in diameter, called tracheoles. It is from these tracheoles that the oxygen diffuses into the tissues. The tracheoles are usually partly filled with liquid and the amount of liquid depends on the activity of the insects. Wigglesworth showed that accumulating waste products in active muscle exert an osmotic pressure that draws fluid from the tracheoles – a neat arrangement ensuring that the oxygen supply in the tracheoles is increased as required. Carbon dioxide escapes mainly through the tissues of the body and out through the body wall.

All adult insects are air-breathers, even the aquatic ones, although many aquatic nymphs and larvae get their oxygen by simple diffusion from the water. Most aquatic adults are either beetles or bugs and they carry bubbles of air under their elytra or trapped by hairs elsewhere on the body. The air is in contact with the spiracles and, as far as breathing goes, the insects might just as well be in the air. An air bubble actually provides more than its original oxygen content because oxygen gradually diffuses in from the water to replace that used up by the insect. In other words, the bubble acts as an inanimate or physical gill. But gases are also lost to the water and the bubble gradually gets smaller, necessitating periodic visits to the surface to renew it. A few aquatic insects have taken this physical gill a stage further and, although still strictly air-breathers, they can remain permanently under the surface. The body is covered with very fine water-repellent hairs which trap a very thin layer of air around it. No air can escape through the dense hairs, so the air film acts as a permanent physical gill. Oxygen continuously diffuses in to make up for that used by the insect. This system is known as plastron respiration and it is employed by the bug *Aphelocheirus* (Pl.11) and by various water beetles. They can live only in well-aerated streams with a high oxygen content.

The Senses

Insects are very active creatures and the nervous system is better developed in them than in any other invertebrates apart from the squids and octopuses. They are very well equipped with sense organs or receptors. The eyes have already been described, together with the role of the antennae in picking up scents. Touch can be detected over large areas of the body but this sense is concentrated on the antennae and legs, where sensitive hairs are connected to nerve fibres. Taste is well developed in many insects, although the taste-receptors are not not confined to the mouth region. House-flies and many other insects have taste-receptors on their feet and determine the suitability of food simply by landing on it. Female butterflies often assess the suitability of food-plants by stamping their feet on them before laying their eggs. Sounds are picked up by a variety of organs. Many of these are little membranes like our own ear-drums, but they are not normally found on the head: the ears of crickets occur on the front legs! Hairs and bristles can also detect sounds. The bushy antennae of male mosquitoes pick up the whining sounds of the females and lead the males to them. Other sense organs can detect heat. Bedbugs, for example, home in on their victims by detecting the warmth of their bodies with heat-detectors on their antennae. Bees and other social insects have temperature-receptors which enable them to monitor the temperature in the nest and take action to maintain it at the right level.

The Insect's Life History

Although a few insects, notably the summer generations of aphids, give birth to active young, the vast majority of insects lay eggs. Protected by a tough shell and one or more internal membranes that render them waterproof, the eggs can survive a wide range of conditions. Many pass the winter freely exposed on twigs, prevented from freezing solid by an assortment of anti-freeze chemicals. When the young insect is ready to leave the egg it either chews its way out or bursts its way out by muscular action, sometimes assisted by spines on the cuticle.

The apterygote insects and some of the secondarily wingless species hatch in a form very like that of the adult except for the lack of reproductive equipment, and apart from an increase in size there is little visible change as the insects grow up. But the development of the winged insects is a much more complicated process. The insect that hatches from the egg is often very different from the adult of the species, one of the principle differences being the absence of wings in the young insect. There may also be differences in the mouth-parts as well as the obvious difference in size. It follows that most young insects must undergo considerable changes before reaching the adult state. These changes are collectively called metamorphosis.

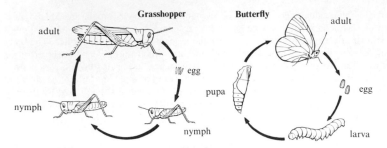

Insect life histories: the partial metamorphosis of the grasshopper - an exopterygote insect - and the complete metamorphosis of the butterfly - an endopterygote

Because of its tough, non-living external skeleton, an insect cannot grow steadily: it has to grow in stages, periodically shedding its coat when it gets too tight. The process is called moulting or ecdysis. The inner layers of the coat are digested away and a new, looser covering is secreted under the old outer skin. By swallowing air or water, the insect then pumps itself up and splits the old skin and crawls out of it. It remains swollen until the new coat has hardened and then, by getting rid of the air or water, it makes room for the next period of growth. An insect may moult anything from once to 50 times during its life, but such extremes are unusual and most insects moult between four and ten times. The stages between moults are called instars.

Winged insects can be split into two groups according to the way in which the wings develop in the young. Among the so-called 'lower insects' – cockroaches, grasshoppers, dragonflies, and so on – the wings develop gradually on the outside of the body and get larger at each moult until they are fully developed. The young stages of these insects are called nymphs and they frequently resemble the adults in general appearance, often inhabiting the same places and eating the same kinds of food. This group of insects is called the Exopterygota, in reference to the external development of the wings. It is also known as the Hemimetabola and, because there is no really dramatic change of form during their lives, the insects are said to undergo a partial metamorphosis.

The other group of winged insects includes the butterflies and moths, beetles, flies, and so on in which the young stages are very unlike the adults. These young stages are called larvae and they often exist on diets quite different from those of

The four basic types of insect larvae

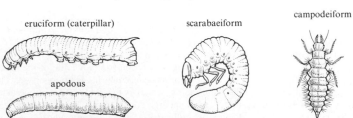

*The two main kinds of pupa: **a**. obtect, in which all the appendages are fixed down; **b**. exarate, in which the appendages are free*

the adults and occupy completely different ecological niches. Instead of undergoing a series of small changes to reach the adult form, the larvae undergo one very dramatic change – so great as to require a resting stage during which the transformation can take place. This resting stage is the pupa or chrysalis and, although capable of a certain amount of movement, it does not feed. The wing buds develop internally in this group and are not visible until the pupal stage, so this group is known as the Endopterygota. It is also known as the Holometabola, and the insects are said to undergo a complete metamorphosis because of the complete change from larval to adult form.

Mayflies, caddis flies, and some flies with aquatic larvae can fly as soon as they leave their nymphal or pupal skins, but most insects need some time to unfurl their crumpled wings. Their first reaction is usually to find a suitable support where the wings can unfurl freely. The unfurling is brought about by pumping blood along the veins. Although the wings may reach their full size in just a few minutes, they usually need another hour or two to harden before the insects can take to the air. Many species time their emergence very efficiently so that their wings are ready for flight at the appropriate time of day. Dragonflies, for example, tend to emerge early in the morning and are ready for flight as soon as the sun warms them, while many moths emerge late in the afternoon and are ready to fly at dusk. The fully developed adult is known as the imago.

When the wings are fully developed, or when sexual maturity has been reached, most insects stop growing and moult no more: small flies do not grow into larger flies, to give an oft-quoted example. The only exceptions to this are the wingless bristletails and springtails, which moult throughout their lives and may undergo as many as 50 moults, and the mayflies. The latter are unique in moulting once more after spreading their wings.

Collecting and Preserving Insects

The aim of this book is to help you to get to know insects in the field and not to fill cabinets and store boxes with them. Nevertheless, a certain amount of collecting will be necessary – especially when dealing with the smaller insects – and this book would not be complete without some guidance in this direction.

Your collection should not be an end in itself, but an aid to understanding the biology and variety of insect life. If earlier collectors had paid more attention to the biology of insects, particularly their habitat requirements, instead of filling their cabinets with rows of colourful specimens, several extinct species might well be with us today. Over-collecting has often been blamed for the extinction of various butterfly species: it may have finished off some species that had already become rare for other reasons, but it is unlikely that any species has been lost purely as a result of collecting. Loss of habitat has always been the greatest threat – and it still is. The destruction of natural habitats has reduced the numbers of many insect species to levels at which further interference with breeding populations could be very serious: a species could take years to build up again, or it could die out altogether. These threatened species are protected by law in many European countries. All but a handful of common butterflies are protected in Germany and Luxembourg and in most parts of Austria. Before embarking on any serious collecting, you should find out which species are protected or threatened in the country concerned. Sensible collecting of other species, taking no more than a couple of specimens of each, is unlikely to harm a healthy population.

If I may quote from Harold Oldroyd's book Collecting, Preserving, and Studying Insects: '...do not be in a hurry to catch and kill the insects, but spend as much time as you can watching them going about their daily life.' Record details of the insects' behaviour in your notebook before reaching for your net. When you have caught your specimens and identified them, or perhaps merely determined their families, you will be able to recognise them again in the field without catching them. In this way you will gradually build up your knowledge of insect species and groups.

After a period of general observation and collection, during which you will familiarise yourself with the various insect orders and many of the families, you may wish to specialise in one particular order or even a family. This is the only way to become a real expert – no-one can ever know everything about all insects – but always try to avoid becoming so 'wrapped up' in your own little group that you never see any other insects.

Collecting methods can be divided into active hunting on the one hand and baiting or trapping on the other, but the exact methods chosen will depend on the habits of the insects you want to catch

Hunting

1. Flying Insects Most insects fly at some time or other but, in the context of collecting methods, flying insects may be regarded as those that spend most of their time on the wing and are caught in flight or during brief periods of rest on the vegetation. The main groups included here are the dragonflies, butterflies and certain moths, flies, and hymenopterans. The principle equipment is, of course, the net. Several patterns are available from dealers (see p. 299), but it is not difficult to make a net. The frame should be light, but strong, and the most favoured material now is

The butterfly net in use: turning the net traps the insect so that it can be examined

Left, The pooter or aspirator in use to pick up small insects. Right, The sweep net in use: the strut across the mouth gives it extra rigidity

nylon or polythene. Wire can be used as long as it is not so thin that it bends when the net is swept through the air. The net should be at least 30cm across – big enough to get your hands and a killing bottle in. The nets sold as butterfly nets in toy shops are virtually useless for catching flying insects. The frame should be attached to a short handle – much easier to use than a long one for general collecting, although provision for attaching a longer handle when necessary would be an advantage.

The net bag must be soft and light, but tough enough to withstand attack by bramble and briar. Re-inforcement is needed at the rim to prevent the frame from wearing through the material. The length of the bag should be at least twice its diameter, as this allows the net to be folded at the end of each stroke to trap any insects caught in it. The colour is not vital, but dark colours – green, brown, or black – are best for butterflies and dragonflies. Paler colours are best for catching flies, mainly because the insects show up better in a pale net.

2. Crawling Insects Under this heading we can consider those insects that spend most of their time sitting or crawling on the ground or vegetation. They include beetles, bugs, grasshoppers and crickets, and many smaller creatures. The simplest method of finding these insects, although not the most productive, is to search for them in likely places. The larger insects can often be collected directly into a pill box but the smaller ones are best picked up with the aid of a pooter or aspirator. This is easily made from pieces of glass and/or plastic tubing (see diagram), but make sure that the lower end of the mouth-tube is covered with gauze – otherwise you will get a mouthful of insects when you suck!

The techniques of sweeping and beating are more productive than searching. Sweeping involves the use of a net and is usually confined to the relatively low herb-

*Two forms of beating tray: in **a** the material is permanently attached to the handle and to the two hinged arms, and when it is looped over the far end the arms automatically swing into place. **b**, which is easier to carry, is attached to a convenient branch and unrolled with the other hand*

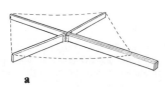 

a   b

age of fields and verges. The net should be swept from side to side in front of you as you walk along. Examine the net contents at frequent intervals to prevent seeds and leaves from damaging the specimens, and also so that you can be fairly sure which plants the insects came from. An ordinary general purpose net such as that described above can be used for sweeping, but a better pattern is shown in the diagram on p. 27. The handle continuing across the mouth of the net provides greater rigidity and allows you to produce a more controlled sweep. Ideally, a sweep net should be made of stout material, with a stout hem to withstand the constant rubbing against the vegetation.

Beating is used to obtain insects from trees and hedgerows. All you need are a stout stick and something in which to catch the insects. A white sheet laid on the ground will do, but it is better to have one stretched on a frame about a metre square. This can be held in one hand and thrust under the branches much more easily than a simple sheet. Give each branch a good whack with the stick to dislodge the insects: one good hit is usually all that is necessary. This is a particularly good method for obtaining caterpillars, but it will also yield bugs, beetles, and many other leaf-eating insects.

3. Soil and Litter Dwellers   Ants, beetles, and apterygotes are the main insects found in these habitats, which are dominated by various arachnids, and the two main collecting methods involve driving them out with heat and light. The simpler method is to spread some of the soil or litter on a white sheet and shine a strong light on it while turning the pieces over by hand. Disturbed insects scurry for cover and are easily picked up with a moist brush or a pooter. But this is a time-consuming process and suitable only for small amounts of litter. A Tullgren funnel can be used to deal with larger amounts of material. It consists of a metal or plastic cylinder 10-15cm in diameter and about 20 cm high, with a sheet of wire or plastic mesh fixed across the bottom. The holes in the mesh should be no more than about 5mm in diameter. The cylinder stands in a large funnel, whose spout leads into a jam jar or similar container with some moist tissue in it. Fill the cylinder with soil or leaf litter and then hang a light bulb just above the surface. The heat will drive the insects and other creatures down through the litter and they will eventually fall into the jam jar. Remember to keep the tissue in the jar moist, for the insects are used to damp conditions and most will shrivel up if they get dry. If you don't want to examine your catch alive, put some alcohol in the jar to pickle the insects straight away.

4. Aquatic Insects   Mayflies, dragonflies, stoneflies, and caddis flies all spend their early lives in the water. Several moths and flies do as well, but the only insects to have mastered the water in the adult state are various bugs and beetles. A net is needed to catch these aquatic creatures, but it should not be the one used for catching flying insects. A much stronger net is needed for use in water, attached to something like a broom handle: water exerts a surprisingly large resistance and a slender handle simply bends when the net is swept through the water. The net frame should have a square end so that it can be pushed along the bottom, rather like a shrimping net. It is not necessary for the bag to be more than about 15cm deep.

Baits and Traps

Night-flying moths are commonly caught by luring them with light or 'sugar' (see p. 243), but almost any kind of insect can be caught by putting out the appropriate bait. Even a bunch of nectar-rich flowers will attract bees and other nectar-feeding insects, while carrion and dung will draw in an assortment of flies and beetles. Jam jars sunk in the soil make good pitfall traps for beetles, especially nocturnal ones, as long as the tops are covered sufficiently to prevent mice and other small mammals getting in to demolish the catch. You can add small pieces of bread or meat as bait, but good catches can be obtained without any bait at all.

One of the most interesting methods of collecting moths is that known as assembling. The bait here is an unmated female, which is placed in a wire or muslin cage and left in an exposed place. Several dozen males may arrive, often from a considerable distance (see p. 16). The emperor moths are the best-known assemblers but they are by no means the only ones and it is worth trying any virgin female as a lure. Unmated females are not easy to find in the wild because many females mate almost as soon as they leave their pupae, but you can use any females that you rear from larvae. The method can also be tried with some of the larger beetles.

Traps are useful for catching the smaller flying insects, including many flies and hymenopterans, which are too small to spot and chase individually. Several designs are available, but one of the commonest and most efficient is the Malaise trap. This is a tent-like structure made of fine netting and it is open on one side. Insects entering the trap instinctively fly or crawl upwards and congregate at the highest point, where there is a narrow tunnel leading to a collecting vessel full of alcohol. Large insects, such as butterflies and moths, can be prevented from entering the collecting chamber by stretching a piece of coarse netting across the tunnel.

Preservation

When they have been caught the insects should be transferred to specimen tubes or boxes so that they can be examined. This avoids the all-too-common fault of killing first and then finding that specimens are not worth keeping. Those required for the collection or for further study can be taken home and the others can be released. Most insects travel better in the living state than when dead, but most flies and some other fragile insects should be killed at once and pinned or properly packed before travel. Cellulose wadding or soft tissue paper should be used for packing. Never use cotton wool, for its fibres become inextricably tangled with the insects' legs.

The standard type of killing bottle is a wide-mouthed bottle with a securely fitting bung and it should be large enough for the largest insects likely to be collected. If you are interested only in small insects you can use glass specimen tubes 20-25mm in diameter. Recommended killing agents include ammonia, chloroform, ethyl acetate, and tetrachlorethane. The last two are probably the best for general use, although they can turn grasshoppers and crickets pink if the insects are exposed to them for too long. Ammonia adversely affects some green insects. Before any of these liquid agents is used the killing bottle or tube should be equipped with a layer of plaster 15-20mm thick. When the plaster has set and dried the bottle is ready for use. Pour in sufficient killing agent to moisten the plaster thoroughly, and insert some bits of tisue to prevent the insects from rolling around. The liquid will gradually evaporate, but the bottle can be recharged again and again and its life is indefinite. Most liquid killing agents destroy plastic, so don't put them into plastic tubes or bottles.

In the absence of a specific killing agent, you can always resort to crushed young cherry laurel leaves, which contain a type of cyanide although they are relatively safe to handle. The crushed leaves have one big advantage over most other killing agents in that they keep the specimens in a soft or relaxed condition for quite a long

Arranging butterflies on a setting board.
The wings are moved into position with a
mounted needle

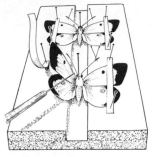

time without allowing them to go mouldy. Laurel leaves may also be used to relax specimens that have already dried. Boiling water is another useful standby killing agent and is the quickest of the lot, but it can be used only for beetles and a few other tough insects. Most insects can also be killed very quickly by popping them into the freezer. Delicate insects die within seconds, but larger and tougher specimens need a bit longer.

Because of their relatively small bodies, most insects can be preserved simply by drying them in the air. Once dried, they will keep indefinitely if protected from mould and other pests. Some large-bodied insects are best cleaned out before drying but there are few of these in Europe, although dragonflies sometimes need special treatment if they are to retain their colours (see p. 64). Drying is not suitable, however, for many of the smaller insects with thin cuticles, including the apterygotes and other soil-living species and the aphids. These insects shrivel on drying and become unrecognisable. They should be preserved in alcohol or else on cavity slides for use with a microscope. Methyl alcohol and industrial meths are the most suitable forms of alcohol, but can be bought only under licence. Isopropyl alcohol is easier to obtain, but it does tend to harden the insects and make detailed examination more difficult. The addition of a small amount of glycerine to the alcohol may help in this respect. In extreme emergencies vodka or gin can be used!

The insects can be put straight into the preservative from the net or pill-box. The bottles should be completely full of liquid to avoid damaging the insects by shaking them about.

Insects that can be preserved in the dry state can be treated in one of four ways: direct pinning, staging, pointing, or carding. In direct pinning the pin passes through the insect, usually through the thorax, and is then fixed into the drawer or store-box. Ordinary pins should not be used because they are too thick and they tend to rust. Specially manufactured entomological pins should be obtained from entomological dealers (see p. 299). English pins come in various length and thicknesses, while continental pins, favoured by most entomologists, are of standard length and various thicknesses. Several sizes will be needed for a general collection. The insects should always be pinned when they are in a relaxed condition, preferably when they are fresh, for the cuticle is then elastic and it grips the pin properly.

Those insects with large or showy wings are usually set after pinning. This involves spreading out the wings and flattening them. Setting boards are normally used for this. They are cork boards of various widths with a groove along the centre to take the bodies. The insects are arranged on the boards as shown in the diagram and their wings are held in position with thin strips of paper. The length of time needed

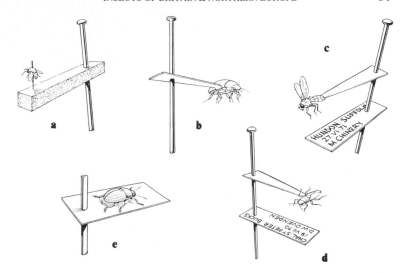

*Methods of dealing with small insects: **a**. staging; **b, c, d**. pointing; **e**. carding*

for drying obviously depends on the temperature and the size of the insects' bodies, but 3-4 weeks is generally sufficient. The insects can then be transferred to the cabinet or store-box. Insects that are usually set include butterflies and moths, dragonflies, mayflies, and lacewings. Some grasshoppers are also set, often just on one side, to show their hind wings. Although bees and wasps and many flies can be set in this way, they are not usually set because this can obscure some of the diagnostic features of the thorax.

Staging is used only for very small insects. The specimens are first pinned directly with very fine, headless pins, but the smallest specimens may simply be impaled on the points or glued to the sides of these micro-pins. Each pin is then stuck into a strip of soft material called the stage, which is then pinned into the store-box with a stouter pin. The traditional material for the stage is polyporus, obtained from bracket fungi, but a new polyethylene material known as Plastazote is now available (see p. 299) and is ideal for this purpose as well as for lining store-boxes and collecting boxes.

Pointing is also very satisfactory for the smaller insects that cannot be directly pinned. The points are small triangles of thin card and the insects are attached to them by small spots of adhesive. The points are then pinned into the store-box. The pins must obviously be put through the points before the insects are attached and the safest way to attach the insects is to put the gum on the tip of the point and then pick the insect up with it. No attempt is made to set these small insects apart from arranging them so that the important features are visible.

Carding is widely used for displaying beetles but it is not really suitable for a scientific collection because the underside of the specimen is obscured. The method involves sticking the specimens to pieces of card and then spreading the legs and antennae out with a lightly gummed brush so that they stick to the card at their tips. Various adhesives can be used, but they must not dry so quickly that you don't have time to arrange the specimens properly. Carding may also be used for earwigs, cockroaches, and most heteropteran bugs if these are being preserved merely for display purposes. Otherwise, the insects should be pinned.

Whatever methods you use for catching and preserving your insects, every specimen should bear a label giving details of place and date of capture, together with any other relevant information about the habitat. It is also usual to add the collector's name to the label. Although all this information may seem unnecessary for a small, personal collection, it all adds to the scientific value of the specimens: there is always the chance that someone may want to make a detailed study of the insect fauna in your area, and fully labelled specimens will provide a background for any future study. The label should always be on the same pin as the specimen so that the two cannot be separated.

Finally, remember that almost everything is eaten by some insect or other, and dead insects are no exception. Booklice and other small insects seem to make their way into the tightest-fitting boxes and can completely destroy a collection if unchecked. Most store-boxes and cabinet drawers have special camphor-cells, into which you can put naphthalene or some other moth-repellent to ward off these pests. If there is no such cell you can pin a small muslin bag into one corner of the box and fill it with the repellent – a moth-ball will work very well. Mould is another common problem, but can be avoided by complete drying of the specimens before storing them and by storing them in a completely dry place. Do not put store-boxes against an outside wall – there is always a chance of damp or condensation, however well the house is built. If mould does strike it can be controlled by dousing the specimens with lighter fuel – this soon evaporates – and then pinning a bag of thymol in the box, but mould-damaged specimens can never be completely restored.

Breeding Insects

This is a very worthwhile occupation because, as well as producing good adult specimens for study, it teaches a good deal about the young stages. Life history details are still poorly known for many of our insects, but they must be discovered if we are to understand the insects' habitat requirements. Breeding insects is not usually difficult, although certain species, notably some of the larger butterflies, are reluctant to pair in a confined space. It is always worth keeping females alive for a while after capture to see if they produce eggs. Rearing the young stages of most species is quite easy as long as you can provide them with the right food-plant and conditions not too different from those they enjoy in the wild. Detailed information on insect breeding is outside the scope of this book, but you will find plenty in the books listed in the bibliography (pp 300–307).

The Classification of Insects and a Key for the Identification of the Orders

The amateur entomologist will often be faced with a bewildering assortment of foreign-sounding names and might well feel like the gnat in Alice Through The Looking Glass: 'What's the use of their having names if they won't answer to them?' Alice's wise reply was 'No use to them but it's useful to the people that name them I suppose', and this is precisely why we name things – so that we can refer to any particular object without going into a lengthy description every time.

Most of our larger and more conspicuous animals – mammals, birds, and so on – have acquired English or common names, but among the insects only the butterflies and larger moths, together with a few large or economically important members of other groups, have common names. The layman cannot distinguish between the smaller and less conspicuous insects and therefore cannot give them common names. He may recognise some as grasshoppers or dragonflies, but most of the others are dismissed as 'flies' or 'bugs' and it is left to the entomologist to name them.

Biologists always use Latin or latinised Greek words when naming plants and animals and, although this may seem rather unfair on the beginner, there are good reasons for it. In the 17th and 18th centuries, when the classification of living things was in its infancy, Latin was the principal written language among educated people and it was automatically used for naming plants and animals. Although Latin was later replaced by modern languages for most purposes, biologists saw no reason for abandoning Latin names, for biology is a world-wide science and there would be disadvantages in using any one modern language. Several European languages are derived from Latin and this reduces the problem involved. If it is to be of the best possible use, a scientific name must give some indication of the nature of the organism. Latin or latinised Greek is usually better at doing this than modern languages because the word stems can be compounded to convey the description in a shorter space. For example, *Hydrometra stagnorum* is a much better way of saying 'water measurer of stagnant water'. Each different kind or species of plant or animal is given a double-barrelled scientific name and more will be said about this binomial system a little later.

Names of the species are not the only ones to confront the entomologist. There are many others referring to orders, families, genera, and other categories in the hierarchy of classification, and these are just as important as the names of the species themselves. Classification is a way of arranging living things in logical groups for convenient use. Each group contains species with certain features in common and each group must have a name. The group name should give some indication of the nature of the component species, just as a species name describes an individual species.

Just imagine what would happen if the insects had not been classified into groups and you wanted to find out if an insect you had found was new to science. You would have to look at every picture and description of every specimen ever collected to be sure that there was no other one like yours. This would clearly be an impossible task, but with classification and the arrangement of the insects in groups the search can be narrowed down straight away. If your specimen has features that place it in the earwig group, then no time need be spent searching the other groups.

The arrangement of insects into named groups according to major structural features also makes it much easier to describe an insect. Merely by reading that a new fly belongs to the genus *Pollenia* in the family Calliphoridae, an entomologist has a fairly good idea what the new insect looks like. All that is necessary to complete the description is a list of features that separate the new species from other species of *Pollenia*. Without any scheme of classification, it would be necessary to describe the new insect in full – number of wings, form of antennae, venation of wings, and so on. Classification is clearly necessary.

The characteristic features of insects and their position in the Arthropoda have already been discussed and we now move on to the classification of the insects themselves. Here the major division is into two sub-classes – the primitive, wingless **Apterygota** and the more advanced **Pterygota** whose members are winged or secondarily wingless. Within these sub-classes there is sufficient structural variation to justify their division into a number of orders. Wing structure is one of the most important features involved in the classification of the Pterygota and many of the order names refer to the nature of the wings. But there is much variation within the orders, and several orders are wingless, so that wing characteristics are not the only ones that have to be taken into account.

Classification, or taxonomy as it is properly called, is not an exact science because much depends on the opinions of the biologists involved. Two main lines can be distinguished among taxonomists – the 'splitters' and the 'lumpers'. The splitters may erect two or more orders for a group which the lumpers regard as a single order. Whether one is a splitter or a lumper depends upon the importance one attaches to certain features. The alder flies, snake flies, and lacewings provide a good example. The major differences between them are in the larvae and the splitter regards these differences as sufficient to split the insects into three separate orders. The lumper, however, feels that the larval differences are less significant than the adult similarities and so includes the three groups in one order – the Neuroptera. Different entomologists may thus recognise different numbers of orders.

The orders themselves can be grouped into several super-orders according to their evolutionary relationships (which are not universally agreed), but this aspect of classification is of theoretical interest only and of no concern here.

The orders recognised in this book and listed below are the 'traditional' 29 orders listed in *Imms' General Textbook of Entomology* (10th Edition: 1977), although many entomologists now question whether three of the apterygote orders really belong with the insects (see p. 45). All but the Grylloblattodea (wingless soil-living insects) and the Zoraptera (minute winged or wingless insects living in decaying wood and humus-rich debris) occur in Europe.

Class Insecta

Sub-class Apterygota These are wingless insects and their thoracic structure suggests that they have never had wings during their history.

Order Thysanura	Silverfish and other bristletails
Order Diplura	2-pronged bristletails – tiny soil-living insects
Order Protura	Minute soil-living insects without antennae
Order Collembola	Springtails

Sub-class Pterygota These are basically winged insects, although a number of them have lost their wings during the course of their evolution.

Division Exopterygota The wings develop externally and there is no marked change during the life history. The young stages, called nymphs, usually resemble the adults in all but size and the absence of fully-developed wings. The division is also called the Hemimetabola.

Order Ephemeroptera	Mayflies
Order Odonata	Dragonflies
Order Plecoptera	Stoneflies
Order Grylloblattodea*	Soil-dwellers of E. Asia and N. America
Order Orthoptera	Crickets and grasshoppers
Order Phasmida**	Stick and leaf insects
Order Dermaptera	Earwigs
Order Embioptera**	Web-spinners
Order Dictyoptera	Cockroaches and mantids
Order Isoptera**	Termites
Order Zoraptera*	Minute insects of uncertain affinity
Order Psocoptera	Booklice or psocids
Order Mallophaga	Biting lice
Order Anoplura	Sucking lice
Order Hemiptera	True bugs
Order Thysanoptera	Thrips

Division Endopterygota The wings develop inside the body of the immature insects and there is a marked change (metamorphosis) during the life history. The young stages are very different from the adults and are called larvae. The change from larval to adult form takes place during a non-feeding stage called the pupa. This division is also known as the Holometabola.

Order Neuroptera	Alder flies, snake flies, and lacewings
Order Coleoptera	Beetles
Order Strepsiptera	Stylopids
Order Mecoptera	Scorpion flies
Order Siphonaptera	Fleas
Order Diptera	True flies (2-winged flies)
Order Lepidoptera	Butterflies and moths
Order Trichoptera	Caddis flies
Order Hymenoptera	Bees, wasps, ants, ichneumons, etc

* denotes orders not found in Europe
** denotes orders not native to the British Isles

There is a good deal of variation within most of the insect orders and they are split into a number of smaller groups. If two or more distinct lines occur within an order they may be designated as sub-orders, but this category is of minor importance in the general scheme of classification. One of the most important categories is the family, often called the natural family to emphasise the fact that it is a natural grouping as opposed to the somewhat artificial and arbitrary higher groups. The family contains species which are clearly related to each other because of detailed similarities.

By convention, family names throughout the animal kingdom end in -idae. When there are several families in an order or sub-order they are often grouped into super-families, whose names always end in -oidea. The members of a superfamily resemble each other more closely than they resemble members of the other superfamilies in the group.

Just as orders are sometimes split into sub-orders, so families are often split into sub-families – with names ending in -inae. All the sub-families share the main features of the family but there are minor differences between them. A genus is an even smaller group consisting of closely related species. The species themselves are the individual kinds of animals – the units of the living world. It is not easy to say just what is a species, but it is usually described as an assemblage of individuals with clear similarities in appearance and structure, inhabiting the same area and breeding freely among themselves.

As mentioned earlier, the scientific name of a species consists of two words. The first, always spelt with a capital letter, is the name of its genus – its generic name. The second is always spelt with a small letter and is the specific or trivial name. These names are usually printed in italics. This binomial system for naming plants and animals was firmly established by the Swedish naturalist Linnaeus in 1753 and it has two great advantages over a single-name system. Firstly, it indicates relationships by giving the name of the genus to which the plant or animal belongs: if we see the names *Colias croceus* and *Colias hyale* in a list of butterflies we know at once that these two insects are related. If the insects had only one name each – *croceus* and *hyale* – we would have no indication of their relationship. The other big advantage of having two names is that the trivial names can be used over and over again with different generic names. Every genus must, of course, have a different name, but a specific or trivial name, describing a particular member of the genus, can be used many times, although never more than once in a given genus. Members of several genera may inhabit similar places and, because the specific name can be used again and again, all can have a name indicating the type of habitat in which they live. For example, the names *Musca domestica* and *Thermobia domestica* immediately indicate that these two insects are associated with domestic premises. If each had only one name, only one insect could be called *domestica* and the domestic nature of the other would not be apparent.

Although the species is regarded as the biological unit, it can be sub-divided. Genetic variation can produce forms which differ widely in appearance, although still able to breed freely with each other. When geographical barriers, such as mountains, seas, or simply unsuitable habitats, divide a population into isolated units differences can evolve between the separated populations. The animals can still interbreed if brought together, but the differences may be sufficiently constant and clear for the species to be split into two or more sub-species or geographical races. This has often happened with British insects cut off from the main populations of Europe. One of the best-known examples is the British race of the Swallowtail butterfly (*Papilio machaon*), which shows several differences from the continental race. When sub-species are recognised a third word is added to the scientific name: the British race of the Swallowtail is appropriately named *Papilio machaon britannicus*, while the continental race is known as *P.m.gorganus*.

The name of the person who first described a species should strictly be added to the scientific name. If this name appears in brackets it indicates that the person concerned originally gave the insect a different generic name from the one it has now.

This leads on to a common cause of complaint among amateur entomologists – name changing.

The scientific naming of animals is strictly governed by the rules of the International Commission on Zoological Nomenclature and one of the most important of these rules is that the first correct name given to a species is the only valid name. When people began to name insects and other animals there was not the degree of communication that we enjoy today. Quite often a name was published but then became buried in the literature. Another entomologist, unaware of the publication, could well have given a different name to the same species. If the earlier publication then comes to light and it is proved that the two names refer to the same species, the law of priority dictates that the earlier name shall be adopted, even if the later name has become well established.

Another major reason for name-changing has been our increasing knowledge of the relationships of insects. The early entomologists tended to be large-scale 'lumpers' and this led to many quite different insects' being grouped in a single genus. Linnaeus actually placed all the dragonflies that he knew in the genus *Libellula*, but later workers pointed out the wide variation in the structure of the dragonflies and created a number of different genera for them. Only two of the eleven British species that Linnaeus described in the genus *Libellula* still retain that name, although they still have the specific names given to them by Linnaeus. Most changes in generic names have arisen through the splitting up of the original genera in this way. This does not conflict with the law of priority mentioned above, as long as there are sound reasons for creating the new genera. Detailed microscopical and even biochemical investigations aid today's taxonomists in sorting out the genera.

The Key

The first thing to do when trying to identify an unknown insect is to assign it to its correct order, and with the help of a lens and the following key you should be able to place most adult European insects in their correct orders. I say 'most' because there is an enormous variation within the orders as well as between them and most orders contain a few atypical members. These cannot be run down with a general key, but you will soon learn to recognise them. In fact, the characteristics of most of the orders are so clear that before long you will be able to place an insect in its order without reference to this key at all. You will be able to say that a particular specimen is a stonefly (or whatever else it is) because it looks like it. A combination of features such as resting attitude or style of flying or simply general appearance will indicate the order without your having to examine the wing structure. These features are less precise and less easy to describe than those in the key but, once known, they are equally important in identification.

In order to use the key, the beginner must always start at the beginning and work through systematically. Each clue has two alternatives. Read these carefully and select the one that applies to the specimen you are investigating. To take the simplest example, clue 1 has as its alternatives 'winged' and 'wingless'. Having selected the appropriate one, look at the figure on the right. For a winged insect you will see the figure 2, and this is the number of your next clue. Follow this procedure with every clue you meet. If you follow the clues accurately and in sequence, each insect examined will fall in with one or other of the alternatives. If you come to a clue neither of whose alternatives appear to fit your insect you may have gone wrong earlier in the key, but more probably you are looking at an immature insect.

Eventually a clue will be followed not by a number but by the name of the order to which your insect belongs. To identify your insect further, turn to the page indicated after the order's name. There you will find a description of the order and usually further keys that will enable you to discover the family or superfamily to which your specimen belongs. Some orders crop up several times in the key because they contain several somewhat different groups.

As with the orders, it is possible to recognise many families by general appearance, and this is where the illustrations play their part. The species illustrated are, in general, those most typical of the family and there are many small diagrams pointing out the differences between related families.

From the descriptions and illustrations, you may even be able to find out the exact name of your insect but, with over 20,000 insect species in Britain alone, only a very small proportion can be included in this book. If you wish to take your identification any further you will have to refer to a specialist work dealing with the order concerned. Appropriate works are listed in the bibliography at the end of the book, but it is as well to remind the reader that the structural differences between individual species, or even genera, are very much smaller than the differences between families. A microscope is essential for work with the smaller insects. More specialised knowledge is usually necessary for identifying insects to species level, and it is hoped that the glossary on p. 287 will provide help in this direction.

Key to the Orders of European Insects
* Denotes orders not found in the British Isles

1.	Insects winged	2
	Insects wingless or with vestigial wings	29
2.	One pair of wings	3
	Two pairs of wings	7
3.	Body grasshopper-like, with enlarged hind legs and pronotum extending back over abdomen	Orthoptera p. 68
	Insects not like this	4
4.	Abdomen with 'tails'	5
	Abdomen without 'tails'	6
5.	Insects <5mm long, with relatively long antennae: wing with only one forked vein	Hemiptera p. 97
	Larger insects with short antennae and many wing veins: tails long	Ephemeroptera p. 52
6.	Forewings forming club-shaped halteres	Strepsiptera p.161
	Hind wings forming halteres (may be hidden)	Diptera p. 170
7.	Forewings hard or leathery	8
	All wings membranous	13
8.	Forewings horny apart from membranous tip	Hemiptera p. 97
	Forewings of uniform texture throughout	9
9.	Forewings (elytra) hard and veinless, meeting in centre line	10
	Forewings with many veins, overlapping at least a little and often held roofwise over the body	11

10.   Abdomen ending in a pair of   Dermaptera p. 78
        forceps: elytra always short

      Abdomen without forceps: elytra   Coleoptera p. 134
        commonly cover whole abdomen

11.   Insects with piercing and sucking   Hemiptera p. 97
        beaks

      ← beak

      Insects with chewing mouths: cerci   12
        usually present

12.   Hind legs modified for jumping   Orthoptera p. 68

      Hind legs not modified for jumping   Dictyoptera p. 82

13.   Tiny insects covered with white powder   14
      Insects not like this   15

14.   Wings held flat at rest: mouth-parts   Hemiptera p. 97
        adapted for piercing and sucking

      Wings held roofwise over body at   Neuroptera p. 127
        rest: biting mouthparts

15.   Small, slender insects with narrow,   Thysanoptera p. 125
        hair-fringed wings: often found in
        flowers

      Insects not like this   16

16.   Head extending downwards into a   Mecoptera p. 163
        beak   ← beak

      No such beak   17

17. Wings more or less covered with minute scales: Lepidoptera p. 213
     coiled proboscis (tongue)
     usually present

     Wings usually transparent, although often hairy   18

18. Wings with a network of veins, including many cross veins   19

     Wings with relatively few cross veins   23

19. Abdomen with long terminal threads   20

     Terminal appendages short or absent   21

20. Forewings much larger than hind wings: Ephemeroptera p. 52
     wings held vertically over body at
     rest: 2 or 3
     terminal threads

     Wings more or less equal in size or   Plecoptera p. 64
     hind wings larger: wings folded
     close to body at rest: 2 terminal
     appendages

21. Antennae very short: body at least   Odonata p. 57
     25mm long

     Antennae longer, greater than width of head   22

22. Tarsi 3-segmented   Plecoptera p. 64

     Tarsi 5-segmented   Neuroptera p. 127

23.   Wings noticeably hairy   24
      Wings not noticeably hairy   25

24.   All wings more or less alike: front   *Embioptera p. 81
        tarsi swollen

      Hind wings usually broader than   Trichoptera p. 245
        forewings: front tarsi not swollen

25.   Tarsi with 4 or 5 segments   26
      Tarsi with 1-3 segments   27

26.   All wings alike   *Isoptera p. 86

      Hind wings much smaller than   Hymenoptera p. 253
        forewings

27.   Hind wings similar to or larger than   Plecoptera p. 64
        forewings: abdomen with cerci

      Hind wings smaller than forewings: no cerci   28

28.   Tiny insects with at least 12   Psocoptera p. 88
        antennal segments

      Never more than 10 antennal   Hemiptera p. 97
        segments: piercing and sucking
        beak present

      ← beak

29. Insects with slender, twig-like body   *Phasmida p. 77

     Insects not like this   30

30. Insects with grasshopper-like body   Orthoptera p. 68
     and long back legs

     Insects not like this   31

31. Small, soft-bodied insects living on   Hemiptera p. 97
     plants, often under a protective
     shield or scale

     Insects not like this   32

32. Minute soil-living insects, < 2mm   Protura p. 48
     long and without antennae

     Insects not like this   33

33. Insects with cerci or other abdominal appendages   34

     Insects without such appendages   41

34. Abdominal appendages long and conspicuous   35

     Abdominal appendages short or hidden under body   38

35. Appendages forming pincers   36

     Appendages not forming pincers   37

36. Tarsi 3-segmented   Dermaptera p. 78

     Tarsi 1-segmented   Diplura p. 47

37. Abdomen with 3 long terminal   Thysanura p. 45
     appendages

     Abdomen with only 2 terminal   Diplura p. 47
     appendages

38. Tiny jumping insects with head   Mecoptera p. 163
     produced downward into a beak:
     vestigial wings present

     No sign of a beak   39

39. Small or minute insects with a   Collembola p. 48
     forked springing organ under
     rear end: generally found
     in soil or decaying
     vegetation

     Insects not like this   40

40. Tarsi usually 4-segmented   *Isoptera p. 86

     Tarsi 3-segmented: front tarsi   *Embioptera p. 81
     swollen

41. Parasites in fur or feathers: insects generally flattened   42
     side-to-side or dorso-ventrally

     Insects not parasitic and not usually flattened   46

42. Jumping insects flattened from side   Siphonaptera p. 165
     to side

     Insects flattened dorso-laterally   43

43. Insects of moderate size: head partly withdrawn into thorax   44

     Small or minute insects: head not withdrawn into thorax   45

44. Antennae short: very 'leggy' insects   Diptera p. 170
     with strong claws well suited to
     clinging to host mammal

     Antennae long: body somewhat   Hemiptera p. 97
     circular, with less prominent legs
     and claws

                                   prothorax

45. Prothorax distinct: biting mouths   Mallophaga p. 95

     Thoracic segments fused into one   Anoplura p. 96
     unit: sucking mouths

46. Abdomen with pronounced 'waist': antennae often elbowed   Hymenoptera p. 253
     No such features   47

47. Body > 5mm long, clothed with flattened hairs and scales: Lepidoptera p. 213
     wing vestiges present

     Body usually < 5mm long, naked or occasionally scaly: 48
     wing vestiges rarely present.

48. Head as wide or nearly as wide as   Psocoptera p. 88
     body: biting mouthparts: insects
     often found among dried
     materials

     Head narrower than body: sucking   Hemiptera p. 97
     mouthparts: abdomen often with a
     pair of tubular outgrowths near
     hind end: insects found on
     growing plants

THE APTERYGOTE INSECTS

The sub-class Apterygota (= without wings) contains a rather heterogeneous assortment of wingless insects. Some 3,000 species are known but, because of their small size and secretive habits, many more undoubtedly await discovery, even in Europe. Most of the species live in the soil and among decaying vegetation.

It is believed that the apterygotes are the most primitive insects and that they have never had wings in their evolutionary history. Detailed study of the thorax of these insects has revealed no vestige of the wing-bearing apparatus such as is found in the wingless lice and fleas. More evidence for their primitive origin is provided by the presence in many apterygotes of abdominal appendages other than the normal cerci and genitalia. These indicate a possible affinity with or even descent from some multi-legged ancestral arthropod.

Four orders have long been recognised in the Apterygota, but their relationship to each other is not clear. They may well have evolved independently from more than one ancestral type. Only the bristletails of the order Thysanura can be regarded as close to the main line of insect evolution. The other orders, especially the springtails and proturans, are so distinct that many biologists no longer consider them to be insects at all – not even aberrant off-shoots – and treat them as separate classes within the Arthropoda.

Metamorphosis among the apterygotes is slight or absent, with the young stages resembling their parents in all but size and reproductive organs. Mating is a simple affair without any actual copulation. The male simply deposits a packet of sperm and the female picks it up in her genitalia.

The soil-living apterygotes may be collected in the usual ways (see p. 28) and preserved in alcohol. Slide mounts can be made with whole specimens of the smaller species.

Order Thysanura – Bristletails

Recognition features Wingless insects up to about 20mm long, with carrot-shaped bodies clothed with shiny scales. Long, thread-like antennae and three long, segmented tail filaments at the rear.

The bristletails are the most familiar of the apterygotes because they include the largest species and also a number of household species. Most people have seen silverfish darting away from spilled flour in a neglected corner of the kitchen cupboard

The Silverfish - a typical bristletail

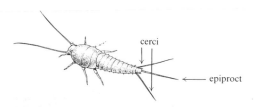

cerci

epiproct

or scurrying for shelter when an infrequently-used book is taken from the shelf. The bristletails are extremely primitive insects with simple biting mouths. The flattened, tapering body is usually covered with minute, shiny scales – hence the name Silverfish for our common household representative. Try to pick up one of these insects and you are likely to retain nothing but a coating of scales on your fingers, the insect itself slipping quietly away. The slender antennae are often longer than the body. The tarsi have two, three, or four segments and most of the abdominal segments carry small appendages. The last abdominal segment carries two long, jointed cerci and a central, segmented 'tail' known as the epiproct. These processes are fringed with bristles and are responsible for the name of the order, derived from the Greek *thysanos* (a fringe) and *oura* (a tail).

The only insects with which the thysanurans are likely to be confused are the two-pronged bristletails of the order Diplura (p. 47), but the latter lack the epiproct and have a rather different body-shape. They also have 1-segmented tarsi. Size is also a useful clue in the British Isles, where all thysanurans are over 9mm long *when adult* and the diplurans are never more than 5mm long.

Thysanurans all start life as eggs, but metamorphosis is slight. The main external change is the appearance of scales after the first few moults. There are at least six instars and often many more. Many members of the order continue to moult throughout their lives, which may be four or five years. This is unusual because insects normally stop growing and moulting once they reach maturity.

The order contains about 600 known species and there are two main families. The **Machilidae** is the larger of the two and its members may be recognised by their large eyes and small ocelli, together with a strongly arched thorax. Members of the **Lepismatidae** have very small eyes and no ocelli and the thorax is not arched. There are also small, but significant differences in the mouth-parts, as a result of which the two families are placed in separate sub-orders. Some entomologists even recommend splitting the thysanurans into two separate orders on this basis.

Members of the Machilidae live under stones or among moss and leaf litter. They are agile insects and they often jump when disturbed. *Petrobius maritimus* is the largest and most frequently seen of the seven British species. It is a metallic-coloured insect about 18mm long and it lives on organic detritus on the sea shore.

The two British members of the Lepismatidae both live in buildings. The Silverfish (*Lepisma saccharina*) is a common insect in food cupboards and similar places, where it feeds on scraps of paper, the glue of cartons, spilled flour, and other starchy materials. The Firebrat (*Thermobia domestica*), as one would expect from its name, frequents warmer places such as bakeries and kitchens where, like the Silverfish, it feeds on carbohydrate materials. It can be distinguished from the Silverfish by its much longer antennae and cerci. Several other members of the family live in buildings and out of doors in southern and central Europe. The family **Nicoletiidae**, whose members lack both eyes and ocelli, is closely related to the Lepismatidae. The only European species is *Atelura formicarius*, which lives in the nests of various ants.

The Firebrat

Order Diplura – Two-pronged Bristletails

Recognition features Small wingless soil or detritus-living insects with two cerci. British species never more than 5mm long.

A typical dipluran of the family Campodeidae

These insects, of which there are just over 400 known species, were formerly grouped with the bristletails in the order Thysanura, but they are sufficiently different in structure to merit an order of their own. The diplurans have no epiproct and their thoracic segments are much more clearly separated than those of the thysanurans, but the most constant and important differences concern the mouth-parts: those of the diplurans are partially sunk into the head capsule, whereas those of the thysanurans (and all the pterygote insects) are free. Many entomologists consider this difference in the mouth-parts so fundamental that they now separate the diplurans (and the similarly-equipped proturans and springtails) from the insects and place them in distinct classes.

The diplurans live in soil, under bark, and in other dark and humid places. Most of them feed on decaying plant matter. They are all pale in colour and have neither compound eyes nor ocelli. Their antennae are relatively stouter than those of the thysanurans and their segments are more clearly visible. The tarsi are one-segmented. Like the thysanurans, the diplurans have paired appendages on most of the abdominal segments, although these are not visible without a microscope.

Several families are represented in Europe, but only the **Campodeidae** occurs in the British Isles. Twelve species have been discovered in these islands so far, all in the genus *Campodea*. They all have long, slender cerci. The other families are primarily tropical but have a few members in southern Europe. *Anajapyx* species have short, stout cerci to match their sturdy antennae. *Japyx* species, which reach lengths of about 16mm, have stout, pincer-like cerci which they use to capture other small creatures.

*Two diplurans from southern Europe: **a.** Japyx solifugus (Japygidae), with pincer-like cerci; **b**. Anajapyx vesiculosus (Anajapygidae)*

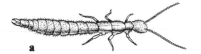

a   b

A typical proturan

Order Protura

Recognition features Minute white soil-living creatures generally under 2mm long. Antennae, eyes, and ocelli absent. Front legs held forward in the manner of antennae.

These tiny creatures, with little resemblance to the normal insect pattern, were not discovered until 1907 but since then they have been uncovered in all parts of the world. About 70 species have been recognised so far and 12 of them occur in the British Isles. They can be found in leaf litter and in moist soil with plenty of organic matter but, with the largest known species being little more than 2mm long, a microscope is almost indispensable for the search. It is certainly essential for any detailed observation of the proturans. The name Protura means 'simple tail' and refers to the simple, pointed telson. There is no common name for the group.

The head is rather conical, pointed at the front and ending in piercing mouth-parts which, like those of the diplurans (see p. 47), are partially sunk into the head. They are used for piercing fungal hyphae and taking juices from decaying vegetable matter. There are no eyes or antennae but the front legs are held forward at the sides of the head and they fulfil a sensory role. Only the middle and hind legs are used for walking. The tarsi are one-segmented and each ends in a single claw. The cylindrical abdomen has the full complement of 11 segments in the adult, but the young proturan has only eight abdominal segments plus the pointed telson. Segments 9, 10, and 11 are added during development, so there is a slight metamorphosis. This increase in segments during post-embryonic development is not found in other insects but it is a feature of arthropods in general, so here is another reason for thinking that the proturans should not be regarded as insects.

The first three abdominal segments each bear a pair of tiny appendages and the classification of the order into families depends upon the structure of these appendages. Three families occur in Europe and all are represented in the British Isles. The only satisfactory way of preserving these creatures is by making slide mounts.

Order Collembola – Springtails

Recognition features Small wingless insects, rarely more than 5mm long and usually much less. Body cylindrical or globular and usually provided with a forked springing organ at the rear that enables the insects to leap into the air when disturbed. Living mainly in soil and leaf litter.

This is by far the largest order of the Apterygota, containing about 2,000 known species. Just over 300 of these occur in the British Isles. The order has a world-wide

A typical litter-inhabiting springtail (superfamily Entomobryoidea) with its 'spring' released

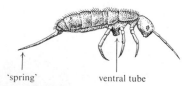

'spring'   ventral tube

distribution and certain species even occur beyond the permanent snow lines of the Arctic and Antarctic regions, apparently feeding on sparse algae or pollen grains deposited by the wind. A number of species live openly on plants and some of them may damage crops, but most springtails are very susceptible to drying and they generally live in soil or leaf litter where they feed on decaying matter. Some species live on the surface of still water. Greys and browns are the main colours, although some springtails are white and many litter-living species are mottled with brown and pale yellow. The body is often clothed with hairs or scales and many species have a prominent collar of bristles just behind the head.

Springtail mouth-parts are of the biting type and are partially sunk into the head capsule like those of the diplurans and proturans (see p. 47). The antennae are variable in length although never with more than six segments: four is the usual number. There are no compound eyes, but a number of ocelli are usually present and are often surrounded by a pigmented area that gives the impression of a true eye. The thoracic segments are not readily distinguishable from those of the abdomen apart from the fact that they carry legs, but the legs themselves are unusual in that they have no tarsal segments: the tibiae end in single or double claws.

The abdomen contains only six segments, compared with eleven in all other adult insects, and this is a major reason for placing the springtails in a class of their own. In all springtails the first abdominal segment bears a characteristic organ called the ventral tube, formed by the fusion of the appendages of that segment. The tube contains eversible sacs or vesicles that are expanded by forcing blood into them. Sometimes thought to have a respiratory function, the tube has now been shown to play a role in regulating the water balance of the insects, by absorbing or secreting water as necessary. It also acts as an adhesive organ. Springtails confined in a glass tube can be seen pressing the tube against the glass as they climb the smooth walls. The name Collembola refers to this adhesive function (Greek *kolla* = glue and *embolos* = peg).

The third and fourth abdominal segments are concerned with the springing action which gives the group its common name. The forked springing organ is formed by the partial fusion of the appendages of the fourth abdominal segment and is known as the furcula. When not in use it is folded forward under the abdomen and held in place by the appendages of the third abdominal segment, which again are partly fused and are known as the hamula or retinaculum. When the animal is disturbed the hamula releases the furcula, whose muscles then contract and pull it backward and downward on to the ground. The force of this action drives the whole insect forward through the air. This springing organ is well developed in most springtails, but is small or absent in a few genera. Jumping is not, of course, the usual method of locomotion because the insects commonly live in confined spaces. They normally walk or run jerkily through the leaf litter, with their antennae continually on the move as they seek out food or pathways through the leaves.

There are usually six to eight instars in the springtail's lifespan, although the insects reach sexual maturity before they reach maximum size. The changes taking place during the life history are so slight that we can say metamorphosis is absent. Under normal conditions there are probably several generations in a year.

Key to the Main Groups of European Springtails

1. Body more or less elongate (sub-order Arthropleona)   2

    Body more or less globular (sub-order Symphypleona)   3

2. Pronotum similar to other tergites and quite   Superfamily Poduroidea p. 50
    visible from above: cuticle granular or tuberculate

    Pronotum reduced and often   Superfamily Entomobryoidea p. 51
    invisible from above: cuticle with
    hairs or scales

3. Antennae shorter than head: ocelli absent   Family Neelidae

    Antennae as long as or longer than head: ocelli present   4

4. Antennae elbowed between 3rd and 4th segments   Family Sminthuridae p. 51

    Antennae elbowed between 2nd and 3rd segments   Family Dicyrtomidae p. 51

The superfamily **Poduroidea** contains mostly very small springtails with slaty colouring and relatively short legs and antennae. Many members of this group live on or near water. The small, black *Podura aquatica* scavenges on the surface of ponds

*The four major groups of springtails, seen from the side and from above with their
'springs' extended: **a**. Poduroidea; **b**. Entomobryoidea; **c**. Sminthuridae; **d**. Neelidae*

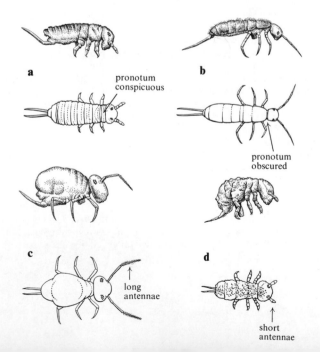

a

pronotum
conspicuous

b

pronotum
obscured

c

long
antennae

d

short
antennae

and other still waters, while *Hypogastrura viatica* and *Anurida maritima* live on the seashore. The four families within this group are not easily separated.

The superfamily **Entomobryoidea** contains larger springtails with relatively long appendages. The antennae are longer than the body in *Tomocerus longicornis* and a few other species. The insects are very common in leaf litter, where their brown and mottled colours make them difficult to see even on the examination table. Four families are generally recognised. Members of the **Isotomidae** have hairs but no scales. They include the hairy black *Isotoma saltans*, which is often so abundant on the alpine snow-fields and glaciers that the ice looks black. Members of the other families usually have scales, with or without hairs. *Seira domestica* is a white, silky-haired species that occasionally appears in damp houses and cellars.

The sub-order Symphypleona contains three families of very small, globular springtails, separable with the aid of the above key. Many of the species are only about 1mm long. There is little sign of segmentation, with the thorax and abdomen being more or less fused into a single unit. Many of these tiny springtails live on growing plants. The yellowish *Sminthurus viridis*, often known as the Lucerne Flea, frequently damages clovers, peas, and various other crops, including forage grasses. *Sminthurides aquaticus* is a green or yellowish species that feeds on duckweed. The family **Dicyrtomidae**, which has only recently been separated from the **Sminthuridae**, contains a number of minute debris-feeding springtails. The reddish brown *Dicyrtoma fusca* is abundant in leaf litter and under loose bark.

THE PTERYGOTE INSECTS

The sub-class Pterygota contains all the winged insects and it is a far larger division than the Apterygota. Although pterygote means 'with wings', the sub-order does contain many wingless creatures, including the fleas and lice. The reason for their inclusion is that they are clearly descended from winged ancestors. Most of them have lost their wings during their evolutionary history as a result of adaptation to parasitic life or to life under the ground.

Order Ephemeroptera – Mayflies
Plates 1 & 2

Recognition features Small, medium, and large-sized insects with two or three long 'tails' and one or two pairs of delicate wings. The hind wings, when present, are always considerably smaller than the front pair. Antennae short. Usually found in the vicinity of water.

The stoneflies, caddis flies, and lacewing flies are the only other insects with which the mayflies might be confused, but the short antennae of the mayflies should distinguish them. Other useful distinctions are: the large hind wings of the stoneflies, the few cross veins of the caddis flies, and the similarity of the two pairs of wings in the lacewings. In addition, a feature that can be seen only in life, the mayflies are quite unable to fold their wings back along their bodies: the wings are always held vertically over the body at rest, a position unknown in these other insects except when just emerged from their nymphal or pupal skins. Most mayflies are less than 12mm across and, apart from the entomologist, the fisherman probably knows them better than anyone, for the mayflies spend most of their lives in the water and are extremely important items in the diet of many fish. Mayflies, in fact, are the models for many of the angler's artificial flies and are therefore often called fishing flies.

Despite their common name, the mayflies are by no means confined to the month of May and one species or another can be found throughout the summer. They are all weak fliers and, except when carried by the wind, they are rarely found far from water. The adult mayfly has a very slender body and delicate transparent wings. The hind wings are always considerably smaller than the front pair and may be absent

Left , A typical mayfly at rest. Right, Forewing venation of Ephemera

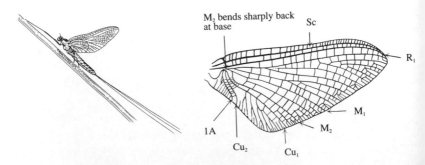

altogether. As would be expected in an insect whose forewings are dominant, the mesothorax is the largest thoracic region, the pro- and metathoracic segments being rather insignificant.

None of our species can be called colourful, the dominant colours being brown and yellow. The wings of some species appear to have a metallic sheen when light hits them at certain angles, but the colours fade after death and identification by colour is not at all easy. Mayfly classification depends primarily on the wing venation, but there are problems here too because the veins are often so faint as to be almost invisible. A good lens and suitable lighting, however, will allow one to make out most of the veins.

The front legs of male mayflies are relatively long and are used to hold the female during pairing. Otherwise, the legs are weak and slender and used only for holding on to vegetation. The 'tails' consist of a pair of long filamentous cerci, with or without a central filament. The number of tails is constant for individual families, though one or more may be damaged or missing in a particular individual. Male mayflies also have a pair of claspers or forceps at the rear end. Part of the genital apparatus, they are used to hold the female abdomen firmly during copulation.

The compound eyes are larger in males than in females and in some genera the male eye is divided into an upper part with large facets and a lower part with small facets. In the Baetidae the upper part of the male eye is expanded to form a flat-topped turret. Such eyes, thought to enhance the ability to spot females in flight, are known as turbinate eyes. The antennae are always small. Adult mayflies do not feed and their mouthparts are greatly reduced.

Mayflies are unique among insects in moulting after attaining the winged state. Final instar nymphs stop eating and after a short while they climb plant stems or, more usually, float or swim to the water surface. Here, within a few seconds, the nymphal skin splits and a winged insect emerges. In contrast to most freshly emerged insects this one can fly right away, although the direction of its flight is largely governed by air currents. But this winged insect is not the mature mayfly: it is the sub-imago (the fisherman's dun) and it is rather dull in colour. This is due to a covering of very fine hairs, which are thought to assist emergence from the nymphal skin by preventing wetting. The sub-imagos that reach a suitable resting place moult within a few hours (in some species it is only minutes) and turn into the shinier mature imagines known as spinners.

The spinner's life is a short one and is responsible for the name Ephemeroptera (Greek *ephemeros* = living a day). Many species live for less than a day in the adult state: they emerge in the evening and are dead by morning. Others may live for up to a week. During this brief aerial existence the insects ensure the continuance of their species by mating and laying eggs. The males swarm in large numbers, dancing up and down over and around the water. Any female that comes near the swarm is seized by a male and mating takes place in the air. The eggs are usually laid within an hour or so, although bad weather may delay laying for several hours. The eggs are dropped singly or in batches into the water, but some species may descend into the water to lay their eggs on submerged plants and, having fulfilled their purpose, the spent gnats are eagerly devoured by fishes. Bats, swallows, and dragonflies also take their share of mayflies before they fall into the water.

Most mayfly species are widely distributed, but each has its preferred habitat and the nymphs are admirably adapted to their particular niches. We can recognise cy-

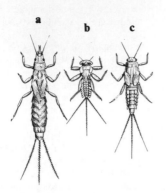

*Three types of mayfly nymphs: **a**. Ephemera;*
***b**. Ecdyonurus; **c**. Ephemerella*

lindrical burrowing forms, rather rugged forms that crawl on the vegetation, stream-lined swimmers, and flattened forms that cling tightly to stones in fast streams. Clear, fresh water, moving or still, is more likely to hold mayflies than stagnant ponds with lots of organic material.

The nymphs are basically herbivorous, feeding on plant debris and algae, although some take animal food as well. They breathe by means of plate-like tracheal gills that grow out from the sides of the abdomen. There are usually seven pairs of these gills and they contain tiny tracheae that are continuous with those of the rest of the body. Oxygen diffuses into them from the water. All mayfly nymphs have three tails, even if the adult has no median filament.

The short adult life is preceded by a much longer nymphal development. *Ephemera danica* takes two years to mature, but most mayflies complete their life cycles in one year and some, particularly in the warmer regions, have two broods in a year. Up to 27 moults have been recorded for mayfly nymphs.

Fourteen families are represented in Europe, totalling about 200 species. Eight families, with 47 species, live in the British Isles.

A Key to the Families of European Ephemeroptera

1.	Insects with 3 long tail filaments	2
	Insects with 2 long tail filaments	7
2.	Hind wings absent	Caenidae p. 56
	Hind wings present	3
3.	Hind wing lacking cross veins	†Oligoneuriidae p. 56
	Hind wing with cross veins	4
4.	Forewing with dark blotches	Ephemeridae p. 56
	Forewing without blotches	5

5. Vein M_2 of forewing bends sharply   Potamanthidae p. 56
     backwards at base

M_2

Cu_1

     Vein M_2 of forewing does not bend sharply backwards   6

6. Vein Cu_2 of forewing midway   Leptophlebiidae p. 56
     between Cu_1 and 1A at the base
     or nearer to 1A

Cu_2 midway between →
Cu_1 and 1A

1A

Cu_2

Cu_1

     Vein Cu_2 of forewing nearer to Cu_1 Ephemerellidae p. 56
     than to 1A at the base

Cu_2 very close →
to Cu_1

1A

Cu_2

Cu_1

7. Wings cloudy   8

    Wings clear and shining   9

8. Wings brownish, spanning about 6cm   [†]Palingeniidae p. 56

    Wings white, spanning only about 3cm   [†]Polymitarcidae p. 56

9. Vein Cu_2 of forewing almost parallel to rear margin   [†]Isonychidae p. 56

    Vein Cu_2 of forewing not parallel to rear margin   10

10. Hind wing very small (less than 1/5th length of forewing)   Baetidae p. 56
     or absent

    Hind wing about 1/3rd length of forewing   11

11. A number of wavy veinlets run   Siphlonuridae p. 56
     obliquely from vein Cu_1 to rear
     margin of forewing

Cu_1

wavy veinlets

    Forewing has no such veinlets   12

12.   One pair of intercalary veins between Cu_1 and Cu_2 in   [†] Metretopodidae p. 56
       forewing: hind wing distinctly oval

       Two pairs of intercalary veins between Cu_1 and Cu_2 Heptageniidae p. 56

[†] indicates families not occurring in the British Isles.

Care must be taken when using this key to ensure that the correct number of tails is known. Broken stumps will be present where tails have been lost accidentally.

The **Ephemeridae**, typified by *Ephemera danica* (Pl. 1), have dark brown wing markings. The nymphs are burrowers and these species are therefore found principally in slow-moving or still water where the mud accumulates. The nymphal gills are rather feathery and are bent over the abdomen in response to the burrowing habit. There are three British species. The **Potamanthidae**, with a single European species, is very similar but has clear wings (Pl. 1).

The **Caenidae**, typified by the genus *Caenis* (Pl. 1) are all very small mayflies with no hind wings. The forewings are fringed posteriorly with small hairs and the venation is reduced, there being only a few cross veins arranged in a vague zig-zag line across the wing. The nymphs are slow-moving, bottom dwelling forms and at least partly carnivorous. They can be recognised by the enlarged second gill that forms a protective cover over those behind it. There are six British species. The **Leptophlebiidae** contains medium-sized species, between about 10 and 25mm across, with brown or yellow bodies and clear or smoky brown wings. *Leptophlebia vespertina* (Pl. 1) is typical of the six British species. The **Ephemerellidae** is very similar but the two families can be separated by their wing venation (see key). *Ephemerella ignita* (Pl. 1) is the commoner of the two British species.

The **Baetidae** (Pl. 1) has four genera: *Baetis* and *Centroptilum* with hind wings and *Cloeon* and *Procloeon* without. All are under 25mm across. The nymphs are swimmers but the first two genera prefer running water and the other two are more often found in ponds and canals, or even in water butts. There are 14 British species.

The **Siphlonuridae** are confined largely to hilly regions, where the nymphs frequent lakes and rivers. Commonest of the four British species is *Siphlonurus lacustris* (Pl. 1). The **Isonychidae**, with its single European species *Isonychia ignota* (Pl. 1), is often regarded as a sub-family of the Siphlonuridae.

Members of the **Heptageniidae** vary from 10 to 35mm across and are fairly widely distributed, although commoner in upland regions where the streams are faster and the lakes are clearer. The nymphs are of the flattened type, adapted to clinging to stones on the river bed. *Ecdyonurus dispar* (Pl. 1) is a typical member of the family, which contains 11 British species.

The **Palingeniidae** has only two European species, including *Palingenia longicauda* (Pl. 2), which is Europe's largest mayfly. *Oligoneuriella rhenana* (Pl. 2) is the only species in the **Oligoneuriidae** and is easily recognised by its few wing veins, while *Ephoron virgo* (Pl. 2), the only European member of the **Polymitarcidae**, is readily identified by its cloudy white wings. The **Metretopodidae**, with its distinctly oval hind wings, is confined to Scandinavia, where *Metretopus norvegicus* (Pl. 2) is the commonest species. The **Ametropodidae**, with a few species in central Europe, is very similar and the two families have only recently been separated by taxonomists.

Collecting and Preserving

Searching waterside vegetation can be very productive. Mayflies generally do not fly readily and are reasonably easy to capture. A soft net material is necessary for taking them in flight to avoid damaging the delicate wings. Emerging duns can be scooped from the water with a piece of muslin stretched over a wire frame. Nymphs collected from the water and kept in an aquarium may be expected to provide duns and spinners at a later date. Specimens for the collection may be killed in the normal way. The larger ones can be pinned and set like butterflies, but the smaller species are extremely fragile and are best preserved on microscope slides or in alcohol. Mayfly colours rapidly deteriorate and specimens should be brought home alive if the colours are to be used for identification. Many species can be identified by colour or venation alone, but microscopic examination of the genitalia is often necessary to separate closely related species. If this sort of examination is intended the specimens must be preserved in alcohol.

Order Odonata – Dragonflies
Plates 2 & 3

Recognition features Long, slender-bodied insects. Two pairs of wings with an intricate network of veins. Very large compound eyes. Antennae short and inconspicuous. It is unlikely that the dragonflies will be confused with any other insects, although the ant-lions (Pl. 14) are rather similar.

Like the mayflies, dragonflies spend their early lives in water and few stretches of permanent water are without them, although most species favour still or slow-moving water. Many of the adults, however, are very strong fliers and they are by no means confined to the vicinity of water. Despite such names as 'horse-stinger' – given to them perhaps because of their large size, swift flight, and the rustling of their wings as they swoop about – dragonflies are harmless and certainly have no sting. In fact, they do a great deal of good by keeping down mosquitoes and other small flies which make up the bulk of their food.

The colours of dragonflies, produced by pigments and/or structural effects, are some of the most striking in the whole animal kingdom. In life, many species can be recognised by colour alone, but colour is not always a good guide. For one thing,

A dragonfly (left) and a damselfly at rest

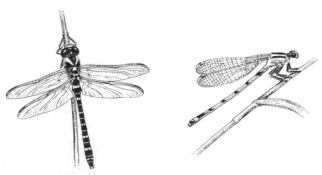

colours fade after death and preserved specimens, unless specially treated, never really retain the colours of the living insects. Females often differ in colour or pattern from the males and, above all, the insects change colour as they get older: freshly emerged (teneral) specimens are much paler than older ones. Several species gradually develop a powdery bloom or pruinescence on the body surface as they get older, especially among the males. This bloom is whitish or powdery blue and can completely alter the appearance of a specimen in two or three days.

There are 113 European species, of which 40 are resident in the British Isles. They fall easily into two sub-orders – the ZYGOPTERA or damselflies (Pl. 2) and the ANISOPTERA or true dragonflies (Pl. 3). The wings of the damselflies are all more or less alike, with a narrow stalk, whereas in the true dragonflies the hind wings are broader than the front pair.

Dragonflies are generally day-flying insects and they rely almost entirely on sight for carrying out their daily lives. In many species the head appears to consist of little but the compound eyes, which may have up to 30,000 facets. The eyes of the true dragonflies generally meet or almost meet on top of the head. The hemispherical eyes of the damselflies are smaller and are set widely apart on the sides of the broad head, giving the head and body a resemblance to a tiny hammer. The head is able to swivel round on the slender neck, giving the insects all-round vision. The large number of facets makes the eyes extraordinarily sensitive to movements in the surroundings and allows the insects to see and catch small insects in full flight. It also makes the larger dragonflies extremely difficult to catch. The antennae, seat of the senses of touch and smell, are poorly developed. The mouth-parts have strongly toothed mandibles and are well adapted for a carnivorous diet.

The prothorax is small and distinct but the other two thoracic segments are welded together into a very prominent pterothorax, in connection with the strong powers of flight of many species. The pterothorax has undergone distortion during evolution so that the leg-bearing ventral surface is tilted forward and the wing-bearing dorsal surface is tilted back. The prominent 'shield' in front of the wings is actually formed

Forewings of a dragonfly (top) and a damselfly, showing the main features of the venation

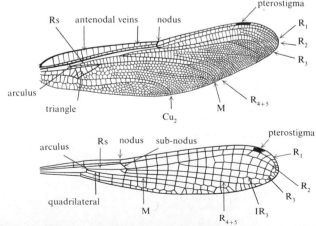

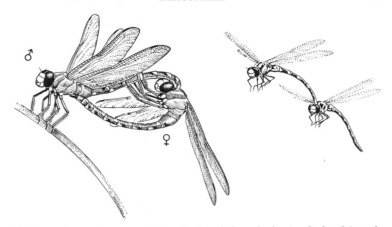

*Left, The mating position or copulation wheel, with the male clasping the female's neck.
Right, The tandem position*

by the upward extension of the episterna (sides) of the second thoracic segment. In this way the second and third pairs of legs are brought forward close to the front legs and are all available to form the 'basket' that scoops the dragonfly's prey from the air and holds it while the jaws get to work. The legs are also used for clinging to supports, but the insects do not walk.

The basic wing venation is the same in both orders, although not all entomologists agree on naming the veins. The system used here is based on the work of Tillyard and Fraser. Somewhere along the front edge of the wing (costa) there is a small kink called the nodus, and just behind it there is a prominent cross vein. Towards the tip of the wing there is usually a dark area called the pterostigma, or simply the stigma. The radius and media arise as a single vein from which vein R_1 is given off and runs to the wing-tip. Between the wing base and the nodus, the vein R_1 is joined to the costal margin by a number of antenodals. Those that run straight across the sub-costa to the wing margin are said to be complete, the others incomplete. At the junction with R_1, vein R+M bends sharply backwards and, together with a small cross vein behind it, forms the arculus. Rs and M separate here, Rs sending three branches to the wing margin. Supplementary veins may occur between these branches. Just beyond the arculus there is in the damselflies a somewhat rectangular cell called the quadrilateral. In the anisopterans this area is divided into two triangular cells, the triangle and supratriangle. This region is important in identification. There are numerous cross veins, generally developed to a greater extent in the anisopterans than in the damselflies, and there are also various additional or supplementary longitudinal veins.

The resting damselfly holds its wings vertically over the body or partly spread, whereas the true dragonflies always rest with wings outspread. The wings work independently in flight and the insects are very manoeuvrable, even able to hover and fly backwards.

The abdomen is relatively long and slender in all dragonflies, although the anisopterans are somewhat stouter in general than the damselflies. There are 10 recognisable segments and some vestiges of the eleventh. All males bear a well-developed

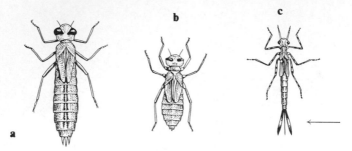

*Nymphs of Odonata: **a** and **b**. dragonflies; **c**. damselfly, distinguished by the external gills at the rear*

pair of appendages on segment 10 and the males are unique among insects in having special reproductive organs on segments 2 and 3 of the abdomen. An ovipositor is present in segments 8 and 9 in the females of certain species, and among the Anisoptera many females also have a prominent pair of appendages on segment 10.

Before pairing the male transfers sperm from the genital opening on segment 9 to the special organs on segments 2 and 3. He then sets off in search of a female and grabs her by the neck with his claspers on segment 10. The female then curves her body round until the tip of her abdomen touches the male's reproductive organs and collects the sperm. This position is known as the copulation wheel. The insects can fly in this position, but usually rest on the vegetation. After copulation a mated pair often fly in the tandem position, with the male towing the female. In some species, particularly among the damselflies, the eggs are laid while the male still holds the female's neck. The zygopterans and some anisopterans lay their eggs in the tissues of water plants, usually putting their abdomens below the water surface in order to make contact with suitable plants. The ovipositor is used to make a suitable slit and the eggs are inserted. Other dragonflies merely scatter their eggs by skimming over the water and dipping the tip of the abdomen into the water at intervals.

The nymphs that hatch from the eggs breathe by means of tracheal gills – thin-walled plates containing tracheae. Those of the true dragonflies are concealed within the abdomen, but those of the damselflies are developed by modification of the cerci and a central projection from the end of the body. There is therefore no difficulty in distinguishing nymphs of the two sub-orders. Those of the Anisoptera are considerably stouter than the zygopteran nymphs.

The head of a dragonfly nymph showing the mask at rest (left) and in use to catch a worm

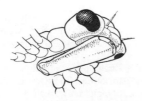

All dragonfly nymphs, like the adults, are carnivorous and the lower lip (labium) is cleverly modified for catching food. It is greatly elongated and hinged in the middle. The palps are modified as movable claws at the end of the labium and the whole arrangement is called the mask because when not in use it is folded back under the head and conceals the rest of the face. When food is sighted the mask is thrust forward and the prey is impaled on the claws.

Apart from the development of the wings and the gradual enlargement of the eyes, there is little visible change during nymphal life. The length of the nymphal life depends to a great extent on the prevailing temperatures and the availability of food, but almost all our damselflies complete their life cycles in one year. True dragonflies may take anything from one to five years and possibly even longer. There are usually between 10 and 15 moults during the nymphal life.

When a nymph is about to moult into a mature, winged dragonfly it crawls up a suitable stem. After a short rest, the skin splits and out come the adult's head and thorax. Another rest follows before the abdomen is pulled clear of the nymphal skin. The wings and body then expand to their full size. Many dragonflies emerge early in the morning, while it is still dark, and the early riser can see them clinging to their supports. As soon as they are warmed by the sun the newly emerged insects fly away, leaving only their cast skins as evidence of the transformation.

SUB-ORDER ZYGOPTERA (Plate 2)

These are very slender and delicate insects with weak powers of flight. Their movement appears to be more of a silent drift from reed to reed than an active flight and they get much of their prey by plucking it out of the vegetation rather than by chasing it through the air. They can be found resting on the vegetation around the water for most of the time. Four families are represented in Western Europe and all occur in the British Isles. They can be separated with the aid of the following key.

1. Wings coloured: 5 or more complete antenodals   Calopterygidae p. 62

    Wings colourless: only 2 complete antenodals   2

2. Stigma elongate   Lestidae p. 62

nodus

    Stigma diamond-shaped   3

3   Quadrilateral   nodus   Platycnemididae p. 62
    sub-rectangular

    Quadrilateral with acute distal angle   nodus   Coenagriidae p. 62

Members of the **Calopterygidae** have brilliant metallic blue or green bodies. Their wings are less abruptly narrowed than those of other damselflies and also differ from them in being coloured. The females have only a yellowish colour on the wings but the males, when seen at certain angles, reflect a brilliant blue sheen. There is no stigma. The males indulge in prolonged fluttering courtship dances and the insects almost always breed in running water. There are two British species, *Calopteryx virgo* differing from *C.splendens* (Pl.2) in having the male wings completely coloured. They are often called demoiselles.

The **Lestidae** contains six species of *Lestes* with metallic green bodies. Two of them occur in Britain. The males have prominent claspers and in two species they have a strong tendency to pruinescence. They usually breed in ponds, bogs, and other stagnant waters, where the female lays her eggs on plants well below the surface. The family also contains two brownish species of *Sympecma*, which are the only European dragonflies passing the winter in the adult state.

Members of the **Platycnemididae** generally have expanded white tibiae on the middle and hind legs. *Platycnemis pennipes*, the only British species, is called the White-legged damselfly. The insects breed in still or slow-moving water, the eggs being laid on submerged or floating vegetation.

The **Coenagriidae** is the largest damselfly family, with 22 European species. Twelve of them occur in Britain. They are mostly red or blue with varying amounts of black, the females usually being much blacker than the males. They live in various habitats but are rarely associated with fast-moving water. Some species produce two generations in a year in southern Europe. Common genera include *Coenagrion, Pyrrhosoma*, and *Ischnura*.

A fifth family – the **Euphaeidae** – occurs in the extreme south-east of Europe. Its single European species, *Epallage fatime*, can be recognised by the brown tips to its otherwise colourless wings.

SUB-ORDER ANISOPTERA (Plate 3)

These dragonflies are much more robust than the damselflies and are much faster fliers. Adults are often found several miles from water and many species seem to have a regular beat, hawking up and down a particular stretch for hours on end. The stiff wings frequently make a rustling sound as they fly. The five European families can be separated with the aid of the following key.

1.   Triangles similar in both wings   2

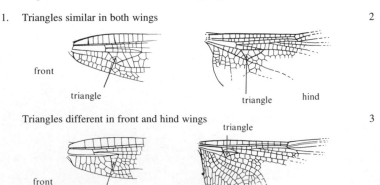

Triangles different in front and hind wings   3

2. Eyes in broad contact on top of head   Aeshnidae p. 63

     Eyes widely separated: abdomen swollen   Gomphidae p. 63

     Eyes only just touching   Cordulegasteridae p. 63

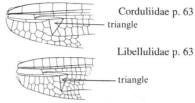

3. Triangle of forewing with front side about as long as basal side: body metallic   Corduliidae p. 63

     Triangle of forewing with front side much shorter than basal side   Libellulidae p. 63

The **Aeshnidae**, with eight British species, are all long-bodied dragonflies sporting blues, browns, greens, and yellows on darker backgrounds. They favour the still waters of ponds and canals, where the nymphs hunt among the water weeds. The adults can be watched for hours as they fly steadily up and down regular beats along streams and hedgerows. *Anax imperator*, commonly known as the Emperor dragonfly, is one of the largest and most colourful of our dragonflies. *Aeshna* is our largest genus, with ten European species. *Brachytron pratense* is a very hairy species that flies earlier in the year than most other dragonflies. It is sometimes on the wing at the beginning of April.

Members of the **Gomphidae** are easily recognised by their widely separated eyes. In addition the male abdomen is slightly swollen at the rear. The insects breed mainly in running water and the rather flat nymphs bury themselves in the mud or sand to wait for prey. Unlike most dragonflies, the adults like to bask on the ground, often congregating in large numbers at favourable spots. *Gomphus vulgatissimus* is the only British species.

The **Cordulegasteridae** has just two very similar black and gold species in western Europe, with only *Cordulegaster boltonii* occurring in Britain. The insects breed in fast-running streams, where the females use their long ovipositors to bury their eggs well in the sand or silt. The nymphs burrow and lie in wait for their prey.

The metallic green *Cordulia aenea*, recognisable by the thick yellow hairs on its thorax, is the commonest of the nine European members of the **Corduliidae**. It can be found near large ponds and other stretches of still water. There are three British species in this family.

Members of the **Libellulidae** are shorter than most other anisopterans. They rarely reach 50mm in length, but a flattening of the abdomen makes many of them appear rather stout. Instead of patrolling a regular beat like the hawkers of the Aeshnidae, most of them spend long periods on a perch from which they dart out to investigate passing flies. For this reason they are commonly known as darters. Bronze and red are the dominant colours, but there is a strong tendency for the older males to develop the blue bloom. This is particularly noticeable in *Libellula* and *Orthetrum* species. Other genera in this family include *Sympetrum* and *Leucorrhinia*. There are 14 British species, including an infrequent visitor. Several species in this family are great migrants.

Collecting and Preserving

The weak-flying damselflies can be collected quite easily by sweeping waterside vegetation, although it is better to net them as they fly up after disturbance. The larger dragonflies, literally with eyes in the backs of their heads, are not so easy, but their habit of patrolling a beat or perching in a particular place allows one to sit in wait, and then a quick upward sweep of the net from behind may be rewarded. Freshly-emerged or teneral specimens, whether collected in the field or bred in captivity, are quite unsuitable for the cabinet as they are very soft and pale. Even if kept alive for a few days in captivity, they rarely attain their full colours.

Dragonflies intended for the collection can be killed with the usual agents but they should not be killed for a day or two after collection. They can be slipped into paper envelopes and kept cool until wanted. This treatment appears to do no harm to the insects, but during confinement they get rid of most of their gut contents and this makes for quicker drying and better preservation. It is essential to pin the insects through the pterothorax at right angles to the wings. Do not pin through the 'shield' or the wings will not lie flat. A normal setting board can be used, or the insects can be set upside-down on a flat sheet of cork. Dragonfly colours fade rapidly after death but quick drying will help to preserve them and anyone with access to a desiccator that can be connected to a vacuum pump can expect good results. Some collectors recommend slitting the abdomen and withdrawing the gut, and then immersing the specimen in alcohol for several hours before drying.

Order Plecoptera – Stoneflies
Plate 4

Recognition features Medium-sized insects usually with two pairs of membranous wings, of which the hind pair are the larger. The soft body is somewhat flattened and this feature is often accentuated by the way in which the wings are folded flat over the body at rest. The antennae are long and slender and there are often long cerci at the hind end, although these are greatly reduced in some species. Structurally, the stoneflies resemble the grasshoppers and cockroaches, but there is never any great thickening of the forewings. Caddis flies and some lacewings could be confused with stoneflies, but their wing venation and the positions of their wings at rest should distinguish them.

The stoneflies are a relatively small order with about 3,000 known species. About 150 live in Europe but only 34 have been recorded in Britain. They are little known outside entomological and angling circles because they are rather secretive and inactive creatures and their colours merge very well with the background.

Like the mayflies and dragonflies, the stoneflies spend their early lives in the water and the nymphs are important items in the diet of fish. The adults are also eaten, thus making them of interest to the fly fisherman, who has names for many of them and uses them as models for his artificial flies. Stonefly nymphs have a distinct preference for running water, only a few being found in still or slow-moving stretches. Most species and greatest numbers are found in those streams with stony or gravelly bottoms and the stoneflies are therefore found principally in hilly regions,

A typical stonefly showing the way in which the wings lie flat over the body at rest

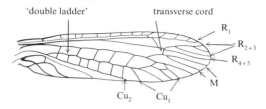

The forewing venation of a typical stonefly, showing the 'double ladder' characteristic of most families

although certain chalk streams in southern England are well stocked with them. They are very intolerant of pollution and are quite absent from stagnant water where the oxygen content is low.

Adult stoneflies live for two or three weeks, which they spend crawling among the waterside stones (hence the name) or on the adjacent vegetation. Their mouth-parts are weak biting structures and many of them do not feed as adults, although some scrape algae from stones and tree trunks or take pollen from flowers. When disturbed they fly weakly and soon come to rest again.

The long, slender antennae consist of up to 80 tiny segments. The compound eyes are well developed and there are usually three ocelli. All three thoracic segments are of similar size, the prothorax being well formed. The legs are sturdy and the three-segmented tarsus ends in a strong claw used for clinging to stones. All the wings are membranous, there being little or no hardening of the forewing which is relatively narrow. The hind wings are usually considerably broader than the forewings. The males of some species are almost wingless, and short-winged (brachypterous) forms occur in several species, especially among those species living at high altitudes. The two pairs of wings are widely separated at the base and there is no wing-coupling mechanism. One of the most noticeable features, characteristic of most stoneflies, is the double 'ladder' formed by cross veins running between veins M and Cu_2 in the forewing. The width of the hind wing is produced largely by the development of the anal area, supported by the branched anal veins. There is much irregularity among the smaller cross veins, even to the extent of the two sides of one individual being different. At rest, the wings are either held flat over the body or rolled tightly round it. The name Plecoptera means 'folded wings' (Greek *plekein* = to fold) and refers to the fan-like folding of the hind wings when at rest.

The abdominal cerci are usually long, many-segmented threads but in some families they are reduced to scarcely visible stumps. The abdomen, like the rest of the body, is soft and fleshy with poorly developed sclerites.

Pairing in stoneflies takes place on the ground or on the vegetation and the females then either fly over the surface and dip their abdomens periodically into the water to wash off a batch of eggs, or they actually swim across the surface and lay eggs as they go. The short-winged forms simply crawl into the water or even lay their eggs at the water's edge. Each female may lay several hundred eggs.

Apart from the lack of wings, stonefly nymphs are very similar to the adults. Their flattened bodies are admirably suited to their life of clinging to stones in running water and in this respect they resemble certain mayfly nymphs. They can be distinguished from the latter, however, by the absence of the plate-like tracheal gills and by the possession of only two 'tails' – all mayfly nymphs have three tails. Even those

A stonefly nymph

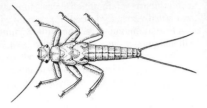

stonefly species in which the adult cerci are reduced have two well-developed tails in the nymphal state.

Stonefly nymphs obtain much of their oxygen by simple diffusion through the body surface but some species have accessory gills which are like tufts of tiny hairs on various parts of the body. They are primarily vegetarians, feeding on algae and mosses on the stream bed, but some of the larger ones are carnivorous and eat nymphs and larvae of other aquatic insects.

Most of our stoneflies complete their development in one year but a few take two or three years. One of our larger species, *Dinocras cephalotes*, has been known to undergo 33 moults during its three-year nymphal life, but most species probably have considerably fewer moults. When fully grown the nymphs move to the edge of the water and crawl out before the adults emerge. Stoneflies can be found at most times of the year, although most species have a fairly definite season.

A Key to the Families of European Plecoptera

The following key, based on that given by Kimmins in the R.E.S. Handbook, will allow the European species to be placed in their correct families.

1.	Cerci short and inconspicuous	2
	Cerci long	4
2.	2nd tarsal segment as long as the others	Taeniopterygidae p. 67
	2nd tarsal segment shorter than the others	3
3.	Apical marginal space of forewing has oblique cross vein	cross vein in apical space Nemouridae p. 67
	No such cross vein	Leuctridae p. 67
4.	No obvious 'ladder' of veins in forewing: basal tarsal segment as long as third	Capniidae p. 67
	Usually a clear 'ladder' of veins in forewing: basal tarsal segment shorter than third	5

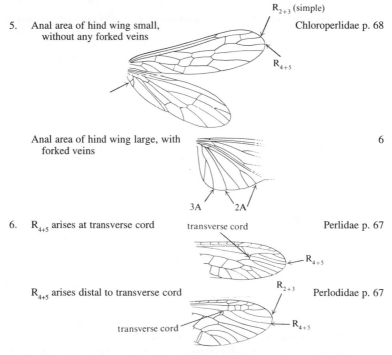

5. Anal area of hind wing small, without any forked veins — Chloroperlidae p. 68

R_{2+3} (simple)

R_{4+5}

Anal area of hind wing large, with forked veins — 6

3A   2A

6. R_{4+5} arises at transverse cord — Perlidae p. 67

transverse cord

R_{4+5}

R_{4+5} arises distal to transverse cord — Perlodidae p. 67

R_{2+3}

transverse cord

R_{4+5}

The families **Taeniopterygidae, Nemouridae**, and **Leuctridae** all contain small brown or black stoneflies with short, inconspicuous cerci. The insects, of which there are 21 British species, rarely exceed 12mm in length. *Leuctra* species are often called needle flies because, when at rest, the wings are wrapped around the body to give them a very slender appearance. *Nemoura* species are rather similar, but their forewings are slightly less pointed and they are not wrapped around the body at rest. *Taeniopteryx nebulosa*, the angler's February Red, is unusual in preferring muddy streams and rivers and it is absent from typical stonefly areas.

The family **Capniidae** contains small blackish stoneflies which are easily recognised because their wings lack the 'ladder' of veins found in most other stoneflies. They emerge quite early in the year and are often called winter stoneflies. *Capnia bifrons* is the commonest of the three British species.

The **Perlidae** contains several quite large insects, such as *Dinocras cephalotes*, whose wings may span 50mm or more. Freshly-emerged insects can often be found sitting beside their empty nymphal skins on waterside stones, especially around upland streams. Despite their large wings, their flight is very weak. They don't feed, although they drink plenty of water. Their nymphs are carnivorous. There are only two British species. *Perla bipunctata* is similar to *D. cephalotes* but the pronotum is largely yellow.

The **Perlodidae** contains several large species resembling those in the Perlidae but they can be distinguished by the network of veins near the tip of the forewing. *Perlodes microcephala*, whose male has very short wings, is a typical example. It is the only large stonefly commonly found in chalk streams. The family also contains a number of smaller green or yellowish species such as *Isoperla grammatica*. There are five British species, although one of these may now be extinct. The **Chloroperlidae**, represented by *Chloroperla torrentium*, contains a number of small yellowish stoneflies with narrow hind wings and unforked anal veins. There are three British species.

Collecting and Preserving
Examination of tree trunks and walls around suitable stretches of water will yield a fair selection of stoneflies, and more can be found by looking on and between stones at the water's edge. The larger species can be pinned and set in the normal way but the soft body soon shrivels and, although the wings remain in good condition, the genitalia and other features necessary for specific identification are damaged or destroyed. Insects intended for permanent storage or study should be preserved in spirit.

Order Orthoptera – Grasshoppers and Crickets
Plates 5 & 6

Recognition features Medium to large insects with a stout body, large blunt head, and conspicuous saddle-shaped pronotum. The hind legs are usually enlarged and modified for jumping. There are typically two pairs of wings, the front pair of which are tough and leathery, although one or both pairs may be reduced or absent. The shape of these insects is so characteristic that, once known, it is impossible to confuse them with members of any other order.

There are more than 17,000 known species in this order, but they are mostly tropical insects and most of the 650 or so species found in Europe are confined to the south. Only 30 species live in the British Isles, and only seven of these reach Scotland. The insects are quite numerous, however, and few grassy places are without these chirpy creatures in the summer. Their relatively large size and the ease with which they can be kept in captivity make them ideal insects for study, and the fascination of their songs adds greatly to their interest. In the warmer parts of Europe the Field Cricket is sometimes kept as a family pet on account of its song, which is less varied than that of a canary but certainly no less pleasant.

The name Orthoptera, derived from the Greek *orthos* meaning straight or rigid, refers to the rather straight forewings of these insects, but this feature is also exhibited by the cockroaches and mantids (Order Dictyoptera) and some entomologists advocate dropping the name Orthoptera in favour of Saltatoria. Derived from the Latin *saltare*, meaning to leap, this name is certainly more descriptive of the grasshoppers and crickets. There are seven European families, although some entomologists recognise a lot more, and they differ considerably in both structure and habits.

The large head is usually hypognathous, meaning that it has a vertical face with the biting jaws below the rest of the head (fig. p. 14). The compound eyes are large

A typical grasshopper showing the enlarged hind legs used for jumping

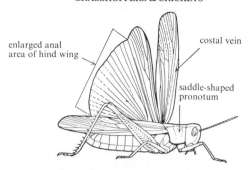

enlarged anal
area of hind wing

costal vein

saddle-shaped
pronotum

*A typical grasshopper showing the saddle-shaped pronotum, the rather straight and
narrow forewing, and the greatly enlarged anal area of the hind wing*

and most species have two or three ocelli. The antennae vary from very short to
several times the length of the body.

Behind the head, the pronotum is always large and well developed, bending down
at right angles to cover the sides as well as the top of the prothorax. In the groundhoppers the pronotum reaches almost or quite to the end of the abdomen. Many
species have reduced wings or no wings at all, but when wings are present the front
ones are tougher and are sometimes called tegmina (singular tegmen). They overlap
to a greater or lesser extent in the middle line and are bent downwards to cover the
sides of the body. The hind wings are delicate, membranous structures and are folded
neatly under the forewings at rest. They are generally of a drab or neutral colour,
but some continental grasshoppers have brightly coloured hind wings. Venation is
fairly complete and there is normally a greatly enlarged anal area in the hind wing.
The costal vein of the forewing does not follow the front margin.

Many grasshoppers, including the notorious locusts, can fly well, but flight is not
usually maintained for any great length of time. Even narrow stretches of water form
effective barriers to these insects, and this explains why there are so few British
species compared with the continental fauna. Many orthopterans are, of course, completely flightless, especially those living at high altitudes.

The legs are well developed and carry efficient claws. The hind legs are normally
much larger than the other two pairs and endowed with powerful muscles in connection with the jumping habit, although not all species jump with equal readiness:
crickets and bush-crickets are just as likely to crawl or scuttle away as to jump.

The ovipositor is normally well developed and externally visible, but the male
genitalia are partly concealed. The cerci vary in length, being long in the true crickets
and short in most other groups, although in some males, especially among the bush-
crickets, they form large claspers which are used to hold the females during mating.

Metamorphosis in this order is slight, the young stages being recognisable almost
from the very beginning. The eggs are laid singly or in batches and are placed under
the ground, in crevices, or in plant tissues, the ovipositor being used to seek out or
cut a suitable hole. When they first leave the eggs the young insects are worm-like,
but this is merely a transitional stage lasting only long enough for the insect to reach
the open air. There the shroud-like covering is immediately discarded to reveal the
little nymph. There are normally four to six nymphal instars among the grasshoppers,
but the crickets undergo up to ten moults or even more before becoming adult. An

*A grasshopper nymph showing how the wing
buds are reversed in the last two nymphal
instars*

interesting feature of all orthopterans is that in the two final nymphal instars the developing wing buds become twisted so that the front margin of the wing is uppermost and the hind wings cover the front ones.

Most of our orthopterans complete their life cycles in one year, the adults dying in the autumn and leaving only eggs to survive the winter and produce the next year's insects. A few species take two years to mature and pass at least one winter as nymphs, and a few species actually overwinter in the adult state. Some bush-crickets regularly spend two winters in the egg stage.

Grasshoppers feed primarily on grass, but animal material features quite largely in the diets of the crickets.

The 'songs' of the crickets and grasshoppers fascinate many people. They are produced by a process known as stridulation, which involves the rubbing of one part of the body called the file over another part called the scraper. The file is provided with a series of pegs or ridges that strike the scraper in turn and set up vibrations. You can imitate the action by drawing a comb over the edge of a piece of card. Grasshoppers stridulate by rubbing their hind legs against their wings, while crickets do it by rubbing their wings together. The complete passage of the file over the scraper is usually very rapid and produces a short pulse of sound (strictly speaking there are several pulses, one for each peg as it strikes the scraper, but these small pulses follow each other so quickly that we can regard each passage of the file as producing a single pulse). This is the basic sound-producing mechanism in all the stridulators, but the pattern of the song varies enormously. The pulses come in bursts, or chirps, of varying duration, caused by repeated passage of the file over the scraper. The Common Green Grasshopper (*Omocestus viridulus*) produces a continuous chirp for 20 seconds or more and its whole body quivers as the legs move up and down as much as 20 times every second. Very different is the song of the Field Grasshopper (*Chorthippus brunneus*), which consists of a series of 6-10 half-second chirps spread evenly over about 12 seconds. All of our grasshoppers have a fairly fixed song length at a given temperature and the song is repeated at irregular intervals, but the crickets have no fixed song length and in warm weather they go on singing indefinitely. Most orthopterans are quiet in cool weather.

Volume and pitch vary from species to species just as the song pattern does, and one can liken the various songs, when amplified, to the sounds of motor mowers, sewing machines, motor cycles, and so on. In fact, it is usually easier to identify grasshoppers, in which there is great colour variation, by their songs than by their appearances.

Stridulation is confined largely to the males. Some females can do it, although their songs are normally quieter than those of the males. When in the presence of females, many males break into their 'courtship songs', often very different from the 'isolated male songs' which are most frequently heard and which presumably attract any females that happen to be in the neighbourhood. The females, of course, respond only to the songs of their own species. The 'ears' with which the insects pick up the sounds are tiny membranes, at the base of the abdomen in grasshoppers and on the front legs in crickets.

The 'ear' of a cricket is just below the 'knee' - the femur-tibia junction - of the front leg

'ear'

The seven European families of the Orthoptera can be identified with the aid of the following simple key.

Key to the European Orthoptera

1. Front legs greatly enlarged and used for digging   Gryllotalpidae p. 71

   Front legs not so modified: hind legs large and normally used for jumping   2

2. Antennae longer than body   3
   Antennae shorter than body   5

3. Palps very long: insects always wingless   Rhaphidophoridae p. 74
   Palps shorter: insects often winged   4

4. Tarsi 4-segmented: cerci short   Tettigoniidae p. 73
   Tarsi 3-segmented: cerci long   Gryllidae p. 72

5. Pronotum extends back to cover all or most of abdomen   Tetrigidae p. 76

   Pronotum does not extend back in this way   6

6. Front tarsi 3-segmented   Acrididae p. 74
   Front tarsi 2-segmented   Tridactylidae p. 76

Family Gryllotalpidae: Mole Crickets
Plate 5

Only the Common Mole Cricket (*Gryllotalpa gryllotalpa*) lives in the northern half of Europe. It is one of our largest insects, with a length of 35mm or more. It is almost entirely clothed with fine hairs and it has enormous front legs. These are strongly toothed and used for digging, for these insects spend most of their time tunnelling in the soil – hence the name mole cricket. The insect favours damp ground in the vicinity of water and, although widespread on the continent, it is now very rare in Britain.

The forewings are short, but the hind wings are fully developed and extend beyond the tip of the abdomen when folded. There is no external ovipositor and the female lays 200-300 eggs in an underground nest. Unlike most insects, she guards her eggs and also tends the young that hatch in two or three weeks. After a month or so the nymphs leave the nest and begin to fend for themselves, eating plant roots and insect grubs. The latter probably make up the bulk of the diet, so the damage done to crop roots is probably more than offset by the destruction of pests. There are about 10 nymphal instars and the nymphs do not become adult until the year after hatching. Insects hatching in late summer may even spend two winters as nymphs and not reach the adult state until nearly two years after hatching.

Male mole crickets stridulate like the other crickets by rubbing their forewings together. The song, described as 'long bursts of a subdued churring noise', may be heard on warm, summer evenings, at which times the insects occasionally take to the air with a rather clumsy flight. *Gryllotalpa vineae* from southern Europe builds a special singing burrow with two funnel-shaped openings which act like megaphones. Its piercing 'song' can be heard more than 500 metres away, making the insect a good candidate for the title of the world's noisiest animal!

Family Gryllidae: True Crickets
Plate 5

These insects appear more flattened than the other orthopterans because the bulk of the forewing is placed horizontally over the body instead of vertically. The forewings are also relatively short and the rolled-up hind wings, when present, extend beyond them. The female's ovipositor is usually long and needle-like and the cerci are long in both sexes. The eggs are laid singly in the soil or in crevices and the nymphs follow the usual path of development, varying only in the length of time taken to reach maturity. They are omnivorous creatures, although vegetable material predominates in their diets.

The males stridulate by rubbing their forewings together. The wings are held a little way above the body and a toothed ridge on the underside of the right forewing is drawn across the hind edge of the left forewing. Cricket songs are prolonged and relatively musical, having a much higher pitch than grasshopper songs.

The commonest cricket in most parts of Europe is the House Cricket (*Acheta domesticus*), a native of Africa and the Middle East which is now well established in buildings all over Europe. It is found in kitchens, bakeries, and other places where the temperatures are above normal, and it also exists, sometimes in enormous numbers, on rubbish dumps which are kept warm by the fermentation of refuse. Unlike many native crickets, it is fully winged and flies well. Britain's only two native crickets – the Field Cricket (*Gryllus campestris*) and the Wood Cricket (*Nemobius sylvestris*) – are both rare and confined to the southern counties of England, but they are common on the continent, where the Field Cricket's bird-like warble can be heard in the fields from April until August. Whereas most crickets are crepuscular, the

a. Field cricket with wings raised in singing position; b. the file on the field cricket's wing: c. the stridulatory pegs on the hind leg of a grasshopper

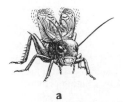

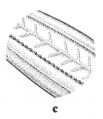

a

b

c

field and wood crickets are active mainly by day. Their hind wings are vestigial or absent, so the insects cannot fly. The wingless Scaly Cricket (*Pseudomogoplistes squamiger*) occurs in many coastal areas of southern Europe and also in a small area on the southern coast of England.

The pale and delicate Italian Cricket (*Oecanthus pellucens*) lives in the southern half of Europe, where it sits on the vegetation at night and brings forth one of the sweetest of all insect songs – a bubbling sound, fairly high pitched and consisting of the phrase gri-i-i-i repeated over and over again. It is very difficult to track down the insect, however, because it alters the volume of the song at the slightest disturbance and the sound appears to come from another place. Fabre described the effect on the would-be collector as '...complete confusion!'.

Family Tettigoniidae: Bush-crickets
Plate 5

These insects used to be called long-horned grasshoppers because of their very long, thread-like antennae, but bush-cricket is a much more appropriate name. The insects are more closely related to the true crickets than to the grasshoppers and they are more likely to be found in bushes and other scrubby vegetation than in open grassland. They can be separated from the true crickets by their 4-segmented tarsi and short cerci. There are ten British species.

The degree of wing development varies from species to species and only five of the British species can fly. Some, including the Great Green Bush-cricket (*Tettigonia viridissima*), fly very well, but most make just short flights and many are just as likely to walk away when disturbed. All the winged species fly more readily in warm weather. Like the true crickets, the bush-crickets sing by raising their wings and rubbing them together, but the arrangement of the wings is reversed, with the left forewing carrying the teeth and lying on top of the right one. The sound is often very high pitched and some bush-crickets, including *Conocephalus* species, go on singing for long periods without a break. It is normally only the males that sing, but the female Speckled Bush-cricket (*Leptophyes punctatissima*) has a weak song with which she attracts the males after they have alerted her with their own high-pitched chirps. *Ephippiger* females also sing quite well. As in the true crickets, the 'ears' are situated on the front legs (fig. p. 71).

The male cerci are curved inwards and are used to hold the female during mating. They are usually quite small, but in some species, including the Oak Bush-cricket, they are very prominent. Their shape is often useful in identification. The female is endowed with a fearsome-looking, broad-bladed ovipositor but, although it strikes terror into many people, it is quite harmless and is used solely for placing the eggs in suitable places. Many ovipositors are equipped with small teeth, which are used to cut slits in plants prior to laying the eggs there. The eggs are laid singly or in small batches and they do not usually hatch until the following year.

Bush-crickets are more nocturnal than grasshoppers, becoming active in the afternoon and continuing to sing well into the night. The Dark Bush-cricket (*Pholidoptera griseoaptera*) produces his staccato psst-psst-psst all through the night. The Oak Bush-cricket (*Meconema thalassinum*) is a common nocturnal visitor to lights in the vicinity of trees. This is one of our commonest bush-crickets and it is in no way confined to oak trees. It has no song and the male summons a mate by stamping his back feet on a leaf: it makes a surprisingly loud noise!

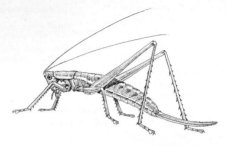

The fiercely carnivorous Saga pedo *comes from the Mediterranean region and, at 10cm in length, is one of Europe's largest insects. Males are unknown and the females reproduce parthenogenetically.*

Visitors to southern Europe will hardly escape without meeting, or at least hearing, the famous tizi (*Ephippiger ephippiger*). This large green or brown insect sits in low bushes and uses its stubby golden wings to utter the short double chirp from which it gets its common French name of tizi. Both sexes produce the sound, although the female chirp is softer than that of the male. There are several other *Ephippiger* species in southern Europe, all with the raised pronotum accommodating the tiny wings. Unlike most of the bush-crickets, the tizi is active all through the day. The same is true of another large continental species, *Decticus albifrons*. This sturdy brown and white insect has a wing-span of over 10cm and flies very well when disturbed. It frequents dry places and produces a very shrill chirp which sounds more like a bird than an insect.

Most bush-crickets eat a mixture of plant and animal matter, but animal matter, in the form of other insects, usually predominates and some of the larger bush-crickets are entirely carnivorous. A few, including some *Ephippiger* species, are largely vegetarian and some damage vines and other crops in southern Europe.

Family Rhaphidophoridae: Cave Crickets
Plate 6

These are completely wingless and rather hump-backed insects with extremely long antennae and a long, almost leg-like pair of palps. They are omnivorous creatures, but they prefer animal food. *Dolichopoda azami* is one of several similar cave-dwelling species living in southern Europe. There are no native species in the British Isles, but the Asiatic *Tachycines asynamorus* has become established in some market gardening areas where there are extensive heated greenhouses. It is often called the Greenhouse Camel Cricket and, although usually regarded as an undesirable alien, it probably does good by eating other insects.

Family Acrididae: Grasshoppers
Plate 6

These are the insects that serenade us with their chirpy songs as we walk through the meadows in the summer, and they are the most familiar of the orthopterans. There are eleven British species, of which ten are fully winged and able to fly. The exception is the Meadow Grasshopper (*Chorthippus parallelus*), in which the hind wings are vestigial. Many other flightless species occur on the continent and some of them

The hind end of the abdomen of a male (left) and a female grasshopper

have virtually no wings at all, especially among the females. *Oedipoda* species and some other grasshoppers have brightly coloured hind wings. When disturbed, they fly on an erratic course and flash the colours. Then they drop to the ground and cover their hind wings, leaving a pursuing bird (or an entomologist) searching in vain for brightly coloured insects.

The antennae are short and stout, in great contrast to those of the bush-crickets, and there are no hearing organs on the legs: the tympana occur on the sides of the abdomen. The pronotum bears a keel along the mid-line. The ovipositor is small and often partly concealed, but the sexes are easily distinguished because the hind end of the abdomen is always turned up in the male, rather like the prow of a boat.

As their name suggests, grasshoppers frequent grassy places and other low-growing vegetation, but many of them have very definite habitat preferences. For example, the Large Marsh Grasshopper (*Stethophyma grossum*) is found only on peat bogs. On the other hand, the Meadow Grasshopper is found on any grassland that is not too dry and, despite its inability to fly, it must be our most abundant grasshopper. Almost all grasshoppers are pure vegetarians, feeding on grasses and a few other plants.

The eggs are laid in groups of about a dozen just under the soil or at the bases of grass tufts. When laid, they are covered with a frothy substance that hardens into a protective envelope or pod and protects them through the autumn and winter. The eggs start to hatch in the spring and adult grasshoppers begin to appear in May or June after four nymphal instars. A few southern species pass the winter as adults.

Sound production in grasshoppers involves the hind legs, which usually carry the stridulatory pegs on their inner surfaces. The singing grasshopper moves its legs up and down, rubbing the pegs against a hardened vein on each forewing. A few species, none of them British, have the stridulatory pegs on their wings and a ridge on each hind leg, while the Large Marsh Grasshopper has a method all of its own: it produces a string of ticking or popping sounds simply by flicking its hind legs against the tips of its wings. The females of some grasshoppers can sing, but their stridulatory pegs are smaller than those of the males and the sounds produced are much softer.

Locusts are large grasshoppers with strong powers of flight. From time to time their populations explode and vast swarms emigrate from the population centres, causing enormous damage to crops wherever they land. Several species are centred on North Africa and the Middle East and these often find their way to Europe. The Migratory Locust (*Locusta migratoria*) is resident in southern Europe but it does not often build up to dangerous numbers there. For much of the time the insects exist in the solitary phase, which can be distinguished by a distinct hump on the pronotum. These solitary insects are often largely green.

Family Tetrigidae: Groundhoppers
Plate 6

At first sight these little insects look like grasshoppers, but they are readily distinguished by the backward extension of the pronotum to cover the abdomen. The forewings are reduced to small scales. The hind wings are often fully developed and the
insects fly readily in warm weather, although the Common Groundhopper (*Tetrix
undulata*) has small hind wings and is flightless. Groundhoppers can be found where
the grass cover is not too extensive (this would favour grasshoppers at the expense
of the groundhoppers) and often occur around the edges of ponds and streams. Several of them actually swim quite well. Like the grasshoppers, they are active by day
and their activity depends very much on temperature. They have no audible chirp
(or hearing organs) and their predominantly brown coloration makes them rather difficult to find on the ground. They feed mainly on mosses and algae.

The eggs are laid in batches, stuck together but not forming pods as in the grasshoppers. They are laid in the ground or in moss and they hatch within a few weeks.
The insects pass the winter as nymphs or young adults. There are three British
species.

Family Tridactylidae: Pigmy Mole Crickets
Plate 6

This family is represented in Europe only by three or four species of *Tridactylus*,
none of which occurs in Britain. All are rare insects under 10mm long that burrow
in moist sandy soil. They can be recognised by their hind femora, which are almost
as large as the abdomen. *T.variegatus* occurs as far north as Switzerland and is the
commonest of the European species.

Collecting and Preserving

Although the crickets and grasshoppers jump well, catching them is not a difficult
task. Tracked down by their songs, many species can be induced to jump or crawl
into large glass tubes. A net may be used for the more active species. Most killing
agents are suitable, and the insects should be pinned through the pronotum and left
to dry after arranging the legs and spreading the wings if desired. As with many
other large-bodied insects, the preservation of body colour is difficult, but rapid
drying, preferably in a desiccator, should give reasonable results.

Grasshoppers and crickets are very easy to keep alive in a large glass container.
An old fish tank is ideal. A layer of moist sand in the bottom will provide a suitable
medium for the eggs of most species. Regular supplies of fresh grass will keep the
grasshoppers happy, while the addition of a bit of bread or fruit will be welcomed
by the crickets. Most bush-crickets will appreciate an occasional feed of aphids or
other small insects. Kept on a window-sill, but not in the full sun, the males will
usually oblige with a song, and if a suitable window-sill is not available you can
provide the necessary warmth and light by shining a small reading lamp on to the
cage for a few hours each day.

Order Phasmida – Stick Insects
Plate 7

Recognition Features Long slender insects with long legs and (in the European species) no wings. Biting mouth-parts are present. The insects cannot be confused with any other group.

This order contains some 2,000 species and includes both stick insects and leaf insects. The latter are remarkable insects with flattened bodies and leaf-like flaps on their limbs. They look just like leaves. The stick insects are slender, twig-like insects, generally green or brown and very difficult to spot as they sit in bushes and other vegetation. Most members of the order occur in the tropical and oriental regions, but a few stick insects live in southern Europe.

The head is prognathous and carries a pair of slender antennae with as many as 100 segments. All phasmids are vegetarians and they have strong biting jaws. The pronotum is small – in contrast to that of the grasshoppers and cockroaches – but the meso- and metanota are very long and between them they may account for nearly half the body length. All the legs are more or less alike and carry five tarsal segments, except when legs have been lost and regenerated. Wings are not found in the European species, although many tropical species are winged. The abdomen carries a pair of short cerci at the hind end.

Many stick insect species have no known male sex, and males are extremely rare in many others. Reproduction is then parthenogenetic, the females laying fertile eggs without mating. The eggs are like small seeds and each is normally provided with a 'lid' which comes off when it hatches. The eggs are simply dropped to the ground and they often take many months to hatch. Some may not hatch for two or three years. Apart from an increase in size, there is little change during the development of the nymphs. Where males exist they are considerably shorter than the females and much more slender.

Only three species are at all widely distributed in Europe. *Bacillus rossius* and *Clonopsis gallica*, both in the family Phyllidae, are fairly common, but *Leptynia hispanica*, which belongs to the Phasmatidae, is less frequent. The first two species rarely produce males, but the sexes are more or less equally represented in *Leptynia*. The two families are separated on the basis of minor differences in the ornamentation of the legs. *B. rossius* can be distinguished from *C. gallica* by its long antennae. Those of *C. gallica* are hardly larger than the head.

Although there are no native stick insects in the British Isles, four exotic species have established small colonies. Three of them – *Acanthoxyla geisovii, A. inermis,* and *Clitarchus hookeri* – hail from New Zealand and probably arrived with imported plants. They are established only in the Scilly Isles and a few other places in southwest England and southern Ireland. *A.geisovii* has sharp spines on the head and tho-

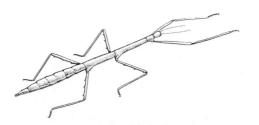

A typical stick insect

rax and is called the Prickly Stick Insect, but the other two are smooth. Males of all three are unknown in Britain, where the females reproduce parthenogenetically, but males of *C.hookeri* are common in New Zealand. The fourth introduced species is the Indian or Laboratory Stick Insect (*Carausius morosus*), which is commonly kept as a pet. A native of the orient, it has managed to establish itself only in greenhouses in the British Isles. Males are rare and the females reproduce parthenogenetically. All four introduced species belong to the Phasmatidae.

Stick insects are best preserved by pinning them through the metathorax, about half way along the body.

Order Dermaptera – Earwigs
Plate 7

Recognition features Elongate brownish insects, usually with short leathery fore-wings meeting in the middle line and reaching only a short way down the body, although many species are entirely apterous. The cerci are modified into stout forceps, strongly curved in the male. The general shape of these insects is such that they may be confused with certain of the rove beetles (Staphylinidae), but the forceps will always distinguish the earwigs.

The earwigs are a small order with only about 1,000 known species. About 45 species occur in Europe, but only four are native to the British Isles and only *Forficula auricularia* and *Labia minor* are at all common in these islands. Other species arrive with imported materials from time to time and some of these have been known to form temporary colonies in and around ports and warehouses in Britain.

Earwigs bring the shudders to many people on account of the superstition that they seek out human ears and bite through the eardrums. There is no truth in the last part, although many campers' ears have been investigated by earwigs and it seems certain that the name earwig (and similar names used in other countries) arose from the occasional finding of one of these insects in the ear. Such visits would presumably have been much more common in the days when people slept on straw mattresses. Earwigs are nocturnal insects and they seek out dark, narrow crevices for their daytime rest. They like to feel both upper and lower surfaces of the body in contact with something when at rest and this allows us to trap them with straw-filled, inverted flower-pots in the garden. As omnivorous scavengers, the insects do more good than harm, but they do have the annoying habit of chewing flower petals – especially those of our prize blooms!

The broad head carries long, slender antennae, containing up to 50 segments. The compound eyes are large, but there are no ocelli. The jaws are of the simple biting

A typical earwig

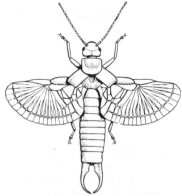

An earwig showing the delicate semi-circular wings, which are folded many times before they can be tucked under the small elytra

type, associated with the insects' omnivorous habits: carrion and living insects are eaten just as readily as flower petals. The prothorax is well developed and clearly visible but the meso- and metathoracic segments are generally hidden by the short, veinless forewings (elytra). The latter carry minute hooks under the inner margin and these engage with similar hooks on the metanotum to hold the elytra firmly in place. The hind wings are relatively large, almost semi-circular in shape, and extremely thin, having very much the texture of the skin that we shed after getting sun-burned. The name Dermaptera means skin-winged (Greek *derma* = skin) and refers to this soft texture of the hind wings.

Most of the hind wing consists of the enlarged anal area, the pre-anal part being reduced to a narrow, thickened strip. The wings are folded very elaborately under the elytra and this thickened strip often projects a short way behind them. If you try to unfold the wings of an earwig you will realise just how elaborately they are folded to get them under the small elytra: there are about 40 thicknesses of each wing when completely folded. The Small Earwig (*Labia minor*) flies frequently, but the other species are reluctant to fly and it is tempting to think that the earwig finds it too much trouble to get its wings out and then put them away again! A number of species have dispensed with hind wings and many of them lack elytra as well.

The abdomen ends in the characteristic forceps, strongly curved in the male and almost straight, perhaps just meeting at the tips, in the female. These forceps are probably defensive structures, for they are raised scorpion-like over the body when the insects are disturbed, but they are also used on occasion to capture prey. Male *Labidura* wrestle fiercely with their forceps when they meet, especially if two males are confined in a small space. There are also reports of the forceps' being used by some species to open their elytra prior to flight and to tuck the hind wings away again afterwards.

Insects are not noted for maternal care, but the female earwig is an exception. *F. auricularia*, which is the best-known earwig in this respect, lays 20-50 eggs in the soil and looks after them through the winter. Experiments under artificial conditions have shown that the female will even collect up her eggs if they are removed and scattered over the surrounding soil. The eggs hatch in early spring, but the nymphs do not leave their winter quarters until they reach the second instar. They are fed and tended by their mother, even after coming above ground, until they are well able to fend for themselves and it is quite common to see such family groups in the spring.

Left, The asymmetrical forceps typical of male members of the Anisolabididae. Centre and right, the forceps of Forficula auricularia, *showing the clear differences between the male (centre) and female (right)*

Apart from the development of wings in those species that possess them, there is little external change in the growing insects. The antennae get more segments and the forceps gradually thicken and assume their adult form, but otherwise the nymphs look very much like the adults. White earwigs often intrigue people, but these are not freaks – just freshly-moulted individuals that have not yet developed their normal pigmentation. There are normally four nymphal instars and the earwigs reach maturity in late summer. Mating takes place before the insects seek out their winter resting places.

The European earwigs may be placed in their correct families with the aid of the following key.

Key to European Earwigs

1. 2nd tarsal segment heart-shaped and surrounding base of 3rd segment: antennae generally with 11-15 segments   Forficulidae

   2nd tarsal segment normal   2

2. Insects usually very dark and completely wingless or with just narrow, scale-like elytra at sides: male cerci often asymmetrical   Anisolabididae

   Elytra always well developed: hind wings usually present as well   3

3. Last abdominal segment wider than the rest: antennae with 20-30 segments   Labiduridae

   Abdomen widest in the middle: antennae with 11-12 segments: body normally under 9mm long   Labiidae

The **Forficulidae** is Europe's largest earwig family and most of its members are fully winged. It contains three British species. *Forficula lesnei* and *Apterygida media* are easily separated from *F. auricularia* because their hind wings do not show beyond the elytra, and easily distinguished from each other by the shape of the male forceps. Both are confined to southern England. The **Labiidae** contains just two small European species, including *Labia minor* which commonly lives in manure and compost heaps. The **Anisolabididae** contains three European species, all totally wingless and all living in damp places. *Euborellia annulipes*, with yellow legs and dark rings on the femora, has occasionally established itself around ports and on rubbish dumps in Britain. The **Labiduridae** has two European species, including our largest earwig *Labidura riparia*. Up to 25mm long, this species is most common in coastal areas and by rivers, where it tunnels in the sand under stones and driftwood. It used to occur around the south coast of Britain, either as a native or an introduced alien, but it is now probably extinct.

Collecting and Preserving
Many earwigs can be collected by sweeping vegetation, by beating branches, or by setting traps of the type described earlier in this chapter, but others prefer to stay on the ground and are normally found by turning over logs and stones. The insects are best preserved by pinning. Attempts should be made to unfold the wings of at least one specimen.

Order Embioptera – Web-spinners

Recognition features Small to medium-sized insects with soft brownish bodies and biting jaws. The basal segment of the front tarsus is swollen. Wings may be present in the males, but are normally absent in European species. The insects live under logs and stones in little silken tunnels.

The Embioptera is a small and little known order of insects, with about 170 known species distributed in all major regions. The insects are known as web-spinners because they make silken webs and tunnels under stones and in the soil. They live in and around their tunnels and withdraw into them very rapidly when disturbed. During the colder months they go deeper into the soil. Web-spinners often live in communities of a dozen or more individuals and, although the individuals do not co-operate, their tangled webs probably give them extra protection from centipedes and other predators. The silk is produced in special glands in the swollen basal segment of the front tarsus.

The head is as broad as the body and carries typical biting jaws. These differ in the two sexes, the male having sharper ones than the female. It is likely that the male is carnivorous and the female feeds more on vegetable matter. Female web-spinners are always wingless, and several species have wingless males as well. In some species the males may be winged or wingless. When wings are present the two pairs are alike, smoky brown and clothed with fine hairs. The radial vein is greatly thickened, but the other veins are weak. Web-spinners do not fly well, although some males come to light at night. The abdomen bears a pair of short cerci, which are generally asymmetrical in the male and useful in the identification of the species.

The eggs are relatively large and oval and they are laid in the tunnels. The female looks after them and the young nymphs for a while. Metamorphosis is more or less absent in the females and only slight in the males.

The few European species are rarely seen and they are confined to the southern parts. Examples include *Haploembia solieri* (family Oligotomidae) and *Embia amadorae* (family Embiidae), the latter sometimes producing winged males. *E. ramburi* is probably the commonest species. It resembles *E. amadorae*, but has a rounder

A typical wingless web-spinner showing the swollen front tarsus

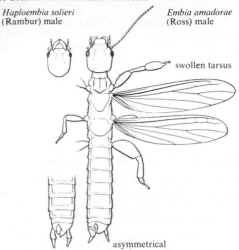

Haploembia solieri
(Rambur) male

Embia amadorae
(Ross) male

swollen tarsus

asymmetrical
cerci

*Above, Hind tarsi of
web-spinners: **a.** Embia,
with one tubercle on the
basitarsus; **b.**
Haploembia, with two
tubercles. Right, Two
European web-spinners
showing the different
head shapes and the
peculiar cerci of the
males. Female cerci are
straight and unmodified.*

head and never has wings. The two genera can be separated only by microscopic examination of the hind tarsi, as shown in the diagram.

Web spinners must be preserved in alcohol because their soft cuticle becomes greatly distorted when dried.

Order Dictyoptera – Cockroaches and Mantids
Plate 7

Recognition features Small, medium, or large insects of rather flattened appearance. Usually two pairs of wings, of which the front ones are leathery and held flat over the back. The antennae are long and slender and the legs are long and spiky. Cerci are conspicuous. Cockroaches have a large shield-like pronotum extending forward and covering most of the head. Mantids have a long, slender pronotum and can also be recognised by their greatly enlarged, spiky front legs. Cockroaches can be distinguished from crickets by the lack of jumping legs. There might be some confusion with beetles – the name 'black beetle' for the Common Cockroach indicates this – but beetle elytra meet in the mid-line as a rule and do not normally overlap. Furthermore, beetles have no cerci. Some of the heteropteran bugs resemble small cockroaches, but here again there are no cerci, and the sucking beaks of the bugs will always distinguish them.

A typical cockroach

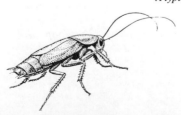

SUB-ORDER BLATTODEA – THE COCKROACHES

The cockroaches are a mainly tropical group and most of the cockroaches seen in Europe are introduced species living only under artificial conditions. The Common Cockroach or 'black beetle' (*Blatta orientalis*), the American Cockroach (*Periplaneta americana*), and the German Cockroach (*Blattella germanica*) are all common pests here. Indeed, they are common all over the world as a result of man's commercial activities. Coming originally from the warmer parts of the world (*B. germanica* is not a native of Germany), these insects find ideal homes in warehouses, kitchens, breweries, and so on where there is warmth and an abundance of food, and they are joined by several other cosmopolitan species. They are all omnivorous insects, although dead animal material is probably their main food in the wild. In captivity they readily devour their dead brothers and sisters, but they will not attack and kill each other for food.

Cockroaches are nocturnal creatures and they hide during the daytime behind skirting boards, under floors, in ventilating ducts, and in other out-of-the-way places. They can build up considerable populations before they are noticed. The harm they do lies not so much in the material they actually eat – this consists largely of scraps – but in the contamination of other materials with a characteristic smell. Large quantities of food have to be thrown away because of this contamination. Cockroaches also carry a number of disease-causing viruses and bacteria.

There are over 4,000 known cockroach species, of which about 130 are native to Europe. These natives are rather small and inconspicuous insects. Three species of *Ectobius* extend into the British Isles, but do not reach beyond the southern counties of England and Wales. They live among the vegetation in a variety of habitats.

The cockroach head (fig. p. 14) is hypognathous and rather primitive in structure. The simple biting jaws are strongly toothed in connection with the omnivorous diet. The antennae are long and the compound eyes are well developed, while two pale patches on the top of the head are believed to represent degenerate ocelli. When the insects are viewed from above most of the head is concealed by the large pronotum, which also extends laterally. The pronotum does not turn down to cover the sides of the prothorax as it does in the grasshoppers and crickets.

Two pairs of wings are normally present, although the females of some species have reduced wings. The forewings, sometimes called tegmina, are leathery and they overlap in the middle line to protect the membranous hind wings. The venation of the hind wing is quite complex, with many branches of the radius and, as in the grasshoppers, a large anal area. The name Dictyoptera means net-wings (Greek *dictyon* = net), but this refers more to the extinct species, which had many more cross veins than living cockroaches.

Most of our cockroaches can fly, but they seem reluctant to do so and they are essentially ground-living insects, although several can be found in the trees. The legs are not modified for jumping but they are relatively long and slender, making the cockroaches elusive runners and very difficult to catch. The tarsi are 5-segmented and the abdomen ends in a pair of short, but quite visible cerci. There is no external ovipositor.

Cockroaches lay their eggs in little purse-shaped containers called oothecae and these can often be seen projecting from the female abdomen. Most cockroaches deposit their purses soon after they are formed but *B. germanica* carries hers around until the eggs are about to hatch. The number of eggs in a purse varies from about 12 to 50, with each species having its own range and average. The nymphs are worm-

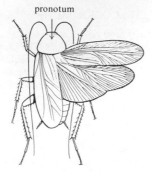

pronotum

An American cockroach showing the large pronotum almost concealing the head and the complex venation of the wings

like when they first hatch, but as soon as they reach the air they shed their skins and emerge as tiny cockroaches. Metamorphosis is slight and there are between 5 and 12 moults, according to species. The nymphs take several months to mature.

The German Cockroach and most of our native species belong to the family **Blattellidae**, while the Common Cockroach and the American Cockroach belong to the **Blattidae**. The main anatomical differences between these families concern the genitalia, but there is also a difference in the way that the oothecae are carried. In the Blattellidae they are carried on their sides, but in the Blattidae they are carried vertically with the keel uppermost.

SUB-ORDER MANTODEA – THE MANTIDS

The mantids, often called praying mantids, are readily distinguished from the cockroaches by their strongly-spined raptorial front legs. They also have a long, narrow prothorax which forms a movable neck. At rest, the prothorax is usually raised a little and the front legs are held folded in front of the face. The resemblance to a person in prayer has led to the common name of the insects. Many mantids are green and they are well hidden as they sit motionless among the vegetation and wait for food. Some tropical species are brightly coloured and have bizarre outgrowths on limbs and body. They bear striking resemblances to certain flowers and are hard to see as they sit on the blossoms. Some are actually so flower-like that they don't even have to sit on flowers: other insects mistake them for flowers and pay with their lives.

All mantids are carnivorous and they use their front legs to catch their food. Flies, butterflies, grasshoppers, and many other insects are eaten. The mantis shoots out its front legs at great speed and snaps them shut around the prey. The spines hold the victim firmly while the mantis devours it greedily with the aid of its strong, sharp mandibles. Even the heavily sclerotised head capsule of a wasp is no problem for a mantis – the jaws munch straight through it.

Mating among mantids has been compared to that among spiders because the male is usually somewhat smaller than his mate and often ends up as her next meal, although the smaller species, such as *Ameles spallanzania*, are not cannibalistic. The eggs are laid in oothecae of various kinds. One common type starts off as a frothy secretion pumped out of the abdomen with the eggs, and then it hardens into a tough spongy material. These oothecae are attached to twigs and branches or hidden under stones, and a female may produce a dozen or more during her lifetime. Like the cockroaches, the mantids are worm-like when they hatch, but they soon shrug off their

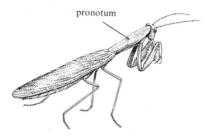

A praying mantis showing the spiky front legs and the very long pronotum

first skins to reveal their true nature. Most mantids pass the winter in the egg stage, although *Empusa* species overwinter as nymphs.

Mantids, like cockroaches, are mainly tropical insects and only about a dozen of the 2,000 or so known species reach Europe. The best known European species is *Mantis religiosa* – the original 'praying mantis' – which occurs throughout the southern half of Europe. It is brown or green, up to 8cm long, and flies readily in warm weather

Collecting and preserving

Our native cockroaches can be collected quite easily in their known haunts by sweeping low-growing vegetation or by sifting leaf litter. The introduced species can be trapped with fruit or syrup when droppings and greasy marks suggest their presence. Insecticidal treatment – to be used with great care where food is prepared – usually sends the insects back to their hideaways to die. Cockroaches are easily kept in captivity as long as warmth is provided. Food presents no problem – kitchen scraps are all that are needed. The mantids can be obtained by careful searching or by sweeping the vegetation. They live well in captivity as long as they have a supply of flies or other insects to eat. Bluebottles, bred from fishermen's maggots, are ideal for the larger mantids.

The smaller cockroaches may be preserved in alcohol or staged on micro-pins, but the larger species and the mantids are best pinned through the meso- or meta-thorax, with the wings spread on one side.

Several species of Empusa *live in southern Europe and are easily recognised by the very slender neck and the crest on the head. They belong to the family Empusidae, whereas most other European mantids belong to the Mantidae*

Order Isoptera – Termites

Recognition features Small to medium-sized insects, with or without wings and with biting mouths. The body is soft and pale and bears short cerci. Wings, when present, are long and narrow with the anterior veins thickened. Both pairs are alike. The insects live in colonies, with several different castes.

A winged termite

The termites are basically tropical insects and only two of the 2,200 or so known species are native to Europe. They are often called white ants because of their pale colour and their social life, but there are many differences between the termites and the true ants and the two groups are not at all closely related.

The mouth-parts of the termites are rather like those of the cockroaches, with tough biting jaws. Some species eat grass and fungi, but most termites feed on wood and they are extremely destructive insects. Some members of the colony get their food at second hand after it has been at least partly digested by the workers. The soldiers and the reproductive castes are always fed in this way, and so are some of the young stages. Food is regurgitated by the workers, or else they pass partly-digested faecal pellets which are consumed by the other termites. Wood is not an easily digested material, and the termites rely on armies of protozoans or bacteria in their stomachs to break down the tough cellulose. Young termites receive their micro-organisms in the food they receive from the workers.

Only the head capsule is at all hard in the termites, the cuticle of the rest of the body being soft and more or less transparent. The head is large and rather oblong or pear-shaped in the soldier castes, but small and rounded in the others. Compound eyes are present in the reproductive castes, but may be greatly reduced or absent in the others, especially in species that remain below ground.

The pronotum is clearly separated from the rest of the thorax and its shape is important in the classification and identification of the insects. The wings, when present, are all alike (Isoptera means 'equal wings') and their anterior veins are thickened. There are few regular cross veins, but the wings often carry a network of small veins and vein-like wrinkles. The wings normally extend well beyond the body when at rest. A pair of short cerci is present in all castes.

The termites differ from the ants and other social insects in having males and females present in more or less equal numbers. All castes contain both males and

Forewings of Kalotermes flavicollis *(left) and* Reticulitermes lucifugus, *showing the extremely fine venation. Front and hind wings are almost identical*

females, and the colony is normally headed by a 'king' as well as a 'queen'. These are members of the primary reproductive caste and they are winged to start with. Their bodies are also more heavily sclerotised than those of the other castes. The primary reproductives emerge from their nests at certain seasons and have a brief aerial life on their weak wings. This may be sufficient to carry them away from the vicinity of their own nests, and then they come down to earth and break off their wings. When opposite sexes meet they excavate a small nuptial chamber and a new colony begins. The king and queen are long-lived insects and they may live together in their colony for many years – 50 years has been quoted for some species. They mate frequently during this time and the queen may get very large – up to 10cm in length in some species – as her abdomen swells with eggs. The colony builds up slowly at first, but then speeds up and colonies of the more advanced families may contain over a million termites. Colonies of the more primitive families contain only a few hundred individuals.

As in all the social insects, the workers are the most numerous members of the colony. They look after the royal couple, tend the eggs and young, forage for food, feed the soldiers, and build and maintain the nest. The work force of the more primitive termites is composed of juvenile insects of various ages and there is no definite worker caste. The majority of these working juveniles never grow up, but they can change into soldiers or reproductive forms if necessary. Further up the termite scale we find the work being carried out more and more by the later instars only, and in the highest termite families, unrepresented in Europe, there is a distinct worker caste. These workers are still juveniles, however, and they never develop wings.

Soldier castes are found in almost all genera of termites. They have large heads and their job is to defend the colony. There are two types of soldier – one with large and powerful jaws and the other with small jaws and a pointed head. The latter type, not found in the European species, ejects poisonous, repellent liquids from glands in the head and this keeps ants and other potential enemies at bay. The soldiers of most termite species lack functional eyes. If anything should happen to the king or queen of the colony the workers can rear yet another caste – the supplementary reproductive. This has only small wings and it does not leave the colony, but its members are fertile and they can step into the role of king or queen to ensure that the colony continues. Termites exhibit only a slight metamorphosis during their lives, but the length of development varies from caste to caste and from species to species. Soldiers and workers probably live for up to four years.

Termite nests vary a great deal in construction. The most primitive families simply excavate galleries in dead wood or make underground nests. The most advanced termites build huge mounds, largely with soil excavated from their underground chambers and cemented with saliva. These great termitaria are especially common in Africa and Australia.

The European termites belong to two families – the **Kalotermitidae** and the **Rhinotermitidae**. The former is one of the more primitive families and it is represented by *Kalotermes flavicollis*. This is a dry-wood termite, living in dead trees and logs and occasionally in building timbers. It has no worker caste and it lives in small communities consisting of a royal pair and a few hundred working young and soldiers. The reproductives take over a year to mature, passing through several instars on the way. The soldiers, which account for about 5 per cent of the population, mature more quickly. This species occurs around the Mediterranean coast, from Portugal to Greece and on to the Middle East.

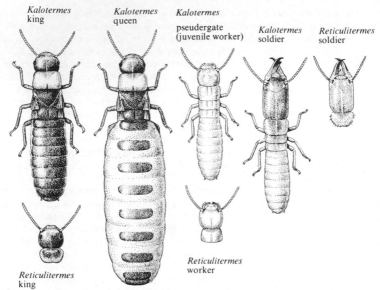

The castes of the two European termites. The pronotum of Reticulitermes *is rounded at the back and almost heart-shaped.* Kalotermes *soldiers have toothed jaws*

The second European species is *Reticulitermes lucifugus*, with a more distinct worker caste. It excavates galleries in trees and shrubs and in building timbers at or below ground level. It does a considerable amount of damage to old buildings. The insects travel more than *Kalotermes* and their colonies are more diffuse. The outer branches may sever their connections with the parent colony and become self-supporting through the production of supplementary reproductives. *Reticulitermes* can survive lower temperatures than *Kalotermes* and it extends north to Bordeaux and northern Italy. An American species, *Reticulitermes flavipes*, has become established in western France and also in Hamburg, but it has so far been found only in buildings.

The European termites can often be found by digging into old logs. Because of their soft cuticles, the insects must be preserved in alcohol.

Order Psocoptera – Psocids or Booklice

Recognition features Small or minute soft-bodied insects rarely exceeding 6mm in length. With or without wings and living in vegetation or among dried materials. Antennae generally long and filiform. Compound eyes often large and protruding from the sides of the head, which itself is quite broad and has a bulging clypeus. Most winged forms, when at rest, hold their wings steeply roof-wise over the body, a position which, with other features, gives the insects a very characteristic appearance. There are never any cerci.

The winged psocids, especially when found in large numbers, may be taken for aphids but the long antennae, broad head, and biting jaws of the psocids easily separate the two groups. They are more often confused with psyllids (p. 120), but the

A typical winged psocid showing the roofwise position of the wings at rest

mouth-parts and wing venation will easily distinguish them. Some of the wingless psocids superficially resemble some of the lice – hence the names booklice and dustlice. Their nearest relatives are probably the biting lice (p. 95), but they are in no way parasitic and are easily distinguished from the lice by their long antennae.

This is a relatively small order of insects with about 2,000 known species, although many more will undoubtedly be discovered. Over 100 species occur in Europe and there are about 90 British species, including several that exist here only in warehouses and similar artificial conditions. The indoor species are mostly wingless or short-winged and live among dried materials such as paper – habits that have given them names such as booklice and dustlice. Undisturbed books frequently harbour these psocids, which feed on minute traces of mould on the paper. The insects are also found in damp houses, where they feed under peeling wallpaper. Entomological collections also suffer from psocid attack and many a prize specimen has been reduced to dust by these little creatures.

The majority of psocid species live out of doors, scraping a living from pollen grains, from algae on bark, and from minute fungi on leaves. The alternative name of barklice refers to the fact that many psocids live on and under bark. Old birds' nests also harbour them. Most of these outdoor species are fully winged. Economically, the order is unimportant, although certain species have been known to carry sheep tapeworms.

The psocid head is relatively wide and very mobile, its width being effectively increased by the large compound eyes which protrude from the sides in most of the winged species. But the eyes are very small structures in the wingless booklice of the family Liposcelidae. Three ocelli are present in winged psocids. The slender antennae mostly contain 13 segments, although some species have 20 or more segments. The mouth-parts are complex pieces of apparatus, the major components being the strong biting mandibles and two rigid rods formed from the inner parts of the maxillae. Sometimes known as picks, these rods are believed to support the head while the mandibles scrape up food particles. The gnawing action of the jaws has led to the order's alternative name of Corrodentia, derived from the Latin verb *rodere* meaning to gnaw.

Winged and wingless psocids or booklice. The swollen hind femora of the wingless Liposcelis *are characteristic of the family Liposcelidae.* Cerobasis, *belonging to the* Trogiidae, *is common on tree trunks (see p. 93)*

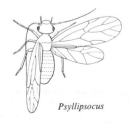

Psyllipsocus

Liposcelis

Cerobasis

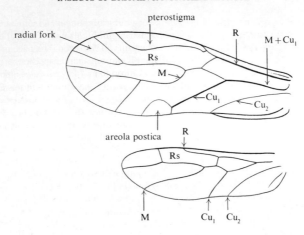

Typical psocid venation

There is a reduction of the prothorax in most winged species and it is commonly concealed from above by the raised mesonotum. The prothorax is larger in the wingless psocids. The wings, when present, are membranous and the forewings are considerably larger than the hind wings. Flight is not common, however, and most species simply scuttle away when disturbed. At rest, the wings are generally held steeply roof-wise over the body, although some species fold their wings flat.

The veins are prominent, although reduced in number. The so-called pterostigma is actually a cell at the front of the forewing and it is frequently pigmented. There is often a certain amount of other marbling on the wings. The radius with the radial sector is 3-branched. The media is also 3-branched in the forewing, although single in the hind wing. The media and cubitus are fused basally and, in the forewing, Cu_1 usually forms a loop to enclose a cell known as the areola postica, which may or may not be connected with the media. There is a notable absence of cross-veins in most species. Wing development commonly varies within a species, with fully-winged, short-winged, and apterous individuals in the same population. Many species have winged males and wingless females.

The legs are simple structures, well suited to running. The tarsi each have two or three segments and each bears two claws. In the family Liposcelidae the hind femora are broad and flat.

The majority of psocids lay small pearly eggs which may be protected by a web of silk or with an encrustation of tiny food particles or faecal matter. The nymphs usually pass through six instars before reaching maturity, although some wingless species have fewer instars. Apart from an increase in size and the development of wings (when present), the main external changes during development are increases in the number of antennal segments and in the relative size of the eyes. There are usually several generations in a year.

On account of their small size, many psocids are difficult to identify and a low power microscope is necessary to identify some of the families with certainty. The following key may be used to separate most of the European families.

Key to the Main Families of European Psocids

1. Insects totally wingless   2
   Insects with at least vestigial wings   4

2. Tarsi 2-segmented   Epipsocidae
   Tarsi 3-segmented   3

3. Very small insects with flattened   Liposcelidae p. 93
   abdomen: hind femora broad

   Insects not flattened: hind femora slender   Trogiidae p. 93

4. Wings vestigial, not extending beyond thorax   5
   Wings fully developed   8

5. Body and winglets covered with scales   Lepidopsocidae
   Insects without scales   6

6. Relatively large species with minute wing vestiges: ab-   Mesopsocidae (females)
   domen distinctly humped, often mottled, and bearing a
   characteristic transverse black band

   Insects not fitting this description   7

7. Winglets rounded (weakly attached and easily lost): maxil-   Trogiidae
   lary palps broad at tip

   Winglets narrow: maxillary palps pointed: hind legs notice-   Psyllipsocidae
   ably long

8. Forewing with just 2 longitudinal   Liposcelidae(some females)
   veins

   Wings normal, with greater number of veins   9

9. Pterostigma and areola postica are   Psyllipsocidae
   simple unpigmented forks: hind
   legs, especially the tarsi,
   noticeably long – reaching well
   beyond tip of abdomen: species
   often brachypterous

   simple fork

   Pterostigma commonly pigmented, both it and areola pos-   10
   tica (if present) with curved margins

10.   Areola postica not present   11

      Areola postica present   12

11.   Pterostigma oblong: cilia present on   Ectopsocidae
      some forewing veins, at least in
      basal half: membrane often with
      dark spots at ends of veins

              oblong pterostigma

                                                        no areola postica

      Pterostigma distally rounded: Peripsocidae
      forewings lack visible cilia:
      membrane often clouded

                                                    no areola postica

12.   Areola postica joined to media in   13
      various ways

                                        free pterostigma

      Areola postica not joined to media: 14
      pterostigma free

                                                    free areola postica
                                        M

13.   Pterostigma joined to Rs   Rs   Stenopsocidae

                                                        M
              areola postica joined to M

      Pterostigma free   Psocidae p. 93

14.   Tarsi 3-segmented   15

      Tarsi 2-segmented   17

15.   Relatively large psocids with globular eyes: forewings   Mesopsocidae (males)
      without cilia

      Smaller psocids with ciliated forewings   16

16.   Cilia short and sparse: hind wing   Elipsocidae
      ciliated only in area of radial fork

      Cilia conspicuous, crossing to form   Philotarsidae
      a lattice around wing-tip: hind
      wing ciliated nearly all round

17.   Wings without visible cilia: pterostigma abruptly termi-   Lachesillidae
      nated and roughly wedge-shaped

      Wings clearly ciliated: pterostigma often long and pointed   18

                                              cross vein

18.   Dark brown insects with elongated   Epipsocidae (males)
      areola postica: cross-vein links Rs
      and M

elongate areola postica

      Areola postica strongly arched: Rs   19
      and M merge

                                             Rs + M

arched areola postica

19.   Rear edge of hind wing carries alternating long and short   Trichopsocidae
      cilia

      Rear edge of hind wing carries only long cilia   Caeciliidae p. 93

There are a number of species that cannot be tracked down with this key because of various departures from the basic family plan. Most of them are rare or obscure in habit and can be ignored in this general account, but there are a few that are likely to come to the notice of anyone who starts looking for psocids. One such species is *Reuterella helvimacula*, a member of the **Elipsocidae** although its tarsi are only 2-segmented. It is a minute insect that spends most of its time in small communal webs on tree trunks. The male is winged, but the female is apterous.

Only about half of the psocid families are at all common and most of our species belong to just four families. The majority of indoor species belong to the **Trogiidae**, whose wings are reduced or absent, and the **Liposcelidae**, all but one of which are wingless. The Liposcelidae includes the commonest of the booklice, *Liposcelis bostrychophilus*. *Lachesilla pedicularia*, with reddish brown bands on its abdomen, is one of the commoner winged species found in houses. Most of our outdoor species belong to the **Psocidae** and the **Caeciliidae**, but *Cerobasis guestfalica* (fig. p. 89) is a very common member of the Trogiidae. Easily recognised by its densely speckled body, it is abundant on tree trunks and fences. It also gets into houses. Males are almost unknown in this species.

Collecting and Preserving

Outdoor species can be collected very easily by sweeping herbage and beating trees. Searching under loose bark or in old birds' nests is also profitable. Indoor species can be found in dim, neglected corners, especially where there is a musty smell.

Their soft bodies dictate that psocids must be preserved in spirit if any structural detail is to be retained.

Orders Mallophaga and Anoplura – Lice

These are small and minute insects that live ectoparasitically on birds and mammals. Their bodies are generally flattened and they are usually provided with strong claws, two features that enable them to cling closely to the host's body and resist all but the most vigorous scratching. In association with the flattening, the spiracles have come to lie on the dorsal surface of the body. The lice spend their whole lives on their hosts, although they may move from one individual to another if two hosts comes into contact, and it is not surprising that wings have disappeared during the course of evolution. As in other parasitic animals, the sensory organs are poorly developed, the eyes being small or absent and the antennae short.

Lice feed either on blood or by scraping the surface of the skin and taking particles of feathers. In this way they may cause considerable irritation to the host, which must resort to almost continuous scratching when infestation is heavy. This leads to skin damage, loss of blood, and the entry of disease germs, leading in turn to wasting and possible death of the host. Some species of lice also actively transmit certain bacterial and viral diseases. Lice are therefore of great economic importance when they infect domestic livestock and a great deal of effort goes into finding effective control measures. Some species of lice affect a wide range of host animals but other species may be confined to one host or a group of closely related host species. The claws of some lice are so well adapted for gripping the hair of the host that they are unable to attach themselves to other hosts whose hairs are of different diameters. Some species of lice even confine themselves to certain areas of the host animal – the head and neck for example. The insects soon die if removed from their hosts.

The evolution of lice has gone hand in hand with that of their hosts – a not unexpected situation in view of the constant association between the two. Lice are undoubtedly passed from parent to offspring in the nest and from one member of a herd or family group to another, but apart from this there will be little interchange of lice. One strain of lice will therefore tend to stay with one particular strain of host animal and the two will evolve together. To take a simple example, the lice of man and apes are much more closely related to each other than they are to those of rodents, paralleling the relationships of the host animals themselves. Lice have actually aided systematists in determining the relationships of some birds. An oft-quoted example is that of the flamingos: these birds might appear closer to storks than to ducks, but their lice suggest that they are more closely related to the ducks and this relationship has been confirmed by other methods.

All lice are superficially similar and some entomologists place them in a single order – the Phthiraptera. But much of the similarity is due to their mode of life and other entomologists, stressing differences in the mouth-parts, recognise two separate orders – the Mallophaga and the Anoplura. All probably share a common ancestor with the Psocoptera.

Order Mallophaga – Biting Lice and Bird Lice

Recognition features Small and minute wingless, generally flat-bodied parasites, mainly associated with birds. Eyes very small. Antennae with 3-5 segments and often concealed. Biting mouth-parts. Although superficially similar to some of the wingless psocids, the lice may be distinguished by their short antennae. Biting lice are easily separated from the sucking lice of the order Anoplura by the general body shape and by the prominant prothorax.

These parasites are found primarily on birds – hence the name bird lice – although some species infest mammals. Biting lice feed mainly on particles of skin, fur, and feathers. Some species take blood, sometimes puncturing the skin with their own mandibles but more often feeding at wounds made when the hosts scratch themselves.

The largest biting lice are about 1cm long although very few reach this size and most species are less than half this length. The body is usually flat and quite hard and the head is comparatively large. There are no ocelli and the compound eyes are reduced. The antennae are very short and concealed in grooves on the sides of the head in the sub-order AMBLYCERA, but longer and clearly visible in the sub-order ISCHNOCERA. The large, toothed mandibles are held either vertically or horizontally. The prothorax is usually distinct from the other two thoracic segments, which may or may not be fused together. Each leg bears one or two claws with which the insect clings tightly to the host, although these lice are no sluggards when it becomes necessary to avoid capture. Lice living on the head and neck of birds, where they are out of reach of the beak, are often short and somewhat globular, but those living elsewhere on the body are longer and flatter and well able to scuttle away between the feathers.

The female louse lays between 50 and 100 eggs, which she cements to the feathers or hair of the host. The nymphs pass through three instars before reaching the adult state with no obvious metamorphosis. The whole process from egg to adult takes three to four weeks in the constant temperature environment of the host's body.

Nearly 3,000 species of biting lice are known, but it is certain that many hundreds have yet to be discovered. About 700 species, representing six families, occur in Europe and about 500 of these have been recorded in Britain. The **Menoponidae** (sub-order Amblycera) and **Philopteridae** (sub-order Ischnocera) are the two largest families and both include important poultry pests, such as the Shaft Louse (*Menopon gallinae*). The family **Trichodectidae** (sub-order Ischnocera) is much smaller but it includes the very important genus *Damalinia*, whose species cause much loss among sheep, goats, cattle, and other hoofed mammals in various parts of the world. None of the biting lice affects man.

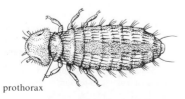

prothorax

A biting louse (Menopon), showing the broad head and distinct prothorax of this group of lice. Like all bird lice, it has two claws on each leg. Most mammal-infesting species have only one claw on each leg

Order Anoplura (= Siphunculata) – Sucking Lice

Recognition features Small and minute wingless parasites of mammals. The head is usually narrow and the eyes are reduced or absent. Antennae short. Mouth-parts modified for blood-sucking and retractable into the head when not in use. The thoracic segments are fused together and each leg ends in a strong claw. The sucking lice are distinguishable from wingless psocids by their short antennae and from the biting lice by their fused thoracic segments, there being no free prothorax.

All sucking lice are parasitic on mammals and they all feed exclusively on blood which they obtain by piercing the skin with their highly-specialised mouth-parts. These consist of a toothed proboscis and three stylets. The proboscis maintains a hold on the skin while the stylets pierce it. Muscular movements of the pharyngeal region cause the blood to flow up the channel formed by the stylets. Apart from the mouth-parts and the method of feeding, the habits of the sucking lice are very similar to those of the biting lice and it seems likely that the sucking lice evolved from some kind of biting louse.

   The head is generally narrower than that of the biting lice and the thorax differs in that the segments are all fused, there being little sign of segmentation other than in the abdomen. The sturdy legs each end in a single claw, like those of some of the mammal-inhabiting biting lice. The claw is hinged in such a way that it can be drawn up tight against the tarsus to grip the host's hair. The curvature of the claw and tarsus closely follows that of the hair and the parasite gets a very firm hold.

   As with the biting lice the eggs are usually cemented to the host's hair, although the Human Louse will also attach its eggs to clothing or even scatter them loosely. The life history is very similar to that of the biting lice, although some species mature much more quickly. The Human Louse has been known to mature just eight days after hatching.

   About 500 species of sucking lice are known although, as with all the smaller and less 'popular' insects, many more must await discovery. Less than 50 species are known from Europe, with one of our five families being confined to seals. The best known family is the **Pediculidae**, on account of its human-infesting species. The Human Louse (*Pediculus humanus*) exists as two distinct races – the Head Louse (*P. h. capitis*) and the Body Louse (*P. h. humanus*). The Body Louse is the larger of the two in general and the two races keep very much to their respective parts of our anatomy. Some entomologists now regard the two races as separate species. The Body Louse is not much of a problem where frequent washing and changing clothes is the rule, but infestation is quite common where less attention is paid to hygiene.

The Human Louse, showing the dorsal spiracles and (right) the structure of the single claw present on each leg

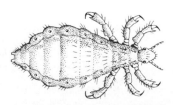

The bite of this louse can be very irritating and the insect is the vector of several diseases, including typhus. There is always a risk of typhus outbreaks after earthquakes and similar tragedies when people are herded together, sharing sleeping accommodation and getting little chance to keep clean.

Head lice are much more common than body lice and children seem to be more susceptible to them than adults. Heavy infestations frequently occur among school children, but this does not imply any lack of attention to hygiene, for the lice and their eggs can stand any amount of washing and combing. Luckily, the Head Louse does not seem to carry any diseases.

The only other human-infesting louse is the Crab Louse (*Pthirus pubis*), which is confined to the lower parts of the body and has not so far been found to carry any disease. The most important of the other sucking lice are those of the genus *Linognathus* (family **Linognathidae**), which affect sheep and cattle.

Collecting and preserving
The only satisfactory way of collecting lice in any numbers is to obtain living or freshly-dead host animals and to search them with the aid of a brush and comb. The lice can be picked up with forceps or with a brush dipped in alcohol. The insects should be preserved in spirit or, for permanent display, mounted on microscope slides after clearing slightly in potassium hydroxide. The small size of the lice and the difficulty of collecting them have not helped the study of the group and anyone with a microscope and a good supply of host animals and patience can contribute quite a lot to our knowledge of these parasites.

Order Hemiptera – The True Bugs*
Plates 8-13

Recognition features Minute to large sized insects of widely differing shapes and habits but all possessing piercing mouth-parts adapted for sucking the juices of plants or other animals. The needle-like mandibles and maxillae are sheathed in the labium and the whole beak or rostrum is normally held horizontally under the body when not in use. The antennae may be quite long in relation to the size of the body, but they have only a few segments – usually four or five and rarely more than ten. Two pairs of wings are normally present, the front ones often being hardened to some extent.

The great variety of shapes and habits assumed by the bugs makes it impossible to give a general recognition pattern: the only really constant feature is the rostrum. There are, however, only three other orders with which the bugs might be confused and none of these has sucking mouth-parts. Beetles and cockroaches resemble some of the bugs, but beetles can be distinguished because their elytra do not overlap and cockroaches can be recognised by their fine, many-segmented antennae. Many psocids resemble aphids, but again the many-jointed antennae of the psocids will distinguish them.

---

*   *Among non-entomologists the word bug is often synonymous with insect, and even the entomologist accepts this use of the word, being quite happy with his 'bug-hunter' title. When talking about hemipterans, therefore, it is wise to talk of 'true bugs' rather than 'bugs' in order to avoid any possibility of confusion.*

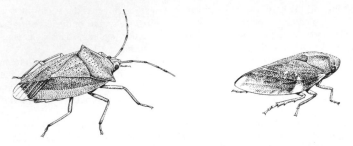

Left, A shieldbug – a typical heteropteran. Right, a froghopper – a typical homopteran

The true bugs form a large order of insects with about 70,000 species, of which over 7,000 live in Europe. About 1,650 occur in the British Isles. The majority feed on plants and there are among them some very serious agricultural pests, including the aphids which not only damage the plants directly but transmit many viral diseases. The order is divided into two quite distinct sub-orders – the HETEROPTERA and the HOMOPTERA – which differ considerably in wing structure and in the position of the rostrum. These two groups are given separate ordinal rank by many entomologists.

When present, the forewing of the heteropteran bug is clearly divided into two regions – a tough, leathery basal area and a membranous tip – and this is responsible for the name Heteroptera (Greek *heteros* = different). It is also responsible for the name Hemiptera given to the whole order because, when at rest, the insects appear to have only half of each wing (Greek *hemi* = half). The hind wings are always membranous and in the Heteroptera both pairs are folded flat over the body at rest. The rostrum or beak clearly arises from the front part of the head. This sub-order contains both herbivores and carnivores and includes such insects as the colourful shieldbugs, the mirid or capsid bugs, bedbugs, and all those bugs that live on or in the water.

The homopteran forewing is not divided into two regions and is either membranous or stiffened throughout (Greek *homos* = uniform). Again, the hind wings are membranous, but in this sub-order all four wings are normally held roof-wise over the body when the insects are at rest. The rostrum arises from the rear part of the head and often appears to spring from between the two front legs. All the members of this sub-order are plant-feeders and they include the cicadas, leafhoppers, and aphids. Our cicadas may reach lengths of 4cm and have wingspans of 10cm, but the other European homopterans are very much smaller and most are under 5mm long.

SUB-ORDER HETEROPTERA – Plates 8-11

The bodies of these insects are generally flattened and the wings are folded flat over the body at rest. Beyond this, however, there is little uniformity of shape. Most of our heteropterans are cryptically coloured, with greens and browns being dominant, but some exhibit brilliant warning colours. Many families produce pungent secretions in special 'stink glands' near the hind legs and this secretion taints the plants on which the bugs crawl as well as giving the insects themselves an unpleasant taste. The stink glands are particularly efficient in the shieldbugs, which are often known as stinkbugs.

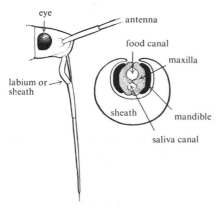

The head of a bug, showing the beak or rostrum, together with a section through the rostrum to show the canals formed by the mouth-parts

The head is rather variable in shape but is usually held horizontally and is normally clearly visible from above. Compound eyes are always present and there are two ocelli in most of the land bugs, but water bugs have no ocelli. The antennae never have more than five segments and those of the water bugs are concealed under the head.

The mouth-parts vary little throughout the order on account of the uniform feeding habits. The mandibles and maxillae are in the form of needle-like stylets and rest in the grooved labium which is known as the rostrum or proboscis. The labium is not grooved at its upper end, but here the stylets are protected by the overlying labrum. At the lower end of the rostrum the walls of the groove curve right over the stylets and hold them firmly in their sheath. The rostrum itself has a sensitive tip and is used to select a suitable feeding site: then, having guided the stylets into position, it is drawn back and the stylets are plunged into the host. It has been shown that the saw-edged mandibles make the first incision and that the more slender maxillae follow them into the wound. The four stylets are arranged concentrically, with the mandibular ones surrounding the maxillary ones. The latter are held tightly together and their inner surfaces are so shaped that the central cavity is divided longitudinally into two fine canals. Food is sucked up through one and saliva is pumped down the other. The hypopharynx, which is small and insignificant in insects with biting jaws, plays an important role here because it forms part of the pumping chamber which draws up the liquid food. When not in use the whole rostrum is folded back under the body, often extending beyond the base of the back legs.

The prothorax is always large and prominent in the heteropterans, the pronotum occupying most of the visible part of the thorax when viewed from above. Apart from the scutellum – the prominent triangular region between the wing bases – the mesothorax is concealed beneath the pronotum and wings. The small metathorax is also concealed from above. In some species the scutellum is very large and extends backwards and sideways so that even the wings are covered and the insects appear wingless.

Because the forewings are only partially hardened, they are called hemelytra – elytra being the name given to the hardened forewings of beetles. The hardened or cornified area is itself divided into two or more regions, the primary division being along the claval suture which separates an anterior corium from a posterior clavus

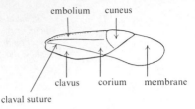

The forewing of an anthocorid bug showing the major regions of the wing

– the region next to the scutellum when the wings are folded. This division is present in all winged heteropterans. A narrow strip along the anterior border of the wing is sometimes marked off as the embolium and, more commonly, a triangular region is marked off at the apex of the corium to form the cuneus. These divisions are used in the classification of the bugs.

The venation of the forewings is very indistinct but in all species it is considerably reduced. Veins R, M, and Cu are often unbranched and no veins at all may reach the membrane. The venation is also reduced in the membranous hind wings. Several species are quite or almost wingless, and many more exist mainly as short-winged or brachypterous individuals. A few species, including the pond skaters of the family Gerridae, regularly produce both long-winged and short-winged individuals.

The legs of the heteropterans are generally unremarkable, except that many predatory species, such as the Water Scorpion (*Nepa cinerea*), have raptorial front legs for catching their prey. The femur is toothed in these legs and the tibia closes tightly against it to hold the prey. Minor differences in spininess, number of tarsal segments, and so on are used in the classification of the bugs.

The abdomen varies in the number of segments visible, but modifications are few. Cerci are absent from all the bugs, but one feature worth mentioning is the respiratory siphon or breathing tube found in the water scorpions and their relatives in the family Nepidae (p. 112). Parts of the abdomen are sometimes modified for sound production and, although the most famous of the 'singing bugs' – the cicadas – belong to the Homoptera, a number of heteropterans stridulate modestly by rubbing legs or wings over roughened patches on the body. *Reduvius personatus* (Plate 9) stridulates by rubbing the tip of its beak along a striated furrow on the prosternum, while the corixids (p. 113) make surprisingly loud noises by rubbing their front legs against their faces.

Heteropteran eggs are usually attached to plants and are often placed inside the tissues. The egg is very often adorned with delicate sculpturing and is frequently provided with a special detachable lid to aid the escape of the young nymph. The nymphs may look rather unlike the adults at first but, being members of the Hemimetabola, they change gradually and get more like the adults at each moult. Most species have five nymphal instars and there are often considerable colour changes from one instar to the next. This is especially true of the change from the last nymphal instar to the adult state. Other external changes include increases in the number of antennal and tarsal segments, alterations to the shape of the pronotum, and the development of wings. The wings buds are not usually obvious until the fourth nymphal instar. Like the adults, the nymphs feed entirely by sucking and their diet is essentially the same as that of the adults of the species. Most of the plant-feeding bugs contain symbiotic bacteria in their digestive tracts. Their function is not fully understood, but an antibiotic role has been suggested for them. Bugs take in liquid food and there is no question of cellulose breakdown such as occurs in the termites and many herbivorous mammals. In many of the bugs the symbionts are passed to the eggs when they are laid, so the young nymphs have a supply right from the start.

The following key, based on that given in Southwood and Leston, may be used to place most of the European heteropterans in their families. Because of the way in which the wings develop on the outside of the growing nymphs, it is sometimes difficult to distinguish between fully-grown nymphs and short-winged adult bugs. One of the best clues is in the junction between the wings and the scutellum: if it is sharp and well defined your specimen is almost certainly an adult.

Key to the Main Families of European Heteropteran Bugs

1. Antennae visible from above: generally terrestrial or living on the water surface (Geocorisae and Amphibicorisae)*   2

    Antennae small and concealed from above: insects living under water (Hydrocorisae)*   34

2. Head at least 5 times longer than broad   Hydrometridae p. 111

    Head not more than 3 times as long as broad   3

3. Antennae shorter than width of head   Ochteridae p. 112

    Antennae longer than width of head   4

4. Antennae 5-segmented   5

    Antennae 4-segmented   10

5. Bugs 2mm long or less: scutellum not reaching middle of abdomen: living on water surface   Hebridae p. 111

    Bugs over 3mm long: scutellum reaching at least to middle of abdomen: terrestrial   6

6. Tarsi 2-segmented   7

    Tarsi 3-segmented   8

7. Body almost hemispherical: scutellum covers whole of abdomen   [†]Plataspidae p. 105

    Body longer than broad: scutellum smaller and distinctly triangular   Acanthosomatidae p. 105

8. Tibiae strongly spined: largely black or dark brown insects, often with a metallic sheen   Cydnidae p. 105

    Tibiae not strongly spined, or if so insects are very hairy   9

---

*   *This three-fold division into terrestrial, surface-dwelling, and under-water bugs is ecologically useful, but the true division is into the Gymnocerata with visible antennae on the one hand and the Cryptocerata with concealed antennae on the other. Only the Ochteridae (p. 112) do not fit neatly into this scheme.*

9.   Scutellum reaching end of abdomen: pronotum without lat-   Scutelleridae p. 106
       eral projections

       Scutellum not reaching end of abdomen, or if so the prono-   Pentatomidae p. 106
       tum has lateral projections reaching to near eyes

10.   Underside of abdomen densely covered with fine silver   11
       hairs: insects usually living on the water surface

       Underside of abdomen without such hairs: generally terre-   13
       strial insects

11.   Mainly greenish insects with apical   Mesoveliidae p. 111
       claws on front tarsi

       Claws on front tarsi sub-apical: 12
       insects never greenish

12.   Hind femora reaching beyond tip of abdomen: middle legs   Gerridae p. 112
       inserted nearer to hind ones than to front ones

       Hind femora not reaching beyond tip of abdomen: middle   Veliidae p. 111
       legs inserted midway between the other two

13.   Rostrum more or less curved and not pressed flat against   14
       body at rest: body longer than 4.5mm

       Rostrum pressed flat against body at rest, or if curved   16
       body is shorter than 4.5mm

14.   Body almost flat, with broad diamond-shaped abdomen: [†]Phymatidae p. 109
       front legs strongly raptorial with femora almost as
       broad as long

       Insects not fitting this description   15

15.   Rostrum 4-segmented   Nabidae p. 109

       Rostrum 3-segmented   Reduviidae p. 108

16.   Corium and pronotum covered with   17
       netted pattern

       No such patterning   18

17.   Pronotum projecting back and covering scutellum, or head   Tingidae p. 108
       and pronotum black: membrane not distinct

       Pronotum not covering scutellum: membrane distinct, with   Piesmidae p. 107
       cross-veins

18.   Tarsi 2-segmented   19

       Tarsi 3-segmented   21

19.   Bugs under 2.5mm long   Microphysidae p. 109

       Very flat bugs, over 3.5mm long and with robust antennae   20

20.	Forewings almost entirely membranous and not completely covering abdomen	Aneuridae p. 105
	Forewings distinctly horny at base: not completely covering abdomen and sometimes very narrow	Aradidae p. 105
21.	1st and 2nd antennal segments short and thick, less than half as long as 3rd and 4th segments together: 3rd and 4th segments very thin: bugs under 3mm long	Dipsocoridae p. 111
	Antennae not as above	22
22.	Ocelli absent	23
	Ocelli present	25
23.	Bugs extremely flat, brown, and wingless	Cimicidae p. 109
	Bugs not fitting this description	24
24.	Scarlet and black bugs over 8mm long: often brachypterous, but no cuneus if fully winged	Pyrrhocoridae p. 107
	Insects mostly under 8mm long, but if longer they are not scarlet and black: cuneus present in fully-winged insects	Miridae p. 110
25.	Rostrum 3-segmented and curved under head at rest (not flat): embolium and weak cuneus present when fully winged, but insects often short-winged and under 2.5mm long	Anthocoridae p. 109
	Rostrum with 3 or 4 segments and held flat under head at rest	26
26.	Strong cuneus present: rostrum 4-segmented	[†]Isometopidae p. 111
	No cuneus or embolium: rostrum with 3 or 4 segments: insects often brachypterous	27
27.	Rostrum 3-segmented	28
	Rostrum 4-segmented	29
28.	Legs bristly	Saldidae p. 111
	Legs smooth: ocelli on stalked platform on top of narrow head	[†]Leptopodidae p. 111
29.	Membrane with 5 or less ± parallel veins: if short-winged, abdomen is dark brown or black	30
	Membrane with 6 or more veins: if short-winged, abdomen is green or yellowish with red or black markings	31

30. Scutellum distinctly shorter than commissure (the line where the two clavi meet), or if nearly as long the entire upper surface is shiny and strongly punctured: legs usually very slender — Berytidae p. 107

commissure

scutellum

Scutellum as long as or longer than commissure: if about as long the upper surface is not entirely shiny or strongly punctured — Lygaeidae p. 107

31. Antennae, tibiae, and mid and hind femora distinctly banded with black and yellow — Stenocephalidae p. 107

These regions not all distinctly banded — 32

32. 4th antennal segment curved: head nearly as wide as base of pronotum: hind femora strongly spined beneath near apex — Alydidae p. 106

4th antennal segment straight: head much narrower than base of pronotum, or if nearly as wide the hind femora lack spines — 33

33. Forewings with extensive horny region at base: stink gland openings generally ear-shaped and clearly visible from the side between middle and hind legs — Coreidae p. 106

Forewings largely membranous: stink gland openings generally slit-shaped and concealed ventrally between middle and hind coxae — Rhopalidae p. 106

34. Rostrum short and blunt and concealed by labrum: front tarsi spatulate — Corixidae p. 113

Rostrum clearly visible and sharply pointed: front tarsi not spatulate — 35

35. Abdomen with a conspicuous stiff 'tail' – the breathing siphon — Nepidae p. 112

Abdomen without such a 'tail' — 36

36. Front legs raptorial, with broad femora: body generally rather flat — 37

Front legs not raptorial: back-swimming bugs with boat-shaped bodies — 39

37. Very large bugs with 2 retractable appendages at the rear — †Belostomatidae p. 113

Smaller bugs with no such appendages — 38

38. Front legs stout and projecting horn-like from beneath the head: fully winged — Naucoridae p. 113

Front legs more normal (although femora still broad): rarely fully-winged — Aphelocheiridae p. 113

† denotes families not found in the British Isles

SERIES GYMNOCERATA (= NAKED HORNS) – BUGS WITH FREE ANTENNAE

Geocorisae: Terrestrial Bugs

The terrestrial bugs as a whole are essentially a tropical group and several families are right on the edge of their range in Europe, and especially in the British Isles where many species are found only in the southern counties. Britain's damp climate is more to blame for this than latitude, because the bugs reach further north on the continent. Many of our species, particularly the large ones, hibernate among grass tufts or in the upper layers of the soil where they are prone to attack by fungi in damp weather. Continental winters are often colder than British ones, but they are also drier and the bugs survive better. It is significant that most ground-living bugs in Britain are found in the drier areas of the south and east – on the better-drained chalk and sandstone areas – or on coastal sand dunes. Britain's somewhat lower and rather unpredicatble summer temperatures, however, are probably just as important in denying us a richer bug fauna.

Bugs of the family **Aradidae** (Pl.8) are known as flatbugs. They are broad and very flat and they usually live on or under loose bark where they feed on fungi, although the Pine Flatbug (*Aradus cinnamomeus*) feeds on the sap of pine trees. The stylets are long and slender and are coiled inside the head when not in use. Apart from the Pine Flatbug, in which the males have narrow wings and the females are generally brachypterous, most flatbugs are fully winged, although flight is common only at certain times. There are five British species. *Mezira tremulae* is sometimes placed in a separate family – the **Meziridae**. The closely related family **Aneuridae** are the barkbugs, distinguished from the aradids by the largely membranous fore-wings. The insects, typified by *Aneurus laevis* (Pl.8), live under bark and feed on fungal threads. There are two British species.

The shieldbugs, named for their general shield-like shape, belong to the super-family Pentatomoidea and they are often known as stinkbugs on account of the pun-gent odour produced by some of the species. Members of the family **Acanthosomatidae** (Pl.8) differ from most of the other shieldbugs in having only two tarsal segments. There are five British species. The Hawthorn Shieldbug (*Acan-thosoma haemorrhoidale*) is a common representative whose main food is hawthorn fruit, although leaves sustain the over-wintered adults in the spring. The Parent Bug (*Elasmucha grisea*), which frequents birch woods, is of interest because the female lays a diamond-shaped egg mass on a leaf and then sits over it until the eggs hatch. Even after hatching, parent and offspring move about in a family group and the mother actively protects her young. This maternal care may reduce parasitism, es-pecially of the eggs which are well protected under the female's body. The family **Plataspidae** also has only two tarsal segments, but its sole European member, *Cop-tosoma scutellata* (Pl.10), is easily recognised by its hemispherical shape. The enor-mous scutellum covers virtually the whole of the abdomen and the wings. The insect is quite common on leguminous plants in southern Europe.

Members of the **Cydnidae** (Pl.8) can be distinguished by their spiny tibiae and their generally dark and often metallic colouring. The insects feed on various low-growing plants and generally lay their eggs in the soil. The adults also hibernate in the soil, and the insects are therefore most common in sandy and chalky regions where the soil is light and well drained. There are nine British species. The Pied Shieldbug (*Sehirus bicolor*) feeds on white deadnettle and other labiates. The Negro Bug (*Thyreocoris scarabaeoides*), easily recognised by its rounded shape and large scutellum, is widespread on chalkland, where it lives among the leaf litter and short vegetation.

The **Scutelleridae** (Pl.8) is a mainly tropical family whose main feature is the huge scutellum which reaches the tip of the abdomen and almost completely covers the wings as well. There are five British species, of which *Eurygaster testudinaria* is the commonest. It occurs on grasses and rushes in most parts of southern England and is widely distributed elsewhere in Europe. *E.integriceps* is a serious pest of wheat in Europe and Asia but is not found in Britain. *Odontoscelis dorsalis*, which is mainly coastal in Britain, has spiny legs like those of the previous family but it can be distinguished by its hairy appearance.

The **Pentatomidae** (Pl.8) is the largest shieldbug family. The scutellum is generally triangular and the whole body is clearly shield-shaped, more so than in the other families in the group. Although some of its members are abundant in southern Europe, it is near the edge of its range in Britain, where there are only 17 native species and none of them is really numerous. It seems that hot summers are necessary for the insects' well-being, perhaps more so than dry winters, because we usually get increased numbers of these bugs after a run of good summers. Several species, including *Picromerus bidens*, are largely or entirely carnivorous, but most species are sap-feeders. The insects cause a certain amount of damage to crops in warmer areas, although numbers are not sufficient for them to cause any damage in Britain.

The Forest Bug (*Pentatoma rufipes*) is a common tree-living species. The European Turtle Bug (*Podops inuncta*), which is common in many grassy places, differs from the rest of the family in that its scutellum covers almost all of the abdomen, but it can be distinguished from the Scutelleridae by the possession of two tiny horns on the front of the pronotum. *Graphosoma italicum* from southern Europe has an atrocious taste and advertises the fact well with its bold warning colours. *Sciocoris cursitans* is of interest because of the male's very loud stridulation.

Members of the **Coreidae** (Pl.8) are collectively called squash bugs as a result of the serious damage caused by some of them to squash fruits in America. They are almost all fruit or seed feeders. They have a broad pronotum and they are somewhat shield-shaped, but they are narrower than most pentatomids and the scutellum is less prominent. The antennae are 4-segmented, whereas those of the shieldbugs are 5-segmented. Stink gland openings are clearly visible on the sides of the body between the middle and hind legs (fig. p. 104). In most species the abdomen is expanded posteriorly, giving the insects a characteristic shape, although *Philomorpha laciniata* is unusual in having several separate abdominal bulges. *Coreus marginatus*, the commonest of the ten British species, feeds mainly on sorrels and docks.

Alydus calcaratus (Pl.8), the only British member of the **Alydidae**, occurs in coastal areas and other sandy places. It readily takes flight and is one of the fastest of the bugs. Its wings are very dark, but the upper surface of the abdomen bears a bright orange patch which is visible when the insect is in flight. This is an example of flash coloration, designed to confuse predators (see p. 239). *Camptopus lateralis* from southern and central Europe is similar but it has a much squarer pronotum.

The family **Rhopalidae** (Pl.9) is very similar to the Coreidae, but is distinguished by the ventral position of the stink gland openings between the middle and hind coxae. The forewings are often largely membranous. Most of the species are red and/or black and the family is typified by *Rhopalus subrufus*, a not uncommon woodland and hedgerow insect. *Chorosoma schillingi* is rather atypical on account of its narrow shape, but this is associated with its life among marram and other duneland grasses and is not a fundamental difference. There are eight British species.

Members of the **Pyrrhocoridae** are mainly seed-eaters. The commonest European species, and the only one found in Britain, is the Fire Bug (*Pyrrhocoris apterus*) (Pl.9). This bug is generally brachypterous but it also has apterous and fully-winged forms. Large clusters can often be seen feeding on the ground in the spring.

The spurge bugs of the family **Stenocephalidae** are something of a link between the coreid and lygaeid bugs. The legs are banded and the forewing membrane has at least six veins. The two British species, *Dicranocephalus medius* (Pl.9) and the very similar *D.agilis*, are both found on various spurges.

The ground bugs of the family **Lygaeidae** (Pl.9) are a large group of slender or oval bugs, all under about 12mm long. Most are brownish, but *Lygaeus saxatilis* and several others display classic black and red warning coloration. Ground bugs bear many resemblances to the coreids but they can be distinguished by having only a few veins in the wing membrane: the coreids have at least six veins in the membrane. Some ground bugs also resemble the mirid bugs, but the latter have a softer body and lack ocelli. The mirids also have a conspicuous cuneus. Some ground bugs are predatory, but most are herbivorous and, although none is a serious pest in Europe, the family contains a number of economically important species in other parts of the world. The Chinch Bug (*Blissus leucopterus*), for example, is particularly injurious to cereals in the United States. The bugs often hibernate in masses and may be found in winter by opening up tufts of grasses and rushes. *Megalonotus chiragra* and *Scoloposthetus decoratus* are two of the commoner of Britain's 70 or so species. *S.decoratus* is widespread on heathland.

Members of the **Berytidae** (Pl.9) are commonly called stilt bugs because most of them, including *Berytinus minor*, have very long, slender legs. The family does, however, contain the short-legged *Cymus* species, which are superficially similar to the lygaeid bugs. Stilt bugs range up to about 12 mm in length and are generally to be found on leguminous plants. There are 13 British species. Some are superficially similar to the long-legged assassin bugs, such as *Empicoris* (p. 108), but the rostrum is strongly curved in these latter insects and they often have raptorial front legs.

The beet bugs of the family **Piesmidae** (Pl. 9) resemble the lace bugs but the similarity is only superficial and confined to the lace-like pattern on the wings and pronotum. The insects are actually more closely related to the ground bugs. They feed almost entirely on plants of the beet family (Chenopodiaceae). The two British species, *Piesma maculatum* and *P.quadratum* are primarily insects of salt-marshes and other coastal habitats where sea purslane and other chenopods grow, but they are now quite widespread in old gravel pits and similar waste land. *P. quadratum* is

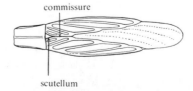

commissure

scutellum

The body of Berytinus *showing the tiny scutellum - much shorter than the commissure. This feature is characteristic of most members of the Berytidae, although some* Cymus *species, recognised by their shiny and strongly punctured surface, have a relatively long scutellum*

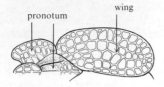

*The lace-like pattern of a lacebug
(Tingidae), with the scutellum completely
covered by the pronotum*

found over much of Central Europe, where it interferes with sugar beet cultivation by carrying a viral disease. The males of this species stridulate loudly by rubbing their wings against certain abdominal sclerites. All the beet bugs are very small.

Members of the family **Tingidae** (Pl. 9), called lace bugs on account of the delicate sculpturing of the wings and pronotum, can be distinguished from the beet bugs because in most lace bugs the pronotum extends backwards to cover the scutellum. It also extends forwards and sideways to some degree, forming the hood and the lateral margin. The wing membrane is indistinct, in contrast to the definite membrane of the beet bugs. The insects often have a greyish colour caused by a layer of powdery wax that develops on the surface. All lace bugs are plant feeders and they don't exceed about 6mm in length. Many of them live in moss, and the majority of these are short-winged. The Spear Thistle Lace Bug (*Tingis cardui*), a widespread species found on various thistles, is the commonest of the 23 British species.

The assassin bugs of the family **Reduviidae** (Pl.9) are, as their name suggests, predatory bugs feeding mainly on other arthropods. Many can give painful jabs with their beaks when handled, but relatively few feed regularly on mammalian blood. The family is a large one, but most of its members are tropical and only six reach the British Isles. Our commonest species is the Heath Assassin Bug (*Coranus subapterus*), which is usually brachypterous. *Reduvius personatus* lives in and around human habitations where it feeds on bedbugs and other small insects. Like the previous species, it can stridulate quite loudly by rubbing the rough tip of its curved rostrum along a ridged groove in the prosternum. *Rhinocoris iracundus* can often be seen prowling over vegetation in search of prey in southern and central Europe. The legs are relatively long in all the assassin bugs, but especially so in *Empicoris vagabundus* which resembles a large mosquito when at rest. It is one of several species with raptorial front legs. Another is the wingless *Ploiaria domestica*, which captures small flies at night in southern Europe and is sometimes found in houses.

Left, Ploiaria domestica, *a delicate assassin bug, 7–8mm long, that catches small flies with the aid of its raptorial front legs. Right, A typical phymatid bug, showing the strongly raptorial front legs.*

The **Phymatidae** is a small family of predatory bugs related to the assassins. The front legs are strongly raptorial, with a broad femur and a narrow, opposable tibia. The abdomen is diamond-shaped and projects far beyond the wings on each side. There are two species in southern and central Europe, both about 6mm long.

The damsel bugs of the family **Nabidae** (Pl.9) resemble the assassins in several ways, but the rostrum is 4-segmented instead of 3-segmented as in the assassins and the damsel bugs are actually more closely allied to the bedbugs. Damsel bugs are long-legged and rather slender, but they are fiercely carnivorous and they feed on a wide range of other insects. The Marsh Damsel Bug (*Dolichonabis limbatus*) is a widespread species, by no means confined to marshland despite its common name. *Himacerus apterus* lives in trees and, like the previous species, is usually micropterous. There are 12 British species, all of them some shade of brown.

The family **Cimicidae** (Pl.10) contains the blood-sucking bedbugs, which are parasites of birds and mammals. They are always micropterous and chestnut brown in colour and they reach about 6mm in length. *Oeciacus hirundinis* lives on house martins and often finds its way into houses from their nests in the autumn, although it rarely feeds on man. The true Bedbug (*Cimex lectularius*) feeds mainly on man and also infests various animals in zoos. It is very widespread, although less common since the introduction of synthetic insecticides. The insects usually feed at night and hide in crevices or among clothing by day. Although the bedbug's bite is very annoying, there is no proof that the insect regularly transmits any diseases. Related species are found on bats and on various birds.

Members of the family **Anthocoridae** (Pl.10) are generally small and fully winged predators of other insects, although some will draw blood from people if they get the chance. They are clearly related to the bedbugs and are sometimes placed in the same family. It is possible that the bedbugs evolved from some kind of anthocorid ancestor. One group of these insects is found mainly on flowers and leaves and its members are called flower bugs. One of the commonest species is *Anthocoris nemorum*, which can be found attacking other insects on the vegetation throughout the summer. Like most of its relatives, it spends the winter resting under bark and in other concealed spots. The other main division of the family is typified by *Xylocoris galactinus*, which lives in granaries, manure heaps, and other accumulations of vegetable debris. These insects, which may be called debris bugs, feed on psocids, springtails, and other small arthropods. Flower and debris bugs may be distinguished from mirids and ground bugs found in similar places by the distinct embolium. There are about 27 British species.

The tiny bugs of the family **Microphysidae**, typified by *Loricula elegantula*, are usually found among lichens and mosses on tree trunks, where they are thought to

Left, Forewing of a mirid bug (Miridae), showing the small cells commonly present in the membrane of this family. Right, forewing of an anthocorid bug (Anthocoridae), showing its distinct embolium

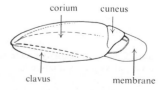
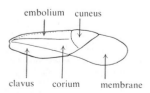

*Loricula elegantula is only about 2mm long.
The male is fully winged and more slender
than the female pictured here*

feed on psocids and other minute insects. There are only seven known British species, but as these tiny insects are so easily overlooked it is quite possible that more will be added to the list.

The **Miridae** (Pl.10) is the largest family in the Heteroptera, with over 6,000 known species. Just over 200 species occur in the British Isles – nearly two thirds of all the British heteropterans – and the range of habitats exploited by them is almost as wide as that occupied by the rest of the heteropteran families. Mirids are found from mountain top to seashore and in all kinds of vegetation from high forest to almost bare ground. The majority of mirids, also known as capsids and leaf bugs, are rather delicate plant-feeders, but a number are at least partly predatory. Mimicry is well exhibited in the family and there are two excellent ant-mimics in the European fauna – *Myrmecoris gracilis* and the female *Systellonotus triguttatus*, both of which are illustrated on Pl.10. These mimics are normally micropterous and they live on heathland, frequently in association with their ant models. Although they have not been known to attack living adult ants, they readily feed on dead ones and larval ants probably contribute to their diet.

The mirid bugs usually have a well-marked cuneus in the forewing and this serves to distinguish them from most other bugs. The flower bugs have a cuneus, but they have a well-marked embolium as well. As to be expected in insects that live primarily among vegetation, greens and browns are the dominant colours.

Many of our mirid species are very common and can be taken in numbers by sweeping or beating herbage in summer: almost every umbellifer head supports one or more of these insects. The developing fruits and seeds are their main targets and the family contains many species of economic importance. The Common Green Capsid (*Lygocoris pabulinus*) is a common pest of fruit trees, producing blemishes on leaves and fruit. The eggs overwinter on the trees and the young nymphs feed there for a while in spring before moving to the various herbaceous plants on which the summer generations exist. The latter insects return to the trees in autumn to feed and lay their eggs. The Black-kneed Capsid (*Blepharidopterus angulatus*) is another common fruit tree mirid, easily recognised by the black marks around its 'knee-joints'. It is mainly predatory and feeds on the red spider mites which themselves do so much damage to the plants. It is thus one of the better mirid bugs to have in the orchard. The Tarnished Plant Bug (*Lygus rugulipennis*) is a common garden pest, causing white spots on the leaves where it feeds. *Capsus ater*, easily identified by the swollen 2nd segment of the antennae, occurs in grassy places almost everywhere, while *Halticus apterus*, which sometimes has fully-developed wings, is often a pest of clovers and other legumes.

The **Isometopidae** is a small family, closely related to the mirids but differing in possessing ocelli. *Isometopus mirificus* (Pl.10), from the southern half of Europe, feeds on psocids and aphids on lichen-covered tree trunks.

Members of the family **Dipsocoridae** are all predatory insects under 2.5mm long. They live in wet places, such as the gravel at the edges of streams. *Cryptostemma alienum* is the commonest of the three British species.

Members of the **Saldidae** (Pl.10) are predatory bugs almost always found at the water's edge – around coastal marshes, ponds, bogs, and so on. They are commonly known as shore bugs. The head is rather broad and the eyes are very prominent. The 3-segmented beak and the general presence of four or five long, closed cells in the membrane will help to identify this family. *Saldula saltatoria* is the commonest of the 22 British species. It is found around muddy ponds. Its brown pattern merges with the mud when it is at rest, but it runs, jumps and flies when disturbed. The **Leptopodidae** is a small family related to the Saldidae but distinguished from them by having the ocelli on a raised platform. The prothorax is also much narrower. *Leptopus marmoratus* (Pl.10) lives under stones in damp places in the southern half of Europe.

Amphibicorisae: Pond Skaters and other surface-living water bugs (Pl.11)

The surface-living bugs are classified with the terrestrial ones in the Gymnocerata because they possess free, visible antennae – in contrast to the hidden antennae of the true water bugs – but the families concerned form a very distinct ecological group specially adapted for life on the water surface. One of the main features is the coating of fine, water-repellent hairs that clothe at least the undersides of the insects and prevent their getting wet. All are predatory insects, finding food by sight and/or by sensing vibrations in the surface film.

The **Mesoveliidae** and the related **Hebridae** are much less specialised for life on the water surface than the other skaters and they retain more features of their terrestrial ancestors. For example, both families have apical claws on their tarsi, although this feature is also shared by the Hydrometridae. The two families are represented in Britain by just three species, all under 3mm long. *Mesovelia furcata*, green and black and usually wingless, spends much of its time on the floating leaves of pondweeds. *Hebrus pusillus* and *H.ruficeps* – the latter usually with vestigial wings – are both found on mosses at the edges of streams.

The Water Measurer (*Hydrometra stagnorum*) belongs to the **Hydrometridae**, a family characterised by great elongation of the head. The insects are usually micropterous and they are found on still and slow-moving water. Unlike most surface-dwelling bugs, the water measurers spear food through the surface film and hold it with the rostrum instead of with the front legs. It would appear, therefore, that the elongation of the head is associated with this method of feeding. Water fleas and mosquito larvae make up the bulk of the water measurer's food. There are just two British species.

The family **Veliidae**, typified by the Water Cricket (*Velia caprai*), resembles the Gerridae in many ways, but the middle and hind legs are relatively shorter than those of *Gerris* and the water crickets are altogether stouter. They are brownish insects, up to 8mm long and generally wingless. They are very common on ponds and streams, where they feed on small creatures that fall on to the water. They probably

Tarsi of Mesovelia *(left) and* Gerris, *showing the position of the claws. The sub-apical claws of* Gerris *allow the insect to skate more easily over the water surface*

apical claws   sub-apical claws

also take mosquito larvae from under the surface film. The prey is held on the rostrum rather than by the legs. There are five British species.

The **Gerridae**, typified by the Common Pond Skater (*Gerris lacustris*), is the most advanced family of surface-dwelling bugs. They are the true pond skaters or water-striders, *G. lacustris* being found on almost all stretches of still fresh water. The insects row themselves across the surface at high speed by means of the long middle legs. The hind legs trail behind and act as a sort of rudder. This arrangement leaves the short front legs free to catch food in the form of small insects that fall on to the water. The claws, like those of the Veliidae, are situated just before the apex of the tarsi and the apical position is occupied by a pad of water-repellent hairs, making for more efficient movement over the surface. *Gerris* is usually fully winged and a good flier, but short-winged individuals are regularly found in most populations. The forewings are always homogeneous in texture, there being no distinct membrane. There are nine British species. Although not in the European fauna, the genus *Halobates* deserves mention as one of the few insect groups that have conquered the sea. The insects are found on floating seaweed, and on the water surface itself, hundreds of miles out in tropical and sub-tropical seas.

SERIES CRYPTOCERATA (= HIDDEN HORNS) – TRUE WATER BUGS (Plate 11)

The members of this group almost all have their antennae concealed in pits or furrows under the head. They nearly all live under the water surface and the protection of the antennae is associated with this mode of life. These aquatic bugs are also collectively known as Hydrocorisae (see p. 101). The constituent families are rather diverse in structure and it is not possible to pinpoint their origin from terrestrial bugs, although there is a clear sequence from the tube-breathing nepids, through bubble-carriers, to the plastron-breathing *Aphelocheirus*. Most water bugs are predatory and many can inflict painful bites if handled.

The family **Ochteridae** (Pl. 10), containing only about 20 species throughout the world, is an aberrant member of the Cryptocerata in that the antennae are visible. They are very short, however, and the family is otherwise clearly a member of this group. *Ochterus marginatus* lives around the edges of ponds and streams in southern Europe, where it feeds mainly on fly larvae. It flies strongly in sunshine.

Members of the **Nepidae** are easily recognised by the long 'tail', which is actually the respiratory tube or siphon. At intervals the siphon is pushed up to the water surface and air is thereby conducted to the abdominal spiracles. The insects possess hydrostatic receptors which help them to maintain a suitable depth in the water for correct functioning of the siphon. The family is mainly tropical, but Europe has the flat, bottom-living Water Scorpion (*Nepa cinerea*) and the slender, stick-like *Ranatra linearis* which lives among the water weeds. Neither species is a good swimmer and the insects rely mainly on crawling. Both species are winged, but generally unable to fly because the wing muscles are poorly developed. The front legs are raptorial, particularly so in *Nepa*, and well suited to catching food. *Nepa* feeds on other insects, tadpoles, and even small fishes, while *Ranatra* normally takes smaller prey such as water fleas and other small arthropods.

The **Belostomatidae** contains the giant water bugs – broad, flat insects at least 3cm long and reaching lengths of more than 10cm in some species. They are fierce predators with strongly raptorial front legs. A pair of retractable appendages at the tip of the abdomen carry air from the surface to the reservoir under the wings. The insects fly well at night and are often attracted to lights. Most of these bugs live in the tropics, but *Lethocerus* (=*Belostoma*) *niloticus*, which reaches lengths of about 8cm, lives in a few lakes in south-east Europe. It has also been found swimming in the sea.

The Saucer Bug (*Ilyocoris cimicoides*), the only British representative of two very similar European members of the **Naucoridae**, is easily identified by the enormous front femora projecting horn-like from the front of the body. Up to 15mm long, it lives in muddy ponds. It is a bubble-breather, but can stay under water for longer than most bugs before needing to renew its air supply.

Aphelocheirus aestivalis is sometimes included in the Naucoridae, but many entomologists now give it a family to itself – the **Aphelocheiridae**. It has a narrower head than the naucorids and less strongly raptorial legs. The wings are usually very short or even absent, but fully-winged individuals occur from time to time, mainly in the south. The main feature of *Aphelocheirus*, however, is its plastron-respiration (see p. 23), which means that it is confined to well-oxygenated waters. Bubble-carrying bugs that rely on air from the surface can, of course, live in foul water with very little oxygen.

The backswimmers of the family **Notonectidae** are among the fiercest of the bugs. They are represented in the British Isles by four species of *Notonecta*, of which *N.glauca* is the most common. The insects swim on their backs – ventral side uppermost – and use their long, hair-fringed back legs as oars. The upside-down position, together with the very long back legs, immediately distinguishes the backswimmers from the corixids. Light, not gravity, controls the swimming position, and if backswimmers are put into a tank lit only from below they will swim right-way-up. Backswimmers are bubble-breathers and must come to the surface quite frequently to renew their air supplies. Tadpoles, small fishes, insects, and other arthropods are all consumed by backswimmers. The insects are strong fliers.

Plea atomaria, the only British member of the **Pleidae**, is closely related to the backswimmers and, like them, it swims on its keel-shaped back. It is less than 3mm long.

The **Corixidae** or water boatmen differ from the other water bugs in being largely herbivorous, feeding on plant debris and unicellular algae from the bottom of the pond. The material is scooped up and filtered by the flattened front tarsi and then sucked in through the short, blunt rostrum. Typified by *Corixa punctata*, the corixids are superficially similar to the backswimmers but they do not swim on their backs and the dorsal surface is much flatter. The hind legs are used for swimming and are fringed with hairs, but they are relatively shorter than in the backswimmers and little longer than the middle legs. Water boatmen spend much of their time on the bottom of the ponds, rising only to renew their air supplies. Except in the small *Micronecta*, the scutellum is completely covered by the wings. The insects generally fly well – by day and by night – although some individuals have reduced flight muscles and cannot take to the air. Male water boatmen produce a 'courtship song' by rubbing their hairy front legs against a ridge on each side of the face, and when confined in a small dish the sound is surprisingly loud. There are about 30 British species.

Take care when meeting the name water boatmen: it is widely used for both notonectids and corixids. Although most authors now favour the name backswimmers for the notonectids, some retain the name water boatmen for this family and use the name lesser water boatmen for the corixids.

SUB-ORDER HOMOPTERA (PLATES 12 and 13)

The members of this sub-order are a rather diverse collection of insects bearing little resemblance to the heteropteran bugs. Only the striking similarities in their mouth-parts link the two groups together. The homopterans themselves, ranging from the large cicadas on the one hand to minute aphids and scale insects on the other, would probably be split into several orders were it not for their mouth-parts. As it is, two distinct divisions or series are recognised within the sub-order: the AUCHENORRHYNCHA (cicadas and hoppers) with short bristle-like antennae, and the STERNORRHYNCHA (aphids and others) in which the antennae are generally long and thread-like.

The head of the homopterans is usually strongly deflexed or hypognathous so that mouth-parts come to lie below and behind the eyes, thus appearing to arise from the back of the head. Among the Sternorrhyncha the rostrum actually appears to come from between the front legs. Apart from this more posterior position, however, the homopteran mouth-parts are very like those of the heteropteran bugs.

Compound eyes are usually present and clearly visible, although they often have only a few facets. Two or three ocelli are also usually present and many aphids possess accessory eyes or ocular tubercles. The antennae generally have four or five segments, although psyllids have ten and some male scale insects have 25 segments. The form of the antennae is an important guide to the identification of some families.

Whereas the prothorax of the heteropteran bugs is large and conspicuous, that of the homopterans is generally small, forming little more than a collar behind the head. The exceptions to this are the treehoppers of the family Membracidae, in which the pronotum extends backwards and upwards to form a hood. The meso- and metanota are usually well-developed, but the scutellum is never as conspicuous as in the heteropterans.

It is in the wings that the two sub-orders of bugs differ most noticeably: the forewings of the homopterans are never divided into leathery and membranous areas. They may be membranous, as in the aphids, or tough and leathery, as in some hoppers, but they are always uniform in texture. At rest, the wings are generally held roofwise over the body, whereas those of the heteropterans are folded flat. The venation is fairly complete in the cicadas and hoppers, but much reduced in the other families. Female scale insects and certain generations of aphids are regularly wingless, but most other homopterans are fully winged.

Most cicadas and hoppers possess broad, sabre-like ovipositors with which they place their eggs in crevices or in slits cut specially in the plant tissues. Aphids and most other sternorrhynchans have no special ovipositors and they simply lay their eggs on the plant surface. Homopteran eggs are far less ornate than those of the heteropterans and the nymphal life is more variable, there being from three to seven instars in the various families. Viviparity and parthenogenesis occur regularly among the aphids. The majority of species overwinter as eggs.

All homopterans are plant feeders and the sub-order contains some very serious pests, especially among the aphids and leafhoppers. These insects weaken the plants by taking large amounts of sap and many also inject toxins which destroy chlorophyll and reduce the plants' food-making activities. Some produce blockages in the plants' food-conducting tubes, so that regions beyond the injury wither and die. But the greatest importance of these insects lies in their ability to transmit viruses. Leafhoppers are not serious pests in Europe, but aphid-borne viruses cause huge losses. The virus particles pass down through the rostrum and infect each new plant on which the insect feeds. The wise potato grower selects 'seed' potatoes from Scotland or some other cool region where aphids are less common: the potatoes are then less likely to carry viruses at the time of planting.

An interesting habit displayed by many homopterans, notably the aphids and other sternorrhynchans, is the production of a sweet secretion called honeydew. This is exuded through the anus – although it was once thought that the paired cornicles on the aphid abdomen were responsible – and consists largely of excess sugars derived from the plant sap. It is this substance that makes greenfly and other aphids so attractive to ants. Honeydew – often produced so copiously that it can be seen falling from aphid-infested trees – is also responsible for the sooty appearance of many plants in late summer. Nothing is wasted in nature and a black fungus utilises the dried honeydew as a food material. Many woodland butterflies also feed largely on honeydew.

Waxy substances are also produced by many homopterans from glands on the abdomen. In the form of waxy powders or strands, the secretions help to keep the insects dry in what is often a very wet habitat. The abdominal cornicles of the aphids exude a waxy fluid when attacked and this deters many of their smaller predators. In addition, the odour of this fluid appears to warn neighbouring aphids of the danger and they rapidly crawl away or drop to the ground out of harm's way.

The following key may be used to place most of the European homopterans in their correct families, although the psyllids, aphids, and scale insects are taken only to their superfamilies.

1. Antennae very short, with terminal arista: rostrum clearly arising from head: tarsi 3-segmented (Series Auchenorrhyncha) — 2

    Antennae longer: rostrum (if present) appears to arise from between front legs: tarsi with 1 or 2 segments (Series Sternorrhyncha) — 12

2. Pronotum extended back over abdomen — Membracidae p. 117

    Pronotum not so extended — 3

3. Veins 1A and 2A of forewing do
    not unite distally: middle coxae
    short and close together: hind
    wing with peripheral vein
    running parallel to margin, at
    least in posterior half of wing   4

    2A 1A

    Veins 1A and 2A of forewing unite
    distally: middle coxae usually
    longer and well separated: no
    peripheral vein in hind wing   6

    1A + 2A

4. Insects at least 15mm long, with clear wings and 3 ocelli   Cicadidae p. 117

    Insects smaller, usually with opaque, coloured wings: 2   5
    ocelli or none

5. Hind tibia rounded and bearing only   Cercopidae p. 118
       a few spines

    Hind tibia angular, with one or more   Cicadellidae p. 118
       rows of spines

6. Hind tibia with large moveable spur   Delphacidae p. 119
       at apex

    No such spur, although several smaller fixed ones may be   7
    present

7. Forewing ± membranous and transparent, with well-   8
       defined veins

    Forewing generally tougher and opaque, with less distinct   10
    veins

8. Head prolonged into a sharp point well in front of eyes: †Dictyopharidae p. 120
       forewing with marked reticulate venation towards tip

    Head not markedly elongated, but if pointed the venation   9
    is not strongly reticulate

9. Forewings meet in mid-line at rest   Cixiidae p. 119
    Forewings overlap slightly at rear   †Achilidae p. 119

10. Forewings distinctly pitted: eyes small   Tettigometridae p. 120
    Forewings not pitted: eyes relatively large   11

11. Forewing sharply angled about 1/3rd of way back: rear   Issidae p. 120
       edge of pronotum almost straight: scutellum pointed at
       rear

    Forewing smoothly rounded: rear edge of pronotum in-   †Tropiduchidae p. 120
       dented: rear edge of scutellum appears rounded

12. Tarsi with 2 segments of about equal length: insects al-   13
       ways fully winged and with well-developed legs: anten-
       nae 7-10-segmented

Adults often wingless and legs sometimes greatly reduced: 14
  tarsi (when present) 1-segmented or else with 2 seg-
  ments of which the basal one is very small: antennae
  usually with 3–6 segments (up to 25 in male scale insects)

13. Forewings rigid and with prominent veins   Superfamily Psylloidea p. 120

     Forewings soft and whitish, with reduced venation   Aleyrodidae p. 121

14. Tarsi, when present, usually   Superfamily Coccoidea p. 123
     1-segmented and bearing a single
     claw: females almost always
     wingless, males with or without
     wings but never with more than 1
     pair

     Tarsi usually present and having 2   Superfamily Aphidoidea p. 121
     segments and paired claws:
     winged or wingless and often
     bearing 2 tiny tubes on the
     abdomen

[†] denotes families not found in the British Isles

SERIES AUCHENORRHYNCHA (Pl.12)

The cicadas of the family **Cicadidae** are easily recognised by their large size – European species are at least 15mm long – and by the two pairs of transparent, membranous wings which are held roofwise over the body at rest. Most feed on trees of one kind or another by plunging their long beaks into the twigs and branches. Young cicadas are subterranean creatures and have greatly enlarged front legs with which they burrow through the soil from one root to another. They spend several years feeding on the roots before emerging as adult insects. One American species takes 17 years to grow up but, despite this long period of development, the nymphs pass through only seven instars.

Adult cicadas sit on trees or among other vegetation and the males give out their shrill, monotonous whistle which is produced by two small membranes called tymbals. These are situated in two resonating cavities, one on each side of the abdomen, and they are vibrated rapidly by the action of two tiny muscles. The noise is emitted almost continuously and can be quite deafening where cicadas are numerous. This method of sound production is almost unique among insects. Similar organs are found in certain leafhoppers but they do not produce anything like the volume emitted by the cicadas.

Several species of cicadas live in Europe, mainly in the south where *Tibicen plebejus* is the largest and noisiest species. Only *Cicadetta montana* reaches Britain, where it is confined to the New Forest and particularly associated with hazel trees. It has a much softer song than the larger cicadas.

The family **Membracidae** is characterised by the backward extension of the pronotum to form a sort of hood over the rest of the thorax and abdomen. It is primarily a tropical family whose members live largely in the trees. They are commonly called treehoppers and they show many examples of protective resemblance. The hood of

The Buffalo Treehopper Stictocephalus
bisonia, *with a strongly domed pronotum,
occurs on a wide range of woody and
herbaceous plants and often causes
damage to fruit trees*

the tropical thornhopper, for example, is shaped and patterned like the prickles on
the insect's food-plant and it is not easy to pick out the insect. Four species live in
Europe, including the Buffalo Treehopper – a bright green species introduced from
North America and now widely distributed in southern Europe. *Centrotus cornutus*
and *Gargara genistae* are the only British species.

Members of the **Cercopidae** are known mainly through the nymphal habit of living in a mass of froth or spittle. Their common names therefore include spittlebugs
and cuckoo-spit insects. They are also known as froghoppers, from their leaping abilities and the vaguely frog-like appearance of some of the adults. The froth which
surrounds the nymphs protects them from drying up and also gives them some protection from predators. It is produced by the nymphs themselves by forcing air into
a fluid exuded from the anus.There are ten British species. *Philaenus spumarius* is
one of the commonest froghoppers, but the dull brown adult is less well known than
the red and black *Cercopis* species, of which there are several in Europe. *Cercopis*
nymphs live underground, feeding communally on roots and surrounded by solidi-
fied froth. Some entomologists restrict the Cercopidae to *Cercopis* and its allies in
which the anterior margin of the pronotum is straight. The other froghoppers, in
which the front edge of the pronotum arches forward between the eyes, are then
placed in the family Aphrophoridae.

The family **Cicadellidae**, also known as the **Jassidae**, contains the leafhoppers,
so called because they are usually found on leaves. It is a large family, with over
250 British species, and is often divided into several smaller ones. The insects are
generally small and often brightly coloured although greens are the dominant colours. The leafhoppers resemble small, narrow froghoppers, but they can be distinguished by the very broad hind coxae, which reach almost to the sides of the
abdomen, and by the one or more rows of small spines on the hind tibiae. The tibiae
are also more angular than those of the froghoppers. The leafhoppers jump extremely
well for their size and they also fly readily.

Leafhoppers are extremely numerous insects and large numbers can be beaten
from almost any bush or tree during the summer. Grasses and other herbage are also

Ledra aurita, *easily recognised by the ear-like
lobes on the pronotum, is up to 18mm long
and is our largest leafhopper. It feeds mainly
on oak trees*

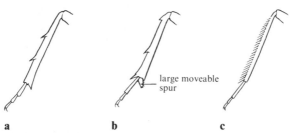

a   b   c

Hind legs of homopteran bugs showing the different arrangements of the spines in three families: **a.** *Cercopidae;* **b.** *Delphacidae;* **c.** *Cicadellidae*

well stocked with them, although each species has a fairly restricted range of foodplants. The insects cause a great deal of damage to crops in the warmer parts of the world but they are not serious pests in Europe, although *Eupteryx aurata* is common on potatoes. By removing sap and destroying chlorophyll, the leafhoppers produce characteristic pale blotches around their feeding sites. During a severe attack these blotches may join up and the whole leaf appears pale. Many leafhoppers also produce honeydew. The numerous genera include *Jassus, Penthimia, Elymana, Thamnotettix, Macropsis*, and *Macrosteles*.

The remaining families of the Auchenorrhyncha belong to the superfamily **Fulgoroidea** and were at one time all included in a single family. Many of these insects resemble leafhoppers, but they differ in that veins 1A and 2A of the forewing unite distally. There are other smaller differences, notably the origin of the antennae below the compound eyes in the Fulgoroidea. Collectively called planthoppers, these insects feed on all parts of plants although none is a really serious pest in Europe.

The **Delphacidae** is the largest family of the group and contains about 70 British species. Its members, typified by *Delphax pulchellus*, can be recognised by the large apical spur on the hind tibia. The **Cixiidae** has over 20 European species. Twelve of them occur in the British Isles, including the common *Cixius nervosus*. The forewing is largely transparent and strongly veined. The pronotum is collar-like and deeply indented on the rear edge, appearing almost like an inverted V. The adults are associated with a wide range of vegetation, including many trees, but the nymphs feed mainly on grass roots. The nymphs often carry tufts of waxy threads at the rear end. The **Achilidae** is a closely related family in which the forewings overlap towards the tip instead of meeting in a straight line. *Helicoptera marginalis* lives in southern Europe, where its nymphs feed under loose bark.

Homopteran forewings showing how veins 1A and 2A unite to form a Y-shaped vein in the Delphacidae and other families of the Fulgoroidea (left), but not in the froghoppers and leafhoppers (right)

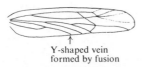

The **Dictyopharidae** is easily recognised by the pointed head. *Dictyophara europaea* is common on many plants in southern Europe, together with the brachypterous *Bursinia genei* which ranges from yellow to deep brown. The **Tettigometridae**, recognised by its densely pitted forewings, has about 30 European members, although only *Tettigometra impressopunctata* occurs in the British Isles. The nymphs are largely subterranean, taking sap from roots or else associating with ants and feeding on honeydew.

Members of the **Issidae** can usually be recognised by the bulging forewings, although there are several brachypterous species in the family. Only two species, including *Issus coleoptratus*, occur in Britain but several others live in southern Europe, where they feed on a wide range of plants. Some can be mistaken for small beetles. The **Tropiduchidae** is related to the Issidae, but the forewings do not bulge and the rear edge of the pronotum is indented instead of straight. The rear edge of the scutellum appears rounded, not pointed as in almost all other hoppers.

SERIES STERNORRHYNCHA (Pl.13)

Members of the superfamily **Psylloidea** are small or minute insects, usually only 2-3mm long and bearing a strong resemblance to miniature cicadas. They are quite numerous insects, found particularly on trees. Many species keep to one particular kind of tree – a glance at a check list will reveal Alder Psyllid, Apple Psyllid, Birch Psyllid, and many others – and several are responsible for gall formation. The shape and resting attitude of the insects are quite characteristic, but the most diagnostic feature is the venation of the forewings. Veins R, M, and Cu_1 are all fused basally so that most of the veins appear to come from a central stalk. There are no cross-veins. The forewings are somewhat thicker than the hind wings and may or may not be mottled. Psyllids do not fly well, but they are excellent jumpers and they are commonly known as jumping plant lice.

There are five nymphal instars and the life history is very easy to follow by opening a series of red-veined leaf galls from ash trees (Pl.13). These are caused by *Psyllopsis fraxini* and can be found wherever ash grows. The eggs hatch as the buds open and the nymphs start to feed on the leaves. Their activity causes the leaves to swell and roll and the veins to turn red, and the psyllids continue to grow inside these galls. The flat, greenish nymphs, their stages recognised by the increasing number of antennal segments, are covered with fluffy wax threads and look like tiny pieces of cotton wool. From June onwards the brownish adults can be seen in the galls, amid masses of tiny balls of fluid. This fluid is honeydew, but the droplets are coated with wax from special abdominal glands and this prevents the insects from getting sticky.

Psylla mali, often called the Apple Sucker, is a very common psyllid which does a certain amount of damage by attacking the growing points and flowers of apple trees. The pale brown *Homotoma ficus* is a large psyllid found on figs and it is easily

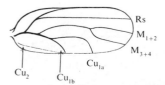

The forewing venation of a psyllid

Livia juncorum, *showing the flat, elongated head that makes this genus look rather different from other psyllids.* L. juncorum *induces the growth of red, tassel-like galls on rushes in summer*

identified by its flattened, hairy antennae. *Livia* species, recognised by their flat, elongated heads, induce galls on sedges and rushes.

Until recently, all psyllids were assigned to the family Psyllidae, but they have now been split into several smaller families according to the shape of the head, the structure of the antennae, and the venation. The **Psyllidae**, represented by *Psyllopsis fraxini*, remains the largest family, with about 40 British species.

The **Aleyrodidae**, the only family in the superfamily Aleyrodoidea, is easily recognised because its members are covered with a fine white waxy powder, giving them their common name of whiteflies. All are tiny insects with wingspans ranging up to about 5mm and, because of their opaque wings, they resemble minute moths. The wing venation is greatly reduced. The life histories of these insects differ from those of typical bugs because there is something in the nature of a pupal stage. The flat, oval nymph – perhaps more correctly called a larva – is active in the first instar, but legs and antennae degenerate after the first moult and the next two stages are spent motionless, often protected by their cast skins or by a waxy secretion. The insect continues to feed throughout this period and then enters the 'pupal' stage. It also feeds during the early part of this stage, but then stops while the adult appendages develop inside the body.

Whiteflies are most abundant in tropical regions, but about 30 species are found in Europe and about 20 of these occur in the British Isles – including several introduced species that are found only in glasshouses. The Cabbage Whitefly (*Aleyrodes proletella*) is often common on brassicas in the spring – and even in the depths of winter – but it does not seem to do much direct harm to crops. Its worst effect is to cover the leaves with sticky honeydew. The introduced Greenhouse Whitefly (*Trialeurodes vaporariorum*) is a more damaging pest, affecting a wide range of greenhouse and indoor plants, especially tomatoes and cucumbers. Like all whiteflies, it is usually found on the undersides of the leaves.

The superfamily **Aphidoidea** contains over 4,000 known species, generally known as aphids, plant lice, greenfly, or blackfly. These insects feed mainly on the sap of leaves and tender young shoots, and their immense reproductive abilities make many of them serious pests.

Aphids are all minute insects, the majority being only 2-3mm long. The body is typically pear-shaped, with a narrow head and bulbous abdomen. Greens and browns are the dominant colours. The wings, when present, are usually clear and membranous, the front ones being much larger than the hind ones. The venation is reduced but fairly constant in all aphids, the most obvious feature being a broad vein running

The forewing venation of an aphid

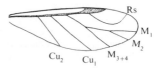

near the costal margin. This broad vein is believed to represent all the principal veins fused together, for the only other veins are branches from this one. At rest, the wings are usually held roofwise over the body, but they are occasionally laid flat or held vertically upwards. Polymorphism is very common and wingless forms occur in most species.

Although greatly reduced in gertain genera, the paired abdominal cornicles are the most characteristic features of the aphids and will usually serve to distinguish them from other small insects. The tubes, once thought to exude honeydew, are the openings of specialised wax glands. The wax protects the aphids from some of their enemies (see p. 115) but, luckily for us, it seems to have little effect on ladybirds, lacewings, and hover fly larvae, all of which eagerly devour the aphids. Many aphid species also produce fluffy or powdery wax in dermal glands.

Aphids pass through several generations in a year and their annual cycle involves a sequence of several different forms. The basic cycle is as follows. The insects over-winter as eggs on the host plant, and these eggs hatch in the spring to produce wing-less, parthenogenetic females known as stem-mothers or fundatrices. When mature, these stem-mothers reproduce without mating and they are generally viviparous, bringing forth several active young each day. The insects of the new generation differ slightly from the stem-mothers and a few winged forms may occur. Several gener-ations of these parthenogenetic females are produced during the summer, the winged forms, which spread the species from plant to plant, usually alternating with a num-ber of wingless generations. As autumn approaches, the aphids produce both male and female offspring. The females are oviparous and lay the overwintering eggs after mating. The occurrence of parthenogenesis in several successive generations, together with the production of large numbers of almost sessile individuals, is re-sponsible for the rapid build-up of aphid colonies in spring and summer. Numbers are kept in check, however, by the predators already mentioned and by various bra-conid and chalcid parasites. The condition of the plant host also affects the aphid population, by affecting the numbers of young produced and by determining whether winged or wingless forms are produced.

Superimposed on the basic life cycle there is often a pattern of migration. A few species of aphids are able to live on a wide variety of plants and the winged indi-viduals distribute themselves at random through the vegetation. Other species, how-ever, are more restricted in their diet and some require a regular alternation of hosts. It is in this latter group, typified by the Black Bean Aphid (*Aphis fabae*), that regular migration occurs. The eggs of *A. fabae* are laid on the spindle tree (*Euonymus eu-ropaeus*) or on *Viburnum* or *Philadelphus*, which are known as the primary hosts. This aphid is very unusual in having three such primary hosts: almost all other aphids have only one. The stem-mothers produce a generation of wingless offspring, but the following generation are the migrants and they are almost all winged. They fly to the summer (secondary) hosts – which include beans, spinach, docks, and many other plants – where they reproduce parthenogenetically and viviparously to give rise to the black masses so common on these plants. These summer generations may be winged or wingless, the winged ones spreading the species throughout the popu-lations of its summer hosts. Migration back to the primary hosts takes place in the autumn. Winged parthenogenetic females fly there and bring forth wingless sexual females. The males are produced on the summer hosts and they fly to the trees to mate with the wingless females. After mating, each sexual female lays just a few large eggs and the cycle starts again. The insects can also go on breeding asexually throughout the year in suitable situations if the temperatures do not fall too low.

The Peach-Potato Aphid (*Myzus persicae*), which is a common potato pest in the summer, is another migratory species. Its primary host is the peach, although it will also pass the winter on various herbaceous plants. The greyish green Cabbage Aphid (*Brevicoryne brassicae*) is a non-migratory species, spending its whole life cycle on cruciferous plants and often causing severe damage to cabbages and other brassicas.

All the aphids mentioned so far belong to the **Aphididae**, which is by far the largest family. There are nearly 500 British species. The cornicles are always clearly visible and there are at least four oblique veins in the forewing. The **Pemphigidae**, with about 40 British species, also has four oblique veins in the forewing, but the cornicles are very small and generally invisible in this family. *Pemphigus bursarius* is one of several gall-causing species. It is responsible for the little pouch-like swellings on the stalks of poplar leaves (Pl.13). The Woolly Aphid (*Eriosoma lanigerum*), often found on apple trees, is one of those aphids that cover themselves with fluffy strands of wax.

Members of the **Adelgidae** have only three oblique veins in the forewing and there are no cornicles. The insects are confined to conifers. *Adelges abietis* causes the development of cone-like 'pineapple galls' on spruce twigs (Pl.13). All generations in this family are oviparous. There are ten British species. Members of the **Phylloxeridae** have stout, 3-segmented antennae and their wings, when present, lie flat over the body at rest. There are only three oblique veins in the forewing. The insects lack cornicles and all generations are oviparous. *Viteus vitifolii* is a serious vine pest, introduced from North America and now well established in Europe, while *Phylloxera glabra* is often abundant under oak leaves in the summer. Some recent classifications place the last two families in a separate superfamily – the Adelgoidea.

The scale insects and mealybugs of the superfamily **Coccoidea** are atypical insects: indeed, the females of most species are hardly recognisable as insects at all, for they are usually wingless and often legless as well. The antennae are also greatly reduced. These females remain motionless, attached to the host plant by the rostrum, which is just about the only external feature that links them with the rest of the insect world. The insects are covered with a hard or waxy scale, or with a mass of waxy threads. These coverings are secreted by the insects themselves and are responsible for the common names given to the group. Males are more normal in appearance, usually winged and not unlike small midges – a resemblance that is heightened by the fact that the hind wings are reduced to tiny halteres. The scale insects can be distinguished, however, by the presence of one or more terminal processes on the abdomen and by their atrophied mouth-parts. Male scale insects are, in fact, rarely seen and the classification of the group depends almost entirely on female morphology.

Scale insects are extremely prolific, parthenogenesis and viviparity being quite common. A single female may produce 1,000 eggs or young and, with perhaps six generations in a year, this could theoretically lead to more than 30 million scale insects. The eggs are usually protected with a wax scale, or they may be kept under the mother's body until they hatch. First-instar nymphs are responsible for the dispersal of the insects for, apart from the adult males, only they are mobile. Legs are often lost after the first instar and the nymphs are then sessile, attached only by their mouth-parts.

A wide variety of host plants is attacked by scale insects, although some species are restricted to one or two closely related plants, and scale insects include some of the most important insect pests in the world. The female scales often occur in such numbers that whole trees are killed. In their natural homes they are kept down by parasites and predators, but they are so easily transported on plant material that many species now have a world-wide distribution. Freed from their natural controls, many have become serious pests. Others have become pests simply through the increased cultivation of their host plants.

There are about 170 species of scale insects and mealybugs in Britain, including several introduced species that exist only in glasshouses, and they are distributed in ten families. The Mussel Scale (*Lepidosaphes ulmi*) is one of the more damaging of our native scale insects. It is a hard-shelled species looking just like a miniature brown mussel shell and it often completely covers the bark of its host trees. These include apple and many other fruit and ornamental trees. The insect has also become a pest in North America, where it is known as the Oystershell Scale. Mealybugs of the family **Pseudococcidae** are among the least specialised members of the group, with the females retaining their legs and a certain amount of mobility. Segmentation is clearly visible under the waxy secretions and the mealybugs look, at first sight, rather like small white woodlice. The Citrus Mealybug (*Planococcus citri*) is an American species that has become firmly established as a citrus pest in southern Europe.

The control of scale insects is a rather difficult matter because, under their scales, the females are protected from most sprays. Fumigation with cyanide was widely used in the United States, but many scales have now become resistant to cyanide and other methods have to be employed. One of the most successful examples of biological control involved the Cottony Cushion Scale or Fluted Scale (*Icerya purchasi*). Introduced into America from Australia, this scale quickly became a serious pest in the citrus-growing regions. It is kept in check in Australia by the ladybird beetle *Rodolia cardinalis*, and large numbers of these beetles were taken to America in an attempt to control the scale there. The beetles soon became established and quickly reduced the *Icerya* population.

There are also a few useful coccids. Shellac, cochineal, and various waxes are obtained from certain species, and the manna of biblical stories is believed to have been the syrupy honeydew exuded by coccids: in warm, dry climates it quickly solidifies into sugar lumps as the water evaporates.

Collecting and Preserving

Beating, sweeping, and detailed examination of herbage are the best ways of collecting the terrestrial bugs. Water bugs can be taken fairly easily with a small net, but the surface-dwellers are more difficult. They can sometimes be attracted with greenfly scattered on the water, and then skilful wielding of the net might result in a few captures. Many bugs, especially the mirids, are very delicate and must not be shaken about in large containers, either before or after despatch. Small tubes are best for collecting these insects.

The heteropteran bugs, together with most of the auchenorrhynchans, are best preserved in the dry state. Carding can be used for simple display, but this method conceals the rostrum and other useful identification guides. Pinning is a more satisfactory method. The ventral surfaces of the thorax and abdomen are particularly important in specific identification and when pinning – through either the scutellum or hemelytron – take care to leave one side of the body undamaged. The smaller bugs may be mounted on points in the normal way.

Aphids are best preserved in spirit because their soft bodies soon shrivel when dried. They can be put straight into collecting fluid in the field. Winged specimens are normally necessary to ensure correct specific identification. Other sternorrhynchans may also be preserved in spirit, although practice enables one to display psyllids and whiteflies suitably on pins or points. Female scale insects not required for detailed anatomical study can simply be dried on part of the host plant. Otherwise they should be kept in spirit.

Order Thysanoptera – Thrips

Recognition features Minute insects, usually brown or black, with very slender bodies and usually with two pairs of narrow, fringed wings. Commonly found in flowers. The thrips, especially the winged ones, are unlikely to be confused with any other insects.

Unless you are an ardent flower-sniffer, your first meeting with a thrips is quite likely to be when one gets in your eye, for these tiny insects are rarely noticed unless they intrude into our lives in this way. They live on the vegetation, under loose bark, and in flowers. Examination of a dandelion will usually reveal a dozen or more of these insects deep down among the florets, where they feed by piercing the plant cells with their mouths and sucking out the sap. A few suck the juices of other insects and some live on fungi and decaying material, but the majority feed on living plants and, although the individual insects are small, they exist in such immense numbers that several species are agricultural pests. One such pest is the Pea Thrips (*Kakothrips robustus*), which is responsible for the mottled silvery appearance of many pea pods. The insects pierce and scrape the outer cells to get at the sap and the collapsed cells give the surface its silvery appearance. When the thrips attack the flower or the early stages of the pod the latter becomes deformed and there is a considerable crop loss. Other species damage wheat and ornamental flowers. The nymphs and young adults of *Limothrips cerealium* feed in the ears of wheat and other cereals, causing shrivelling of the grain and distortion of the ears. They remain in the ears until the ripening grain becomes too hard and dry for them. In addition to the direct damage done by the thrips, some species are able to transmit plant diseases. The damage is offset to some extent, however, by the pollinating services carried out by the insects as they wander among the flowers.

The head carries a pair of small but prominent compound eyes and, in winged thrips, three ocelli. The antennae are rather short and are placed close together on

A thrips showing the feathery nature of the wings. Most of our thrips are only 1-2mm long, but some tropical species reach about 14mm. Most are dark in colour, but some are yellowish or pale grey

the front of the head. They contain between 6 and 10 segments. The piercing mouth-parts are unusual in that they are not symmetrically developed. There is a short coni-cal beak, composed mainly of the upper and lower lips and enclosing three piercing stylets. The latter are derived from the left mandible and the inner arms of the two maxillae. The right mandible is missing. The mandibular stylet makes the first inci-sion, and then the maxillary stylets are inserted. Sap is sucked up through a canal between the two maxillary stylets.

The prothorax is distinct but the meso- and metathoracic segments are completely fused. The wings, when present, are very narrow, with few or no veins. They are fringed on both front and rear edges with relatively long bristles which more than double the effective width of the wings. The name Thysanoptera, derived from the Greek *thysanos* meaning a fringe, simply means fringed-wings. The wings are coupled by tiny hooks on the hind wings. Many species are wingless, but wing development is very variable and even within a species there may be wingless, short-winged, and fully-winged individuals.

In view of the delicate structure of their wings, the thrips are surprisingly good fliers and many of them take to the air on warm, still days. This is when they get into our eyes and hair and, despite their small size, they can cause considerable ir-ritation. These flying thrips are often called thunder flies or thunder bugs because of their association with thundery weather. They are particularly common in mid-summer when the cereal thrips are leaving their host plants, and this is when every-one living in arable areas starts to complain about them.

The eggs of most species are laid on or in plant tissues, many females having well-developed saw-like ovipositors which are used to slit the plants before deposi-ting the eggs. The first two nymphal instars are quite normal, resembling the adults but without wing pads, and then, at the second moult, the insects go into a short, non-feeding stage called the prepupa. Small wing buds are visible on the prepupae of most thrips (sub-order Terebrantia), but not in the sub-order Tubulifera. The pre-pupa moults after a few days to reveal the pupa, in which the wing buds and other appendages are more or less of adult size. Tubuliferan thrips pass through a second pupal stage before emerging as adults. Most thrips pupate in the soil or in debris, but some pupate on their food-plants. Some species spin cocoons around themselves before pupation, although most pupae are free and, like the prepupae, they can move slowly when disturbed. Although the thrips pass through these resting stages during their development, their wings develop externally and they are clearly exopterygotes and not closely related to the other orders with pupal stages. Many species pass the winter as adults, in soil or turf or even in our houses. Others over-winter as pupae.

Some 5,000 species of thrips are known, of which over 300 occur in Europe. About 150 are native to the British Isles. The three families to which our thrips be-long may be separated with the aid of the following simple key.

1.   With a saw-like ovipositor, or with
     abdomen bluntly rounded:
     wings ± parallel at
     rest (sub-order Terebrantia)

     No ovipositor: abdomen tubular at
     tip: wings overlapping at rest
     (sub-order Tubulifera)

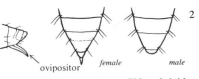

ovipositor   *female*   *male*

Phlaeothripidae

2.   Body flattened: wings narrow and pointed   Thripidae

      Body not flattened: forewings broader and rounded at tip   Aeolothripidae

Members of the **Phlaeothripidae** have stouter bodies than most other thrips and the majority of them are fungus-feeders or predators. Relatively few cause any damage, although *Haplothrips tritici* is a cereal pest in some parts of the world. *Liothrips oleae* damages olives in southern Europe.

The other two families contain most of the injurious species. The broad-winged **Aeolothripidae** often have coloured bands on the wings and are therefore called banded thrips. Most of our species, however, belong to the **Thripidae**. In both of these families the female's ovipositor juts conspicuously from the underside of the abdomen. It curves downwards in the Thripidae and upwards in the Aeolothripidae.

Collecting and preserving
Beating and sweeping vegetation are the best methods of obtaining thrips, although it is not always possible to know exactly which plants the insects came from when using this method. Flower-frequenting thrips can be picked up quite easily with an alcohol-moistened brush, and litter-inhabiting species can be obtained in the normal way. Spirit-preservation and slide-mounting are the only satisfactory ways of dealing with these tiny insects.

Order Neuroptera – Alder Flies, Snake Flies, and Lacewings
Plates 14 & 15

Recognition features Small, medium and large soft-bodied insects, generally brown or green. Two similar pairs of flimsy wings covered with a delicate network of veins and held roofwise over the body at rest. Antennae conspicuous. Compound eyes usually large.
Some of the brown species resemble caddis flies, but the latter are much more hairy and their wings have very few cross veins. The ant-lions and ascalaphids are superficially like dragonflies, but the latter have very short, bristle-like antennae.

These insects undergo a complete metamorphosis during their lives and in this respect they are more advanced than those dealt with earlier in this book. The order is, nevertheless, an ancient one and it contains some of the most primitive living endopterygotes. Nearly 5,000 species are known, of which just over 200 occur in Europe. About 60 live in the British Isles.

The green lacewings (Pl.15) are the most familiar members of the order, being attracted to light and often finding their way into houses. The smaller brown lacewings often come with them, but the diurnal alder flies and snake flies have to be sought among the herbage. They are all predatory insects and the lacewings are important allies of the gardener on account of the hordes of greenfly and other small insect pests that they destroy. The insects are mostly weak fliers, travelling with a slow, drifting motion although their wings beats quite rapidly.

A typical lacewing at rest, with its wings held roofwise over the body

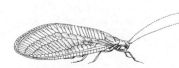

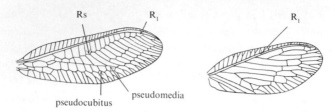

Left, The forewing of a green lacewing (family Chrysopidae), showing the reduction in the longitudinal veins (see p. 132). Right, the forewing of a brown lacewing (family Hemerobiidae). Both wings exhibit the terminal forking of the veins characteristic of this order

There are considerable differences, particularly in the young stages, between the alder flies and snake flies on the one hand and the rest of the Neuroptera on the other, and many entomologists place the insects in two separate orders. Here they are treated as a single order, with the alder flies and snake flies in the sub-order MEGALOPTERA and the lacewings in the sub-order PLANIPENNIA. Snake flies are easily recognised by the long prothorax, which can raise the head above the rest of the body in the manner of a snake about to strike. The alder flies have a shorter prothorax, but their wing venation and generally stouter appearance easily distinguish them from the lacewings.

All adult neuropterans have biting mouths, although some of them rarely seem to feed. The antennae are long and slender, except in the ant-lions, the individual segments being more conspicuous (moniliform condition) in some families than in others (filiform condition). Compound eyes are always present and are especially well developed in the ant-lions and the fast-flying ascalaphids. Ocelli may or may not be present.

The prothorax, already noted as being long in the snake flies, is more or less square in the alder flies and appears to merge with the head. That of the lacewings, however, generally tapers towards the front, and the back of the head is rounded to produce more of a 'neck' in these insects. The meso- and metathoracic segments are both well developed and the two pairs of wings are generally very similar. The venation is fairly complete, although in the green lacewings (family Chrysopidae) there is a secondary reduction of the main veins by fusion. There are usually numerous fine accessory veins and the name Neuroptera (Greek *neuron* = nerve) refers to this nerve-like network. The name was originally used by Linnaeus for all insects with delicate, netted wings – including the exopterygote mayflies and dragonflies.

A long ovipositor is present in female snake flies and dilarids, and prominent claspers occur in male ant-lions and ascalaphids, but abdominal appendages are otherwise absent in the adult neuropterans.

The larvae are rather shuttle-shaped and have three pairs of well-developed legs. The abdomen carries a number of bristles, but true appendages are absent except in the aquatic larvae, in which the appendages form tracheal gills. The larvae, like the adults, are entirely carnivorous, but the fundamental difference between the larvae of the two sub-orders is that those of the Megaloptera have biting jaws whereas those of the Planipennia have sucking mouths. But the sucking mouths of the lacewing larvae are of a very unusual type and many of them have such powerful-looking mandibles that one might be excused for thinking that they are biting jaws. Each mandible, together with part of the corresponding maxilla, forms a tube which is sunk into the victim's body. The larva then sucks out the juices as if through two tiny drinking straws.

The internal anatomy of the planipennian larva is interesting in that the hind intestine is closed and there is no through passage from the digestive region to the anus. This is associated with the liquid diet of the larva and with the unusual method of silk production in these insects (see below). The small amount of solid ingested accumulates in the digestive tract and is not voided until the insect becomes adult.

Some lacewings have two or even three generations in a year, but most other neuropterans are single-brooded. Three larval instars are usual and there is, as in other endopterygote insects, a prepupal stage – little more than a shrunken and inactive larva – prior to pupation. The prepupal stage is very short in the summer generations, but many neuropterans overwinter in this stage. Pupation always takes place on land, even in those species with aquatic larvae. The pupae of the planipennians are enclosed in silken cocoons, the silk being produced not from the salivary glands but from modified excretory tubules which have acquired openings into the hind gut. The silk is thus extruded at the anus. Megalopteran pupae are naked.

The European neuropterans may be placed in their correct families with the aid of the following key.

1.	Hind wings long and ribbon-like	[†]Nemopteridae p. 133
	Wings not like this	2
2.	Front legs raptorial	[†]Mantispidae p. 133
	Front legs not raptorial	3
3.	Small insects covered with white powder	Coniopterygidae p. 131
	Insects not like this	4
4.	Prothorax long and forming a neck	Raphidiidae p. 130
	No such neck	5
5.	Antennae thickened or clubbed at tip	6
	Antennae not thickened or clubbed at tip	7
6.	Antennae over half the length of forewings	[†]Ascalaphidae p. 132
	Antennae less than half the length of forewings	[†]Myrmeleontidae p. 132
7.	Antennae feathery in male: female with prominent ovipositor	[†]Dilaridae p. 133
	Antennae not feathery: no visible ovipositor	8
8.	Veins forking conspicuously at outer wing margins	9
	Veins not forking conspicuously at wing margins	Sialidae p. 130
9.	Large insects with mottled wings	Osmylidae p. 131
	Wings not patterned: insects generally smaller	10

10. Vein Sc joins distally with R_1: costal veinlets of forewing rarely forked: all small brown insects

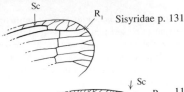

Sisyridae p. 131

Vein Sc does not join R_1 (beware of cross-veins): costal veinlets of forewing mostly forked, especially in basal half

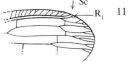

11

11. Medium-sized insects, usually green, with filiform antennae and few longitudinal veins

Chrysopidae p. 131

Small grey or brown insects with moniliform antennae and several longitudinal veins

Hemerobiidae p. 131

† denotes families not found in the British Isles

SUB-ORDER MEGALOPTERA

The alder flies – family **Sialidae** – are easily distinguished from other neuropterans by their venation, which shows no sign of forking at the wing margins. It is true that the coniopterygians also lack this feature, but they cannot be confused with the much larger, smoky-winged alder flies. *Sialis lutaria* (Pl.15) is the commonest of Europe's three alder flies. Only two of them occur in the British Isles.

The eggs are laid around the waterside in batches of 200 or more, and the larvae fall or crawl into the water. The larvae are provided with seven pairs of feathery tracheal gills on the abdomen and there is also a terminal filament of similar appearance. The larvae prefer still or slow-moving water, where they feed on a wide range of smaller insects. Pupation takes place in the soil and the pupae work their way to the surface before the imagos emerge. The life cycle takes about a year, with winter being spent in the larval state. The adults are usually found in spring and early summer.

The snake flies of the family **Raphidiidae** are completely terrestrial, the larvae living mainly under loose bark where they feed on other insects. The female has a

a. *the larva of an alder fly, showing the feathery abdominal gills;* **b.** *a green lacewing larva;* **c.** *the stalked eggs of a green lacewing*

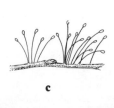

long ovipositor with which she places her eggs in suitable crevices. About 20 species live in Europe, but only four – all *Raphidia* species (Pl.15) – occur in the British Isles. The adults are most likely to be taken from oaks and pines during the summer months, although they are not common insects.

SUB-ORDER PLANIPENNIA

The members of the **Coniopterygidae** differ considerably from the rest of the Neuroptera in appearance, being very small and covered with a waxy, white powder. They are often found in groups and they look more like whiteflies (p. 121) than typical lacewings. They resemble the megalopterans in retaining a forked sub-costal vein, although the venation in general is reduced. Over 20 species occur in Europe, including eight British species, but because these tiny insects are easily overlooked or assumed to be something else it is quite possible that more will be discovered. *Conwentzia psociformis* (Pl.15), readily identified by its very narrow hind wings, is our commonest species. It is usually associated with oak trees, where it feeds on small aphids and scale insects and probably also on mites.

Osmylus fulvicephalus (Pl.15) – the only European representative of the **Osmylidae** – is Britain's largest lacewing. With mottled wings spanning about 50mm, it is a beautiful and unmistakable insect. The larvae live near water, hiding among mosses and stones, and the adults are found mainly near shady streams. It is a local insect, although widely scattered, and is on the wing in spring and early summer.

The **Sisyridae**, with three British species, is closely related to the previous family, although its members are rather different in appearance. Typified by *Sisyra fuscata* (Pl.15), they are all small and brownish. They resemble members of the Hemerobiidae, but the costal veinlets are fewer in number and they rarely fork. The adults are found near water during the summer. The larvae are aquatic and they feed entirely on freshwater sponges. They have seven pairs of abdominal gills.

The **Hemerobiidae**, typified by *Hemerobius humulinus* (Pl.15), is the largest of our neuropteran families, with over 40 European species. About 30 of them occur in the British Isles. All are small brown or greyish insects, often very hairy, and they are commonly known as brown lacewings. The forked costal veinlets readily separate the family from the Sisyridae. Adults and larvae all feed on aphids and other small insects, but the larvae are more slender and less bristly than those of the green lacewings.

The most familiar of our neuropterans are certainly the green lacewings of the family **Chrysopidae**, which has 14 British species. The body and wing veins are generally a delicate shade of green and the prominent eyes have a brilliant metallic appearance – hence the insects' alternative name of golden-eyes. The main feature

Wing tips of Sisyra *(left) and* Hemerobius, *showing how vein Sc meets* R_1 *in the Sisyridae but not in the Hemerobiidae*

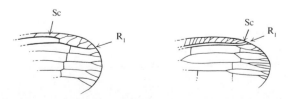

of the wing venation is the reduction of the longitudinal veins. Rs is present as a zig-zag vein, but its various branches fuse with those of the media and cubitus to form two composite veins – a straight pseudomedia and a zig-zag pseudocubitus (fig. p. 128). Two zig-zag veins known as gradates cross the outer part of the wing. *Chrysopa septempunctata* (Pl.15) is a large, bright green lacewing, identified by the seven tiny black spots on its head. *Chrysoperla carnea* is a smaller species which is very common in gardens. It becomes flesh-coloured in the autumn, at which time it often enters our houses. It is one of the few lacewings that pass the winter in the adult state. As well as these familiar green lacewings, the family contains several brown species, including *Nothochrysa capitata* (Pl.15), which is usually associated with coniferous trees, and *Italochrysa italica* whose larvae live in ant nests and feed on the ants' grubs. But these brown lacewings are fairly large insects and their venation readily distinguishes them from the hemerobiids.

Unlike the other lacewings, the chrysopids lay their eggs at the ends of threads of mucus. The threads harden on contact with the air, so that each egg has a slender stalk. Neighbouring threads may or may not coalesce. The larvae of some green lacewings cover themselves with the drained skins of their aphid victims and thus come to resemble just another piece of rubbish – a simple and effective way of protecting themselves against attack by birds.

Members of the **Ascalaphidae** are swift-flying insects with long, clubbed antennae. There are several European species, mainly in the south. Most have patterned wings like the *Libelloides* species illustrated on Pl.14, but there are some clear-winged species. Most of the species are diurnal, catching other insects as they dart to and fro in the sunshine. They often bask on the vegetation with their wings open, but as soon as the sun disappears they close their wings steeply over the body and assume a triangular shape with the antennae held out in front. Their larvae have sharply-toothed mandibles and they hunt their prey among the leaves and stones on the ground.

The ant-lions of the family **Myrmeleontidae** are superficially like dragonflies because of their long wings and their long, narrow bodies, but they are easily distin-

Left, an ascalaphid in its typical resting position. Right, an ant-lion larva, showing its powerful jaws

guished by their stout clubbed antennae. *Palpares libelluloides* (Pl.14) is the largest of the European species, most of which have clear wings. The name ant-lion refers to the larva, particularly that of *Myrmeleon formicarius*. This lives in sandy soil and excavates a little pit. It buries itself at the bottom, leaving only its strong jaws above the sand. Small insects falling into the pit cannot climb out again and the ant-lion grabs them and sucks them dry. Most ant-lions feed in this way, although not all species make pits. Many larvae merely hunt among the debris on the ground, while others, including that of *P. libelluloides*, burrow in loose soil or sand and dart out to capture passing insects. Adult ant-lions fly with a lazy rising and falling motion and rarely move far at one time. Most fly at dusk or by night, although *P. libelluloides* is active by day. The insects are found mainly in the tropics, but several species occur in southern Europe and two of them, including *M. formicarius*, reach Scandinavia.

Members of the family **Nemopteridae** are easily recognised by their long, ribbon-like hind wings. They fly mainly at dusk, when the males dance up and down rather like mayflies. Their trailing hind wings, marked with contrasting bands of colour, are thought to attract the females. The insects also flutter lazily about during the daytime, rarely more than a few centimetres above the ground and rarely moving more than a few metres at a time. They commonly rest on flowers, where they may eat smaller insects or nibble pollen grains. The larvae feed on various small creatures in the turf and leaf litter. Three species, typified by *Nemoptera coa* (Pl.14), occur in southern Europe.

The mantis flies of the family **Mantispidae** are readily identified by the raptorial front legs with which they capture a variety of insect prey. These front legs are very much like those of the praying mantis, but the wings are quite different and the overall similarity of the insects is due simply to convergent evolution. Most of the mantis flies live in the tropics but a few species reach southern Europe, where *Mantispa styriaca* (Pl.14) is widely distributed around the Mediterranean. The larvae seek out the egg cocoons of wolf spiders and enter them to prey on the young spiderlings.

Members of the **Dilaridae** are medium-sized insects with rounded and somewhat hairy wings. They can be recognised by the feathery antennae of the male and the long ovipositor of the female. *Dilar meridionalis* (Pl.14) is fairly common in Spain and southern France.

Collecting and preserving

As to be expected from the habits of these insects, the best way to collect them is to beat and sweep the vegetation – in the neighbourhood of water for those species with aquatic larvae. Many species also come to light. Crushed cherry laurel is one of the best killing agents, for it does not harden these delicate insects. Specimens can be set in the normal way, but quick drying is necessary to preserve the greens. The soft bodies shrivel considerably on drying and any specimen needed for anatomical work must be preserved in spirit.

Order Coleoptera – Beetles
Plates 16-25

Recognition features Minute to large insects, normally with two pairs of wings of which the front ones are hard and horny and generally meet neatly along the mid-line of the dorsal surface. The hind wings are membranous and usually folded away out of sight beneath the forewings. Hind wings are sometimes absent, while a few species have no wings at all. The prothorax is normally large and mobile. Mouthparts are always of the biting type.

Most beetles can be recognised as such by the form of the forewings (elytra). The most frequent confusion is with the heteropteran bugs, but these have overlapping forewings, usually with a membranous portion at the tip, and tubular, sucking mouthparts. Some of the beetles with short elytra look like earwigs but they never have abdominal pincers like earwigs.

With more than 350,000 known species, this is the largest of all insect orders. Over 20,000 occur in Europe, and more than 4,000 of these occur in Britain. In the tropical Hercules and Goliath beetles, with weights in the region of 100 grams, the Coleoptera contains the bulkiest of all insects. But such is the range of form and size within the order that it also contains some of the smallest insects, less than 0.5mm long. Beetles are abundant as individuals as well as in terms of species, although this may not be apparent to the casual observer because of the small size and secretive or nocturnal habits of many species. Most beetles can and do fly well but relatively little time is spent in flight: beetles are very much insects of the ground and low vegetation.

Within the limitations imposed by their biting mouth-parts, the beetles have invaded all available habitats – including the sea – and exploited all possible food sources. The order includes plant-feeders – with many important wood-borers – scavengers, predators, and parasites: few natural organic materials escape the attentions of one or other of these groups. Many species are serious pests: chafers and many other beetles damage our growing crops; several species infest stored grain and flour; carpets and other fabrics are attacked by carpet beetles; and timber is weakened and destroyed by the infamous woodworm and other beetles. Much of the damage is done by the larvae but the adults often do their share, although many prefer pollen or nectar. On the credit side, many beetles are useful allies in combatting other insect pests. The aphid-eating ladybirds are especially important in this respect, while the dung-beetles and burying beetles that consume animal dung and carrion form important links in the nitrogen cycle.

The success of beetles is due largely to their tough elytra and the hardness of the cuticle in general. The elytra allow the beetles to live under stones and in litter, thus making use of the shelter provided yet still retaining the delicate wings necessary for dispersal. The hard cuticle makes the beetles resistant to injury and desiccation,

A typical beetle, showing the large prothorax and the tough elytra covering the whole abdomen

thus allowing them to live in drier places than most insects – granaries, for example. The elytra also enable the beetles to live in water, the space between the body and the elytra acting as an air-tank. The biting jaws, although primitive in themselves, have also contributed to the beetles' success because they have remained adaptable and usable for a wide variety of functions and not just for feeding.

The beetle head is a heavily sclerotised capsule and, with a few notable exceptions, its structure is fairly constant throughout the order. The main exceptions are the weevils, in which the head extends forward to form the rostrum or snout, with the antennae inserted at some point along its length. Beetle antennae themselves are basically 11-segmented, although this number is often reduced (rarely increased). The form of the antennae varies considerably and is an important aid to classification and identification. Many species have clearly 'elbowed' antennae, with a long first segment. Compound eyes are usually present, although often small, but ocelli are found only in a few groups. The mouth-parts are all fully developed, usually with prominent biting mandibles, although this does not mean that the beetles take only solid food: many of them macerate their food and moisten it with digestive juices before ingestion. Others lap up nectar and sap oozing from trees, while the larvae of several species have tubular mandibles with which they suck up liquid food.

The prothorax is large and usually quite mobile, with the whole of the pronotum visible from above. The mesothorax – largest of the three segments in most flying insects – is the smallest in beetles because there are no functional flying wings on this segment. It is fused with the metathorax, which is relatively large in all beetles. All but the mesoscutellum is covered by the elytra when the beetle is at rest.

The elytra themselves are highly modified forewings, horny or leathery and usually rather tough. The name Coleoptera refers to the elytra and means sheath-wings (Greek *koleos* = sheath). In some flightless weevils and other beetles the hind wings are absent and the two elytra have become fused together to form a single protective shield. The elytra are usually long enough to cover the whole of the abdomen when the beetle is at rest, but in some families they are shorter and leave a number of abdominal segments uncovered. Usually only the last two or three segments are exposed in this way, but the rove beetles of the family Staphylinidae (Pl. 18) reveal as many as seven segments. There is often a delicate pattern of furrows or rows of pits on the elytra and this ornamentation is of great value when identifying beetles, particularly below the family level. Other decorations include hairs, scales, and metallic sheens.

In flight, the elytra play no active part in propulsion and are held rigid at an angle to the body. They may provide some lift, but the propulsion comes entirely from the membranous hind wings. At rest, the hind wings are folded neatly beneath the elytra and are not often seen. The venation is reduced but is sometimes of use in classification.

The underside of a beetle, showing the excavate hind coxa into which the femur fits when the leg is folded

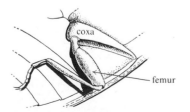

The legs are of normal construction, but exhibit great variation according to the habits of the beetles and we find modifications for digging, swimming, and running. The shape and arrangement of the coxae and their cavities are important in classification. The coxae may be longer than they are broad, in which case they project from their cavities, or they may be broader than long (transverse). If the two measurements are about the same the coxae are said to be rounded. The hind coxae are often hollowed out behind (excavate) to receive the femora when the legs are folded. The normal number of tarsal segments is five on all legs, giving a tarsal formula 5,5,5, but there is often some reduction from this. A common variation is the reduction of the fourth segment to a minute structure visible only under magnification, and then the legs are said to be *apparently 4-segmented*. When the fourth segment is reduced in this way the third segment is normally enlarged and it is this enlargement that conceals the fourth segment. There are other apparently 4-segmented legs, however, in which it is the basal segment that is minute.

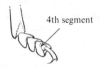
4th segment

The apparently 4-segmented tarsus of a leaf beetle (Chrysomelidae), showing how the minute 4th segment is concealed within the heart-shaped 3rd segment

There is nothing unusual about the beetle abdomen, although certain features are used in the classification of these insects. The two main sub-orders are separated by the structure of the first abdominal sternites (see p. 137), and several smaller divisions depend upon the number of visible abdominal sternites.

Beetle eggs are generally quite plain and typically egg-shaped, without fancy decoration. The number laid by each female depends on the species and varies from a dozen or so to several thousand. Some species lay their eggs carefully where the larvae will find food: others simply scatter them. Very few beetles care for their eggs, but there are a few species that exhibit some form of parental care by watching over both eggs and larvae. The larval head is always well developed and carries biting jaws very much like those of the adult. Adults and larvae often eat the same kind of food. Thoracic legs are usually present in the larvae but most weevil larvae, living in seeds, buds, and other places where they are surrounded by food, are legless. Other

A variety of beetle larvae: **a.** *campodeiform larva of a ground beetle;* **b.** *scarabaeiform larva of a cockchafer;* **c.** *eruciform (caterpillar-like) larva of a leaf beetle;* **d.** *apodous larva of a weevil*

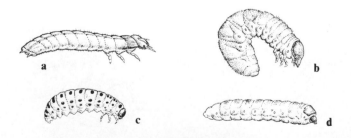

beetle larvae may be campodeiform, scarabaeiform, or eruciform, with the campodeiform larvae being typical of the more primitive beetles.

The pupa is normally of the exarate type, with free appendages. Boring larvae
usually pupate in their larval quarters after tunnelling to a point near the surface of
the stem or whatever they are in. Others pupate in the soil or in flimsy cocoons above
ground. Most of our beetle species probably have only one generation each year,
spending the winter as young larvae, pupae, or adults. Relatively few seem to overwinter in the egg stage.

European beetles belong to two main sub-orders – the ADEPHAGA and the
POLYPHAGA, which are easily distinguished by looking at the hind coxae (see following key). A third sub-order – the MYXOPHAGA – is represented in Europe only
by *Sphaerius acaroides*. This is a minute beetle under 1mm long and no further mention will be made of the group. A fourth sub-order – the ARCHOSTEMMATA – is
unrepresented in Europe.

The following key to superfamilies is a greatly simplified one, ignoring many of
the small species and a good number of 'odd-men-out'. Nevertheless, a large proportion of European beetles should be correctly placed with its aid. Because several
of the superfamilies contain lots of families with rather diverse appearances they
crop up several times in the key.

A Simplified Key to the Sub-orders and Superfamilies of European Beetles

1. Hind coxae immovably articulated
    to metasternum and completely
    dividing 1st visible abdominal
    sternite: antennae 11-segmented,
    usually filiform or moniliform
    (sub-order Adephaga)

    Hind coxae usually movably
    articulated to metasternum and
    very rarely completely dividing
    1st visible abdominal sternite:
    antennae of various types
    (sub-order Polyphaga)

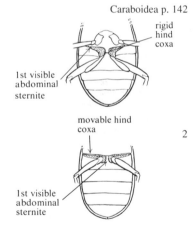

Caraboidea p. 142

rigid
hind
coxa

1st visible
abdominal
sternite

movable hind
coxa   2

1st visible
abdominal
sternite

2. Head more or less prolonged into a snout or beak, or else   Curculionoidea p. 158
    small, cylindrical insects often with elytra hollowed out
    at the back (Pl. 25): antennae generally clearly clubbed
    and elbowed, the 1st segment (the scape) retractable
    into a groove in the snout

    Insects not fitting this description   3

3. Antennae with 9-11 segments, the   Scarabaeoidea p. 147
    last 3-7 expanded on one side to
    form a lamellate club

    Antennae not like this   4

4. Antennae small, usually less prominent than maxillary   Hydrophiloidea p. 145
    palps and terminating in a small club: mostly water
    · beetles

    Antennae normally larger than palps   5

5. Tarsi all apparently 4-segmented   Chrysomeloidea p. 157
    (segment 4 is minute – see p.
    136): antennae not clubbed

    Tarsi not all apparently 4-segmented, or if so the antennae   6
    are clubbed

6. Head almost or quite as broad as thorax: antennae 10-seg-   Eucinetoidea p. 149
    mented, the last 2 forming a club: minute insects
    < 2mm long

    Insects not fitting this description   7

7. Elytra sharply truncated at rear, exposing at least 3 ab- Staphylinoidea p. 146
    dominal segments, but always meeting neatly in mid-
    line: antennae rarely clubbed

    Elytra longer: if sharply truncated no more than 2 abdomi-   8
    nal segments are exposed or else antennae are strongly
    clubbed

8. Last few antennal segments noticeably wider than the rest,   9
    forming a distinct club

    Antennae not abruptly clubbed, although they may thicken   26
    gradually towards tip

9. One or more abdominal segments exposed   10
    Abdomen completely covered by elytra   12

10. Antennal club often with 4-5 segments: tarsi all 5-seg-   Staphylinoidea p. 146
    mented and often strongly lobed on front legs: front
    coxae distinctly projecting: mostly sturdy beetles 10mm
    or more long

    Generally smaller beetles: antennal club rarely with more   11
    than 3 segments: front coxae often transverse or
    rounded, but if projecting the hind tarsi are 4-segmented

11. Strongly rounded beetles with at least 2 abdominal seg-   Histeroidea p. 145
    ments showing

    More elongate beetles with only the last abdominal seg-   Cucujoidea p. 154
    ment showing

12. Antennal club asymmetric (on one side of axis)   13

     Antennal club symmetrical   14

13. Prothorax virtually covers head   Bostrichoidea p. 153
     from above: tarsi all 5-segmented

     Head clearly visible: tarsi 4-segmented: largely aquatic,   Dryopoidea p. 150
     with spiny legs

14. Rounded or oval beetles with elytral margins distinctly   15
     convex

     More slender beetles with elytra parallel-sided for much   19
     of their length

15. Hind coxae strongly excavate   16
     behind

     Hind coxae not excavate behind   17

16. Middle coxae widely separated from   Byrrhoidea p. 150
     each other: elytra usually
     distinctly striated

     middle coxae

     Middle coxae not widely separated: elytra not usually stri-   Dermestoidea p. 152
     ated

17. Front coxae projecting: rather flat beetles with bristly   Cleroidea p. 154
     hairs around the edges

     Front coxae not projecting, or if so the insects have no   18
     prominent hairs

18. Antennal club often with 4-5 segments: sturdy beetles,   Staphylinoidea p. 146
     usually black with slightly striated elytra: tarsi usually 5-
     segmented

     Antennal club rarely with more than 3 segments: hind leg   Cucujoidea p. 154
     usually with less than 5 tarsal segments: elytra not stri-
     ated

19. Rather cylindrical beetles with prothorax extending for-   Bostrichoidea p. 153
     ward and concealing head from above (see couplet 13)

     Head clearly visible from above   20

20. Rear edge of pronotum much narrower than front of elytra   21

Rear edge of pronotum about the same width as front of   24
elytra

21. Water beetles with long palps: tarsi 4-segmented   Staphylinoidea p. 146

Beetles not like this   22

22. Pronotum very square: antennal club 2-segmented   Bostrichoidea p. 153

Antennal club with more than 2 segments: pronotum not   23
square

23. Insect with prominent bristly hairs; often brightly col-   Cleroidea p. 154
oured: tarsi either all 4-segmented or all 5-segmented

Insect without prominent hairs: tarsi either all 3-seg-   Cucujoidea p. 154
mented or all 4-segmented

24. Hind coxae excavate behind   Dermestoidea p. 152

Hind coxae not excavate behind   25

25. Antennal club generally with more than 3 segments: tarsi Staphylinoidea p. 146
all 5-segmented: very small beetles, mostly about 1mm
long or less

Antennal club generally with 3 segments or less: hind   Cucujoidea p. 154
tarsi mostly 3-segmented or 4-segmented

26. Elytra shorter than abdomen or gaping to some extent to   27
reveal part of abdomen or hind wings

Elytra completely covering abdomen   31

27. Elytra meet neatly in mid-line (but always rounded at the   28
back and exposing no more than 2 abdominal segments
– see couplet 7)

Elytra separated for much of their length, or else overlap-   30
ping at front

28. Hind tarsi 4-segmented   Cucujoidea p. 154

Hind tarsi 5-segmented   29

29. Beetles with bristly hairs, at least on head: often metallic: Cleroidea p. 154
tarsal claws with spine-like appendages below

No long bristles on head: never metallic, although often   Cantharoidea p. 151
brightly coloured

30. Tarsi: all 5-segmented: very slender beetles with antennae Lymexyloidea p. 154
no more than twice as long as pronotum: male palps
with feathery branches

Hind tarsi 4-segmented: antennae usually much longer   Cucujoidea p. 154
than pronotum: elytra often metallic

31. Antennae comb-like or toothed on one side   32

    Antennae thread-like or composed of bead-like segments   35

32. Hind tarsi 4-segmented: brilliant red insects with elytra   Cucujoidea p. 154
    widest at rear

    Hind tarsi 5-segmented: elytra not widest at rear   33

33. Insects clothed with long, bristly hairs   Cleroidea p. 154

    Insects without long hairs, although elytra are often downy   34

34. Rear corners of pronotum extend backwards and are   Elateroidea p. 151
    sharply pointed: elytra often downy: antennae some-
    times strongly comb-like

    Rear corners of pronotum not sharply pointed: upper sur-   Buprestoidea p. 150
    face generally hairless and shiny, often with brilliant
    metallic colours

35. Head clearly visible from above   36

    Head more or less concealed from above   43

36. Pronotum with marginal keels   37

    Pronotum without such keels on the sides   42

37. Rear of elytra drawn out to a blunt point   38

    Rear of elytra smoothly rounded   39

38. Terrestrial beetles, generally over 2cm long   Cucujoidea p. 154

    Aquatic beetles under 5mm long   Dryopoidea p. 150

39. Hind tibiae gently curved   Cantharoidea p. 151

    Hind tibiae more or less straight   40

40. Elytra parallel-sided for much of their length   Cucujoidea p. 154

    Elytra more or less oval   41

41. First 4 tarsal segments lobed below   Dascilloidea p. 150

    Only the 4th tarsal segment is lobed   Eucinetoidea p. 149

42. Tarsi all 5-segmented and unlobed   Bostrichoidea p. 153

    Tarsi often with bilobed segments: hind tarsi generally 4-   Cucujoidea p. 154
    segmented

43. Elytra more or less parallel-sided: sometimes bright red   Cantharoidea p. 151

    Elytral margins strongly convex   Bostrichoidea p.153

SUB-ORDER ADEPHAGA

This is the more primitive of the two sub-orders and contains predominantly carnivorous species living on land and in fresh water. The larvae are campodeiform and
are generally predatory like the adults. Both stages are generally very active. There
is only one superfamily – the **Caraboidea** – and it has eight European families, separable with the aid of the following key based upon that given by Crowson in the
R.E.S. Handbook (see p. 303).

Key to the Families of European Adephaga

1.	Terrestrial insects with projecting sensory bristles on various parts of the body: hind coxae not extending laterally to meet elytra	2
	Aquatic insects without such sensory bristles and with the hind coxae extending laterally to meet elytra	4
2.	Antennae stout and hairy	Rhysodidae p. 142
	Antennae more slender	3
3.	Elytra without regular striae: antennae inserted on top of head, just in front of eyes	Cicindelidae p. 143
	Elytra usually with regular striae: antennae inserted at sides of head, between eyes and jaws	Carabidae p. 143
4.	Compound eyes each completely divided into upper and lower halves: middle and hind legs forming short, broad, paddles	Gyrinidae p. 143
	Insects not like this	5
5.	Elytra with rows of distinct elongate punctures: hind coxae forming large plates: insects under 6mm long	Haliplidae p. 144
	Elytra not so marked: hind coxae not forming large plates: insects often over 6mm long	6
6.	Beetles 8-12mm long with prominent bulging eyes: body extremely convex below	Hygrobiidae p. 144
	Eyes never bulging much from the general outline of the head	7
7.	Dorsal surface strongly convex but ventral surface almost flat: scutellum concealed: antennae rather stout, especially in male, and hardly longer than width of head	Noteridae p. 144
	Ventral surface never flat: scutellum often visible: antennae usually much longer than width of head	Dytiscidae p. 144

The family **Rhysodidae** is found mainly in the tropics, but a few species, typified by
Rhysodes sulcatus (Pl. 16), occur in southern Europe. The beetles have a deeply grooved
prothorax and stout, moniliform antennae. Both adults and larvae live in rotten wood.

Members of the **Cicindelidae** are commonly called tiger beetles. They are closely related to the Carabidae and often treated as a sub-division of that family, although they differ in the position of the antennae and in the lack of elytral striation. All are long-legged, fast-running beetles fond of sunning themselves on the ground. When disturbed they launch into a noisy buzzing flight, but they rarely fly far at one go and soon return to earth. Both adults and larvae are fierce carnivores, the larvae making little burrows in which they lie in wait for prey. In association with this burrowing habit, the tiger beetles occur mainly in areas of light, well-drained soil. The Green Tiger Beetle (*Cicindela campestris*) (Pl. 16) is the commonest of the five British species.

The **Carabidae** (Pl. 16) is a large family, with about 350 British species. Its members are commonly known as ground beetles because they spend much of their time on or under the ground. Like the tiger beetles, the insects are good runners. Some of them also fly well, but many lack hind wings and in several species the elytra are fused together. The fused elytra give the beetles added protection as they scramble about. Each elytron normally has nine longitudinal ridges, separated by furrows or rows of dots, and this ornamentation is important in specific identification. Black is the main colour among these beetles, although many species have beautiful metallic sheens. The shape of the body is fairly constant throughout the family and many ground beetles, especially the larger ones, can be recognised as such on sight. Most ground beetles are nocturnal and they can be found under logs and stones during the daytime. Both adults and larvae are primarily carnivorous but the larvae do not burrow: they go out and actively hunt for worms, slugs, and insect prey.

Our largest ground beetles – up to about 40mm long – belong to the genus *Carabus*, in which the rear corners of the pronotum are extended backwards to form pointed lobes. There is also commonly a flattened rim around the outer edge of each elytron. The genus *Calosoma* shares these features but the outer margins of the elytra are rather straight: in most *Carabus* species they are strongly curved. *Calosoma sycophanta* is a brilliant green beetle which spends much of its time searching for caterpillars in trees. Unlike most ground beetles, it flies very well and is active mainly by day. Many ground beetles, although not *Carabus* or *Calosoma*, have a conspicuous notch in the front tibia which is used for cleaning the antennae.

The Bombardier Beetle (*Brachinus crepitans*), which has bluish or greenish elytra, is named for its defensive behaviour: when alarmed, it fires a stinging, volatile liquid from its rear end, producing a puff of smoke and an audible pop. *Dyschirius globosus* has an unusual shape for a ground beetle. It is one of many similar flightless species which use their spiny front legs to burrow in soft ground. Other common ground beetle genera include *Pterostichus*, *Leistus*, *Elaphrus*, *Dromius* and *Amara*.

Members of the **Gyrinidae**, typified by the common *Gyrinus natator* (Pl. 17), are known as whirligig beetles because they spend most of their adult lives skimming round and round on the surface of still or slow-moving water. They are all small, shiny black insects whose middle and back legs are flattened and hair-covered – ideal for skating over the surface and also for swimming. Each eye is divided into two parts – an upper part for looking over the surface and a lower part for seeing down

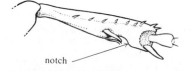

notch

The notched front tibia with which many ground beetles, especially those in the sub-family Harpalinae, clean their antennae

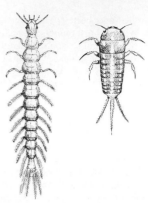

Larvae of a whirligig beetle (left) and a screech beetle

into the water. Whirligig beetles feed mainly on small insects that fall on to the water surface, but they occasionally dive after things. They also dive when alarmed. The beetles can be seen in huge numbers in late summer, but then they disappear into the mud for the winter. Eggs are laid on water plants when the beetles reappear in the spring. There are about twelve British species.

The **Haliplidae** contains a number of small beetles that are often called crawling water beetles because they do not swim much and prefer to creep among the masses of *Spirogyra* and other algae on which they feed. The beetles, typified by *Haliplus fulvus* (Pl. 17), are easy to recognise because the hind coxae form broad plates that cover half of the ventral surface of the abdomen. The elytra all carry a distinctive pattern of elongate punctures. There are about 18 British species.

The Screech Beetle (*Hygrobia hermanni*) (Pl. 17) is our only member of the **Hygrobiidae**. It is about 12mm long and has a very convex body. The prominent eyes are the most distinguishing features, but the living insect will identify itself when picked up by squeaking. It does this by rubbing the tip of the abdomen against the undersides of the elytra. The larva is a strange-looking creature, with three feathery tails, found in muddy ponds.

The **Dytiscidae** (Pl.17) has about 150 European species, and about 110 of these occur in the British Isles. These water beetles range from about 2mm to 40mm in length. *Dytiscus marginalis* is one of the largest and best-known species. Most members of the family are rather dark in colour. The broad, hairy hind legs are used for swimming and the body is well streamlined, with the head drawn back into the prothorax to give a clean outline. Both adults and larvae are fierce carnivores. The large *Dytiscus* species can make short work of frogs, newts, and sticklebacks, and if they get into garden ponds they will have the goldfish as well. The larvae are even more ferocious than the adults, but they feed in a different way. The larval mandibles are sharply pointed and each encloses a narrow canal. The mandibles are thrust into the prey and the larva then injects digestive juices and sucks its victim dry. Other familiar genera include *Acilius, Platambus, Deronectes,* and *Laccophilus.*

The family **Noteridae** is closely related to the Dytiscidae and its members are sometimes placed in that family. They are all small beetles – rarely over 5mm long – and they are best distinguished from the dytiscids by their very flat undersides and rather stout antennae. *Noterus clavicornis* (Pl. 17) is the commoner of the two British species.

SUB-ORDER POLYPHAGA

This is by far the largest sub-order of beetles and, as might be guessed from the name (Polyphaga means 'eating many things'), it contains a very varied assortment of insects. Apart from all being beetles, there is little to link them together and, although the families are fairly well defined, the higher groupings are far from settled. There are still several large and rather heterogeneous superfamilies, such as the Cucujoidea which includes such diverse insects as the ladybirds and the oil beetles (Pl. 22).

Superfamily Hydrophiloidea

The members of this superfamily were once included in a group called Palpicornia. This name, referring to the prominent palps, is perhaps more descriptive of the group than the modern name Hydrophiloidea because, although most of the species are aquatic, there are several terrestrial ones. The adults are almost all vegetarians, feeding mainly on decaying plants, but many of the larvae are carnivorous. Although most of them live in stagnant water, these beetles are not good swimmers and they have no flattened, oar-like legs. They spend most of their time crawling on water plants. As a group, they are sometimes called silver water beetles because the underside of the body is clothed with fine hairs that hold a layer of air and give the insects a silvery appearance. The true colour of the insects is usually black or dark brown. As well as the air film carried on the underside, the beetles carry a bubble under their elytra, but the method of replenishing this air supply is peculiar. Whereas most water beetles come up tail-first to take in air, the hydrophilids come up head-first and use their hairy antennae to break the surface film. The hairs are water-repellent, so there is a continuous tract of air from the surface, along the antenna, and into a groove along the side of the thorax. This groove leads along the body and connects with the spiracles and both dorsal and ventral reservoirs. There is, of course, a groove along each side of the insect, but the beetles normally come to the surface slightly on one side and only one antenna is involved at any one time. The enlarged palps of these beetles take over the normal functions of the antennae.

There is a single family – the **Hydrophilidae** – with something over 150 species in Europe, although some entomologists split the group into five smaller families. There are about 90 British species. The best-known species is the Great Silver Beetle (*Hydrophilus piceus*) (Pl. 17) which, with a length of 50mm, is one of Europe's largest beetles and certainly our largest water beetle. Although a vegetarian, it can inflict a nasty wound on unwary fingers with a sharp spine on the underside of the body. Other genera in the family include *Spercheus, Laccobius, Enochrus,* and *Hydrochus.*

Superfamily Histeroidea

The members of this group have strongly clubbed and usually elbowed antennae. There are over 100 species in Europe and all but one of them belong to the Histeridae. The exception is the rare *Sphaerites glabratus* (Pl. 18), which is distinguished by its non-elbowed antennae and the single visible abdominal tergite. It belongs to the **Sphaeritidae**. The **Histeridae**, typified by *Hister impressus* (Pl. 18), are generally hard, shiny insects with short elytra leaving two abdominal tergites exposed. They are mostly black insects, with or without red markings, and were it not for their short elytra they could easily be taken for small scarabs (see p. 148). When disturbed, they withdraw their appendages into grooves on the underside of the body and appear quite dead. They are scavenging insects, found in dung, carrion, rotting vegetation, and so on, but they appear to feed as much on other scavenging insects as on the refuse itself. The larvae are nearly all predatory. There are about 40 British species.

Superfamily Staphylinoidea

This is a very large group, with about a dozen families in Europe. Most of the 3,500 or so European species are scavengers or predators and they almost all have short elytra, exposing from three to six abdominal segments. Because of these short elytra, the group was once known as the Brachelytra (Greek *brachys* = short). The best-known members are the burying beetles of the family Silphidae and the rove beetles of the Staphylinidae.

The **Silphidae** (Pl. 18) includes the larger members of the group and nearly all its members have strongly clubbed antennae. They are commonly called burying beetles or sexton beetles from the habit of some species of burying small carcases. The best-known burying beetles are the *Nicrophorus* species. These beetles have a good sense of smell and they are attracted to carrion. The first individuals of each sex to arrive at a carcase appear to fight later arrivals and turn them away. Sexton beetles are therefore most often found singly or in pairs at a carcase. After mating, the insects set to work to bury the carcase – bird, mouse, mole, or what-have-you – by removing the soil beneath it. The jaws and spined tibiae are used in this operation, grass roots and other small obstacles being no problem for the strong jaws. Only a narrow shaft is normally dug and the corpse is usually skinned as it is dragged down. The beetles will even amputate limbs to ease the corpse's passage through the soil, and they will also drag a dead animal from its original place to one where the soil is easier to dig. When the carcase has been buried the female beetle excavates a small passage leading off from the burial chamber and lays her eggs there. She then returns to the carcase and feeds. The male may or may not remain with her. She feeds her offspring with regurgitated food at first, but then they start to feed on the carcase themselves. The larvae undergo hypermetamorphosis, there being three distinct larval forms, starting with a typical campodeiform larva and ending with an almost legless maggot. Pupation takes place in individual cells hollowed out near the feeding chamber. Although these burying beetles are usually regarded as scavengers, there is not universal agreement on this point. Some species do eat carrion, but others are definitely carnivorous, feeding on fly larvae and other insects in the carcase. There are about 60 British species in the family, but they do not all bury corpses. *Silpha atrata* is a predator of snails.

Europe has over 2,000 species of rove beetles in the family **Staphylinidae** (Pl. 18), and nearly 1,000 of these occur in the British Isles. They vary in size from the Devil's Coach Horse (*Staphylinus olens*), at about 25mm, down to minute beetles less than 1mm long. The antennae are not clubbed and the elytra are always short, giving the insects a superficial similarity to earwigs although they have no pincers. Despite the short elytra, the hind wings are well developed and flight is good in most species. Many of them can be found in and around animal dung and other decaying matter, but it is probable that most of them are predatory, feeding on the scavenging fly larvae and other insects. Ant nests also shelter a good many rove beetles – or 'staphs' as they are often called by the entomologist. Some of these guests are welcomed because they produce sweet liquids which are enjoyed by the ants; others are merely tolerated, living as scavengers in the nest and sometimes taking the ants' eggs or larvae.

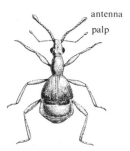

Left, Pselaphus hesei, *under 2mm long and living in damp and decaying vegetation, is one of many ant-like members of the Pselaphidae. The long palps are not found in all species. Right,* Hydraena gracilis, *a member of the Hydraenidae. Only about 2mm long, it lives mainly under moss and stones in upland streams*

Stenus bimaculatus (Pl. 18) and its congeners, recognisable by their bulging eyes, are sun-loving rove beetles usually living near water. They can skim over the surface by exuding oily secretions from the rear end. Other staphylinid genera include *Tachyporus, Paederus, Philonthus, Emus,* and *Creophilus.*

Members of the **Hydraenidae** are aquatic beetles with fully-developed elytra and long palps. They resemble the water beetles of the Hydrophiloidea (p. 145) and are sometimes placed in that group, but current opinion is that the similarities are due to convergent evolution and that the beetles really belong in the Staphylinoidea. The other families in this group contain mainly very small beetles, with or without clubbed antennae. The **Pselaphidae** contains numerous small species, most of which inhabit ants' nests. The insects are very often ant-like themselves and they can usually be recognised by their clubbed antennae and relatively long clubbed palps.

Superfamily Scarabaeoidea

Called the Lamellicornia in the older books, this superfamily is one of the easiest to recognise because of the structure of the antennae. The last three to seven antennal segments are expanded on one side to form a number of flat blades or lamellae which are usually capable of being folded together to form a conspicuous club (fig. p. 16). There are well over 20,000 species, of which nearly 250 occur in Europe. They are heavily-built insects but they are nevertheless mostly strong fliers. The males of many species possess bizarre outgrowths of the head and thorax. The larvae are of the typical scarabaeiform type – soft-bodied, stout, and permanently curved (fig. p. 24). They are usually surrounded by plenty of food – plant roots, dung, or rotting wood for most species – and they do not move much, although their thoracic legs are well developed.

The four families may be distinguished with the following key.

1.	Antennae more or less elbowed: antennal lamellae unable to form a club	Lucanidae
	Antennae not elbowed: antennal lamellae can be drawn together to form a club	2

2.   Elytra roughly sculptured, with hairs, scales, or tubercles   Trogidae

     Elytra not so sculptured   3

3.   Antennae 11-segmented: jaws fully visible from above   Geotrupidae

     Antennae 9-10-segmented: jaws often concealed from   Scarabaeidae
     above

The best-known member of the **Lucanidae** (Pl. 19) is the Stag Beetle (*Lucanus cervus*), which gets its name from the huge, antler-like mandibles of the male. It reaches 50mm in length, but there is much variation in size and some specimens may be only half this length. Although the male looks rather frightening with its large antlers, it is quite harmless because it cannot close them with any force. The small jaws of the female can give a much stronger nip. The male antlers are used mainly for wrestling with other males. The species breeds in rotting tree stumps and other suitably decayed wood and seems to be getting rare in many places. The Lesser Stag Beetle (*Dorcus parallelopipedus*) and *Sinodendron cylindricum* are the only other British members of the family.

The Trogidae and Geotrupidae are often treated as sub-families of the Scarabaeidae but current practice is to give them full family status. The **Trogidae** is represented in Europe by a handful of species of *Trox*, three of which occur in the British Isles. These beetles, none of which is particularly common, can be recognised by their rough sculpturing. They are mainly scavengers in dry animal matter and they lack the broad, digging legs of the Geotrupidae. Several species, including *T. scaber* (Pl. 19), occur in birds' nests.

The **Geotrupidae** (Pl. 19), whose members are commonly known as dor beetles, are mainly dung-feeders. The antennae end in a dull, pubescent, 3-segmented club. The common *Geotrupes stercorarius*, known as the Lousy Watchman because it is often infested with mites, frequents cow dung. Male and female work together to excavate shafts under the dung, and then they haul down bundles of dung and lay eggs in it. The adults also feed on the dung themselves, usually burying far more than they ever eat and thus performing a useful service in removing the dung and hastening the return of its minerals to the soil. The Minotaur Beetle (*Typhaeus typhoeus*) prefers rabbit and sheep dung. The male of this species has prominent thoracic horns and, although he provides some of the dung pellets, he does little or none of the digging – in keeping with the general observation that males with exaggerated horns do little work. The rare *Odontaeus armiger* also feeds on rabbit dung. The male can be recognised by the slender movable horn on its head. There are eight British species in the family.

The **Scarabaeidae** is one of the largest of all insect families, with about 20,000 known species and some 300 representatives in Europe. It also contains the bulkiest species – the tropical Goliath and Hercules beetles – and it is noted for the extraordinary horns that develop on the head and thorax of some species. These horns are usually fully formed only in the male, although some species are horned in both sexes. The mandibles are not out of the ordinary and are usually concealed from above – in contrast to those of the previous family which are usually clearly visible from above. The family can be split into two main groups – the dung beetles or scarabs proper and the plant-eating chafers – and these are divided into several sub-families. There are about 80 British species.

Most of the dung beetles, including the many species of *Aphodius* (Pl. 19), eat and lay eggs in the dung where they find it, but others bury it in some way or other. *Copris lunaris* (Pl. 19) tunnels under cow-pats, with male and female working together to stock the large brood chamber. This species is of particular interest because both parents tend the larvae until they are fully grown. Most dung beetles abandon their burrows when the eggs have been laid. The best-known of the scarabs are the dung-rollers of the genus *Scarabaeus*, several species of which occur in southern Europe. The beetles use their rake-like front tibiae to scrape up the dung, which is then shaped into a ball under the body and rolled along with the hind legs until a suitable burial site is found. The beetles bury dung for themselves as well as to provide food for their offspring, and they can eat almost their own weight of dung in a day. A few other genera of dung-rollers occur in central Europe.

Whereas the scavenging dung beetles are generally useful, the chafers (Pl. 20), distinguished by the exposed tip of the abdomen, are positively harmful. The most familiar of our chafers is the Cockchafer or Maybug (*Melolontha melolontha*), which often comes crashing into lighted windows in early summer. Its large size – up to 35mm long – and buzzing flight make it a little frightening, but it is quite harmless – harmless to us that is: the beetle does untold damage to trees and other plants by eating flowers and foliage. The fat, white larvae are even more destructive. They live in the soil for three or four years and eat plant roots, especially those of cereals and other grasses. The larvae are often called rookworms, for it is said that rooks are particularly fond of both adult and larval cockchafers. Other important chafers include the brilliant green Rose Chafer (*Cetonia aurata*), the Garden Chafer (*Phyllopertha horticola*) and the Pine Chafer (*Polyphylla fullo*). The latter reaches about 40mm in length and is easily recognised by its mottled cream and brown elytra. The male has enormous antennae and both sexes stridulate loudly when touched. The adults cause serious damage to pine foliage. The genus *Hoplia* can be distinguished by the scales on the elytra and by the single claw on each foot. Some species have brilliant colours. The males of *H. caerulea* from southern Europe are sky blue. All these chafers have much the same sort of life history as the Cockchafer.

Superfamily Eucinetoidea

This small group contains only three European families, all rather different but all agreeing in having more or less conical, projecting front coxae and excavated hind coxae. The **Clambidae**, with nine British species, are all minute beetles, under 2mm long, with broad heads and clubbed antennae. They all live in rotting vegetation. The **Scirtidae** are soft-bodied and rather fragile beetles, mostly reddish brown and 2-6mm long with relatively long antennae. They live around ponds and streams and have aquatic larvae. There are about 16 British species. The **Eucinetidae** are oval beetles with strongly pubescent black or reddish brown elytra. No more than about 4mm long, they inhabit dry plant debris. There is only one British species – *Eucinetus meridionalis.*

A typical clambid beetle

Superfamily Dascilloidea

This superfamily has but one species in Europe – *Dascillus cervinus* (Pl. 18), which belongs to the family **Dascillidae**. It is black or brown and clothed with dense yellowish pubescence. It can be found on flowers in spring and summer and is most frequent in upland areas, including the chalk downs.

Superfamily Byrrhoidea

This superfamily contains only one family – the **Byrrhidae**. There are about 50 European species, ten of which occur in Britain. All are rounded or egg-shaped insects ranging from 1.5 to 10mm in length. Legs and antennae can be withdrawn into grooves on the underside of the body in many species and the insects feign death in this manner, often looking just like dried seeds. *Byrrhus pilula* (Pl. 18) is one of our commonest species. Most of them live among mosses and grasses.

Superfamily Dryopoidea

The beetles in this group are nearly all aquatic and rarely exceed 5mm in length. There are over 60 European species, about half of which occur in the British Isles. Although aquatic, these beetles do not really swim. Members of the **Heteroceridae**, typified by *Heterocerus flexuosus* (Pl. 20), burrow in mud at the edges of ponds and streams and their front tibiae are strongly spined in association with this habit. The antennae are unusual in being short and stout with an asymmetrical club. Members of the **Dryopidae** and **Elmidae** are long-legged beetles which spend their time crawling on aquatic vegetation, to which they cling with strong tarsal claws. The dryopids are rather hairy beetles with very short, stout antennae like those of *Heterocerus* but the elmids are smooth and have long, slender antennae. They have prominent marginal keels on the pronotum and their elytra are often constricted at the rear and drawn out to form a blunt point. Many of these beetles live in fast-flowing water and some of the elmids have developed plastron respiration (see p. 23).

Superfamily Buprestoidea

This superfamily contains but one large family – the **Buprestidae** (Pl. 18). There are about 16,000 known species, but most are tropical and only about 120 occur in Europe. Only twelve are British and none is particularly common. They are shiny,

Left, Heterocerus flexuosus, *showing its strongly-spined front tibiae. Right,* Elmis aenea, *showing the pronotal keels and bluntly pointed elytra typical of the Elmidae. The central drawing shows the strong tarsal claws of* Elmis

metallic insects ranging from about 1mm to 35mm in length. The head is sunk deeply in the thorax, the eyes are unusually large, and the antennae are short and toothed. The larvae are mainly wood-borers, tunnelling just under the bark, and many species are serious timber pests. Others tunnel in herbaceous plants and several species induce gall formation. *Agrilus* is the largest European genus. *A. pannonicus*, which ranges from blue to golden green, breeds in oak bark. *Buprestis aurulentis* is an American species which sometimes arrives in Europe with imported timber. Some records suggest that a larval life of nearly 30 years is possible.

Superfamily Elateroidea

The members of this group are generally rather elongated insects with hard integuments. The head is sunk deeply into the thorax and bears toothed or comb-like antennae. The hind angles of the prothorax are sharply pointed and often extended backwards. The major family within the group is the **Elateridae** (Pl.20), whose members are generally known as click beetles or skipjacks from their ability to flick themselves into the air and right themselves when they fall on to their backs. This ability is associated with a very mobile joint between the first and second thoracic sternites. Under normal circumstances a projection on the prosternum rests on the edge of a cavity in the mesosternum. When the insect falls upside-down it begins to arch its back and the peg slips off the edge and springs down into the cavity, producing the familiar click and causing the insect to bounce up into the air. While airborne, the beetle usually manages to right itself.

Most click beetles are brownish and rather dull, although several species have a metallic sheen and a few are bright red. Under a lens they can be seen to have a coating of fine, often greyish hairs. Click beetle larvae – known as wireworms – are responsible for a considerable amount of crop damage, for many of them feed on plant roots. The adult beetles feed on pollen and nectar, and also on the tissues of flowers and leaves. Elaterid genera include *Ctenicera, Athous, Ampedus, Agriotes,* and *Fleutiauxellus.* There are about 65 British species in the family.

The **Cebrionidae** contains some relatively large beetles related to the click beetles. The larvae are like wireworms and live in the soil. Adult females lack hind wings and their short elytra gape open at the rear. A few species live in southern Europe, including *Cebrio gigas* (Pl. 20) whose female never leaves her larval burrow.

Superfamily Cantharoidea

These insects are generally rather narrow, elongated beetles with soft bodies. The elytra are also rather soft and generally covered with short, downy hair. Our largest family is the **Cantharidae** (Pl. 20), with about 150 European species of which around 40 occur in the British Isles. The elytra bear little in the way of striations – a feature that separates this family from the Lycidae (p. 152). Cantharid beetles are frequent flower visitors, being especially attracted to umbellifers, although they are carnivorous insects and probably feed on other flower-visiting species. Many of the

The underside of a click beetle thorax, showing the 'spring' with which these insects flick themselves into the air

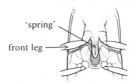

'spring'

front leg

species, including *Cantharis rustica*, are black and red, giving the family its common name of soldier beetles. *Rhagonycha fulva* is a very common species whose reddish colour has given it the misleading name of Bloodsucker in many areas. Cantharid larvae live mainly on the ground, where they feed on a variety of other creatures.

The family **Lampyridae** contains just two British species, including one of the most famous of all insects – the Glow-Worm (*Lampyris noctiluca*) (Pl. 20). The common name is unfortunate, but derives from the appearance of the wingless female which, while not really like a worm, is not much like a beetle either. The male is a more typical beetle, being fully winged and able to fly. In both sexes the pronotum extends forward and completely covers the head. All stages of the life history, including the eggs, give out light but the adult female emits the strongest light. The light-producing organs, consisting of a layer of luciferin backed by a reflector of minute crystals, are carried under her last three abdominal segments. Light is produced by enzymatic oxidation of the luciferin and the process requires both oxygen and water. The luciferin layer is well supplied with tracheae in this connection. The light emitted is pale green and almost all the chemical energy is converted into light – very little heat is produced. The function of the light is to attract the males and all the females have to do is to sit in the grass and turn their bodies so that their lamps are visible to the males flying above. A verge or hedgebank full of glow-worms is an amazing sight, but one which is sadly becoming progressively rarer. Male glow-worms have much better eyes that the females and a glowing female soon attracts a mate. The light can be shut off when required – by reducing the oxygen supply to the luciferin – and the insects glow mainly at dusk. They may switch off if suddenly disturbed, although they often continue to glow if picked up gently and put into a box. Adult glow-worms do not feed much, if at all, but the larva is predatory and feeds on small snails and slugs. It grabs these with its jaws and injects a digestive juice which liquefies the prey ready for ingestion. It is partly the importance of snails in the diet that restricts glow-worms mainly to areas of chalk and limestone – the snails are so restricted by the need for shell-building calcium.

The closely-related European Firefly (*Luciola lusitanica*), which lives to the east of the Rhône in southern Europe, has lights in both sexes, but they do not glow continuously. Males flash their lights as they fly, and the females respond with their own flashes when they see the males overhead. The females are winged, but they never fly. The larvae feed on snails.

The family **Lycidae** contains just a handful of European species, most of which have bright red and strongly ribbed elytra. The beetles breed in rotting wood, where their larvae prey on other insects. There are four British species.

Superfamily Dermestoidea

The **Dermestidae** (Pl. 20), with over 50 European species, is the only important family in this group. Its members range from 1.5mm to 10mm in length and are generally rather sombre in colour. They are covered with downy hairs or scales. Most species possess a large single ocellus on the top of the head, although this is missing in *Dermestes* species. The antennae are distinctly clubbed and, together with the legs, they can be withdrawn into the underside of the body. In this position the insects can easily be taken for lifeless objects. The dermestids are primarily scavengers but several species are of considerable economic importance. *Dermestes maculatus* and the

Bacon Beetle or Larder Beetle (*D. lardarius*) damage hides and dried meat and are more common in warehouses than out of doors, although they can be found in small dried-out carcases in the countryside. These insects can be usefully employed in cleaning animal skeletons for preservation. The Fur Beetle (*Attagenus pellio*) and the various carpet beetles of the genus *Anthrenus* damage furs, fabrics, and stored food. The larvae, which do the damage, are covered with hairs and are commonly called woolly bears. The larva of the Khapra Beetle (*Trogoderma granarium*) is a serious pest of stored grain and cereal products. Many of these beetles, because of their association with stored food and other products, are of world-wide distribution. About 30 species occur in Britain, although about half of these are found only in man-made habitats and are undoubtedly immigrant species.

Superfamily Bostrichoidea

The members of this group can generally be recognised by the hooded pronotum which conceals all or much of the head from above, although this feature does occur in a few other beetles. Most of the species are wood-borers and some are serious timber pests. The larvae are soft and white and more or less scarabaeiform.

Members of the family **Lyctidae**, typified by *Lyctus fuscus* (Pl. 21), are commonly called powder-post beetles because the boring larvae produce a very fine dust quite unlike that produced by the Furniture Beetle (see below). The Lyctidae differs from the other families in the group because the pronotum does not conceal the whole head from above. The antennal club is also 2-segmented, whereas members of the other families have a 3-segmented club or no club at all. Three of the six species occurring in Britain are aliens, established only under artificial conditions.

European species of the **Bostrichidae**, recognised by the asymmetric 3-segmented antennal club, are generally rare, but mention should be made of *Bostrichus capucinus*, a beetle up to 15mm long with a jet black thorax and brick-red elytra. It breeds in decaying tree trunks. It is the only British member of the family, but is now extremely rare and possibly extinct in the British Isles. The Lesser Grain Borer (*Rhizopertha dominica*) (Pl. 21) is a tropical species which is now established in grain stores all over the world.

The **Anobiidae** (Pl. 21) contains two notorious pests – the Woodworm or Furniture Beetle (*Anobium punctatum*) and the Death-watch Beetle (*Xestobium rufovillosum*). The larvae of these beetles tunnel into dead wood – rafters, furniture, or simply dead trees – and can quickly reduce it to sawdust. The adults lay their eggs in any small crevice – well-polished furniture is relatively safe from attack – and the larvae tunnel in. Not until the new adults leave through their 'worm-holes' do we learn of their presence, although the adult Death-watch Beetle can sometimes be detected by

Lateral and dorsal views of Rhizopertha dominica, *showing the hooded pronotum and the asymmetric antennal club typical of the family Bostrichidae*

its knocking. The beetles bang their heads against the wood and, by doing this several times in quick succession, they produce a noise not unlike a scaled-down pneumatic drill. This is believed to be a mating call. Other important members of the family include the Cigarette Beetle (*Lasioderma serricorne*) and the Drug-store Beetle (*Stegobium paniceum*). Both attack a variety of stored products, including tobacco. Many members of this family have no distinct antennal club, but when it is present it is clearly asymmetric. The bases of the antennae are fairly well separated. There are about 27 British species.

The **Ptinidae**, commonly known as spider beetles, are closely related to the Anobiidae but their antennae are inserted close together and are always filiform. Their bodies also tend to be much rounded and their legs are rather long – hence their name of spider beetles. They are scavenging insects and none is a wood-borer. Several are pests of grain, dried fruit, fabrics, and other stored materials. Their natural habitats would appear to be the nests of birds and other animals. There are about 20 British species, including several established aliens. *Ptinus fur* (Pl. 21) is a common example.

Superfamily Cleroidea

This group contains a number of predatory and scavenging beetles – most of them in the **Cleridae**. The members of this family are rather hairy insects and often brightly coloured. The antennae are either strongly toothed or else they end in distinct clubs. The tarsi have membranous flaps or lobes on one or more segments. As larvae, many of the species feed on bark beetles and other wood borers, but *Necrobia rufipes* (Pl. 21) attacks stored bacon and hams. About ten species occur in the British Isles. The Cadelle (*Tenebroides mauritanicus*) (Pl. 21), one of only two British members of the **Trogossitidae**, is not hairy. The last tarsal segment is relatively long and has a small lobe between the claws. This species is a cosmopolitan inhabitant of granaries and other food stores, where it destroys other insects as well as damaging a certain amount of the produce. The family **Melyridae** is a large one, although there are only some 20 British species. Its members are very variable, but generally possess long, bristly hairs on the head. The tarsal claws have teeth or other outgrowths on them. *Anthocomus fasciatus* (Pl. 20) is a common predatory species whose larvae feed on the grubs of various wood-boring beetles.

Superfamily Lymexyloidea

There is only one family in this group – the **Lymexylidae** – and it contains but three European species – *Lymexylon navale, Hylecoetus dermestoides*, and *H. flabellicornis*. Only the first two, both illustrated on Pl. 21, occur in the British Isles. All are narrow-bodied, wood-boring insects characterised by the extraordinary feathered nature of the male palps.

Superfamily Cucujoidea

This is a very large group of beetles, with many diverse families and little to link them together. There are, nevertheless, two fairly distinct sections – the Heteromera, in which the tarsal formula is 5,5,4 in both sexes and the antennae have, at most, a weak club; and the Clavicornia, in which the female tarsi are never 5,5,4 and the antennal club is usually well developed. Only the main families in each section are described in the following pages.

SECTION HETEROMERA

Members of the **Oedemeridae** are rather elongate insects, soft-bodied and often with a metallic sheen. The elytra commonly gape open to reveal the hind wings. The pen-ultimate tarsal segment is bilobed and the males commonly have swollen hind femora. The adults are generally flower-feeders and the larvae are wood-borers. There are seven British species, typified by *Oedemera nobilis* (Pl. 21).

The **Pyrochroidae** contains the cardinal beetles – rather flat beetles with bright red elytra which get wider towards the rear. The antennae are toothed or feathery. There are three European species, all represented in Britain and typified by *Pyroch-roa coccinea* (Pl. 21). They resemble members of the Lycidae (see p. 152), but the latter have five tarsal segments on each leg and their elytra are more or less paral-lel-sided. Cardinal beetle larvae are carnivorous and live under loose bark.

Members of the **Anthicidae** look rather like small ground beetles on first sight although, with lengths in the region of 3-4mm, they are much smaller than most of the ground beetles. Apart from size, the unstriated elytra and four tarsal segments in the hind leg will distinguish the Anthicidae. The rounded head is sharply marked off from the thorax. The beetles live in decaying material and can often be found on the compost heap and in rotting seaweed. There are about a dozen British species, typi-fied by *Anthicus antherinus* (Pl. 21).

The family **Meloidae** (Pl. 22) contains the oil beetles and blister beetles, named for the oily and sometimes blistering secretions released when these insects are dis-turbed. There are nine British species. The blister beetles, such as *Lytta vesicatoria*, are fairly typical beetles, but the oil beetles of the genus *Meloe* are clumsy creatures with short, soft elytra that gape open at the rear. They have no hind wings. The mem-bers of this family are of particular interest because of their complex life histories. The young stages of most of the European species are parasites of solitary bees, but grasshoppers are the main hosts in other parts of the world. The female beetles lay thousands of eggs in the soil in the spring and the eggs soon produce tiny louse-like larvae endowed with strong claws. Those of *Lytta* actively seek out the nests of their host bees, but *Meloe* larvae crawl into spring flowers and await the arrival of their hosts. The lucky ones are carried to the hosts' nests, where they detach themselves and seek out the host eggs. After eating one or more of the eggs, the larvae turn their attention to the bees' stores of pollen and nectar. As they grow, they undergo a series of moults, at each of which they become more and more grub-like, with soft bodies and reduced legs. Pupation takes place in the host nest.

The family **Tenebrionidae** is a large one, although there are less than 100 Euro-pean species and only about 35 of these occur in the British Isles. These insects are commonly called darkling beetles or nocturnal ground beetles, names which reflect their general colour and their habits. Most of the species are black or deep brown and the majority are flightless, often with no hind wings and with the elytra soldered down. There is much variation in size and shape, but the antennae are often thickened or more or less clubbed at the tips. *Tenebrio molitor* (Pl. 21) lives in flour and other cereal products and its larva is the mealworm – a popular food for birds, lizards, and many other small animals. The adult is one of the few flying members of the family. *Blaps mucronata* (Pl. 21), commonly known as the Churchyard Beetle, is a flightless

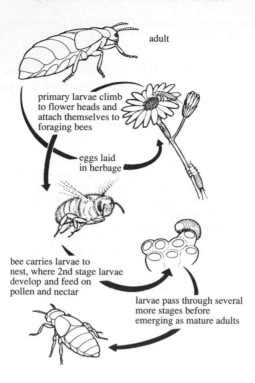

adult

primary larvae climb
to flower heads and
attach themselves to
foraging bees

eggs laid
in herbage

bee carries larvae to
nest, where 2nd stage larvae
develop and feed on
pollen and nectar

larvae pass through several
more stages before
emerging as mature adults

The life cycle of Meloe proscarabaeus, *commonest of the European oil beetles*

species often found in cellars and stables and other damp places, where it feeds on assorted vegetable matter. Many other members of the family are pests in granaries and warehouses and, although now widely distributed in Europe, were probably introduced with food materials. They include *Tribolium confusum* and *Gnatocerus cornutus*, both illustrated on Pl. 22.

SECTION CLAVICORNIA

The family **Nitidulidae** contains many small scavenging beetles, mostly under 5mm long. The antennae usually have a compact, 3-segmented club. The elytra often do not completely cover the abdomen and the tarsi are all 4-segmented. The beetles are found under bark, in decaying plant and animal matter, in fungi, and at oozing sap, but the most familiar members of the family are the little black pollen beetles of the genus *Meligethes* that swarm all over flowers in the summer. The family also contains several stored product pests, such as *Carpophilus hemipterus* (Pl. 22), that attack grain and dried fruit. There are about 100 British species in the family.

The **Cucujidae** also contains scavengers and many species are commonly found in food stores. They are flat insects and the antennal club is sometimes poorly developed. The Saw-toothed Grain Beetle (*Oryzaephilus surinamensis*) (Pl. 22) is one of our commoner granary pests. It gets its common name from the toothed edges of the thorax, a feature present in many members of the family but particularly well developed in this species. Out of doors, many of the species live under loose bark. About 15 members of the family occur in Britain, including several that are restricted to artificial habitats.

The **Cryptophagidae** is another family of scavenging beetles, most of them under 3mm long. There are about 100 British species. The antennae are distinctly clubbed and the somewhat hairy elytra completely cover the abdomen. Loose bark and fungi are the main habitats but, as with the previous families, several species are associated with stored products. *Cryptophagus* species (Pl. 22) are mainly fungus feeders and are often found in damp grain. The **Lathridiidae** is very similar to the last family but its members have only three tarsal segments, compared with four or five in the Cryptophagidae. Fungi, decaying material, dried carcases, and stored foods are the likely places for these beetles, of which there are about 50 British species.

The **Coccinellidae** is certainly the best-known family of the Cucujoidea, because it contains the brightly coloured ladybirds (Pl. 22). They can be distinguished from various superficially similar beetles, especially among the leaf beetles (see p. 158), by the tarsi. These are basically 4-segmented, but the third segment is minute and the tarsi therefore appear to be only 3-segmented. There are nearly 100 species in Europe and 42 of these are resident in the British Isles. Almost all of them are predatory. They destroy huge numbers of aphids and other insect pests, feeding on them in both larval and adults stages. The bright colours – generally red or yellow with black spots – are of a warning nature, advertising the bitter taste of these insects. When handled, most of them exude drops of pungent fluid which stain the hand and taint it with a long-lasting smell. This is an example of reflex-bleeding.

The commonest species in most parts of Europe are the 7-spot Ladybird (*Coccinella septempunctata*) and the much smaller 2-spot Ladybird (*Adalia bipunctata*). Some varieties of the latter are easily confused with the 10-spot Ladybird (*A. decempunctata*), but the leg colour will usually separate them: the legs are black in the 2-spot and brown or yellow in the 10-spot. The above species can be found on a wide range of plants, but the Eyed Ladybird (*Anatis ocellata*) is largely confined to conifers. The 24-spot Ladybird (*Subcoccinella vigintiquattuorpunctata*) feeds on the leaves of various low-growing plants, while the 22-spot Ladybird (*Psyllobora vigintiduopunctata*) nibbles mildews on various plants – especially umbellifers and low-growing shrubs. The specific names, here and in other species, are usually abbreviated to numerals – *24-punctata, 22-punctata,* and so on. The genera *Coccidula* and *Rhyzobius* are not in keeping with the general idea of ladybirds in that they are rather elongate insects, but the other genera are all of the typical hemispherical shape. Colours and patterns vary a lot and cannot be relied on for identifying the species.

Superfamily Chrysomeloidea

The members of this superfamily are almost all plant-feeding beetles and the group was and sometimes still is called the Phytophaga. None of the species has a really distinct antennal club and the tarsi are all apparently 4-segmented, with a very small fourth segment (see p. 136). There are some 40,000 known species, arranged in three families.

The **Cerambycidae** usually have very long antennae and are commonly known as longhorn beetles. Several species are illustrated on Pl. 23. Their larvae tunnel in trees and other plants and some of them do considerable damage to timber. The Wasp Beetle (*Clytus arietis*) is of special interest because of its mimetic resemblance to wasps. Its actual pattern is only a little wasp-like, but the resemblance is completed by the agitated way in which the beetle scuttles over tree trunks and vegetation and taps its antennae just like a wasp. *Hylotrupes bajulus* larvae feed on dead wood and the species is commonly known as the House Longhorn because it is sometimes found in house timbers. About 60 species occur regularly in the British Isles and several others crop up from time to time in imported timber. Many longhorn beetles have been carried around the world in timber.

The **Bruchidae** is a family of seed-eating beetles with about 900 species. The head extends forward a little in front of the eyes, but there is no true rostrum as in the weevils and the antennae are not elbowed. The elytra are often a little shorter than the abdomen, leaving a small part of the latter exposed. Leguminous crops are the main food-plants and many of the bruchids, such as *Bruchus pisorum* (Pl. 24), attack peas and beans in store as well as in the field. About a dozen species occur in Britain, but several of these are found only under artificial conditions.

The **Chrysomelidae** (Pl. 24) contains more than 35,000 species. More than 600 of these occur in Europe and over 250 of them are British. They are almost all leaf-feeders and are commonly called leaf beetles. Most are quite small and many are brightly coloured and often metallic. *Timarcha tenebricosa* is our largest species, reaching lengths of about 20mm. It is black with a violet tinge and may be found crawling over grass in spring and early summer. It has no hind wings and the elytra are fused together. The insect is remarkable for its reflex bleeding, exuding deep red blood from its mouth and various joints when disturbed and earning itself the common name of Bloody-nosed Beetle. The bright red blood warns off the insect's attackers. *Cassida viridis* is one of the tortoise beetles, in which the elytra and thoracic shield completely cover the insect and, by eliminating all shadows, provide it with almost perfect camouflage as it sits on a leaf. Many leaf beetles are serious crop pests, none more so than the Colorado Beetle (*Leptinotarsa decemlineata*). The flea beetles of the genus *Phyllotreta* are well-known enemies of brassica seedlings and other cruciferous plants. *Donacia vulgaris* is one of several similar water-loving species which can be found running about on floating leaves. Their larvae feed on aquatic plants.

Superfamily Curculionoidea

This is an immense group containing the weevils and the bark beetles, almost all of which are plant feeders. The weevils, which make up the bulk of the superfamily, have the head prolonged into a beak or rostrum with the jaws at its tip, and the group is still sometimes known by its old name of Rhynchophora (Greek *rhynchos* = a snout). The rostrum is as long as the body in some species, but it is usually a good deal shorter and in some weevils it is no longer than the width of the head. The antennae are attached part way along the rostrum and they are usually strongly clubbed and sharply elbowed. The elytra are commonly clothed with scales, which give many species their bright colours. Several species lack hind wings and their elytra may be fused together. The larvae are generally legless and most of them feed enclosed in roots, stems, or seeds. *Curculio* species (Pl. 25) grow up mainly in acorns and hazel nuts, while the Grain Weevil (*Sitophilus granarius*) (Pl. 25) is one of several species that have become serious pests of stored grain and other foods. The females of many long-beaked species use their jaw-tipped beaks to bore into their food-plants so that they can lay their eggs in the right places. The long snouts of *Curculio* species – longer in females than in males – are clearly ideal for drilling into nuts. Many other weevils drill into tree trunks, but long snouts don't always mean that the eggs are laid deep inside the host plants. Many short-snouted weevils have root-feeding larvae and don't drill at all. The eggs are laid close to the roots and the larvae have to make their own way inside.

There are more than 50,000 known weevil species, of which over 1,500 occur in Europe. The European species belong to four main families, by far the largest of which is the **Curculionidae** (Pl. 25). The antennae in this family are always strongly elbowed, with the scape almost as long as the rest of the antenna in most species and always longer than the two following segments together. Most species have a long rostrum, on each side of which there is a groove into which the antennal scape can be retracted, but there are also many short-snouted species, such as *Phyllobius viridiaeris* which is common on a wide variety of vegetation. There are over 400 British species in this family.

The **Anthribidae** is a fairly small family whose members don't look much like the other weevils. In many ways they resemble the bruchids (see p. 158), although their elytra completely cover the abdomen. The rostrum is very short and the antennae are not elbowed, but the antennal club and the 4-segmented tarsi clearly link the anthribids to the other weevil families. The Anthribidae is most easily recognised by the tarsal structure, with the second and third segments both bilobed and the third partly sunk into the second. There are eight British species, usually associated with fungi and rotting wood. Some species prey on scale insects and other small bugs.

The **Attelabidae** (Pl. 25) is another relatively small family, whose members can usually be recognised by their rather square elytra. The rostrum varies from very short to about half the body length and the antennae are not elbowed. The scape is not as long as the next two segments together. *Byctiscus populi* is one of several leaf rollers in this family. The female lays her eggs on aspen leaves, which she then rolls up tightly. The larvae feed in relative safety inside the rolled leaves. *Rhynchites aequatus* lives mainly on hawthorn and its larvae develop in the fruits. There are about 20 British species in the family.

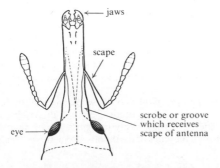

jaws

scape

scrobe or groove which receives scape of antenna

eye

The snout or rostrum of a weevil seen from below and showing the clearly elbowed and clubbed antennae. Not all weevils have such a prominent snout

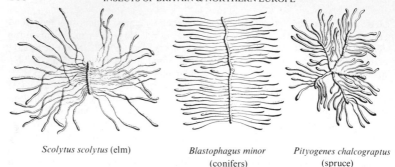

Scolytus scolytus (elm)   *Blastophagus minor*   *Pityogenes chalcograptus*
                          (conifers)   (spruce)

Some bark beetle galleries

The **Apionidae** contains mostly rather small weevils in which the body outline is commonly pear-shaped, with a smooth transition from thorax to elytra. The rostrum is relatively long and usually tapers towards the front. The antennae are not elbowed. *Apion miniatum* (Pl. 25) shows the typical shape of the family, although most species are dark. There are about 75 British species in the family.

The bark beetles of the family **Scolytidae** (Pl. 25) are all dark coloured insects with the rather typical cylindrical appearance of most wood-boring beetles. The rostrum is virtually absent and the whole head is often concealed from above by the pronotum, but the elbowed and clubbed antennae, together with the 4-segmented tarsi, indicate a close relationship with the weevils. The antennae are very short, with the scape being followed almost immediately by the solid, weevil-like club. The elytra are often scooped out at the back and used as shovels for removing the debris from the tunnels. Bark beetle tunnels are, in fact, better known than the beetles themselves, because these are the beetles that make radiating galleries just under the bark of many trees. Heavy infestations kill the trees and the bark falls to reveal the galleries. The beetles themselves are nearly all under 5mm long and it is usually easier to identify them from their galleries than from their own appearances because each species usually makes a distinctive gallery pattern. There are about 60 British species.

Tunnelling starts with the adult beetles making an entrance hole through the bark. The female usually does the boring, but the male is in attendance and helps by removing the debris. Once under the bark, in the nutritious cambium region, the male usually excavates a nuptial chamber where mating takes place. The female (there may be one or more to each male) then starts to tunnel away from the chamber, keeping just under the bark and laying her eggs at intervals along the gallery. When the larvae hatch they tunnel at right angles to the main gallery and so produce the familiar patterns. The mature larvae pupate under the bark and the new adults then emerge through their own exit holes. *Scolytus*, recognisable by the toothed front tibia, is the typical genus of these bark beetles. *S. scolytus* is the infamous Elm Bark Beetle responsible for the spread of Dutch elm disease. *Pityogenes* species attack spruce and fir trees.

The family also includes species that bore right into the wood and feed on the sap and on fungi that grow in the tunnels. These beetles, typified by *Xyleborus* species, are known as ambrosia beetles. *Platypus*, easily recognised by its narrow, cylindrical shape and the deep notches on the sides of the thorax, also burrows deeply

The Colour Plates

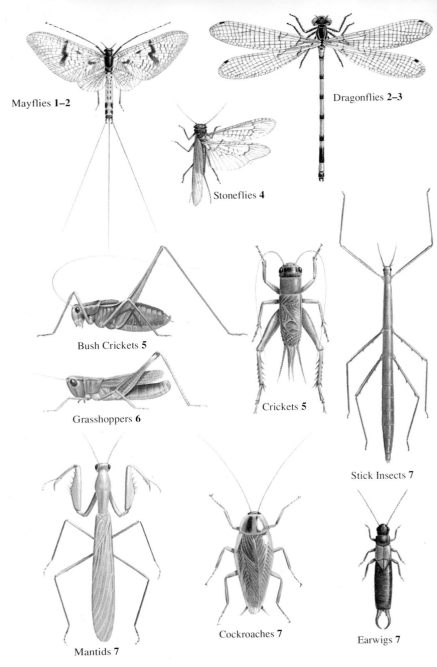

Mayflies **1–2**

Dragonflies **2–3**

Stoneflies **4**

Bush Crickets **5**

Crickets **5**

Grasshoppers **6**

Stick Insects **7**

Mantids **7**

Cockroaches **7**

Earwigs **7**

Figures in **bold** type refer to plates

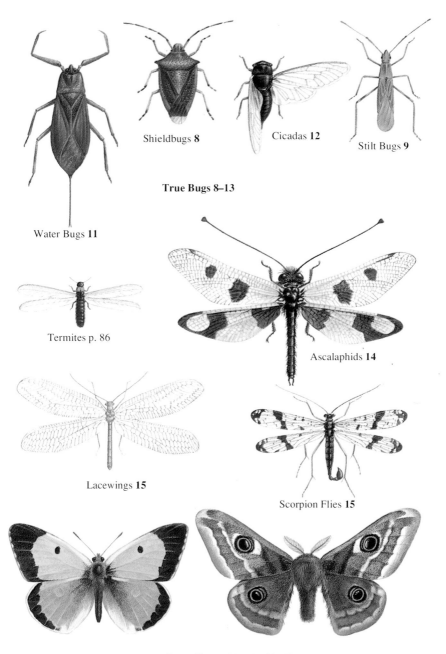

Shieldbugs **8**

Cicadas **12**

Stilt Bugs **9**

True Bugs **8–13**

Water Bugs **11**

Termites p. 86

Ascalaphids **14**

Lacewings **15**

Scorpion Flies **15**

Butterflies and Moths **32–47**

Figures in **bold** type refer to plates

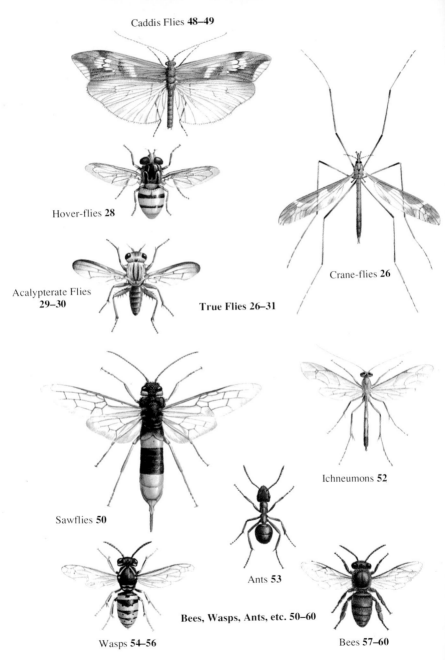

Caddis Flies **48–49**

Hover-flies **28**

Acalypterate Flies
29–30

True Flies **26–31**

Crane-flies **26**

Sawflies **50**

Ichneumons **52**

Ants **53**

Bees, Wasps, Ants, etc. **50–60**

Wasps **54–56**

Bees **57–60**

Figures in **bold** type refer to plates

Illustrations in blue circles are enlarged. Figures in **bold** type refer to plates

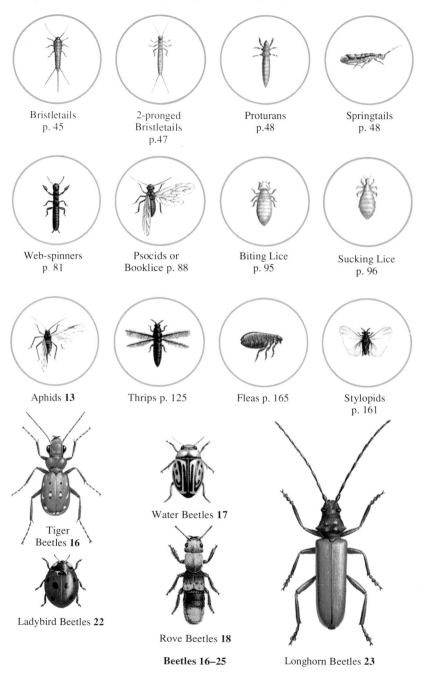

Bristletails
p. 45

2-pronged
Bristletails
p.47

Proturans
p.48

Springtails
p. 48

Web-spinners
p. 81

Psocids or
Booklice p. 88

Biting Lice
p. 95

Sucking Lice
p. 96

Aphids **13**

Thrips p. 125

Fleas p. 165

Stylopids
p. 161

Tiger
Beetles **16**

Water Beetles **17**

Ladybird Beetles **22**

Rove Beetles **18**

Beetles 16–25

Longhorn Beetles **23**

Plate 1

MAYFLIES – Order Ephemeroptera

Delicate insects with long 'tails': hind wings much smaller than forewings and sometimes absent: usually near water. Text p. 52

Ephemeridae p. 56
Fairly large insects with mottled wings: vein M_2 of forewing bends sharply backwards near the base: 3 'tails'
   1. *Ephemera danica* Muller ×1.5

Potamanthidae p. 56
Wings clear: vein M_2 of forewing bends sharply back near base: three 'tails'
   2. *Potamanthus luteus* (L.) ×2

Siphlonuridae p. 56
Vein Cu_1 of forewing with oblique veinlets running to margin: 2 'tails'
   3. *Siphlonurus lacustris* Eaton ×2

Heptageniidae p. 56
2 pairs of intercalary veins between Cu_1 and Cu_2 of forewing: 2 'tails'
   4. *Ecdyonurus dispar* (Curtis) ×2

Caenidae p. 56
Small insects without hind wings: 3 'tails'
   5. *Caenis macrura* Stephens ×3

Ephemerellidae p. 56
Vein Cu_2 of forewing very close to Cu_1 at base
   6. *Ephemerella ignita* (Poda) ×2.5

Forewing of
Ephemerella

A_1 Cu_2 Cu_1

Δ **Isonychidae** p. 56
Vein Cu_2 of forewing parallel to hind margin for most of its length
   7. *Isonychia ignota* (Walker) ×2.5

Baetidae p. 56
Small insects with hind wings very small or absent: 2 'tails'
   8. *Cloëon dipterum* (L.) ×4
   9. *Baetis rhodani* (Pictet) ×2.5

Leptophlebiidae p. 56
Base of Cu_2 in forewing is mid-way between Cu_1 and A_1, or close to A_1: 3 'tails'
   10. *Leptophlebia vespertina* (L.) ×2.5

Forewing of
Leptophlebia

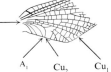

A_1 Cu_2 Cu_1

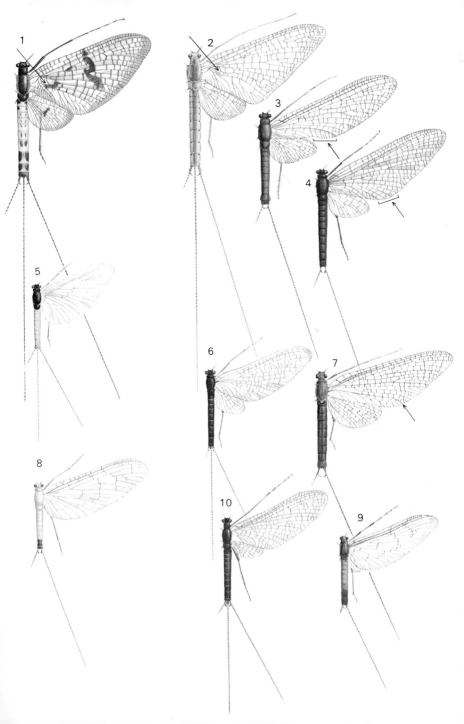

Plate 2

MAYFLIES – Order Ephemeroptera (Cont'd)

Δ **Palingeniidae** p. 56
Very large insects with 2 'tails': vein Cu_1 of forewing bends sharply backwards near base
    1. *Palingenia longicauda* (Ol.)

Δ **Oligoneuriidae** p. 56
Wings with very few veins
    2. *Oligoneuriella rhenana* Imhoff

Δ **Metretopodidae** p. 56
Hind wings very oval: 2 'tails'
    3. *Metretopus norvegicus* (Eaton) ×3.5

Δ **Polymitarcidae** p. 56
Wings white
    4. *Ephoron virgo* (Ol.) ×3.5

DAMSELFLIES – Order Odonata: sub-order Zygoptera

Long, slender insects with large eyes and short, bristle-like antennae: forewings and hind wings of similar shape. Text p. 57

Calopterygidae p. 62
Wings at least partly coloured, with numerous antenodal veins
    5. *Calopteryx splendens* (Harris) male ×1.5

Coenagriidae p. 62
Wings clear, with only 2 antenodal veins: quadrilateral with acute distal angle
    6. *Pyrrhosoma nymphula* (Sulzer) male ×1.5
    7. *Coenagrion puella* (L.) male ×1.5
    8. *Ischnura elegans* (van der Linden) ×1.5

Wing base of *Coenagrion*   Wing base of *Platycnemis*

Platycnemididae p. 62
Wings clear, with 2 antenodal veins: quadrilateral rectangular: tibiae broad and pale
    9. *Platycnemis pennipes* (Pallas) male ×1.5

Lestidae p. 62
Wings clear, with 2 antenodal veins and distinctly elongate stigma: body usually green
    10. *Lestes sponsa* male ×1.5

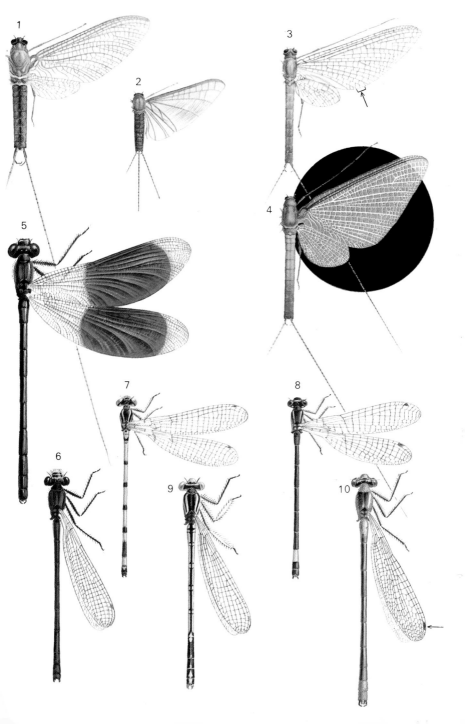

Plate 3

DRAGONFLIES – Order Odonata: Sub-order Anisoptera

Long-bodied insects with large eyes and short, bristle-like antennae: forewings and hind wings differ in shape. Text p. 57.

Aeshnidae p. 63
Triangles similar in both wings: eyes in fairly broad contact
1. Emperor Dragonfly – *Anax imperator* Leach male
2. *Aeshna grandis* (L.)
3. *Brachytron pratense* (Muller)

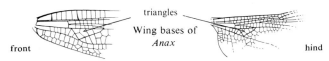

triangles

Wing bases of *Anax*

front   hind

Cordulegasteridae p. 63
Triangles similar in both wings: eyes meet only at a point
4. *Cordulegaster boltonii* (Donovan)

Gomphidae p. 63
Triangles similar in both wings: eyes widely separated
5. *Gomphus vulgatissimus* (L.)

Corduliidae p. 63
Triangles dissimilar in the two wings: forewing triangle with front side about as long as basal side: body metallic
6. *Cordulia aenea* Fraser

Base of *Cordulia* forewing

triangle

Libellulidae p. 63
Triangles dissimilar in the two wings: forewing triangle with front side much shorter than basal side: not metallic
7. *Orthetrum cancellatum* (L.) male
8. *Leucorrhinia dubia* (van der Linden) male
9. *Libellula depressa* L. male
10. *Sympetrum sanguineum* (Muller) male

Base of *Libellula* forewing

triangle

All insects on this plate are about ⅔rds life size.

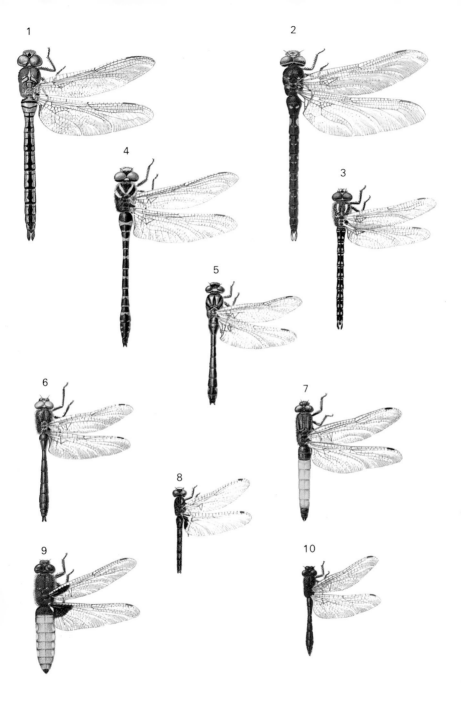

Plate 4

STONEFLIES – Order Plecoptera

Soft-bodied insects, usually found near water: hind wings larger than forewings: wings usually laid flat or rolled round body at rest. Text p. 64. The insects pictured are all females: males often have short wings.

Leuctridae   p. 67
2nd tarsal segment shorter than the others: no oblique vein in apical space
   1. *Leuctra fusca* L., showing the rolled position of the wings at rest ×3.5

Taeniopterygidae   p. 67
All tarsal segments about equal: cerci short
   2. *Taeniopteryx nebulosa* (L.) ×2.5

Nemouridae   p. 67
2nd tarsal segment shorter than others: oblique cross vein in apical space
   3. *Nemoura cinerea* Retz ×3.5

Perlodidae   p. 67
Anal veins of hind wing forked
   4. *Isoperla grammatica* (Poda) ×3.5
   6. *Perlodes microcephala* (Pictet) ×2

Capniidae   p. 67
No double 'ladder' in forewing
   5. *Capnia bifrons* Newman ×3.5

Chloroperlidae   p. 68
Small, yellowish insects with no forked anal veins in hind wing
   7. *Chloroperla torrentium* (Pictet) ×3.5

Perlidae   p. 67
Dark insects with forked anal veins and no yellow stripes on pronotum
   8. *Dinocras cephalotes* (Curtis) ×1.5

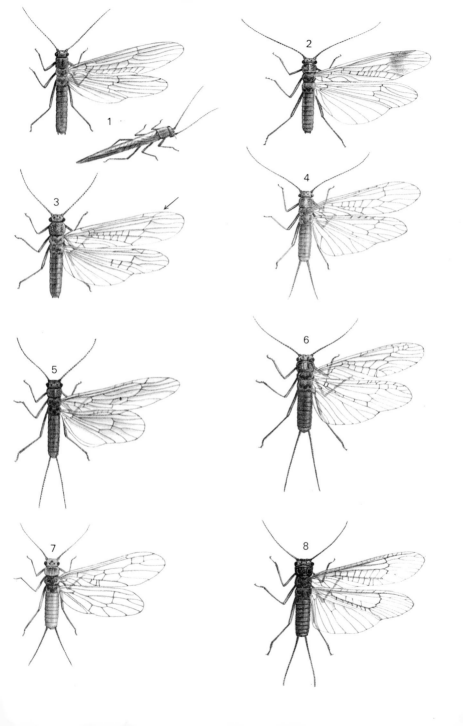

Plate 5

CRICKETS & BUSH-CRICKETS – Order Orthoptera

Stout-bodied insects with an enlarged saddle-shaped pronotum: hind legs usually long and modified for jumping. Text p. 68

Gryllidae – True Crickets   p. 72
Antennae longer than body: tarsi-3-segmented
  1. House Cricket – *Acheta domesticus* (L.) ×1.5
  2. Field Cricket – *Gryllus campestris* L. ×1.5
  3. Wood Cricket – *Nemobius sylvestris* (Bosc.) ×2
  4. Scaly Cricket – *Pseudomogoplistes squamiger* (Fischer) ×2

Tettigoniidae – Bush-crickets   p. 73
Antennae longer than body: tarsi 4-segmented
  5. Long-winged Cone-head – *Conocephalus discolor* (Thunberg) ×2
  6. Oak Bush-cricket – *Meconema thalassinum* (De Geer) ×2
  7. Speckled Bush-cricket – *Leptophyes punctatissima* (Bosc.) ×2
  8a. Dark Bush-cricket – *Pholidoptera griseoaptera* (De Geer) ×2
  8b. Dark Bush-cricket female ×2
▲ 9. *Ephippiger ephippiger* (Fiebig)
  10. Great Green Bush-cricket – *Tettigonia viridissima* L.

Gryllotalpidae – Mole Crickets   p. 71
Front legs enlarged for digging
  11. Mole Cricket – *Gryllotalpa gryllotalpa* (L.)

The insects are all males unless otherwise stated

True crickets and bush-crickets can also be distinguished by looking at the wings if these are fully developed. The left forewing of the bush-cricket normally overlaps the right one, but among the true crickets it is the right wing that is on top.

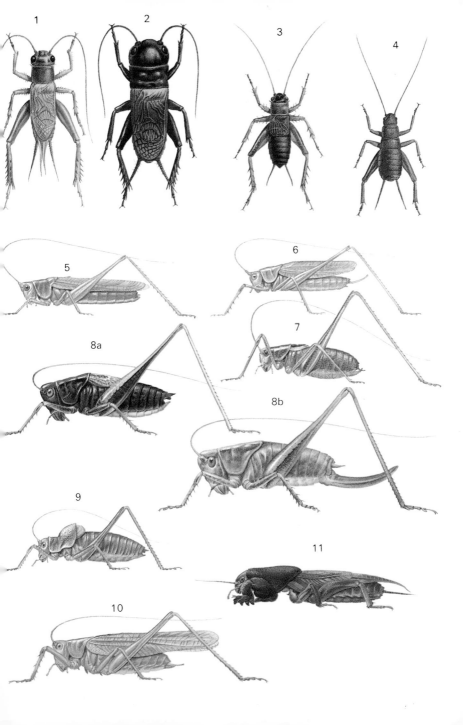

Plate 6

ORDER ORTHOPTERA (Cont'd)

Acrididae – Grasshoppers   p. 74
Antennae shorter than body
   1a. Meadow Grasshopper – *Chorthippus parallelus* (Zetterstedt) ×2
   1b. Meadow Grasshopper female ×2
    2. Field Grasshopper – *Chorthippus brunneus* (Thunberg) ×2
    3. Stripe-winged Grasshopper – *Stenobothrus lineatus* (Panzer) ×2
▲ **4.** *Oedipoda germanica* (Latreille) ×2
    5. Mottled Grasshopper – *Myrmeleotettix maculatus* (Thunberg) ×2
    6. Migratory Locust – *Locusta migratoria* L. – migratory phase

Rhaphidophoridae – Cave Crickets and Camel Crickets   p. 74
Wingless, with very long palps: antennae much longer than body
    7. Greenhouse Camel Cricket – *Tachycines asynamorus* Adelung
▲ **8.** *Dolichopoda azami* Saulcy

Tetrigidae – Groundhoppers   p. 76
Antennae shorter than body: pronotum extends back to tip of abdomen
    9. Common Groundhopper – *Tetrix undulata* (Sowerby) ×2.5

△ **Tridactylidae – Pigmy Mole Crickets**   p. 76
Very small insects with relatively huge hind femora
   10. *Tridactylus variegatus* (Latreille) female ×2.5

The insects pictured are all males unless otherwise stated

Male and female grasshoppers may be distinguished by looking at the hind end of the abdomen. That of the male is turned up and resembles the prow of a boat.

male

female

1a

1b

2

3

4

5

6

7

8

9

10

Plate 7

COCKROACHES – Order Dictyoptera: sub-order Blattodea

Flattened insects with long legs: pronotum covers head. Text p. 83

Blattidae   p. 84
    1. American Cockroach – *Periplaneta americana* (L.) female
    4. Common Cockroach – *Blatta orientalis* L. female

Blatellidae   p. 84
    2a. Dusky Cockroach – *Ectobius lapponicus* (L.) male ×2
    2b. Dusky Cockroach female ×2
    3. German Cockroach – *Blattella germanica* (L.) female ×2

MANTIDS – Order Dictyoptera: sub-order Mantodea

Predatory insects with a long, mobile prothorax and spiky front legs modified for grasping prey. Text p. 84

Δ **Mantidae**   p. 85
    5. *Mantis religiosa* L. female
    6. *Iris oratoria* (L.) female
    7. *Ameles spallanzania* (Rossi) female

EARWIGS – Order Dermaptera

Slender, flattened insects with pincers at the rear. Text p. 78

Labiduridae   p. 80
2nd tarsal segment normal: antennae with 15-30 segments
    8. *Labidura riparia* (Pallas) male

Forficulidae   p. 80
2nd tarsal segment expanded
    9. *Forficula auricularia* (L.) male ×2
    10. *Forficula lesnei* Finot male ×2
    11. *Apterygida media* (Hagenbach) male ×2

Labiidae   p. 80
2nd tarsal segment normal: antennae with 11-15 segments
    12. *Labia minor* (L.) male ×2

STICK INSECTS – Order Phasmida

Slender, twig-like insects. Text p. 77

Δ **Phasmatidae**   p. 77
    13. *Bacillus rossius* (Fabr.) female

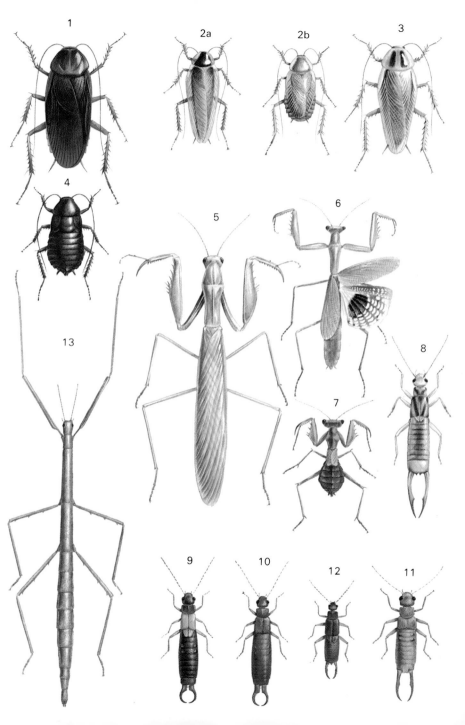

Plate 8

LAND BUGS – Order Hemiptera: sub-order Heteroptera

Insects with a beak or rostrum for sucking plant or animal juices: forewings, when present, are horny with a membranous tip. Text p. 98

Aradidae – Flatbugs p. 105
Very flat bugs with stout antennae: usually fully winged
    1. Pine Flatbug – *Aradus cinnamomeus* (Panzer) ×5
▲ **11.** *Mezira tremulae* Buttn ×2

Aneuridae – Barkbugs p. 105
Very flat bugs with forewings almost entirely membranous
    2. *Aneurus laevis* (Fabr.) ×5

Cydnidae p. 105
Hind tibiae strongly spined
    3. Negro Bug – *Thyreocoris scarabaeoides* (L.) ×5
    4. Pied Shieldbug – *Sehirus bicolor* (L.) ×3

Scutelleridae p. 106
Scutellum enormous, covering all of abdomen and most of wings
    5. *Odontoscelis dorsalis* (Fabr.) ×5
    6. *Eurygaster testudinaria* (Geoffroy) ×2

Pentatomidae – Shieldbugs p. 106
Body generally shield-shaped, with triangular scutellum: tarsi 3-segmented
    7. European Turtle-bug – *Podops inuncta* (Fabr.) ×3
▲ **8.** *Graphosoma italicum* Muller ×2
    9. Forest Bug – *Pentatoma rufipes* (L.) ×2
    10. *Picromerus bidens* (L.) ×2

Acanthosomatidae – Shieldbugs p. 105
Tarsi 2-segmented
    12. Hawthorn Shieldbug – *Acanthosoma haemorrrhoidale* (L.) ×2
    13. Parent Bug – *Elasmucha grisea* (L.) ×2

Coreidae p. 106
Antennae 4-segmented: scutellum generally shield-shaped: abdomen usually extending sideways beyond elytra
    14. *Coreus marginatus* (L.) ×2
▲ **15.** *Philomorpha laciniata* de Vill. ×2

Alydidae p. 106
4th segment of antennae long and curved
    16. *Alydus calcaratus* (L.) ×2

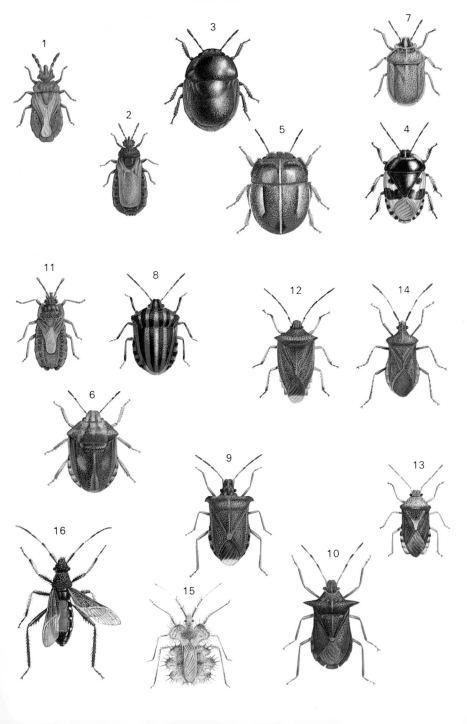

Plate 9

LAND BUGS (Cont'd)

Rhopalidae   p. 107
Forewings largely membranous, otherwise similar to Coreidae
    1. *Chorosoma schillingi* (Schummel) ×2
    2. *Rhopalus subrufus* (Gmelin) ×2

Lygaeidae – Ground Bugs   p. 107
Generally dark bugs, often marked with red: scutellum more or less equal to or longer than commisure
    3. *Megalonotus chiragra* (Fabr.) ×4
    4. *Scoloposthetus decoratus* (Hahn) ×4
▲ **5.** *Lygaeus saxatilis* Scopoli ×2

Berytidae – Stilt Bugs   p. 107
Legs usually very long: scutellum usually no more than half length of commisure
    6. *Cymus melanocephalus* Fieber ×4
    7. *Berytinus minor* (Herrich-Schäffer) ×2

Reduviidae – Assassin Bugs   p.108
Predatory and blood-sucking bugs: 3-segmented beak curved under body at rest
    8. *Reduvius personatus* (L.) ×1.5
▲ **9.** *Rhinocoris iracundus* Poda ×2
    10. Heath Assassin Bug – *Coranus subapterus* (De Geer) ×2
    11. *Empicoris vagabundus* (L.) ×2

Piesmidae – Beet Bugs   p. 107
Pronotum and wings with lace-like pattern: scutellum visible
    12. *Piesma maculatum* (Costa) ×7
    13. *Piesma quadratum* Fieber ×7

Tingidae – Lace Bugs   p. 108
Pronotum and wings with lace-like pattern: pronotum covers scutellum
    14. Spear Thistle Lace Bug – *Tingis cardui* (L.) ×7

Pyrrhocoridae   p. 107
Generally red and black or orange and black
    15. Firebug – *Pyrrhocoris apterus* (L.) – short-winged form ×2

Stenocephalidae – Spurge Bugs   p. 107
At least 6 veins in membrane: legs and antennae distinctly banded
    16. *Dicranocephalus medius* (Mulsant & Rey) ×2

Nabidae – Damsel Bugs   p. 109
Predatory bugs with 4-segmented beak curving under body at rest
    17. Marsh Damsel Bug – *Dolichonabis limbatus* (Dahlbom) ×2
    18. *Himacerus apterus* (Fabr.) ×2

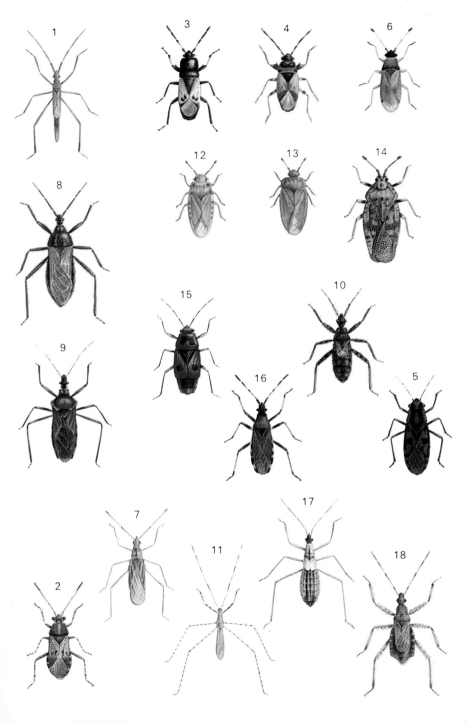

Plate 10

LAND BUGS (Cont'd)

Cimicidae – Bedbugs p. 109

Flattened, blood-sucking bugs with vestigial wings
   1. Bedbug – *Cimex lectularius* L. ×3

Anthocoridae p. 109

Fully-winged predatory bugs, with a distinct embolium and cuneus in the forewing
   2. *Anthocoris nemorum* (L.) ×4
   3. *Xylocoris galactinus* (Fallen) ×6

embolium   cuneus

Forewing of Anthocoridae

Miridae – Mirid or Capsid Bugs p. 110

Generally rather slender and soft-bodied bugs, with a distinct cuneus in fully-winged forms
   4. *Pilophorus perplexus* Douglas & Scott ×3
   5. *Psallus varians* (Herrich-Schäffer) ×4
   6. *Myrmecoris gracilis* (Sahlberg) ×3
   7. *Phylus melanocephalus* (L.) ×3
   8a. *Systellonotus triguttatus* (L.) male ×4
   8b. *Systellonotus triguttatus* female ×4
   9. Tarnished Plant Bug – *Lygus rugulipennis* Poppius ×3
   10. *Capsus ater* (L.) ×3
   11. Black-kneed Capsid – *Blepharidopterus angulatus* (Fallen) ×3
   12. *Amblytylus nasutus* (Kirschbaum) ×3
   13. *Halticus apterus* (L.) ×6

cuneus

Forewing of Miridae

Saldidae – Shore Bugs p. 111

Large-eyed bugs usually found close to water
   14. *Saldula saltatoria* (L.) ×4

Δ **Leptopodidae** p. 111

Similar to Saldidae, but with ocelli on a stalked platform: found near water
   15. *Leptopus marmoratus* (Goeze) ×4

Δ **Plataspidae** p. 105

2-segmented tarsi and an enormous scutellum covering almost the whole body: related to Acanthosomatidae
   16. *Coptosoma scutellata* Fourcroy ×4

Δ **Ochteridae** p. 112

Aquatic or semi-aquatic bugs with visible antennae
   17. *Ochterus marginatus* Latreille ×3

Δ **Isometopidae** p. 111

Large eyed bugs, related to mirids but with ocelli: generally tree-dwelling
   18. *Isometopus mirificus* Mulsant & Rey ×6

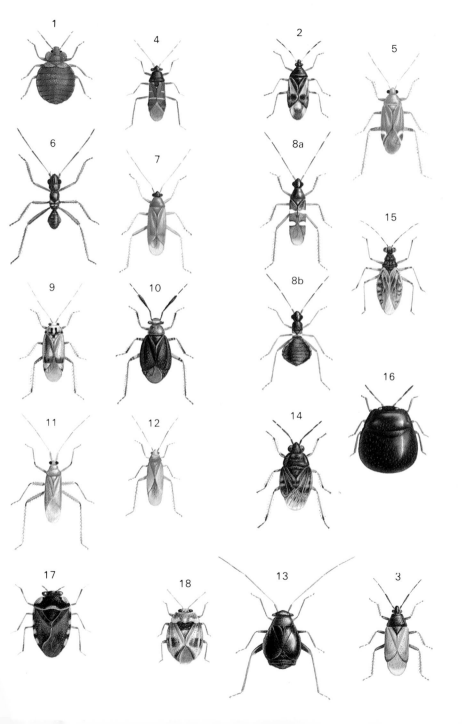

Plate 11

WATER BUGS – Order Hemiptera: sub-order Heteroptera
(Cont'd)

Hydrometridae p. 111
Head 5 times longer than broad
    1. *Hydrometra stagnorum* (L.) ×2.5

Hebridae p. 111
Minute insects with 5-segmented antennae
    2. *Hebrus ruficeps* Thomson ×15

Mesoveliidae p. 111
Tarsi with apical claws: usually wingless
    3. *Mesovelia furcata* Mulsant & Rey ×7

Pleidae p. 113
Minute back-swimmers
    4. *Plea atomaria* (Pallas) ×7

Veliidae p. 111
Skating insects with legs more or less equally spaced
    5. Water Cricket – *Velia caprai* Tamanini ×2.5

Nepidae p. 112
Long breathing siphon
    6. Water Scorpion – *Nepa cinerea* ×2
    7. Water Stick Insect – *Ranatra linearis* ×2

Gerridae – Pond Skaters p. 112
Skating insects with front legs well separated from the others
    8. *Gerris lacustris* (L.) ×2.5

Aphelocheiridae p. 113
Flattened bugs, usually with vestigial wings or none at all
    9. *Aphelocheirus aestivalis* (Fabr.) ×2

Naucoridae p. 113
Bugs with much enlarged front femora
    10. Saucer Bug – *Ilyocoris cimicoides* (L.) ×2

Corixidae – Water Boatmen p. 113
Cylindrical, boat-shaped bugs: middle and hind legs more or less equal
    11. *Corixa punctata* (Illiger) ×2

Notonectidae – Backswimmers p. 113
Boat-shaped bugs that swim on their backs: middle legs much shorter than hind legs
    12. *Notonecta glauca* L. ×2

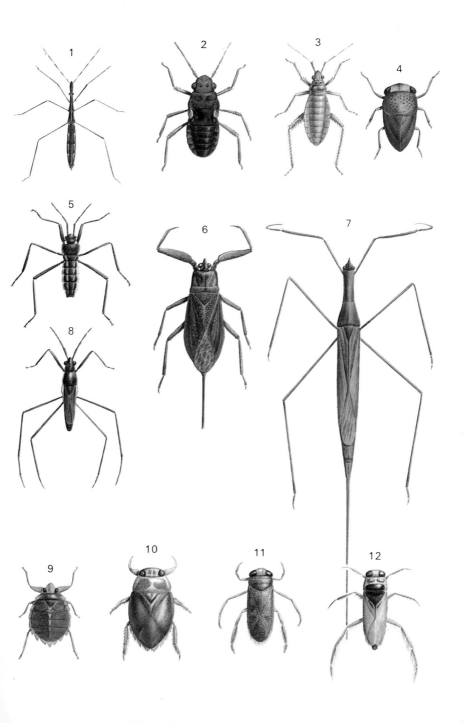

Plate 12

CICADAS AND PLANTHOPPERS – Order Hemiptera
Sub-order Homoptera

Sap-sucking bugs with the beak arising from the back of the head: forewings of uniform texture throughout – all horny or all membranous. Text p. 114

Cicadidae – Cicadas   p. 117
Large insects with clear, largely colourless wings and 3 ocelli
▲ **1.** *Lyristes plebejus* Scopoli
  2. *Cicadetta montana* (Scopoli)

Cercopidae – Froghoppers   p. 118
Forewings opaque and often brightly coloured: hind tibia rounded, with just a few spines
  3. *Cercopis vulnerata* Illiger ×2
  4a. *Philaenus spumarius* (L.) ×2.5
  4b and 4c. varieties of *P. spumarius*

Δ **Dictyopharidae**   p. 120
Head normally with a prominent forward projection   *G. genistae*
  5. *Dictyophara europaea* (L.) ×2

Membracidae – Treehoppers   p. 117
Pronotum extends back over abdomen   pronotum
  6. *Gargara genistae* (Fabr.) ×3.5
  7. *Centrotus cornutus* (L.) ×2.5

C. cornutus

Delphacidae   p. 119
Hind tibia with a large, movable spur
  8. *Delphax pulchellus* (Curtis) ×3.5

Cicadellidae   p. 118
Wings usually opaque and often brightly coloured: hind tibia angular, with one or more rows of spines
  9. *Iassus lanio* (L.) ×2.5
▲ **10.** *Penthimia nigra* Fabr. ×3.5
  11. *Eupteryx aurata* (L.) ×3.5
  12. *Elymana sulphurella* (Zett.) ×3.5
  13. *Thamnotettix confinis* (Zett.) ×2.5
  14. *Macropsis scutellata* (Boheman) ×3.5
  15. *Macrosteles variatus* (Fallen) ×3.5

Tettigometridae   p. 120
Forewings distinctly pitted
  16. *Tettigometra impressopunctata* Dufour ×3.5

Cixiidae   p. 119
Large membranous wings with well-defined veins
  17. *Cixius nervosus* (L.) ×2.5

Issidae   p. 120
Forewings horny, bulging noticeably at the shoulder and covered with a network of fine veins
  18. *Issus coleoptratus* (Fabr.) ×2.5

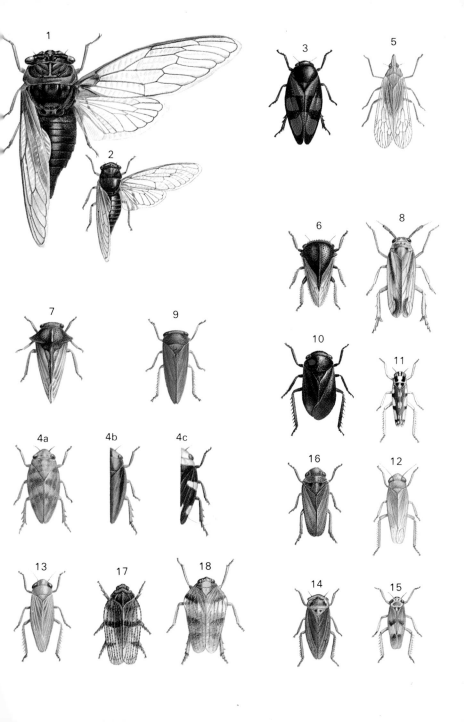

Plate 13

PSYLLIDS, APHIDS, AND SCALE INSECTS – Order Hemiptera: Sub-order Homoptera (Cont'd)

Psyllidae – Jumping Plant Lice or Psyllids p. 120
Jumping insects, with thickened femora: forewings tougher than hind wings
   1. *Psyllopsis fraxini* (L.) ×10 with gall on ash leaf

Aphididae – Aphids p. 121
Tarsi with 2 claws: wings, when present, transparent and all of the same membranous texture: at least 4 oblique veins in forewing: abdominal cornicles usually distinct
   2. Cabbage Aphid – *Brevicoryne brassicae* (L.) ×10
   3. Black Bean Aphid – *Aphis fabae* Scopoli ×10
   4. Peach-Potato Aphid – *Myzus persicae* (Sulzer) ×10

Pemphigidae – Aphids p. 123
Like Aphididae, but cornicles very small and usually invisible: antennae much shorter than body
   5. Woolly Aphid – *Eriosoma lanigerum* (Hausmann) ×10
   6. *Pemphigus bursarius* (L.) ×10 with gall on poplar petiole

Adelgidae – Conifer Aphids p. 123
Only 3 oblique veins in forewing: no cornicles
   7. *Adelges abietis* (L.) ×10 with gall on spruce

Phylloxeridae – Aphids p. 123
Wings, when present, have only 3 oblique veins and are held flat over the body at rest – not roofwise as in other aphids: antennae 3-segmented
▲ **8.** *Viteus vitifolii* wingless female ×30

Aleyrodidae – Whiteflies p. 121
Wings and body coated with white wax: wings held flat over body at rest
   9. Greenhouse Whitefly – *Trialeurodes vaporariorum* (Westwood) ×10

Superfamily Coccoidea – Scale Insects and Mealybugs p. 123
Males with only 1 pair of wings: females wingless and often living under a protective scale: tarsi with only 1 claw
  10a. Mussel Scale – *Lepidosaphes ulmi* (L.) male ×30
  10b. Mussel Scale female ×4
   11. Cottony Cushion Scale – *Icerya purchasi* Maskell female ×4
   12. Citrus Mealybug – *Planococcus citri* (Risso) female ×4

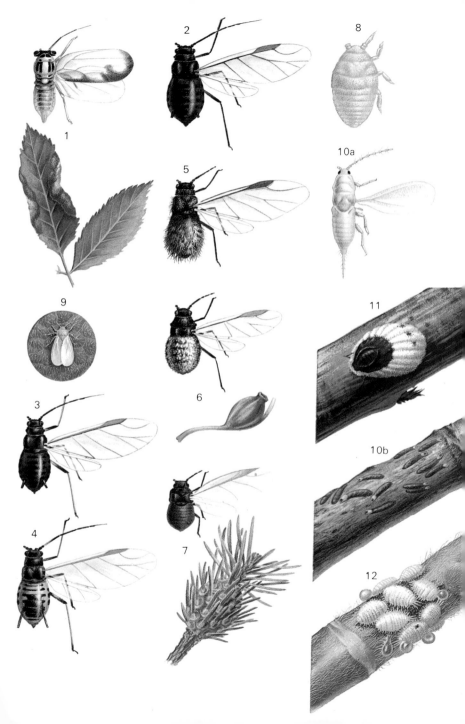

Plate 14
ANT-LIONS AND OTHER NEUROPTERANS
Order Neuroptera

Insects with complex venation, the veins tending to fork at the wing margins. Mostly predatory insects. Text p. 127

Δ **Myrmeleontidae – Ant-lions** p. 132
Long-bodied insects resembling dragonflies, but with much stouter antennae: wings clear or mottled and held roofwise over the body at rest
    1. *Palpares libelluloides* L. male ×1.25

Δ **Nemopteridae** p. 133
Hind wings ribbon-like
    2. *Nemoptera coa* L. ×1.25

Δ **Ascalaphidae** p. 132
Antennae long and clubbed
    3. *Libelloides coccajus* (Schaeff.) ×1.5
    4. *Libelloides macaronius* (Scopoli) ×1.5

Δ **Mantispidae – Mantis Flies** p. 133
Front legs raptorial: distinguished from mantids (Pl. 7) by netted wings
    5. *Mantispa styriaca* Poda ×2

Δ **Dilaridae** p. 133
Male antennae strongly feathered: female with long ovipositor
    6a. *Dilar meridionalis* (Hagen) female ×3
    6b. *Dilar meridionalis* male ×3

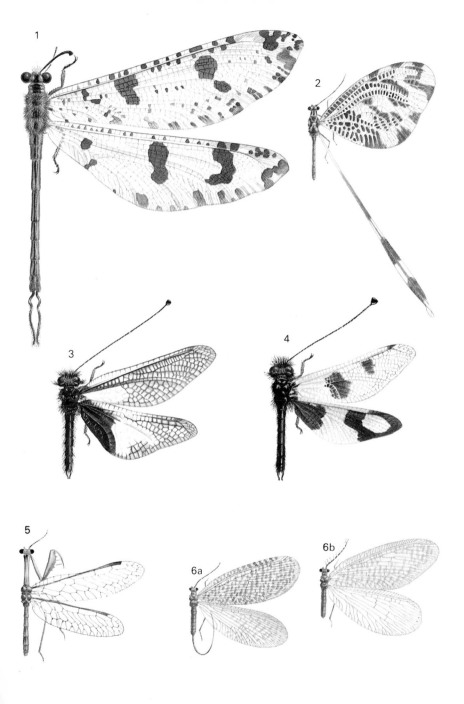

Plate 15

LACEWINGS, ALDER FLIES, AND SNAKE FLIES
Order Neuroptera (cont'd)

Chrysopidae – Green Lacewings   p. 131
Fairly large insects – green or brown – with only a few longitudinal veins
    1. *Chrysopa septempunctata* Wesmael ×2.5
    2. *Nothochrysa capitata* (Fabr.) ×2.5

Sisyridae – Brown Lacewings   p. 131
Rather small insects: vein Sc meets R_1 near
wingtip: costal veinlets rarely fork
    3. *Sisyra fuscata* (Fabr.) ×4

Hemerobiidae – Brown Lacewings   p. 131
Mostly rather small insects: vein Sc does
not meet R_1: costal veinlets nearly all
fork in forewing
    4. *Hemerobius humulinus* L. ×4

Coniopterygidae – White Lacewings   p. 131
Very small insects with powdery white wings, held roofwise over the body at rest
    5. *Conwentzia psociformis* (Curtis) ×6

Osmylidae   p. 131
Large insects with spotted wings
    6. *Osmylus fulvicephalus* (Scopoli) ×2

Sialidae – Alder Flies   p. 130
No marked forking of veins at wing margins
    7. *Sialis lutaria* (L.) ×2.5

Raphidiidae – Snake Flies   p. 130
Elongated prothorax
    8. *Raphidia notata* Fabr. male ×2.5

SCORPION FLIES – Order Mecoptera

Head prolonged into a beak, with jaws at the lower end. Text p. 163

Panorpidae   p. 163
Wings normally blotched: male abdomen turned up in scorpion fashion
    9. *Panorpa cognata* Rambur male ×2.5

Δ **Bittacidae**   p. 163
Legs extremely long and slender, ending in a single claw
    10. *Bittacus italicus* Muller ×2.5

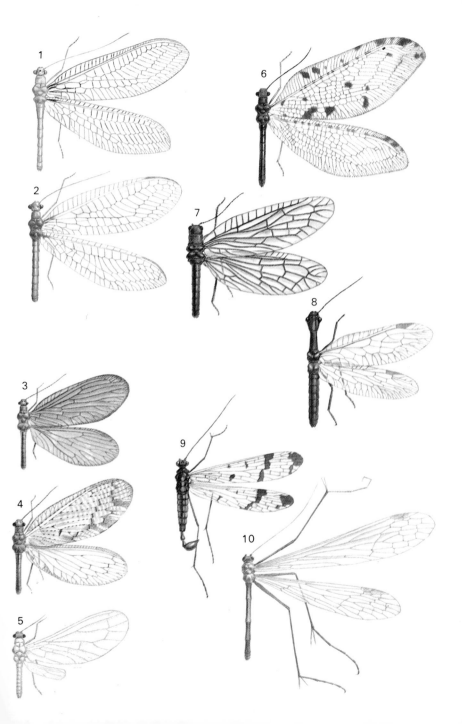

Plate 16

BEETLES – Order Coleoptera

Insects whose forewings (elytra) are tough and horny, covering the hind wings and normally covering the abdomen as well: elytra meet in the mid-line. Text p. 134

Cicindelidae - Tiger Beetles p. 143

Long-legged, fast-running and fast-flying predators: elytra without striations

1. Green Tiger Beetle – *Cicindela campestris* L. ×1.5
2. Wood Tiger Beetle – *Cicindela sylvatica* L. ×1.5

Carabidae – Ground Beetles p. 143

Long-legged, fast-running predators with powerful jaws: elytra generally striated: tarsi 5-segmented: antennae usually 11-segmented

3. *Pterostichus cupreus* (L.) ×1.5
4. *Pterostichus nigrita* (Fabr.) ×1.5
5. *Leistus spinibarbis* (Fabr.) ×1.5
6. *Elaphrus cupreus* Dufts. ×1.5
7. Bombardier Beetle – *Brachinus crepitans* (L.) ×3
8. *Dromius quadrimaculatus* (L.) ×3
9. *Dyschirius globosus* (Herbst) ×6
10. *Amara aulica* (Panzer) ×3
11. *Carabus granulatus* L.
12. *Carabus nemoralis* Muller
13. Violet Ground Beetle – *Carabus violaceus* L.

Δ **Rhysodidae** p. 142

Stout, beaded antennae

14. *Rhysodes sulcatus* (Fabr.) ×3

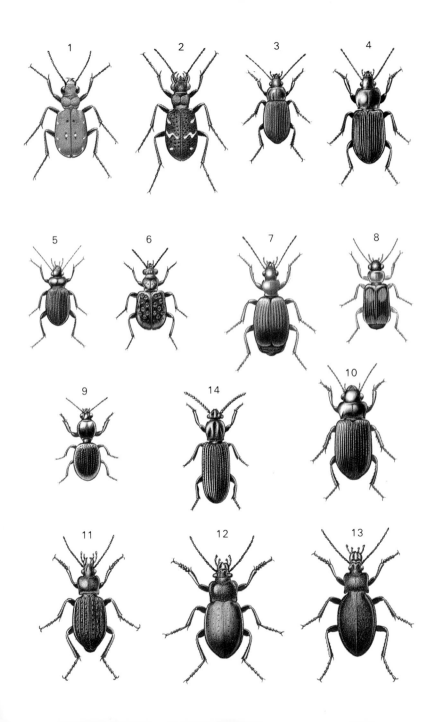

Plate 17

WATER BEETLES – Order Coleoptera (cont'd)

Dytiscidae   p. 144
Elytra without rows of distinct punctures: often large
   1a. Great Diving Beetle – *Dytiscus marginalis* L. male
   1b. Great Diving Beetle female
   2a. *Acilius sulcatus* (L.) male
   2b. *Acilius sulcatus* female
     3. *Platambus maculatus* (L.) ×3
     5. *Potamonectes depressus* (Fabr.) ×4
     6. *Laccophilus minutus* (L.) ×4

Noteridae   p. 144
Underside very flat: antennae very stout
     4. *Noterus clavicornis* (Degeer) ×4

Gyrinidae – Whirligig beetles   p. 143
Middle and hind legs short and paddle-like
     7. *Gyrinus natator* (L.) ×3

Hygrobiidae   p. 144
Prominent eyes
     8. Screech Beetle – *Hygrobia herrmanni* (Fabr.) ×3

Haliplidae   p. 144
Small beetles with distinct elongate punctures on elytra: hind coxae form large plates
     9. *Haliplus fulvus* (Fabr.) ×4

Hydrophilidae   p. 145
Clubbed antennae and long palps
   10. Great Silver Beetle – *Hydrophilus piceus* (L.)
   11. *Spercheus emarginatus* (Schaller) ×3
   12. *Laccobius sinuatus* Mots. ×4
   13. *Enochrus testaceus* (Fabr.) ×4
   14. *Hydrochus elongatus* (Schaller) ×4

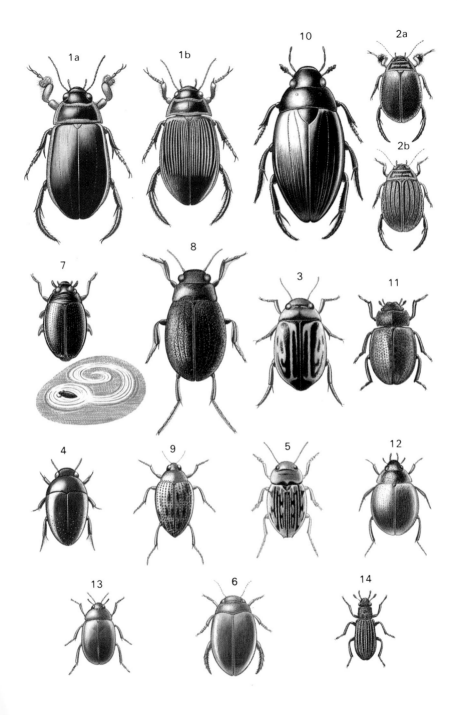

Plate 18

BEETLES – Order Coleoptera (cont'd)

Silphidae – Burying Beetles   p. 146
Strongly clubbed antennae: rear of abdomen exposed
  1. *Nicrophorus humator* (Goeze) ×1.25
  2. *Nicrophorus vespilloides* Herbst ×1.25
  3. *Nicrophorus investigator* Zett. ×1.25
  4. *Silpha atrata* (L.) ×2

Staphylinidae – Rove Beetles   p. 146
Elytra very short, usually exposing 6 abdominal segments: antennae not clubbed
  5. Devil's Coach Horse – *Staphylinus olens* Muller ×1.25
  6. *Tachyporus hypnorum* (Fabr.) ×3
  7. *Stenus bimaculatus* Gyll. ×2
  8. *Paederus littoralis* Grav. ×2
  9. *Philonthus marginatus* (Fabr.) ×2
  10. *Emus hirtus* (L.) ×2
  11. *Creophilus maxillosus* (L.) ×2

Sphaeritidae   p. 145
Shiny beetles with one abdominal segment exposed: antennae strongly clubbed but not elbowed: front tibia not toothed
  12. *Sphaerites glabratus* (Fabr.) ×3

Histeridae   p. 145
Shiny beetles with 2 abdominal segments exposed: antennae strongly clubbed and elbowed: front tibia strongly toothed
  13. *Hister impressus* Fabr. ×2

Buprestidae   p. 150
Metallic insects with head sunk deep into thorax
  14. *Agrilus pannonicus* (Piller) ×3
▲ 15. *Buprestis aurulentis* (L.) ×2

Byrrhidae   p. 150
Rounded or oval beetles which can withdraw their appendages into grooves and appear lifeless
  16. *Byrrhus pilula* L. ×2

Dascillidae   p. 150
Conical front coxae: tarsal segments strongly lobed
  17. *Dascillus cervinus* (L.) ×2

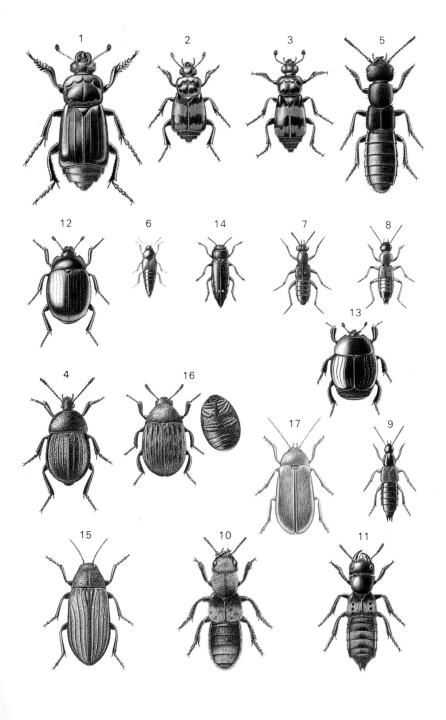

Plate 19

BEETLES – Order Coleoptera (cont'd)

Lucanidae – Stag Beetles p. 148

Antennae more or less elbowed, and with last few segments expanded into flattened lobes

   1a. Stag Beetle – *Lucanus cervus* (L.) male

   1b. Stag Beetle female

    2. Lesser Stag Beetle – *Dorcus parallelopipedus* (L.)

    3. *Sinodendron cylindricum* (L.) ×1.5

Geotrupidae – Dung Beetles p. 148

Antennae 11-segmented and not elbowed, with last few segments expanded into leaf-like flaps which can be drawn together to form a club: jaws visible from above

    4. Dor Beetle – *Geotrupes stercorarius* (L.) ×1.5

   5a. Minotaur Beetle – *Typhaeus typhoeus* (L.) male ×1.5

   5b. Minotaur Beetle female ×1.5

    6. *Odontaeus armiger* (Scopoli) ×1.5

Trogidae p. 148

Antennae not elbowed, but last 3 segments are expanded into leaf-like flaps that can be drawn together to form a club: elytra roughly sculptured and often hairy

    7. *Trox scaber* (L.) ×2

Scarabaeidae – Dung Beetles and Chafers p. 148

Antennae not elbowed and with 9 or 10 segments, the last few of which are expanded into leaf-like flaps that can be drawn together to form a club: jaws not usually visible from above

    8. *Copris lunaris* (L.) male ×1.5

    9. *Aphodius rufipes* (L.) ×2

Plate 20

BEETLES – Order Coleoptera (cont'd)

Scarabaeidae (cont'd) p. 148
1. Common Cockchafer – *Melolontha melolontha* (L.) ×1.25
2. Rose Chafer – *Cetonia aurata* (L.) ×1.25
3. Garden Chafer – *Phylloperthahorticola* (L.) ×1.25
4. *Hopliaphilanthus* Fuessly ×1.25

Cantharidae – Soldier and Sailor Beetles p. 151
Elongated, soft-bodied beetles with lightly hairy elytra
5. *Cantharis rustica* Fallen ×1.25
6. *Rhagonychafulva* (Scopoli) ×3

Lampyridae – Glow-worms and Fireflies p. 152
Elongated beetles with head covered by pronotum: elytra, when present, soft and
hairy: females often wingless
7a. Glow-worm – *Lampyris noctiluca* L. male ×1.25
7b. Glow-worm female ×1.25
7c. Glow-worm larva ×1.25

Elateridae – Click Beetles p. 151
Elongated beetles with hard elytra and sharp angles at rear of pronotum: antennae
often toothed or feathery
8. *Ctenicera cuprea* (Fabr.) ×1.25
9. *Athous haemorrhoidalis* Fabr. ×1.25
10. *Ampedus balteatus* (L.) ×1.25
11. *Agriotes lineatus* (L.) ×3
12. *Fleutiauxellus quadripustulatus* (Fabr.) ×3

Dermestidae – Larder Beetles and Carpet Beetles p. 152
Clubbed antennae and rather downy elytra: usually a single large ocellus on the top
of the head, although not in *Dermestes*
13. *Attagenus pellio* (L.) ×5
14. *Anthrenus fuscus* Olivier ×5
15. Hide Beetle – *Dermestes maculatus* DeGeer ×3
16. Larder Beetle – *Dermestes lardarius* L. ×3
17. Khapra Beetle – *Trogoderma granarium* Everts ×3

Melyridae p. 154
Bristly beetles with teeth or other appendages on tarsal claws
18. *Anthocomus fasciatus* (L.) ×5

Heteroceridae p. 150
Short, thick antennae and heavily spined front legs
19. *Heterocerus flexuosus* Stephens ×5

Δ **Cebrionidae** p. 151
Antennae inserted close to eyes: jaws very prominent
20. *Cebrio gigas* Fabr. male ×1.25

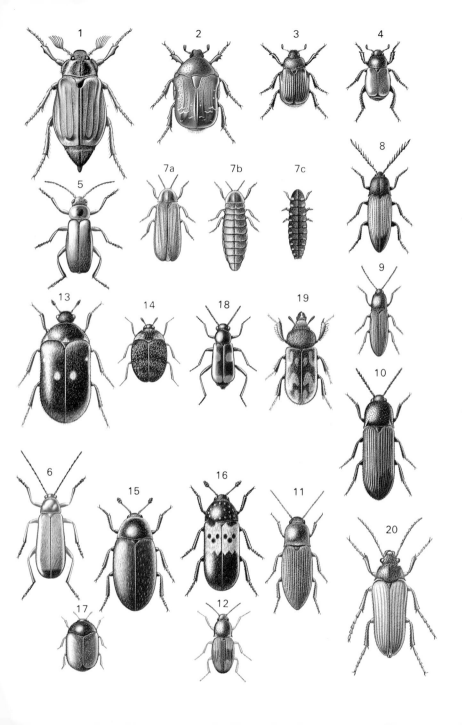

Plate 21

BEETLES – Order Coleoptera (cont'd)

Anobiidae p. 153

Head often covered by a prominent hood formed by the pronotum: antennae usually lightly toothed

    1. Cigarette Beetle – *Lasioderma serricorne* (Fabr.) ×5

    2. Drug-store Beetle – *Stegobium paniceum* (L.) ×5

    3a. Furniture Beetle – *Anobium punctatum* (DeGeer) ×3

    3b. Typical damage by furniture beetle larvae – woodworm

    4. Death-watch Beetle – *Xestobium rufovillosum* (DeGeer) ×3

Ptinidae – Spider Beetles p. 154

Small beetles, often with a globular abdomen: antennae and legs long: head often concealed by thorax

    5a. *Ptinus fur* (L.) male ×5

    5b. *Ptinus fur* female ×5

Cleridae p. 154

Hairy beetles with strongly clubbed antennae: tarsi with membranous flaps or lobes

    6. *Necrobia rufipes* (DeGeer) ×5

Lyctidae – Powder Post Beetles p. 153

Slender beetles with large 2-segmented club at tip of antenna: last tarsal segment very long

    7. *Lyctus fuscus* (L.) ×3

Bostrichidae p. 153

Thorax forms distinct hood over head: antennal club 3-segmented (fig. p. 153)

    8. Lesser Grain Borer – *Rhizopertha dominica* (Fabr.) ×3

Trogossitidae p. 154

Last tarsal segment relatively long and bearing a small lobe between its claws

    9. Cadelle – *Tenebroides mauritanicus* (L.) ×3

Lymexylidae p. 154

Slender, downy beetles: males with elaborately branched palps

    10a. *Hylecoetus dermestoides* (L.) male ×3

    10b. *Hylecoetus dermestoides* female ×3

    11a. *Lymexylon navale* (L.) male ×3

    11b. *Lymexylon navale* female ×3

Anthicidae p. 155

Small beetles with rounded head distinct from thorax

    12. *Anthicus antherinus* (L.) ×3

Pyrochroidae – Cardinal Beetles p. 155

Rather flat beetles, generally red and with comb-like antennae

    13. *Pyrochroa coccinea* L. ×1.5

Oedemeridae p. 155

Soft-bodied, often with metallic colours: hind femora often swollen in male: penultimate tarsal segment bilobed

    14a. *Oedemera nobilis* (Scopoli) male ×1.5

    14b. *Oedemera nobilis* female ×1.5

Tenebrionidae p. 155

Rather dark and stout beetles, often lacking hind wings and with elytra fastened down

    15. Mealworm Beetle – *Tenebrio molitor* L ×1.5

    16. Churchyard Beetle – *Blaps mucronata* Latreille

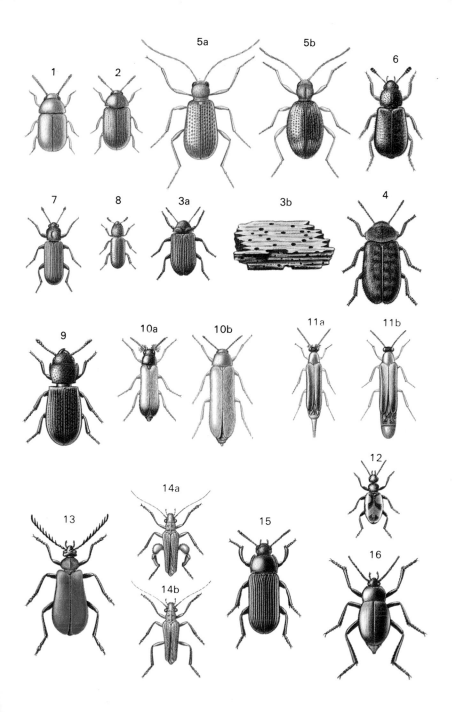

Plate 22

BEETLES -Order Coleoptera (cont'd)

Tenebrionidae (cont'd) p. 155
3. Confused Flour Beetle – *Tribolium confusum* Duval ×4
4. *Gnatocerus cornutus* (Fabr.) ×4

Meloidae – Oil Beetles and Blister Beetles p. 155
Soft-bodied beetles with a narrow neck and often with short elytra
1. *Meloe proscarabaeus* L. ×1.25
2. Spanish Fly – *Lytta vesicatoria* (L.) ×1.25

Nitidulidae p. 156
Antennal club clearly 3-segmented: rear of abdomen often exposed
5. *Carpophilus hemipterus* (L.) ×4

Cucujidae p. 157
Antennae with an indistinct club: sides of thorax often toothed
6. Saw-toothed Grain Beetle – *Oryzaephilus surinamensis* (L.) ×6

Cryptophagidae p. 157
Very small, hairy beetles with distinctly clubbed antennae
7. *Cryptophagus saginatus* Sturm ×6

Coccinellidae – Ladybirds p. 157
Generally rounded insects with head partly concealed from above: often brightly coloured: tarsi 4-segmented, but 3rd segment minute and tarsi appear 3-segmented
8. Eyed Ladybird – *Anatis ocellata* (L.) ×2
9. 7-spot Ladybird – *Coccinella 7-punctata* L. ×2
10. *Coccidula rufa* (Herbst) ×5
11. *Rhyzobius litura* (Fabr.) ×5
12. 22-spot Ladybird – *Psyllobora 22-punctata* (L.) ×5
13. 14-spot Ladybird – *Propylea 14-punctata* (L.) ×5
14. 24-spot Ladybird – *Subcoccinella 24-punctata* (L.) ×5
15a-d. 2-spot Ladybird – *Adalia bipunctata* (L.) ×4
16a-d. 10-spot Ladybird – *Adalia 10-punctata* (L.) ×4

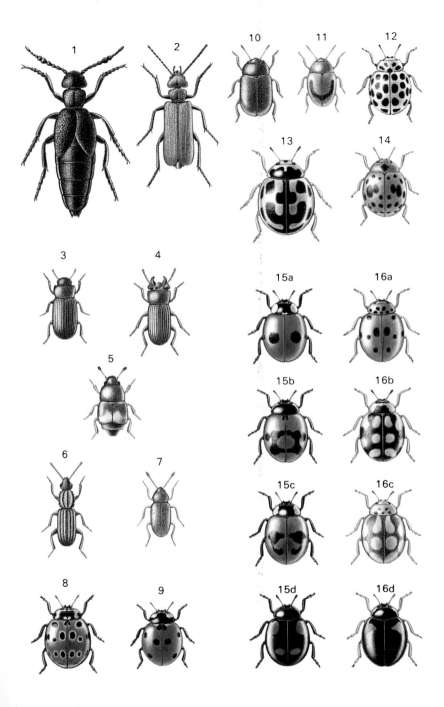

Plate 23

BEETLES – Order Coleoptera (cont'd)

Cerambycidae – Longhorn Beetles p. 158

Antennae usually very long: tarsi apparently 4-segmented, with 3rd segment bilobed – lobes generally larger in males than in females

    1. *Prionus coriarius* (L.)

▲ **2.** *Monochamus galloprovincialis* (Olivier)

    3. Musk Beetle – *Aromia moschata* (L.)

    4. *Saperda carcharias* (L.) ×1.25

▲ **5.** *Cerambyx cerdo* L. ×0.75

    6. *Lamia textor* (L.) ×1.25

    7. Wasp Beetle – *Clytus arietis* (L.) ×1.25

    8. *Agapanthia villosoviridescens* DeGeer

    9. House Longhorn – *Hylotrupes bajulus* (L.) ×1.25

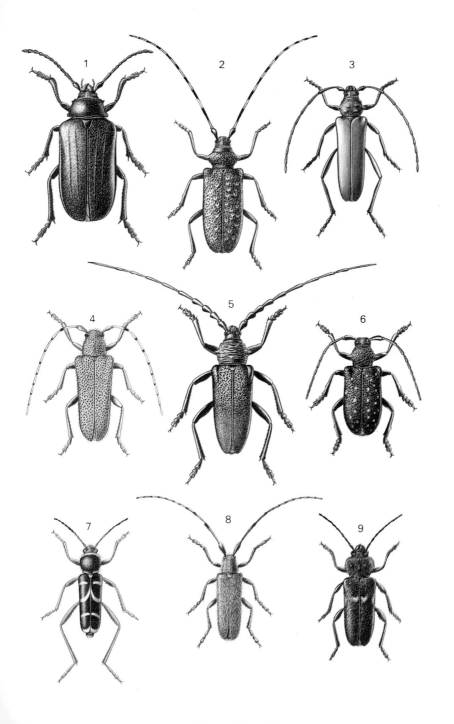

Plate 24

BEETLES – Order Coleoptera (cont'd)

Chrysomelidae – Leaf Beetles   p. 158

Generally rather rounded, with shiny elytra: third tarsal segment expanded and concealing minute 4th segment, so tarsi appear 4-segmented

1. *Galerucella nymphaeae* (L.) ×2.5
2. *Donacia vulgaris* Zschach ×2.5
3. *Chrysolina polita* (L.) ×2.5
4. Green Tortoise Beetle – *Cassida viridis* L. ×2.5
5. *Cryptocephalus hypochaeridis* (L.) ×4
6. *Chrysolina hyperici* (Forster) ×4
7. *Clytra quadripunctata* (L.) ×2.5
8. *Gastrophysa viridula* (DeGeer) ×4
9. Turnip Flea Beetle – *Phyllotreta nemorum* (L.) ×4
10. *Oulema melanopa* (L.) ×4

▲ 11. Colorado Beetle – *Leptinotarsa decemlineata* Say ×1.5
12. Bloody-nosed Beetle – *Timarcha tenebricosa* (Fabr.) ×1.5
13. *Chrysomela populi* (L.) ×1.5

4th segment

5th segment

3rd segment

Bruchidae   p. 158

Antennae distinctly thickened towards tip: elytra often short and exposing rear of abdomen: tarsi apparently 4-segmented

14. *Bruchus pisorum* (L.) ×4

Plate 25

BEETLES – Order Coleoptera (cont'd)

Curculionidae – Weevils
p. 159
Head drawn out into a prominent rostrum, with antennae attached part way along it: antennae usually strongly elbowed
  1. *Otiorhynchus clavipes* (Bonsdorff) ×2
  5. *Phyllobius viridiaeris* (Laicharting) ×4
  6. *Notaris bimaculatus* (Fabr.) ×4
  7a. *Dorytomus longimanus* (Forster) male ×4
  7b. *Dorytomus longimanus* female ×4
  8. *Polydrusus tereticollis* (DeGeer) ×4
  9. *Cryptorhynchus lapathi* (L.) ×3
  10. *Curculio nucum* L. ×4
▲ 11. *Curculio elephas* Gyllenhal ×4
  12. Grain Weevil – *Sitophlus granarius* (L.) ×4
  13. *Cionus hortulanus* (Geoffroy) ×4

Attelabidae – Weevils
p. 159
Elytra rather square in front: antennae not elbowed
  2. *Rhynchites aequatus* (L.) ×4
  3. *Byctiscus populi* (L.) female ×4

Apionidae – Weevils
p. 160
Pear-shaped body: antennae not elbowed
  4. *Apion miniatum* Germar ×4

Scolytidae – Bark Beetles
p. 160
Cylindrical beetles with clubbed antennae: elytra usually scooped out at the back
  14. *Pityogenes bidentatus* (Herbst) ×6
  15. Elm Bark Beetle – *Scolytus scolytus* (Fabr.) ×4

Platypodidae
p. 161
Cylindrical beetles with thorax notched on the sides: 1st tarsal segment very long
  16. *Platypus cylindrus* (Fabr.) ×4

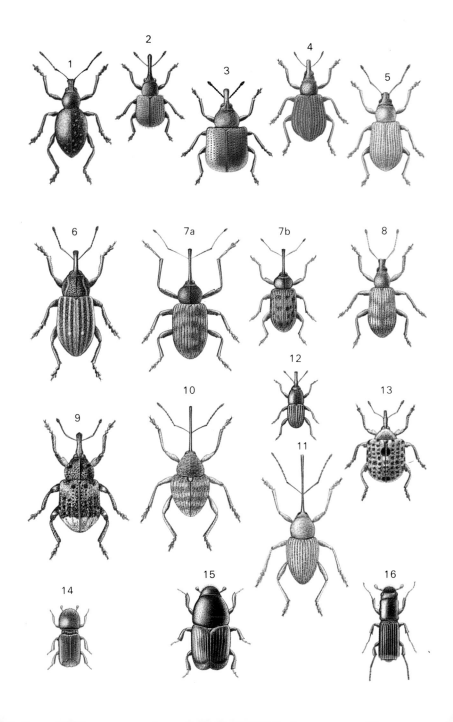

Plate 26

TRUE FLIES – Order Diptera

Insects with no more than two wings, the hind wings being represented by pin-shaped halteres. Text p. 170

Tipulidae – Crane-flies p. 188
Long-legged flies with 2 long anal veins and a V-shaped suture on the thorax
    1. *Tipula maxima* Poda

Trichoceridae – Winter Gnats p. 189
V-shaped suture on thorax: vein 2A short and strongly curved: ocelli present
    2. *Trichocera annulata* Meigen ×4

Culicidae – Mosquitoes p. 190
10 veins reach wing margin: veins and hind margin of wings bear scales
    3. *Culex pipiens* L. male ×4
    4. *Culiseta annulata* (Schrank) female ×4

Anisopodidae – Window Midges p. 189
No V-shaped suture on thorax: wings normally with discal cell: only 1 anal vein reaches wing margin
    5. *Sylvicola fenestralis* (Scopoli) ×4

Simuliidae – Black-flies p. 193
Small, dark flies with very broad wings and short antennae
    6. *Simulium equinum* (L.) ×5

Scatopsidae p. 194
Small dark flies with posterior veins very faint
    7. *Anapausis soluta* (Loew) ×5

Cecidomyiidae – Gall Midges p. 195
Minute flies with no more than 4 veins reaching wing margin: antennae beaded: body often orange
    8. *Taxomyia taxi* (Inchbald) ×6

Sciaridae p. 195
Eyes curve round to meet above antennae: usually a prominently forked vein in middle of wing
    9. *Sciara thomae* (L.) ×4

Ptychopteridae p. 189
Long-legged flies with tibial spurs: deep U-shaped suture on thorax
    10. *Ptychoptera contaminata* (L.) ×2.5

Chironomidae – Non-biting Midges p. 192
Humped thorax and very weak posterior veins: male antennae feathery
    11. *Chironomus annularis* (DeGeer) ×2.5

Bibionidae p. 194
Dark, hairy flies with stout antennae inserted well below eyes: prominent spines on front tibia
    12. Fever-fly – *Dilophus febrilis* (L.) ×3

Δ **Blephariceridae** p. 192
Slender flies with very long legs: a network of very faint folds on wings: usually near swift streams
    13. *Liponeura cinerascens* Loew ×3

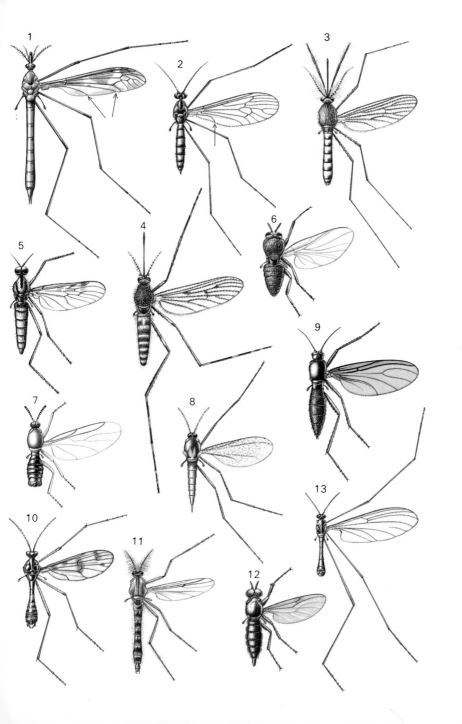

Plate 27

TRUE FLIES – Order Diptera (cont'd)

Stratiomyidae – Soldier-flies
Feet with 3 pads: veins crowded near front of wing
    1. *Oxycera rara* (Meigen) ×3
Tabanidae – Horse-flies
Feet with 3 pads: veins form broad fork across wing-tip
    2. Cleg-fly – *Haematopota pluvialis* (L.) ×3
    3. *Tabanus bromius* L. ×2
    4. *Chrysops relictus* Meigen ×2
Acroceridae
Bulbous bodies and very small heads: venation reduced
    5. *Ogcodes pallipes* (Latreille) ×3
Bombyliidae – Bee-flies
Wings often coloured: only 2 or 3 veins reach wing margin between apical fork and
anal cell: often hairy and bee-like, and often with a long proboscis
    6. *Bombylius major* L. ×2
    7. *Thyridanthrax fenestratus* (Fallen) ×2
Empididae
Bristly flies, often with rigid proboscis: a little nick on inner margin of the eye
    8. *Empis tessellata* Fabr. ×2
    9. *Hilara maura* (Fabr.) ×3   eye nick ——

Δ **Mydaidae**
Large flies with clubbed antennae
    10. *Leptomydas corsicanus* Bequaert female ×1.5
Scenopinidae
Small, naked flies with pendulous antennae
    11. *Scenopinus fenestralis* (L.) ×3
Rhagionidae – Snipe-flies
Long legs: feet with 3 pads:
    12. *Rhagio scolopacea* (L.) ×2
Therevidae
Feet with 2 pads: antennae stout: no groove between eyes
    13. *Thereva nobilitata* (Fabr.) ×2
Lonchopteridae
Small flies with pointed wings and no obvious cross-veins
    14. *Lonchoptera lutea* Panzer female ×4 (male venation differs slightly)
Asilidae – Robber-flies
Medium or large flies, generally hairy and with a groove between the eyes (fig. p.
198): feet with 2 pads
    15. *Asilus crabroniformis* L. ×1.5
Δ **Nemestrinidae**
Large-headed: several veins running parallel to hind margin: often many cells near
wing-tip
    16. *Fallenia fasciata* Meigen ×2
Phoridae
Small flies with obvious veins only near base of wing
    17. *Phora aterrima* (Fabr.) ×4

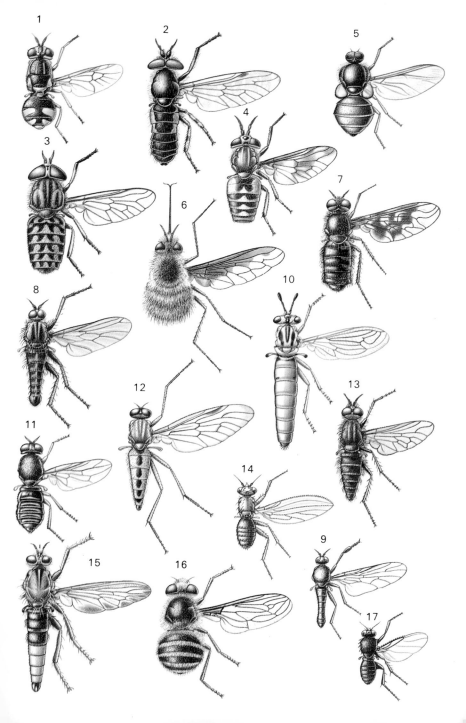

Plate 28

TRUE FLIES – Order Diptera (cont'd)

Dolichopodidae p. 199
Bristly, metallic coloured flies with head long in profile: only 1 obvious cross vein
1. *Sciapus platypterus* Fabr. ×4
2. *Dolichopus popularis* Wiedemann ×3

Dolichopus head from the side

Pipunculidae p. 200
Small dark flies with a very large head – almost all eyes
3. *Pipunculus thomsoni* (Becker) ×3

Platypezidae p. 200
Hind tarsal segments usually dilated
4. *Paraplatypeza atra* (Meigen) ×4

Syrphidae – Hover-flies p. 201
Some veins running parallel to rear edge of wing and
forming a false margin: a spurious vein – a thickening of the wing membrane – runs
through the centre of the wing: flies often brightly coloured
5. *Brachypalpoides lenta* (Meigen) ×2
6a, 6b. Forms of *Volucella bombylans* (L.) ×1.5
7. *Volucella zonaria* (Poda) ×1.5
8. Drone-fly – *Eristalis tenax* L. ×2
9. *Baccha elongata* (Fabr.) ×2
10. *Volucella inanis* (L.) ×1.5
11. *Scaeva pyrastri* (L.) ×2
12. *Syrphus ribesii* (L.) ×2
▲ 13. *Milesia crabroniformis* Fabr.) ×1.5
14. *Leucozona lucorum* L. ×2
15. *Doros conopseus* (Fabr.) ×2

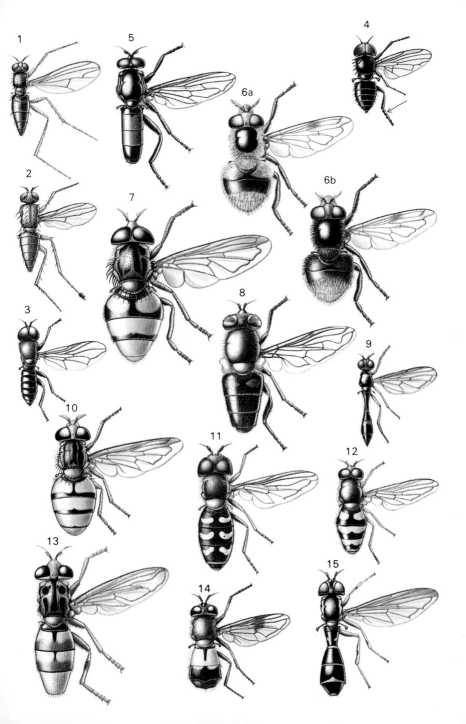

Plate 29

TRUE FLIES – Order Diptera (cont'd)

Gasterophilidae – Bot-flies   p. 208
Large flies with vestigial mouthparts
    1. *Gasterophilus intestinalis* (DeGeer) female ×3

Conopidae   p. 201
Anal cell long and pointed: often a long proboscis and long, clubbed antennae
    2. *Conops quadrifasciata* DeGeer ×3

Otitidae   p. 202
Distinct grooves on face: wings often 'pictured'
    3. *Melieria omissa* (Meigen) ×3

Tephritidae   p. 202
Wings normally 'pictured': vein Sc sharply angled
    4. *Urophora cardui* (L.) ×4

Lauxaniidae   p. 204
Anal cell closed by curved vein
    5. *Calliopum aeneum* (Fallen) ×4

Sciomyzidae   p. 203
2nd basal and anal cells short: tibia has pre-apical bristle
    6. *Tetanocera elata* (Fabr.) ×4

Platystomatidae   p. 202
'Pictured' wings: costa broken near humeral vein
    7. *Platystoma seminationis* (L.) ×4

Dryomyzidae   p. 203
Large wings: 2nd basal and anal cells large (fig. p. 204)
    8. *Dryomyza flaveola* (Fabr.) ×3

Coelopidae   p. 204
Small bristly flies of the seashore: legs stout
    9. *Coelopa frigida* (Fabr.) ×4

Psilidae   p. 203
Ocellar triangle distinct: costal margin clearly broken
    10. Carrot-fly – *Psila rosae* (Fabr.) ×5

Micropezidae – Stilt-legged-flies   p. 203
Legs very long and slender
    11. *Calobata petronella* (L.) ×4

Chamaemyiidae   p. 204
No costal breaks or pre-apical bristle on tibia
    12. *Chamaemyia aridella* (Fallen) ×5

Lonchaeidae   p. 205
Shiny metallic flies: costa broken at tip of Sc: eyes semi-circular in profile
    13. *Lonchaea chorea* (Fabr.) ×4

Sepsidae   p. 205
Constricted abdomen: wings often spotted near tip
    14. *Sepsis punctum* (Fabr.) ×4

Piophilidae   p. 205
Dark, shining flies: costa broken near tip of Sc: eyes circular in profile
    15. Cheese-skipper – *Piophila casei* (L.) ×4

Piophila
head from side

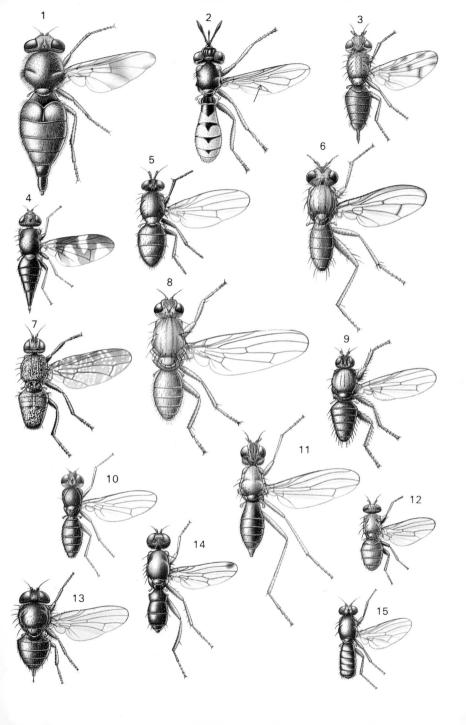

Plate 30

TRUE FLIES – Order Diptera (cont'd)

Heleomyzidae p. 204
Costal margin strongly spined
    1. *Suillia variegata* (Loew) ×4

Anthomyzidae p. 206
Long cilia on costal margin: posterior cross vein near middle
    2. *Anthomyza gracilis* Fallen ×6

Sphaeroceridae p. 205
1st tarsal segment short and fat
    3. *Copromyza similis* (Collin) ×5

Opomyzidae p. 205
1st two long veins converge at wing-tip
    4. *Opomyza germinationis* L. ×6

Ephydridae – Shore-flies p. 206
Small flies with 2 costal breaks and no anal cell
    5. *Psilopa nigritella* Stenhammar ×7

Chloropidae p. 207
Plate-like ocellar triangle
    6. Frit-fly – *Oscinella frit* (L.) ×7
    7. Small Cluster-fly – *Thaumatomyia notata* (Meigen) ×8
    8. *Lipara lucens* Meigen ×4

Carniidae p. 205
Minute flies with a single costal break and just 1 or 2 closed cells
    9. *Meonura obscurella* (Fallen) ×8
    10. *Carnus hemapterus* Nitzsch ×8

Nycteribiidae p. 212
Head folded back on thorax: wingless parasites of bats
    11. *Phthiridium biarticulatum* (Hermann) ×6

Drosophilidae – Fruit-flies p. 206
2 costal breaks: anal cell present: antennae apparently forked at tip
    12. *Drosophila funebris* Fabr. ×6

Antenna of *Drosophila*

Agromyzidae p. 207
1 costal break: post-vertical bristles divergent: lower fronto-orbital bristles pointing inwards

lower fronto-orbital bristles

    13. *Phytomyza ilicis* Curtis ×7

Oestridae p. 208
Well-developed post-scutellum: insects softly hairy
    14. Warble-fly – *Hypoderma bovis* (L.) ×2.5
    15. Sheep Nostril-fly – *Oestrus ovis* L. ×3

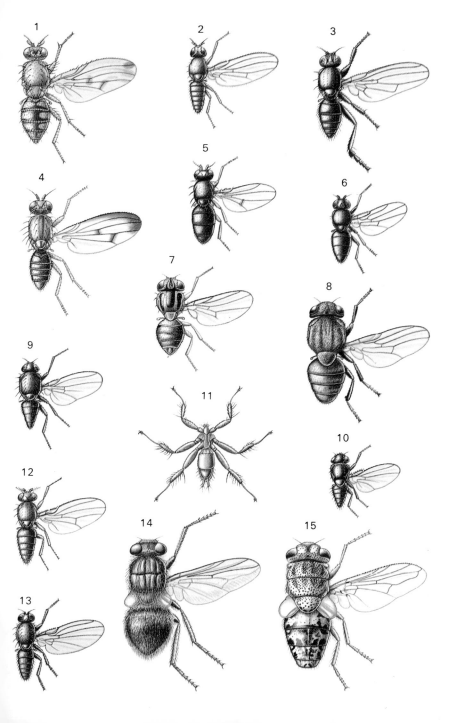

Plate 31

TRUE FLIES Order Diptera (cont'd)

Tachinidae p. 209
Post-scutellum well developed (fig. p. 209): a fan of hypopleural bristles
on each side
    1. *Tachina fera* (L.) ×2
    2. *Gymnochaeta viridis* (Fallen) ×2
    3. *Gonia divisa* (Meigen) ×2
    4a. *Alophora hemiptera* Fabr. male ×2
    4b. *Alophora hemiptera* female ×2

Calliphoridae – Blow-flies p. 209
Post-scutellum small or absent: fan of hypopleural bristles on each side
    5. *Lucilia caesar* (L.) ×2
    6. *Calliphora vomitoria* (L.) ×2
    7. Cluster-fly – *Pollenia rudis* (Fabr.) ×3

Sarcophagidae – Flesh-flies p. 210
Like Calliphoridae, but post-humeral bristle is higher than pre-sutural bristle (see
text and fig. p. 173)
    8. *Sarcophaga carnaria* (L.) ×2

Scathophagidae – Dung-flies p. 210
Thoracic squamae short and usually strap-shaped: halteres clearly visible
    9. Yellow Dung-fly – *Scathophaga stercoraria* (L.) ×2

Muscidae – House-flies p. 211
No fan of hypopleural bristles: posterior calli well developed (fig. p. 208): halteres
concealed
    10. *Mesembrina meridiana* (L.) ×2
    11. Stable-fly – *Stomoxys calcitrans* (L.) ×2
    12. *Eudasyphora cyanella* (Meigen) ×2
    13. House-fly – *Musca domestica* ×2

Hippoboscidae – Louse-flies p. 212
Head sunk back into thorax: large claws: wings often reduced or absent: external
parasites
    14. Forest-fly – *Hippobosca equina* L. ×2
    15. Sheep Ked – *Melophagus ovinus* (L.) ×3

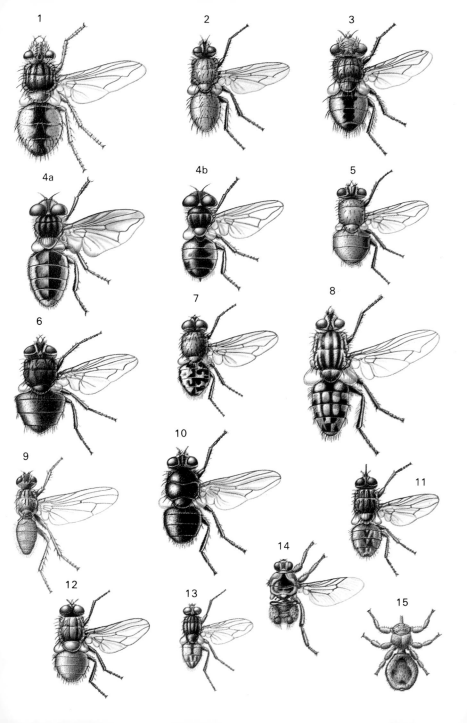

Plate 32

BUTTERFLIES – Order Lepidoptera

Wings covered with minute scales that produce their patterns. Text p. 213

Danaidae p. 225
Large butterflies with front legs incompletely formed: antennae scaled only at base
    1. Monarch – *Danaus plexippus* (L.)*

Papilionidae – Swallowtails and Apollos p. 227
Large butterflies with all legs fully developed: hind wing usually tailed, with a concave inner margin and only 1 anal vein
    2. Swallowtail – *Papilio machaon* L.
▲ **3.** Apollo – *Parnassius apollo* L.

Satyridae – Browns p. 225
Front legs brush-like and useless for walking: anterior veins of forewing swollen near base: antennal club generally weak
    4. Gatekeeper - *Pyronia tithonus* (L.) male
    5. Ringlet – *Aphantopus hyperantus* (L.)
    6. Marbled White – *Melanargia galathea* (L.)

Δ **Libytheidae** p. 226
Very long palps: forewing toothed near apex
    7. Nettle-tree Butterfly – *Libythea celtis* Laicharting

* A sporadic visitor to Britain – see p. 225

Plate 33

BUTTERFLIES – Order Lepidoptera (cont'd)

Nymphalidae p. 226
Front legs useless for walking – brush-like in male: antennal club usually very clear

Front legs of male (left) and female Nymphalidae

1. Silver-washed Fritillary – *Argynnis paphia* (L.) male
2. Pearl-bordered Fritillary – *Boloria euphrosyne* (L.)
3. Small Tortoiseshell – *Aglais urticae* (L.)
4. Red Admiral – *Vanessa atalanta* (L.)
5. Purple Emperor – *Apatura iris* (L.) male
6. Comma – *Polygonia c-album* (L.)
7. White Admiral – *Limenitis camilla* (L.)
8. Peacock – *Inachis io* (L.)

Plate 34

BUTTERFLIES – Order Lepidoptera (cont'd)

Nymphalidae (cont'd) p. 226
    1. Camberwell Beauty – *Nymphalis antiopa* (L.)*

Hesperiidae – Skippers p. 224
Antennae widely separated at base and gradually thickening to form the club, which is often hooked at the tip
    2. Grizzled Skipper – *Pyrgus malvae* (L.)
    3. Large Skipper – *Ochlodes venata* (Bremer & Grey) male
    4. Dingy Skipper – *Erynnis tages* (L.)

Nemeobiidae p. 226
Front leg fully developed in female, but small and useless for walking in male
    5. Duke of Burgundy – *Hamearis lucina* (L.)

Lycaenidae p. 227
All legs functional, although males may have claws missing from front legs: mostly rather small: often metallic
    6. Purple Hairstreak – *Quercusia quercus* (L.) male
    7. Chalkhill Blue – *Lysandra coridon* (Poda) male
    8. Small Copper – *Lycaena phlaeas* (L.)
    9. Common Blue – *Polyommatus icarus* (Rottenburg) male

Pieridae p. 227
All legs functional: hind wing with convex inner margin and 2 anal veins: usually white or yellow
    10. Orange-tip – *Anthocharis cardamines* (L.) male
    11. Clouded Yellow – *Colias croceus* (Geoffroy) male
    12. Brimstone – *Gonepteryx rhamni* (L.) male
    13. Small White – *Pieris rapae* (L.) female

*A casual immigrant to British Isles from the Continent

Plate 35

MOTHS – Order Lepidoptera (Cont'd)

Hepialidae – Swift Moths   p. 229

Antennae very short: venation similar in all wings: jugum present on forewing

Base of wings showing jugum overlapping on to hind wing — jugum

1. Map-winged Swift – *Hepialus fusconebulosa* (DeGeer)
2a. Ghost Swift – *Hepialus humuli* (L.) male
2b. Ghost Swift female
3. Common Swift – *Hepialus lupulina* (L.)
4. Gold Swift – *Hepialus hecta* (L.)

Cossidae   p. 230

Large moths with no large cell in forewing
5. Goat Moth – *Cossus cossus* (L.)
6. Leopard Moth – *Zeuzera pyrina* (L.)
7. Reed Leopard – *Phragmataecia castaneae* (Hubner)

Limacodidae   p. 231

Small moths with no large cell in forewing: no proboscis
8. Triangle – *Heterogenea asella* (Schiff.)
9. Festoon – *Apoda avellana* (L.)

Sesiidae – Clearwing Moths   p. 234

All wings virtually scaleless: forewings very narrow
10. Hornet Moth – *Sesia apiformis* (Clerck)
11. Currant Clearwing – *Synanthedon tipuliformis* (Clerck)
12. Fiery Clearwing – *Bembecia chrysidiformis* (Esper)
13. Red-belted Clearwing – *Synanthedon myopaeformis* (Borkh.)

Zygaenidae – Burnets and Foresters   p. 231

Metallic, day-flying moths with clubbed or toothed antennae and a distinct frenulum
14a. 6-spot Burnet – *Zygaena filipendulae* (L.)
14b. 6-spot Burnet f. *flava*
15. Scotch Burnet – *Zygaena exulans* (Hoch.)
16. Common Forester – *Procris statices* (L.)
17. Transparent Burnet – *Zygaena purpuralis* (Brunn.)
▲ 18. *Zygaena fausta* (L.)

Plate 36

MOTHS – Order Lepidoptera (cont'd)

Cochylidae   p. 233

Wings squared off at ends and almost rectangular: vein Cu_{1b} of forewing arises from the distal part of the cell

    1. *Agapeta hamana* (L.)

    2. *Aethes cnicana* (Westwood)

Forewing of Cochylidae

Tortricidae   p. 233

Like Cochylidae but vein Cu_{1b} arises near centre of cell

    3. *Cacoecimorpha pronubana* (Hubner)

    4. *Tortrix viridana* L.

    5. Codlin Moth – *Cydia pomonella* (L.)

    6. *Croesia bergmanniana* (L.)

Forewing of Tortricidae

Pterophoridae – Plume Moths   p. 232

Slender moths with narrow wings usually split into 2, 3, or 4 feathery plumes; legs long and spiky

    7. White Plume Moth – *Pterophorus pentadactyla* (L.)

    8. *Agdistis bennetii* (Curtis)

Alucitidae   p. 237

Wings each divided into 6 slender plumes

    9. *Alucita hexadactyla* (L.)

Pyralidae   p. 232

Mainly small moths with relatively narrow forewings: vein $Sc+R_1$ of hind wing is fused with Rs beyond the cell: hearing organs on abdomen

    10. Small Magpie Moth – *Eurrhypara hortulata* (L.)

    11. *Pyrausta purpuralis* (L.)

    12. European Corn Borer – *Ostrinia nubilalis* (Hubner)

    13. *Elophila nymphaeata* (L.)

    14. Meal Moth – *Pyralis farinalis* (L.)

    15. Wax Moth – *Galleria mellonella* (L.)

    16. *Scoparia pyralella* (Hubner)

    17. *Crambus pratella* (L.)

    18. *Catoptria pinella* (L.)

    19. *Pempelia palumbella* (Fabr.)

    20. Mediterranean Flour Moth – *Ephestia kuehniella* (Zeller)

    21. *Oncocera semirubella* (Scopoli)

Hind wing of Pyralidae

All ×1.25

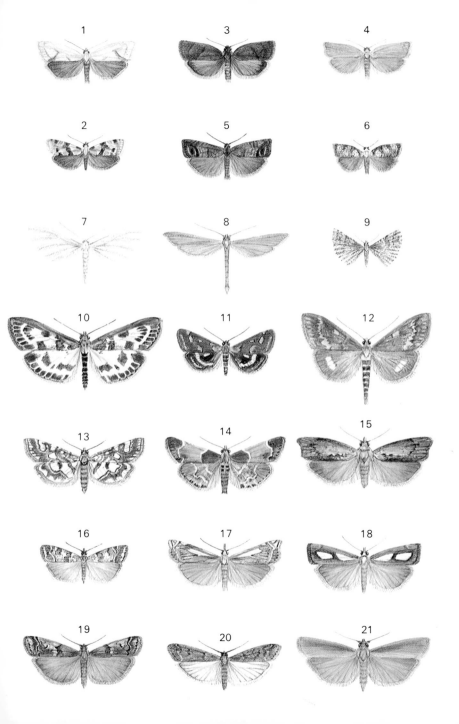

Plate 37

MOTHS – Order Lepidoptera (cont'd)

Micropterigidae Minute, metallic moths with functional jaws　　　p. 228
   1. *Micropterix calthella* (L.)
Eriocraniidae Small, metallic moths without functional jaws　　　p. 229
   2. *Eriocrania purpurella* (Haworth)
Nepticulidae　　　p. 229
Minute moths with 1st antennal segment forming an 'eye-cap': strong frenulum in male
   3. *Nepticula aurella* Stainton
Elachistidae Pointed hind wings　　　p. 235
   4. *Elachista bisulcella* Duponchel
Tineidae – Clothes Moths　　　p. 236
Proboscis reduced or absent: wings often shiny
   5. Case-bearing Clothes Moth – *Tinea pellionella* (L.)
   6. Common Clothes Moth – *Tineola bisselliella* (Hummel)
   7. Tapestry Moth – *Trichophaga tapetzella* (L.)
Yponomeutidae　　　p. 235
Palps long and forward-pointing: antennae often point forward at rest
   8. *Ypsolopha mucronella* (Scopoli)
   9. Diamond-back Moth – *Plutella xylostella* (L.)
   12. *Ethmia bipunctella* (Fabr.)
   13. *Yponomeuta padella* (L.)
Incurvariidae　　　p. 230
Mainly day-flying, with metallic wings: male antennae very long
   10. *Adela viridella* (Scopoli) male
   11. *Nemophora degeerella* (L.) male
Oecophoridae Usually with tuft of hair at base of antenna (fig. p. 235)　　p. 235
   14. *Depressaria pastinacella* (DeGeer)
   15. *Dasycera sulphurella* (Fabr.)
   16. Brown House Moth – *Hofmannophila pseudospretella* (Stainton)
Gelechiidae Up-turned palps: hind wing margin strongly curved (fig. p. 235)　p. 234
   17. Angoumois Grain Moth – *Sitotroga cerealella* (Olivier)
Gracillariidae　　　p. 236
Very small moths with narrow wings: front end raised at rest
   18. *Phyllonorycter alnifoliella* (Duponchel)
Glyphipterigidae Rather square wings, often metallic: large ocelli　　　p. 235
   19. *Glyphipterix haworthana* (Stephens)
Psychidae – Bagworms　　　p. 236
Males with feathery antennae and thinly scaled wings: females wingless
   20. *Sterrhopterix fusca* (Haworth) male
Coleophoridae Narrow pointed wings, almost all fringe　　　p. 236
   21. *Coleophora alticollella* Zeller
Momphidae　　　p. 235
Narrow and often brightly coloured wings
   22. *Glyphipteryx linneella* (Clerck)

All ×2

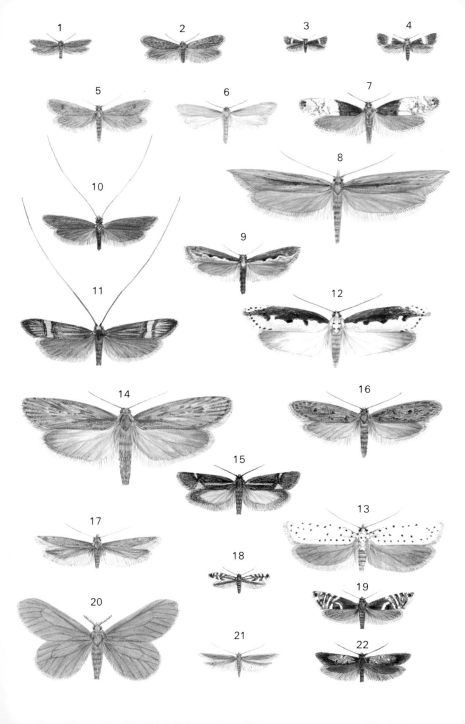

Plate 38

MOTHS – Order Lepidoptera (cont'd)

Notodontidae p. 237

Stout moths with relatively narrow wings: forewings often with tufts of hair on hind margin: vein M_2 of forewing not close to M_3 at base

1. Swallow Prominent – *Pheosia tremula* (Clerck)
2. Buff-tip – *Phalera bucephala* (L.)
3. Iron Prominent – *Notodonta dromedarius* (L.)
4. Puss Moth – *Cerura vinula* (L.)
5. Pale Prominent – *Pterostoma palpina* (Clerck)
6. Sallow Kitten – *Harpyia furcula* (Clerck)
7. White Prominent – *Leucodonta bicoloria* (Schiff.)

△ Thaumetopoeidae – Processionary Moths p. 238

No tuft of hair on hind edge of forewing: female has dense hair tuft at tip of abdomen

    8. Oak Processionary Moth – *Thaumetopoea processionea* L.

△ Ctenuchidae p. 239

Day-flying moths: black or brown with white spots: vein $Sc+R_1$ absent from hind wing

    9. *Syntomis phegea* L.

Arctiidae – Tiger, Ermine, and Footman Moths p. 238

Generally stout moths with bright colours: vein M_2 of forewing is close to M_3 at base: vein $Sc+R_1$ of hind wing usually arises near middle of cell

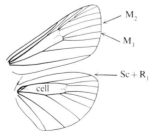

10. Buff Ermine – *Spilosoma lutea* Hufnagel
11. Ruby Tiger – *Phragmatobia fuliginosa* (L.)
12. Rosy Footman – *Miltochrista miniata* (Forster)
13. Common Footman – *Eilema lurideola* (Zincken)
14. Garden Tiger – *Arctia caja* (L.)
15. Cinnabar – *Tyria jacobaeae* (L.)

Plate 39

MOTHS – Order Lepidoptera (cont'd)

Noctuidae p. 239

A very large family with generally rather sombre or cryptically coloured forewings. Veins M_2 and M_3 in the forewing are very close together at the base: vein $Sc+R_1$ of hind wing is joined to cell only at the base

Hind wing

1. Alder Moth – *Acronicta alni* (L.)
2. Common Rustic – *Mesapamea secalis* (L.)
3. Heart and Dart – *Agrotis exclamationis* (L.)
4. Grey Dagger – *Acronicta psi* (L.)
5. Antler Moth – *Cerapteryx graminis* (L.)
6. Smoky Wainscot – *Leucania impura* (Hubner)
7. Green Silver-lines – *Pseudoips fagana* (Fabr.)
8. Cream-bordered Green Pea – *Earias clorana* (L.)
9. Centre-barred Sallow – *Atethmia centrago* (Haworth)
10. Shark Moth – *Cucullia umbratica* (L.)
11. Merveille-du-Jour – *Dichonia aprilina* (L.)
12. Red Sword-grass – *Xylena vetusta* (Hubner)
13. Herald – *Scoliopteryx libatrix* (L.)
14. Large Yellow Underwing – *Noctua pronuba* (L.)
15. Silver-Y – *Autographa gamma* (L.)
16. Red Underwing – *Catocala nupta* (L.)
17. Slender Burnished Brass – *Diachrysia orichalcea* (Fabr.)
18. Golden Plusia – *Polychrysia moneta* (Fabr.)

Plate 40

MOTHS – Order Lepidoptera (cont'd)

Lymantriidae – Tussock Moths   p. 240

Rather hairy moths with feathery antennae in males: proboscis vestigial or absent

    1. Pale Tussock – *Calliteara pudibunda* (L.)

    2. Yellow-tail – *Euproctis similis* (Fuessly)

  3a. Vapourer – *Orgyia antiqua* (L.) male

  3b. Vapourer female

    4. Reed Tussock – *Laelia caenosa* (Hubner)

    5. Black Arches – *Lymantria monacha* (L.)

▲ **6.** Gipsy Moth – *Lymantria dispar* (L.) male

Lasiocampidae   p. 242

Stout moths, mainly brown in colour, with no frenulum and with an enlarged humeral area of hind wing: no proboscis

    7. Oak Eggar – *Lasiocampa quercus* (L.) male

  8a. Drinker – *Euthrix potatoria* (L.) male

  8b. Drinker female

    9. Lappet – *Gastropacha quercifolia* (L.)

  10. Lackey – *Malacosoma neustria* (L.)

Endromidae   p. 242

  11. Kentish Glory – *Endromis versicolora* (L.) – the only member of this family

Saturniidae – Emperor Moths   p. 242

Large moths, with no frenulum: proboscis short or absent: European species all with eye-spots on the wings

  12. Emperor Moth – *Saturnia pavonia* (L.) male

Plate 41

MOTHS – Order Lepidoptera (cont'd)

Sphingidae – Hawkmoths p. 241

Stoutly-built, fast-flying moths with long, narrow forewings

1. Lime Hawkmoth – *Mimas tiliae* (L.)
2. Death's-head Hawkmoth – *Acherontia atropos* (L.)*
3. Pine Hawkmoth – *Hyloicus pinastri* (L.)
4. Hummingbird Hawkmoth – *Macroglossum stellatarum* L.
5. Eyed Hawkmoth – *Smerinthus ocellata* (L.)
6. Poplar Hawkmoth – *Laothoe populi* (L.)

▲ 7. *Proserpinus proserpina* Pallas
8. Privet Hawkmoth – *Sphinx ligustri* L.
9. Convolvulus Hawkmoth – *Agrius convolvuli* (L.)*

* A casual visitor to the British Isles

Plate 42

MOTHS – Order Lepidoptera (cont'd)

Sphingidae – Hawkmoths (cont'd)

p. 241

   1. Spurge Hawkmoth – *Hyles euphorbiae* (L.)*
   2. Oleander Hawkmoth – *Daphnis nerii* (L.)*
   3. Bedstraw Hawkmoth – *Hyles gallii* (Rottenburg)*
▲ **4.** Mediterranean Hawkmoth – *Hyles nicaea* (de Prunner)
   5. Striped Hawkmoth – *Hyles lineata livornica* (Esper)*
   6. Broad-bordered Bee Hawkmoth – *Hemaris fuciformis* (L.)
   7. Elephant Hawkmoth – *Deilephila elpenor* (L.)
   8. Silver-striped Hawkmoth – *Hippotion celerio* (L.)*
   9. Narrow-bordered Bee Hawkmoth – *Hemaris tityus* (L.)
 10. Small Elephant Hawkmoth – *Deilephila porcellus* (L.)

* A casual visitor to the British Isles

Plate 43

MOTHS – Order Lepidoptera (Cont'd)

Thyatiridae p. 240
Relatively stout moths with abdominal hearing organs
  1. Peach Blossom – *Thyatira batis* (L.)
  2. Buff Arches – *Habrosyne pyritoides* (Hufnagel)
  3. Frosted Green – *Polyploca ridens* (Fabr.)

Drepanidae – Hooktip Moths p. 240
Slender moths, usually with hooked wing-tips: hearing organs on upper side of abdomen
  4. Scalloped Hooktip – *Drepana lacertinaria* (L.)
  5. Pebble Hooktip – *Drepana falcataria* (L.)
  6. Chinese Character – *Cilix glaucata* (Scopoli)

Geometridae – Geometer Moths p. 240
Slender moths with hearing organs on lower side of abdomen: wings usually held out flat to the sides of the body at rest
  7. Lime-speck Pug – *Eupithecia centauriata* (Schiff.)
  8. Tawny Speckled Pug – *Eupithecia icterata* (Vill.)
  9. Green Carpet – *Colostygia pectinataria* (Knoch)
  10. Pretty Chalk Carpet – *Melanthia procellata* (Schiff.)
  11. Speckled Yellow – *Pseudopanthera macularia* (L.)
  12. Clouded Border – *Lomaspilis marginata* (L.)
  13. Blood-vein – *Timandra griseata* (Petersen)
 14a. Mottled Umber – *Erannis defoliaria* (Clerck) male
 14b. Mottled Umber female
  15. Early Thorn – *Selenia dentaria* (Fabr.)
  16. Magpie Moth – *Abraxas grossulariata* (L.)
  17. Large Emerald – *Geometra papilionaria* (L.)
 18a. Peppered Moth – *Biston betularia* (L.) normal form
 18b. Peppered Moth melanic form *carbonaria*
  19. Swallowtailed Moth – *Ourapteryx sambucaria* (L.)

Plate 44

BUTTERFLY CATERPILLARS – Order Lepidoptera (cont'd)

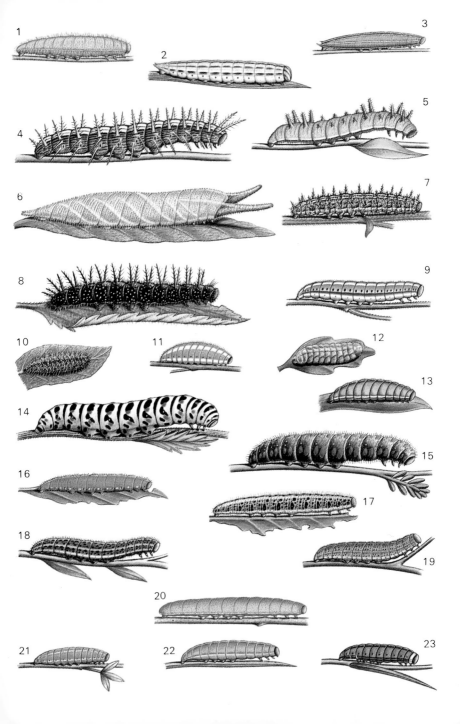

Plate 45

MOTH CATERPILLARS – Order Lepidoptera (cont'd)

Sphingidae p. 241
    1. Privet Hawkmoth – *Sphinx ligustri* L.
    2. Spurge Hawkmoth – *Hyles euphorbiae* (L.)
    3a. Elephant Hawkmoth – *Deilephila elpenor* (L.)
    3b. Elephant Hawkmoth caterpillar displaying

Notodontidae p. 237
    4. Puss Moth – *Cerura vinula* (L.) in threat posture
    5. Buff-tip – *Phalera bucephala* (L.)
    6. Iron Prominent – *Notodonta dromedarius* (L.)
    7. Lesser Swallow Prominent – *Pheosia gnoma* (Fabr.)

Lymantriidae p. 240
    8. Vapourer – *Orgyia antiqua* (L.)
    9. Pale Tussock – *Calliteara pudibunda* (L.)
    10. Yellow-tail – *Euproctis similis* (Fuessly)

Lasiocampidae p. 242
    11. Lackey – *Malacosoma neustria* (L.)
    12. Drinker – *Euthrix potatoria* (L.)

Saturniidae p. 242
    13. Emperor – *Saturnia pavonia* (L.)

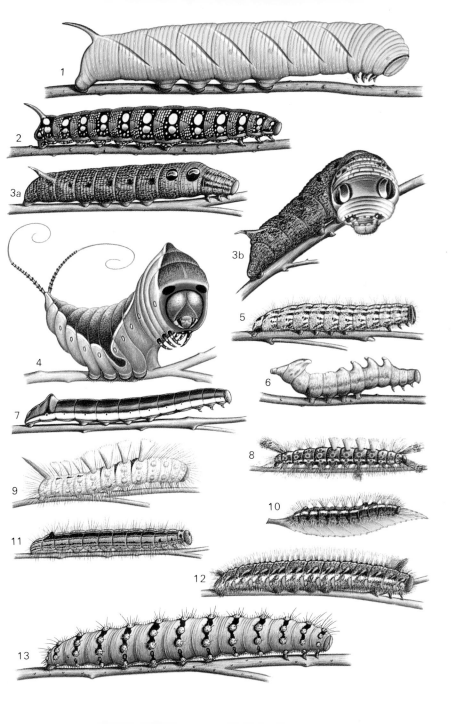

Plate 46
MOTH CATERPILLARS – Order Lepidoptera (cont'd)

Δ **Ctenuchidae**   p. 239
    1. *Syntomis phegea* (L.)

Arctiidae   p. 238
    2. Garden Tiger – *Arctia caja* (L.)
    3. Jersey Tiger – *Euplagia quadripunctaria* (Poda)
    4. Buff Ermine – *Spilosoma lutea* (Hufnagel)
    5. Cinnabar – *Tyria jacobaeae* (L.)

Noctuidae   p. 239
    6. Green Silver-lines – *Pseudoips fagana* (Fabr.)
    7. Alder Moth – *Acronicta alni* (L.)
    8. Grey Dagger – *Acronicta psi* (L.)
    9. Sycamore Moth – *Acronicta aceris* (L.)
    10. Knotgras – *Acronicta rumicis* (L.)
    11. Cabbage Moth – *Mamestra brassicae* (L.)
    12. Large Yellow Underwing – *Noctua pronuba* (L.)
    13. Dot Moth – *Melanchra persicariae* (L.)
    14. Broom Moth – *Ceramica pisi* (L.)
    15. Old Lady – *Mormo maura* (L.)
    16. Small Angle Shades – *Euplexia lucipara* (L.)
    17. Clay Moth – *Mythimna ferrago* (Fabr.)
    18. Hebrew Character – *Orthosia gothica* (L.)
    19. Mullein Moth – *Cucullia verbasci* (L.)

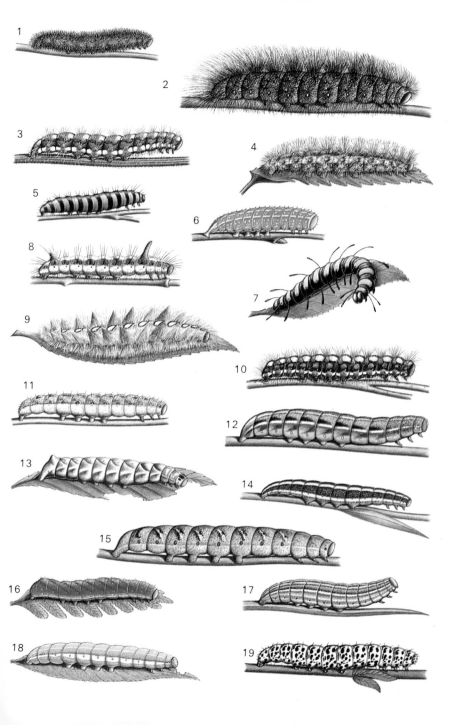

Plate 47

MOTH CATERPILLARS – Order Lepidoptera (cont'd)

Noctuidae (cont'd)   p. 239
  1. The Spectacle – *Abrostola triplasia* (L.)
  2. Herald – *Scoliopteryx libatrix* (L.)
  3. Burnished Brass – *Diachrysia chrysitis* (L.)
  4. Red Underwing – *Catocala nupta* (L.)

Drepanidae   p. 240
  5. Oak Hooktip – *Drepana binaria* (Hufnagel)

Geometridae   p. 240
  6. Treble-bar – *Aplocera plagiata* (L.)
  7. Large Thorn – *Ennomos autumnaria* (Werneburg)
  8. Swallowtailed Moth – *Ourapteryx sambucaria* (L.)
  9. Magpie Moth – *Abraxas grossulariata* (L.)
  10. Mottled Umber – *Erannis defoliaria* (Clerck)
  11. Peppered Moth – *Biston betularia* (L.)

Zygaenidae   p. 231
  12. 6-spot Burnet – *Zygaena filipendulae* (L.)

Hepialidae   p. 229
  13. Ghost Swift – *Hepialus humuli* (L.)

Cossidae   p. 230
  14. Goat Moth – *Cossus cossus* (L.)

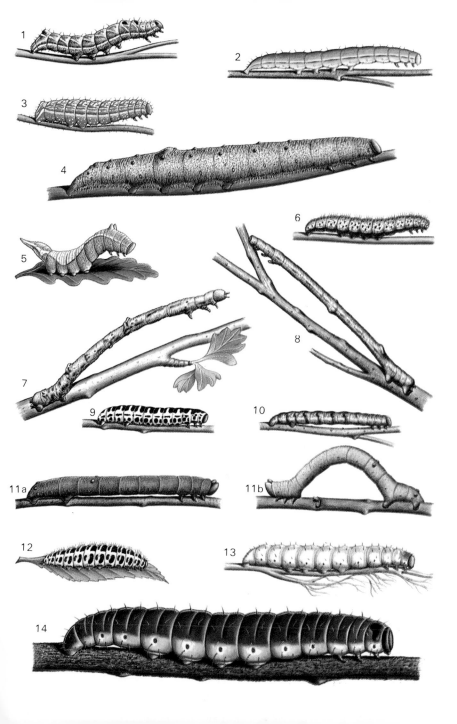

Plate 48

CADDIS FLIES – Order Trichoptera

Insects with hairy wings and few cross veins: wings held roofwise at rest, with antennae held forward: usually near water. Text p. 245

Phryganeidae p. 250
Spurs 2,4,4: very long discoidal cell in forewing
    1. *Phryganea grandis* L. ×2

Philopotamidae p. 251
Last palpal segment longer than all others together: ocelli present: spurs 2,4,4
    2. *Philopotamus montanus* (Donovan) ×3

Palp

Limnephilidae p. 250
1 spur or none on front tibia
    3. *Limnephilus lunatus* Curtis ×2
    4. *Anabolia nervosa* (Curtis) ×2

Brachycentridae p. 251
3 spurs on hind tibia: 1st antennal segment short and hairy
    5. *Brachycentrus subnubilus* Curtis ×3

Hydropsychidae p. 251
Last palpal segment longer than all other together: no ocelli:
spurs 2,4,4
    6. *Hydropsyche contubernalis* McLach. ×3

Polycentropidae p. 251
Last palpal segment much longer than all others together: no ocelli: spurs 3,4,4
    7. *Polycentropus flavomaculatus* (Pictet) ×5

Hydroptilidae p. 251
Very small insects with long fringes on wings
    8. *Hydroptila sparsa* Curtis ×10

The insects illustrated are all males. There are often differences in the shape and size of the wings between the sexes. The drawings in the central column show a variety of larval cases.

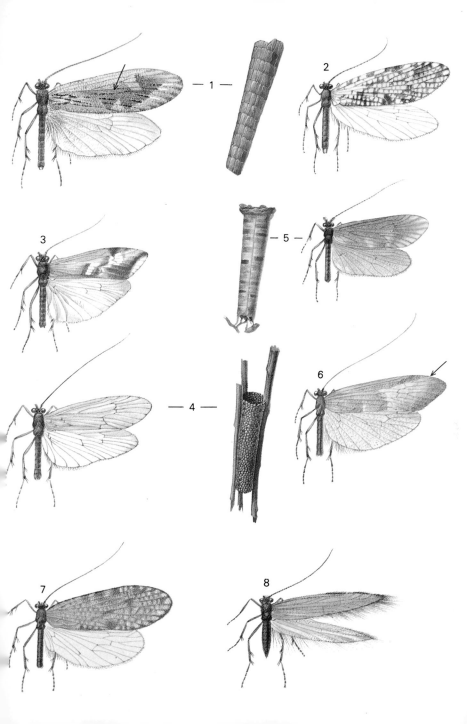

— 1 —

— 5 —

— 4 —

Plate 49

CADDIS FLIES – Order Trichoptera (cont'd)

Rhyacophilidae p. 252
1st and 2nd palpal segments short and thick, with 3rd segment long and thin: no discoidal cell: spurs 3,4,4
    1. *Rhyacophila obliterata* McLach. ×3   Palp

Psychomyiidae p. 251
Last palpal segment much longer than others together: no ocelli: very small discoidal cell: 1st apical fork usually absent
    2. *Tinodes waeneri* (L.) ×4
    3. *Ecnomus tenellus* (Rambur) ×6 – a rare species in which 1st apical fork is present and spurs are 3,4,4 instead of the usual 2,4,4 in this family

Odontoceridae p. 252
Antennae toothed on inner side
    4. *Odontocerum albicorne* (Scopoli) ×3

Leptoceridae p. 252
Antennae very long: only 2 spurs on hind tibia
    5. *Athripsodes aterrimus* (Stephens) ×3

Glossosomatidae p. 252
1st and 2nd palpal segments short and thick, with 3rd segment long and thin: discoidal cell present: spurs 2,4,4
    6. *Agapetus fuscipes* Curtis ×6

Molannidae p. 252
No ocelli: no discoidal cell: spurs 2,4,4
    7. *Molanna angustata* Curtis ×3

Beraeidae p. 252
No ocelli: no discoidal cell: spurs 2,2,4
    8. *Ernodes articularis* (Pictet) ×6

The insects illustrated are all males. There are often differences in the shape and size of the wings between the sexes. The drawings in the central column show a variety of larval cases.

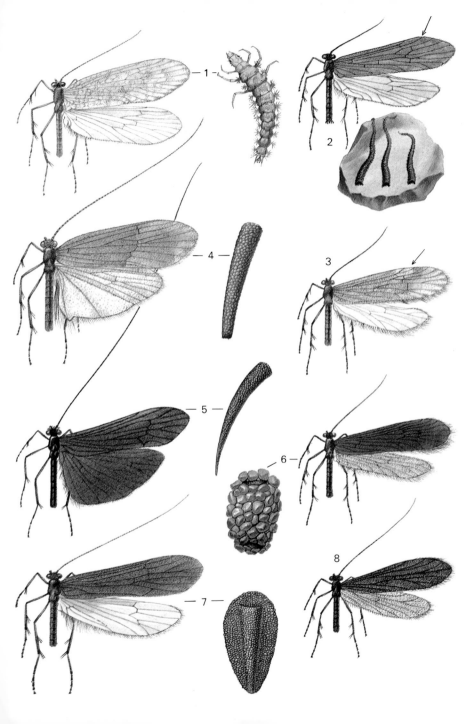

Plate 50

SAWFLIES – Order Hymenoptera
Sub-order Symphyta: insects with no marked 'waist'

Text p. 256

	Cimbicidae	p. 260
	Strongly clubbed antennae	
	1. Hawthorn Sawfly – *Trichiosoma tibiale* Stephens	
	Siricidae	p. 259
	Large, cylindrical insects: vein Rs recurved at tip	
	2a. *Urocerus gigas* (L.) female	
	2b. *Urocerus gigas* male	
	Xiphydriidae	p. 259
	Cylindrical: vein Rs not recurved	
	3. *Xiphydria prolongata* (Geoffroy) ×1.25	
Δ	**Megalodontidae**	p. 259
	Flattened: flabellate antennae: cross vein 2r present	
	4. *Megalondontes klugii* Leach ×1.25	
	Pamphilidae	p. 258
	Flattened: thread-like antennae of 11 or more segments	
	5. *Pamphilus sylvaticus* (L.) ×1.25	
	Tenthredinidae	p. 259
	Antennae normally 9-segmented	
	6a. *Pontania proxima* (Lepeletier) ×1.5	
	6b. *Pontania* galls on willow	
	7a. Gooseberry Sawfly – *Nematus ribesii* (Scopoli) male ×2	
	7b. Gooseberry Sawfly female ×2	
Δ	**Blasticotomidae**	p. 260
	Pear-shaped cell in centre of wing	
	8. *Blasticotoma filiceti* Klug. ×1.5	
Δ	**Orussidae**	p. 258
	Antennae inserted below eyes: no closed sub-marginals in hind wing	
	9. *Orussus abietinus* Scopoli ×2	
	Argidae	p. 260
	Antennae 3-segmented, the 3rd being very long	
	10. *Arge ustulata* (L.) ×1.5	
	Cephidae	p. 259
	Slender sawflies with no cenchri:	
	11. *Cephus pygmaeus* (L.) ×1.5	
	Diprionidae	p. 260
	Male antennae feathery: cross-vein 2r absent	
	12a. Pine Sawfly – *Diprion pini* (L.) male ×1.5	
	12b. Pine Sawfly female ×1.5	
	Xyelidae	p. 258
	Thread-like flagellum beyond 3rd antennal segment	
	13. *Xyela julii* (Brébisson) ×4	

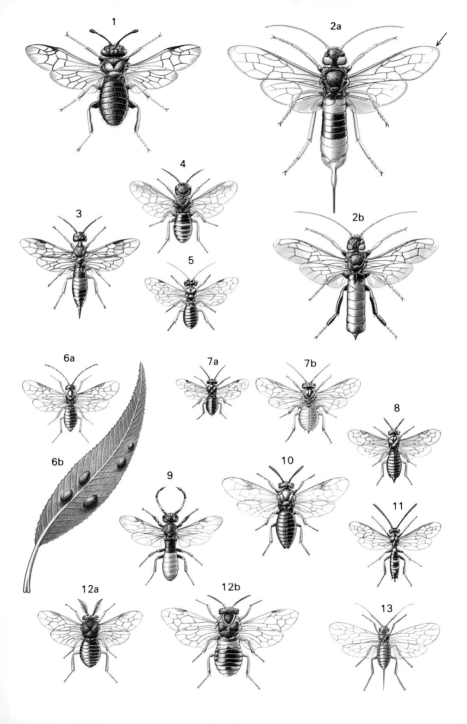

Plate 51

GALL WASPS– Order Hymenoptera (cont'd)
Sub-Order Apocrita: insects with a marked 'waist'

Cynipidae – Gall Wasps p. 266

Small winged or wingless insects with gaster flattened from side to side: characteristic venation in winged insects. The insects induce galls on a wide variety of plants, but are especially common on oaks.

1a. *Andricus kollari* (Hartig) ×1.5
1b. *A. kollari* in resting attitude ×2
1c. Marble galls of *A. kollari* on oak
2a. *Andricus fecundator* (Hartig) ×1.5
2b. Artichoke galls of *A. fecundator* on oak
2c. Sectioned artichoke galls showing inner chambers
3a. *Neuroterus quercusbaccarum* (L.) ×3
3b. Spangle galls of asexual generation on oak leaf
3c. Currant galls of sexual generation on oak catkins
4a. *Diplolepis rosae* (L.) ×3
4b. Bedeguar gall or robin's pincushion on wild rose
4c. Section of old bedeguar gall
5. Pea galls of *Diplolepis eglanteriae* (Hartig) (top) and *D. rosarum* (Curtis) on wild rose
6a. *Diastrophus rubi* (Bouché) ×3
6b. Old gall on bramble stem
7a. *Biorhiza pallida* (Olivier) sexual generation ×3
7b. Oak apple gall of sexual generation on oak twig
7c. Asexual generation ×4
7d. Galls of asexual generation on oak root

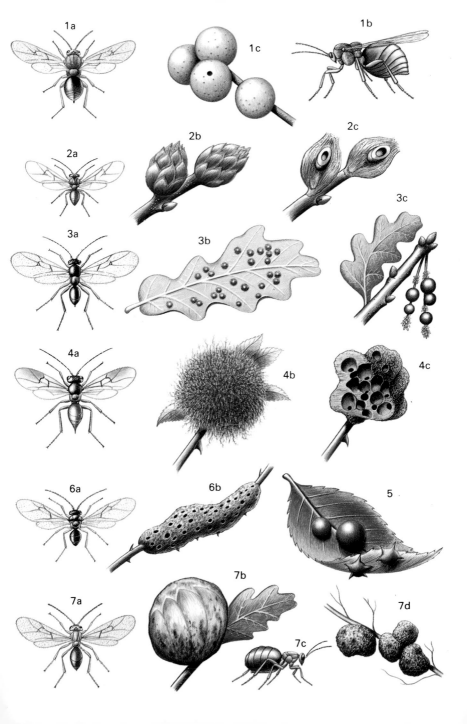

1a

1c

1b

2a

2b

2c

3a

3b

3c

4a

4b

4c

6a

6b

5

7a

7b

7c

7d

Plate 52

ICHNEUMONS & OTHER PARASITES – Order Hymenoptera
Sub-order Apocrita (cont'd)

Evaniidae   p. 264

Gaster short and attached near top of propodeum by a long petiole (fig. p. 264)
    1. *Evania appendigaster* (L.) ×1.25

Gasteruptiidae   p. 265

Long, narrow gaster attached near top of propodeum
    2. *Gasteruption jaculator* (L.) female ×1.25

Aulacidae   p. 264

Pear-shaped gaster attached near top of propodeum by a short petiole
    3. *Aulacus striatus* Jurine female ×1.25

Ichneumonidae – Ichneumons   p. 265

Antennae with over 16 segments: forewing with a stigma and with cross-vein 2m-cu:
costal cell almost obliterated
    4. *Netelia testacea* (Gravenhorst) ×1.25
    5. *Amblyteles armatorius* (Forster) ×1.25
    6. *Ichneumon suspiciosus* Wesmael ×1.25
    7a. *Rhyssa persuasoria* (L.) female
    7b. *Rhyssa* in the act of egg-laying

Forewing of ichneumon

2m–cu

Trigonalyidae   p. 265

Antennae with over 16 segments: costal cell clearly visible
    8. *Trigonalis hahnii* (Spinola) ×2

Pteromalidae   p. 268

Metallic coloured, often with triangular gaster: hind coxae not conspicuously larger
than others
    9. *Pteromalus puparum* L. ×6

Torymidae   p. 268

Metallic coloured: hind coxae much larger than the others: hind femur without a row
of teeth beneath: ovipositor very long
    10. *Torymus nitens* (Walker) female ×6

Platygasteridae   p. 269

Minute insects with virtually no veins: antennae usually 10-segmented and slightly
clubbed
    11. *Platygaster* sp. ×6

Braconidae   p. 266

Antennae with over 16 segments: costal cell of forewing almost obliterated: cross
vein 2m-cu absent
    12a. *Apanteles glomeratus* (L.) ×5
    12b. Larvae and pupae surrounding
       dead host caterpillar

no 2m–cu

Forewing of braconid

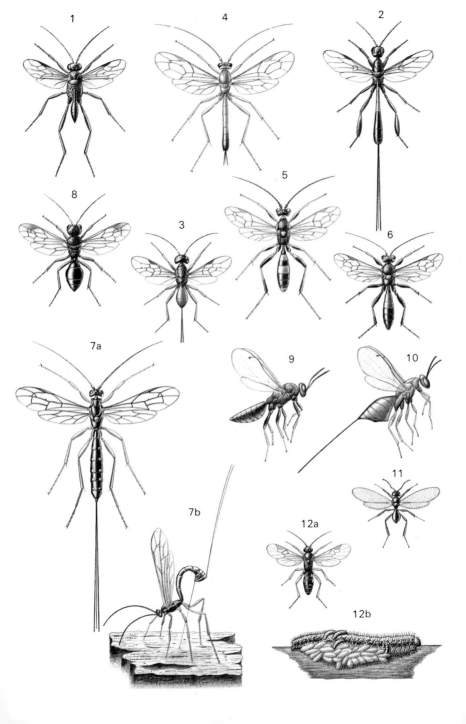

Plate 53

ANTS & ASSORTED PARASITES – Order Hymenoptera
Sub-order Apocrita (cont'd)

Mutillidae – Velvet Ants p. 270

Hairy insects with short, stout legs: pronotum reaches back to tegulae: females wingless

  1a. *Mutilla europaea* L. male ×1.5
  1b. *Mutilla europaea* female ×1.5

Tiphiidae p. 270

Smooth-bodied, with pronotum reaching back to tegulae: females often wingless

  2a. *Methocha ichneumonides* Latreille male ×1.5
  2b. *Methocha ichneumonides* female ×1.5

△ **Scoliidae** p. 270

Large, hairy insects with stout legs and dark wings

  3. *Scolia flavifrons* Fabr. male (female is larger, with an orange head)

Sapygidae p. 270

Both sexes winged, with small jugal lobe on hind wing: pronotum reaches back to tegulae

  4. *Sapyga quinquepunctatum* (Fabr.) ×2

Chrysididae – Ruby-Tailed Wasps p. 269

No closed cells in hind wing: body usually metallic

▲ **5.** *Stilbum cyanurum* Forster ×2
  6. *Chrysis ignita* (L.) ×2

Formicidae – Ants p. 270

Front part of gaster slender, with one or two humps or scale-like outgrowths: antennae normally elbowed: winged or wingless

  7a. Wood Ant – *Formica rufa* L. male ×2
  7b. Wood Ant new queen ×2
  7c. Wood Ant worker ×2
▲ **8a.** Harvester Ant *Messor barbara* L. male ×1.5
  8b. Harvester Ant soldier ×1.5
  8c. Harvester Ant new queen ×1.5
  8d. Harvester Ant worker ×1.5

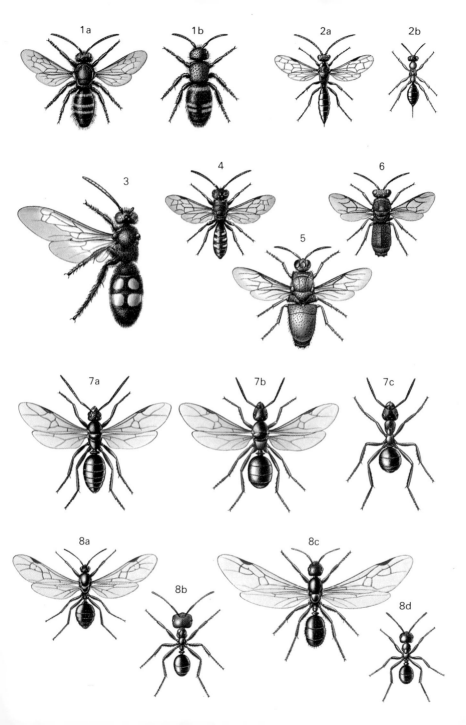

Plate 54

SPIDER-HUNTING & DIGGER WASPS – Order Hymenoptera
Sub-order Apocrita (cont'd)

Pompilidae – Spider-Hunting Wasps   p. 275

Pronotum reaches back to tegulae: wings laid flat at rest: hind femur relatively long

▲ **1.** *Cryptocheilus comparatus* Smith
   2. *Anoplius viaticus* (L.) ×1.5

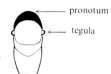

Thorax from above

Sphecidae – Digger Wasps   p. 276

Pronotum does not reach back to tegulae: hind tarsi slender

   3. *Ammophila sabulosa* (L.) ×1.5
   4. *Podalonia hirsuta* (Scopoli) ×1.5
   5. *Argogorytes mystaceus* (L.) ×1.5
   6. *Mellinus arvensis* (L.) ×2
   7. *Pemphredon lugubris* Latreille ×2
   8. *Ectemnius cephalotes* (Olivier) ×2
   9. *Cerceris arenaria* (L.) ×2
  10. *Crabro cribrarius* (L.) ×2

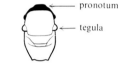

Thorax from above

The black and yellow members of the Sphecidae could be confused with the social wasps (Vespidae) at first, but they can be distinguished by the pronotum and by the fact that the wings are laid flat at rest. The social wasps all fold their wings lengthwise and the wings thus appear very narrow (fig. p. 273)

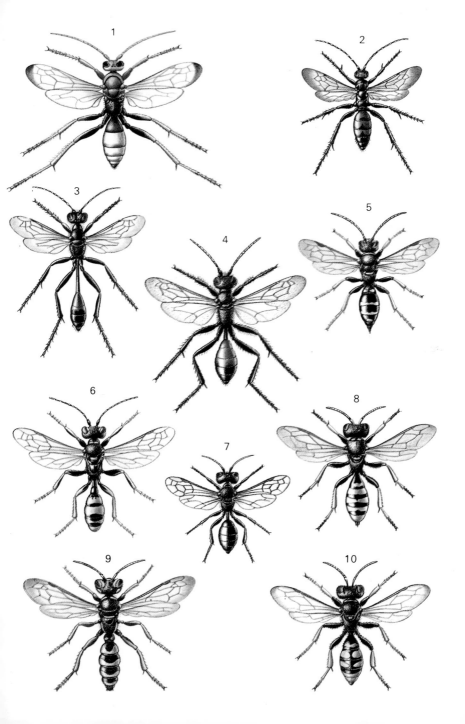

Plate 55

WASPS – Order Hymenoptera
Sub-order Apocrita (cont'd)

Sphecidae (cont'd)

p. 276

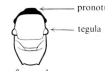

Thorax from above

▲ **1.** *Sphex maxillosus* Fabr.
▲ **2.** *Sceliphron destillatorium* Illiger
▲ **3.** *Bembix rostrata* L.
▲ **4.** *Liris praetermissa* Richards ×2
▲ **5.** *Pison atrum* Spinola ×2

Eumenidae

p. 273

Pronotum extends back to tegulae: eyes deeply notched and almost crescent-shaped: wings folded lengthwise at rest 1 spur on middle tibia

Thorax from above

▲ **6.** *Delta unguiculata* Villers
   7a. Potter Wasp – *Eumenes coarctatus* (L.) ×1.5
   7b. Clay nest of *E. coarctatus*
   8. *Odynerus spinipes* (L.) ×1.5

Vespidae – Social Wasps

p. 274

Pronotum extends back to tegulae: eyes deeply notched and almost crescent-shaped: wings folded lengthwise at rest 2 spurs on middle tibia

▲ **9.** Paper Wasp – *Polistes gallicus* L. ×1.5

folded wing ⟶

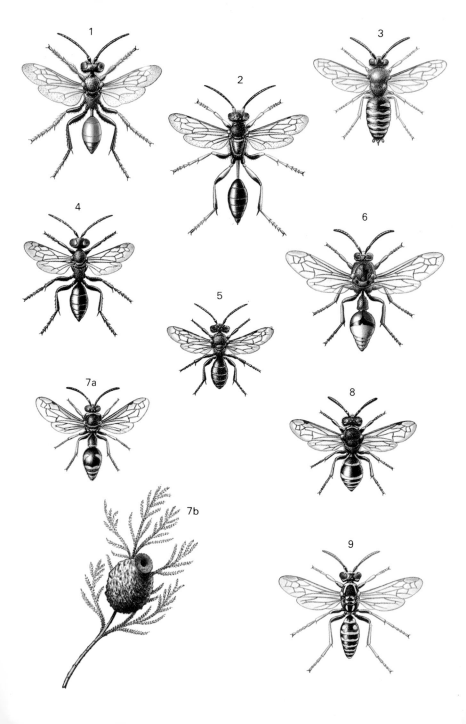

Plate 56

SOCIAL WASPS – Order Hymenoptera
Sub-order Apocrita (cont'd)

Vespidae (Cont'd) p. 274

  1a. Common Wasp – *Vespula vulgaris* (L.) male
  1b. Common Wasp face of worker
  1c. Common Wasp – queen
  1d. Common Wasp – worker
    2. Hornet – *Vespa crabro* L.
    3. *Dolichovespula media* DeGeer
    4. Red Wasp – *Vespula rufa* (L.)
    5. Tree Wasp – *Dolichovespula sylvestris* (Scopoli)
    6. German Wasp – *Vespula germanica* (Fabr.)
    7. Norwegian Wasp – *Dolichovespula norwegica* (Fabr.)
  8a. Cuckoo Wasp – *Vespula austriaca* (Panzer) male
  8b. Cuckoo Wasp female face
  8c. Cuckoo Wasp female

All are workers unless otherwise stated, and all are slightly enlarged.

The social wasps differ mainly in their facial patterns and in the number of yellow thoracic spots. Abdominal patterns are less reliable, as they vary a good deal within a species. Other useful pointers are the length of the cheek between the eye and the jaw, and the colour of the basal antennal segment. It is yellow in all males, but either black or yellow in the workers, according to the species. Males are easily distinguished by their long antennae

Plate 57

SOLITARY BEES – Order Hymenoptera
Sub-order Apocrita (cont'd)

Apidae – Bees   p. 277

Pronotum does not reach back to tegulae: insects generally hairy, with broad hind tarsi

  1. *Hylaeus signatus* (Panzer) ×2
  2. *Colletes succinctus* (L.) ×2
  3. *Panurgus banksianus* (Kirby) ×2
  4. *Dasypoda altercator* (Harris) ×1.5
  5. *Macropis europaea* Warncke ×1.5
  6. *Stelis punctulatissima* (Kirby) ×1.5
  7a. *Coelioxys inermis* (Kirby) male ×2
  7b. *Coelioxys inermis* female ×2
  8. *Chelostoma florisomne* (L.) ×1.5
  9. *Anthidium manicatum* (L.) ×2
▲ **10.** *Anthidium florentinum* Fabr. ×1.5
▲ **12.** *Anthidium variegatum* Latreille ×2

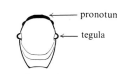

Thorax from above

Plate 58

SOLITARY BEES – Order Hymenoptera
Sub-order Apocrita (cont'd)

Apidae (cont.d) p. 277

   1a. Leaf-cutter Bee – *Megachile centuncularis* (L.) male ×2
   1b. Leaf-cutter Bee female ×2
   1c. Leaf-cutter bee female in flight with leaf fragment
   2a. *Eucera longicornis* (L.) male ×1.5
   2b. *Eucera longicornis* female ×1.5
▲ **3.** *Chalicodoma parietina* L.
   4a. *Osmia rufa* (L.) male ×1.5
   4b. *Osmia rufa* female ×1.5
   5. *Sphecodes spinulosus* von Hagens ×1.5
   6a. Tawny Mining Bee – *Andrena fulva* (Müller) male ×1.5
   6b. Tawny Mining Bee female ×1.5
   7. *Nomada fulvicornis* Fabr. ×1.5
▲ **8.** *Halictus scabiosa* (Rossi) ×2
   9. *Lasioglossum malachurus* (Kirby) ×2
   10. *Ceratina cyanea* (Kirby) ×3

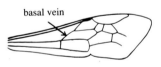

Abdomen of *Megachile*, hollowed in front

Bees belonging to the genera *Halictus, Lasioglossum,* and *Andrena* are often confused, although *Halictus* and *Lasioglossum* rarely have such flat abdomens as *Andrena*. The best way to separate the genera is to look at the basal vein, near the middle of the forewing: This vein is almost straight in *Andrena*, but in the other genera – and in *Sphecodes* – it is quite strongly curved.

basal vein

Andrena   *Sphecodes*

Plate 59

BEES – Order Hymenoptera
Sub-order Apocrita (cont'd)

Apidae (cont'd)   p. 277

   1. *Epeolus cruciger* (Panzer) ×3

   2. *Melecta albifrons* (Forster) female ×1.5

 3a. Honey Bee – *Apis mellifera* L. drone ×1.5

 3b. Honey Bee queen ×1.5

 3c. Honey Bee worker ×1.5

 4a. *Anthophora plumipes* (Pallas) male ×1.5

 4b. *Anthophora plumipes* female ×1.5

▲ **5.** *Anthophora hispanica* Fabr. ×1.5

▲ **6.** *Xylocopa violacea* (L.)

 7a. Buff-tailed Bumble Bee – *Bombus terrestris* L. male*

 7b. Buff-tailed Bumble Bee worker*

 7c. Buff-tailed Bumble Bee queen*

* British race: tail is white on continent

Plate 60

BUMBLE BEES & CUCKOO BEES – Order Hymenoptera
Sub-order Apocrita (cont'd)

Apidae (cont'd)   p. 277

All insects illustrated are queens unless otherwise stated.

All are ×1.25

The species of *Psithyrus* are cuckoo bees, laying their eggs in the nests of other species. Each species of *Psithyrus* is very similar to its normal host species and difficult to separate from it, although the cuckoo bees have much less hair on their abdomens and the shiny body plates show through. Cuckoo bees have no pollen baskets in either sex.

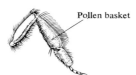
Pollen basket

Hind legs of *Bombus* (left) and *Psithyrus*

into timber in the larval stages. Although sometimes placed in the Scolytidae, it is generally given its own family – the **Platypodidae**. *P. cylindrus* (Pl. 25) is the only European species.

Collecting and Preserving
Beetles can be collected almost anywhere and at any time just by looking. Many of them are rather sluggish and easily boxed. Sweeping the vegetation will produce big hauls of leaf beetles and weevils, while pitfall traps (see p. 29) or simply turning over stones will yield many ground-living species. Most normal killing agents are suitable for beetles, although these are not the easiest insects to kill. Boiling water can be useful for those species that don't have hairs or scales. Direct pinning can be used if the insects are large enough and it is conventional to pin through the right elytron to leave the coxae and other critical features of the underside available for study. The smaller species can be mounted on points and here, so that the underside remains visible for study, it is common practice to bend the tip of the point down and attach it to the right side of the beetle (fig. p. 31). Carding is suitable for a display collection, but the underside of the insect is not then visible. The smallest species are best preserved in spirit.

Order Strepsiptera – Stylopids

Recognition features Minute insects whose early stages are spent as parasites of other insects. Adult males are free-living and have the forewings reduced to tiny club-shaped structures rather like the halteres of the true flies. The hind wings are broad and membranous. Adult females are grub-like and generally remain inside the host.

These tiny parasites are quite common, but they are rarely encountered by the non-specialist and therefore have no common name. There are about 400 known species, of which about 30 are found in Europe. About 20 of them occur in the British Isles. Their most frequent hosts are planthoppers and various bees and wasps, especially bees of the genera *Andrena* and *Halictus*. Attack by stylopids commonly causes ste-rility in the host, especially in the female, and the parasites must play some part in the natural regulation of the host population.
    As far as the adult insects are concerned, the stylopids are a very distinct group, but a study of the larvae and their metamorphosis reveals a number of similarities with some beetle families and some entomologists treat the stylopids as a specialised group of the Coleoptera.
    The male insect is under 4mm long and is dark brown. The head is dominated by the protruding compound eyes and the abnormally thick antennae. These have be-tween four and seven segments, some of which may bear projections giving the an-

A male stylopid, showing the stout antennae and the large, membranous wings

tennae a branched appearance. The mouth-parts are of the biting type, but are very much reduced. The first two thoracic segments are small but the metathorax is well developed, in connection with the development of the hind wings, and may account for more than half the body length. The club-shaped forewings act as balancers like the halteres of the true flies (p. 175). The name Strepsiptera means twisted wings (Greek *strepsis* = a twist) and refers to the twisted nature of these organs. The hind wings are large, white, and delicate and supported by a reduced venation.

In all the European species the female stylopids remain parasitic throughout their lives. They are grub-like, with no eyes, legs, or antennae, and they remain inside the last larval skin. Only the head and thorax are visible, sticking out between two abdominal segments of the host. A few exotic species have free-living females, with eyes, antennae, and legs, although the body remains larviform and wingless.

Males are rare in some species, and reproduction is then largely parthenogenetic, but the following account is fairly typical of those species parasitising bees. The male parasites emerge from their hosts, usually while they are flying, and they seek out bees carrying female parasites. The complex male antennae presumably play some part in this and several males will home in on a single female. On the underside of the female thorax there is an opening leading into the brood canal, which is simply the space between her body and the old larval skin that still surrounds her. Male sperm passes into the brood canal and eventually finds its way into the genital pore at the rear of the female. After fertilisation, the eggs develop and hatch inside the mother's body. The first-stage larvae are minute, active, woodlouse-shaped creatures and they find their way on to the surface of the host. From there they pass to other host insects, probably by way of flowers, but they are not interested in these adult hosts other than as taxis. The young stylopids must get into the hosts' nests and find some larvae. Having entered a host larva, the parasite moults into a legless maggot, living in the body cavity of the host and absorbing food from its blood. The parasite matures soon after the host emerges from its pupa.

Stylopids do not kill their hosts but they have a great effect on them, particularly on the reproductive system and the secondary sexual characters. Male hosts tend to become more female and vice-versa. The size and proportions of the body also alter and stylopised individuals have often been described as new species because of these differences. Male parasites seem to have a much greater effect on their hosts than female parasites.

There are three main families – the **Stylopidae**, whose members parasitise bees and wasps, and the **Halictophagidae** and **Elenchidae** which are mainly associated with planthoppers. Our two commonest genera are *Stylops* and *Elenchus*, parasitising *Andrena* bees and delphacid planthoppers respectively.

Collecting and Preserving
Male stylopids can sometimes be seen drifting around flowers in the sunshine, but the best way to collect these insects is to search for stylopised hosts and try to keep them alive until the parasites emerge. Parasitised hosts can usually be recognised by the swollen abdomen. They also tend to be rather lethargic. The parasites themselves must be preserved in spirit or mounted on microscope slides.

*A typical scorpion fly (*Panorpa *sp.), showing the characteristic beak and the up-turned tail of the male.*

Order Mecoptera: Scorpion Flies (Plate 15)

Recognition features Minute and medium-sized insects in which the head is prolonged downwards into a beak with the biting jaws at the lower end. Two similar pairs of wings are usually present and the tip of the male abdomen is frequently turned up and swollen, giving the insects their common name. The beak makes these insects quite unmistakable.

This is a small group of insects with only about 300 known species but, like the Neuroptera, it is an ancient group. In fact, the oldest known endopterygotes – about 250 million years old – were mecopterans and it is believed that the butterflies and moths, caddis flies, two-winged flies, and fleas all evolved from mecopteran-like ancestors. Some of the present-day Australian scorpion flies appear to have survived with little change since Permian times and they qualify for the title of 'living fossils'.

About 30 species live in Europe, but only four are found in the British Isles. The major family is the **Panorpidae**, in which the terminal segments of the male abdomen are carried scorpion-fashion above the body – hence the common name given to the whole order. Despite their name and appearance, however, the insects are quite harmless. *Panorpa* species are fully winged, but spend much of their adult lives crawling on vegetation in shady places: they are real hedgerow insects. They are largely carnivorous but seem loathe to attack living prey and live mainly on dead insects and other carrion. They even steal food from spiders' webs. They have also been known to nibble at bird droppings and on more than one occasion to take an interest in human sweat. Vegetable matter is not ignored, with over-ripe gooseberries appearing particularly attractive to these insects

The minute Snow Flea (*Boreus hyemalis*) is a member of the **Boreidae**. Under 3mm long, it feeds on mosses and can be found in autumn and winter. It often seen when snow is on the ground, a feature which, added to its jumping ability, is responsible for its common name.

The only other European family is the **Bittacidae**, whose members have very long and slender legs. The tarsi are prehensile and the insects spend most of their time hanging from plants by their front legs. They catch small insects with the tarsi of the hind legs. The hanging insects look very much like crane-flies, but the beak will always distinguish them and the scorpion flies also have four wings. There are two species in southern Europe, *Bittacus italicus* being fairly common.

Boreus, the Snow Flea. The female has a prominent ovipositor and resembles a minute cricket

Bittacus *hanging by its front legs and waiting to catch a passing fly with its hind legs. The 5th tarsal segment snaps back on the 4th segment to grasp they prey, which is held firmly by tiny teeth on the inner margins of these segments*

Although the common name for a member of this order is scorpion fly, only the males of the family Panorpidae have the up-turned abdomen. The diagnostic feature of the order is the beak, formed largely from the clypeus, labrum, and labium. The slender, toothed mandibles are carried at the lower end. The filiform antennae have 40 or 50 segments and the compound eyes are well developed. Three ocelli are normally present, although absent in *Boreus*.

In *Panorpa* the two pairs of wings are very similar and carry a variable amount of dark mottling. They are relatively long and narrow (Mecoptera is derived from the Greek *mekos*, meaning length) but, apart from an unbranched Cu$_1$, the venation is complete – clearly indicating the primitive origin of these insects. There is a simple wing-coupling mechanism consisting of jugal and humeral lobes and a few bristles (fig. p. 18), but flight is very weak and the insects rarely fly far. The wings of *Boreus* have little claim to be wings at all, being reduced to two pairs of bristles in the male and one pair of scales in the female.

The ninth abdominal segment of *Panorpa* males is considerably swollen and, as already described, raised above the rest of the abdomen. The female abdomen tapers considerably towards the rear, although in living specimens the last four segments are usually telescoped inside each other. Both sexes have tiny cerci at the apex. The shapes and relative sizes of the abdominal segments are useful in identifying the various species of *Panorpa*. The degree of spotting on the wings also varies between the species, although it cannot always be relied on for specific identification.

The eggs are laid in the soil. The *Panorpa* larva bears three pairs of thoracic legs and eight pairs of abdominal prolegs. It lives as a scavenger in the soil and leaf litter and pupates in a cavity in the soil. The pupa is of the exarate type and moves to the surface in preparation for the emergence of the adult. *Bittacus* has a similar life history. The larva of *Boreus* is of the curved scarabaeiform type, with no abdominal legs. Like the adult, it lives among mosses and pupates there or in the soil just below.

Collecting and preserving
Beating and sweeping in suitable places between May and August may produce *Bittacus* and *Panorpa*, but *Boreus* must be searched for in autumn and winter. The winged forms can be set in the usual way, but *Boreus* is best preserved in spirit.

Order Siphonaptera – Fleas

Recognition features Small wingless insects, flattened from side to side and living ectoparasitically on mammals and birds. Generally brown or black. Mouth-parts adapted for blood-sucking. The lateral compression of these insects readily separates them from the other orders.

This relatively small order has only about 1,800 known species. Just over 100 occur in Europe and about 60 are established in the British Isles, although not all are natives. Adult fleas show no obvious connection with any other insect order, but specialisation for a parasitic life can be held responsible for removing any similarities there might have been. The larvae, however, are not parasitic and show a number of similarities with certain fly larvae. Fleas are clearly related to winged insects and their skeletal structure suggests a relationship with the scorpion flies of the order Mecoptera.

The whole life cycle is spent in the vicinity of the host, but only the adult fleas are actually parasitic and even these leave their hosts from time to time. There is thus less of a bond between the flea and its host than between the louse and its host, and host-specificity is much less marked among the fleas. Flea larvae live on detritus, including the droppings of their parents, in the nest or home of the host and they require rather precise conditions. What host-specificity there is among fleas is therefore controlled more by the homes and nesting habits of the hosts than by the nature of their blood. Many flea species will feed on a variety of hosts, but they can breed only when they meet one with suitable nesting habits. Fleas are not therefore regularly associated with nomadic animals. Apes and monkeys are basically nomadic and, although often acquiring fleas of one sort or another, have none that they can call their own. It seems that man, too, was flealess until he abandoned his nomadic ways and began to settle down. The Human Flea (*Pulex irritans*) is primarily a parasite of foxes, badgers, and other hole-dwelling mammals and was not introduced to man until he began to live in caves. About 95 per cent of known fleas are parasites of mammals and the rest are associated with birds.

Fleas are small insects, ranging from about 1mm to 9mm in length. The largest European species is the Mole Flea (*Hystrichopsylla talpae*), which is about 6mm long. The characteristic lateral compression of the flea facilitates its movement through fur or feathers and enables it to escape the attentions of the host – and the fingers of would-be flea-catchers. Compare this action with that of the louse, which usually sits tight and resists detachment by pressing itself closely against the skin. Fleas are well known for their jumping powers – long jumps of more than 30cm have been recorded for *P. irritans* – but while actually on the host they usually scuttle around, aided by strong claws that grip the hairs or feathers, and numerous strong,

pronotal comb
↓

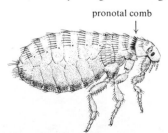

The Cat Flea, Ctenocephalides felis. *The bristles at the rear are thought to detect slight air movements*

backward-pointing bristles that prevent them from slipping backwards on a vertical surface. On the sides of the head and on the pronotum the spines are often very stout, forming the genal and pronotal combs which are useful in identifying certain species. The whole body is strongly sclerotised, hence the difficulty of squashing the insects.

The head, which is not distinctly separated from the thorax, is strongly hypognathous and carries two short, stout antennae partially concealed in grooves. Eyes may or may not be present and are often vestigial. The mouth-parts are adapted for blood-sucking and the piercing stylets are the modified maxillae and epipharynx. The maxillae have serrated edges and their inner surfaces are grooved, fitting tightly together to form a narrow canal through which saliva is ejected. The epipharynx is grooved on its lower surface and the two maxillae fit snugly against it to form a second canal through which the blood is drawn from the host. The labial and maxillary palps cover the stylets when they are not in use but play no part in the actual penetration of the host's tissues.

The three thoracic segments are quite distinct and the pronotum is often decorated by the pronotal comb – a row of stout spines on the hind margin. There are no wings in the adult flea, but the pupae of certain species possess wing-like rudiments on the mesothorax – further evidence of a relationship with winged insects. The legs all have unusually large coxae and long, 5-segmented tarsi. The hind legs are particularly long in association with the insects' jumping abilities. The highly elastic resilin (see p. 13) plays a major part in leaping. Thoracic muscles compress an area of resilin known as the pleural arch – actually a much-modified area of the now-defunct wing articulation – and when the muscles relax again the resilin springs back to its original shape, releasing a burst of energy which is transmitted to the hind legs to send the flea leaping into the air.

The abdomen consists of ten segments with the terga generally overlapping the sterna at the sides. Segments 8 and 9 are modified for reproductive functions, segment 9 of the male carrying a pair of claspers. The shape of these is very important in the specific determination of fleas and may be the only way of separating some species. The dorsal surface of segment 9 in both sexes also bears a sensory area called the sensilium, whose bristles are thought to detect slight air movements. The last segment is very small and inconspicuous.

Adult fleas may lay their pearly white eggs while still on the host or they may leave and lay directly in the nest or other immediate surroundings. The result is the same, because the eggs are not attached to the host and many of them will sooner or later fall into the nest. Several hundred eggs are produced by each female and they normally hatch within a week or two to produce white, worm-like larvae. These have neither legs nor eyes but they are equipped with biting jaws. They live by eating detrital matter in the nest and do not directly affect the host. Blood does, however, seem to be necessary for the proper development of some species and the adult fleas

A flea larva

periodically pass undigested host blood through the anus. Some larvae actually solicit this food by nudging or tugging the adults. The adult fleas' normal droppings also contain partly digested blood, so the larvae are always well supplied. Investigation of the resting places of cats and dogs will usually reveal numerous specks of dried blood released by the fleas in this way.

The length of the larval period varies with the species and season but probably averages two to three weeks, during which time the larva moults twice. When fully grown, the larva spins a silken cocoon among the debris. It remains motionless in the cocoon for two or three days – the prepupal stage – and then moults to reveal the exarate pupa. The length of the pupal stage also depends on temperature and species, and it is likely that many fleas pass the winter as pupae. Mammal fleas often breed throughout the year, although the rate falls during the winter, but bird fleas must restrict their breeding to the breeding season of the host – the only time that the host regularly uses a nest – and this extra problem is reflected in the relatively few flea species that parasitise birds.

Adult fleas need a mechanical stimulus to initiate their emergence from the cocoon and this is generally in the form of vibrations caused by the movements of the host. This neat arrangement ensures that the fleas do not emerge to find no hosts available. If no such stimulus is forthcoming the fleas can remain unharmed in their cocoons for many months – hence the frequent reports of houses, empty for some time, 'coming alive' with fleas as soon as they are occupied. Old birds' nests also yield fleas when disturbed – fleas which matured too late to catch the departing birds.

Newly emerged fleas and fleas that have left their hosts for any reason find new hosts primarily by detecting the warmth of their bodies. Most flea species will jump on to and feed from almost any host but they show a marked preference for their regular host(s), which they detect by chemical means. The insects can certainly detect smells, and recent work suggests that they can even detect the carbon dioxide given off by the host animals. Fleas can go without food for several months, but the females need a blood meal before they can produce eggs and generally require a meal before laying each batch of eggs.

The occasional flea-bite from nursing the family cat or other pet can be very irritating – more so for some people than for others – but the real problem with fleas is their ability to transmit disease. The most serious of the flea-borne infections is plague, caused by the bacillus *Pasteurella pestis*. This disease is primarily one of rats and other rodents, but wherever these animals live in close proximity to man there is the chance of an outbreak through rodent fleas which transfer their attentions to people. It has been estimated that plague has claimed more human victims than all the wars in history.

Transmission of plague may be mechanical, involving simply the contamination of the mouth-parts of the insects, or it may involve regurgitation of infected blood into the puncture. Most infected fleas develop blockages in their digestive tracts as a result of the multiplication of the bacteria, and when they try to feed the blood simply flows back down into the host, taking with it some of the germs from the gut. Because they can't actually get any food down them, the fleas become hungry and try to feed more frequently than they normally would. The result is that the plague spreads even more rapidly. Murine typhus – a less severe form of ordinary typhus – is also carried by rodent fleas.

The identification of fleas is not easy, in view of their small size, but the following key will serve to separate the families occurring naturally in Europe.

1. Hind coxa with a group of short,   Pulicidae p. 168
    stout spines on inner side

                                                                  spines on inside
                                                                  of hind coxa
    No such spines on hind coxa   2

2. Head and thorax without any prominent teeth or combs: Vermipsyllidae
    on large carnivores

    At least a pronotal comb present   3

3. Genal comb present, consisting of several stout bristles   4
    below or behind the eye

    Genal comb absent or consisting of no more than 2 broad   5
    bristles

4. Hind edge of metanotum carries a   pronotal comb   Leptopsyllidae
    few small spines

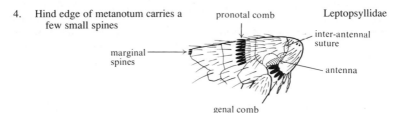

    Hind edge of metanotum smooth and spineless   Hystrichopsyllidae p. 169

5. Genal comb of 2 broad bristles: on bats   Ischnopsyllidae

    Genal comb entirely absent   Ceratophyllidae p. 169

The majority of fleas that come to general notice belong to the **Pulicidae**. *Ctenocephalides felis* is the Cat Flea and this is probably the most numerous of all domestic fleas, although the Dog Flea (*C.canis*) is often quite common. It is quite usual to find cat fleas on dogs and vice-versa and both species are ready to bite man whenever the opportunity arises. They breed very rapidly in warm weather and their control involves treatment of animals with suitable insecticides and regular cleaning of their sleeping quarters to destroy the larvae. *C.canis* is a vector of the dog tapeworm (*Dipylidium caninum*) which can also affect man. The larval fleas are infested with tapeworm eggs from the host's nest and the early stages of tapeworm development take place in the fleas. The worms re-enter the dog when it swallows fleas during grooming. The prominent pronotal and genal combs of *Ctenocephalides* species distinguish them at once from the Human Flea (*Pulex irritans*), a species which is much less common now than it was 100 years ago. The Rabbit Flea (*Spilopsyllus cuniculi*), which is the main vector of the myxomatosis virus in Europe, differs from our other fleas in that the adult females remain more or less permanently attached to their hosts. They select a suitable feeding site – usually the ear – and attach themselves by their mouth-parts.

Our bird fleas belong primarily to the **Ceratophyllidae**, in which there is a complete absence of the genal comb. *Ceratophyllus gallinae* is very widespread and attacks a wide variety of birds. This family, together with the **Hystrichopsyllidae**, also contains a number of rodent fleas, including several species known to carry murine typhus.

Collecting and preserving

Fleas can be collected in much the same way as lice by examining the host animals, although the fleas are considerably more difficult to catch. Combing, or even just blowing through the fur will cause many fleas to jump off the host. But the flea's life cycle and the readiness with which it leaves its host mean that the insects can be obtained simply by examining the homes or nests of the hosts. Old birds' nests (make sure that they *are* old and that the birds have flown) and sweepings from the sleeping quarters of other animals will usually yield all stages of the life cycle. Pupae can usually be relied on to produce adults and, although larvae are more difficult, they too can be bred if kept under the right conditions of temperature and humidity and fed with debris from the appropriate source.

The hard nature of the body means that fleas may be preserved dry if required: pointing is suitable for this purpose. Microscope slides are more suitable for detailed work, but the fleas must first be cleared by immersion in dilute potassium hydroxide solution for a few hours.

Order Diptera – Two-winged Flies or True Flies*
Plates 26–31

Recognition features Minute to large insects in which the hind wings are reduced to club-shaped halteres or balancers, leaving only one pair of membranous wings. A few species are completely wingless, usually in association with parasitic habits. Mouth-parts are always suctorial and frequently adapted for piercing. Many flies resemble bees and wasps as a result of mimicry, but such resemblances are only superficial – involving colour, for example – and closer examination will reveal only two wings, clearly indicating a true fly. Some of the smaller mayflies have only two wings but they never have halteres and their tail filaments should leave no doubt as to their identity.

A typical two-winged fly of the sub-order
Cyclorrhapha

The true flies make up a very large order with somewhere around 90,000 known species, of which over 15,000 occur in Europe. Some 5,200 species are found in the British Isles. Apart from having only two wings – hence the name of the order – there is little to suggest that all these insects belong to a single order. There are the stout-bodied horse-flies and bluebottles, colourful hover-flies, slender crane-flies and mosquitoes, and a host of smaller species indistinguishable to the casual observer and commonly referred to as gnats and midges.

These insects have exploited a very wide range of food materials, from decaying matter on the one hand to nectar or blood on the other, and the order as a whole is of considerable economic importance. Dung-flies and others whose larvae and adults feed on decaying matter perform a useful scavenging role in the economy of nature, while many flower-feeding species are useful pollinators. A number of species, such as the Carrot-fly and some of the crane-flies, are agricultural pests in their larval stages, but it is as enemies of man and his livestock that the flies are most important. Blood-sucking flies are found in many families and they carry several dangerous diseases, including malaria, yellow fever, and sleeping sickness. Blood-feeding is often confined to the female of the species, with the males usually taking nectar and other plant juices. The House-fly, sometimes labelled the most dangerous insect on earth, is not a blood-feeder and does not attack us directly but, because of its liking for both filth and sweet things, it contaminates huge quantities of human food and has been shown to spread a number of human diseases. Veterinary pests include the greenbottles (*Lucilia* spp), whose maggots eat away the flesh of sheep, the wingless, blood-sucking Sheep Ked (*Melophagus ovinus*), and the warble flies (*Hypoderma* spp) whose larvae burrow through the bodies of cattle.

---

*   *A great many insects have the word 'fly' in their common names and, to distinguish between the true flies and these other insects, I follow Oldroyd's suggestion of hyphenating the names of true flies – house-fly, dung-fly, and so on. The other insects' names are spelled without hyphens – dragonfly, alder fly, and so on.*

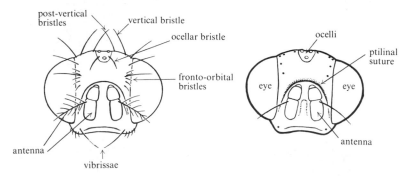

Fly heads, seen from the front to show the ptilinal suture and the positions of the main bristles

The head of a true fly is usually relatively large and a fair proportion of it is occupied by the compound eyes. These are generally larger in the male than in the female and sometimes meet in the mid-line – the holoptic condition. There are usually three ocelli on the top of the head – the vertex – and in many families they sit on a prominent triangular plate called the ocellar triangle. The region of the front of the head between the eyes and reaching down as far as the antennae is called the frons, although this does not correspond with the frons in other insects. The rest of the head, below the antennae, is called the face. The more advanced families all possess a conspicuous suture forming an inverted U around the antennae. This is the ptilinal suture (sometimes called the frontal suture) and it marks the position of the ptilinum, an eversible sac used by these insects to break out of their puparia (see p. 177). The presence or absence of this suture is an important guide when trying to identify the flies.

Among the more primitive flies, such as the crane-flies and the gnats, the antennae are relatively long and are composed of numerous distinct and more or less similar segments. These flies are placed in the sub-order NEMATOCERA, which means 'thread-horns'. The more advanced flies, included in the sub-orders BRACHYCERA and CYCLORRHAPHA, have only two or three distinct antennal segments, the rest being more or less fused to form a spur or a bristle. The antennal structure is very important in the classification of the flies.

The flies are all liquid-feeders, but even so there is great variation in their feeding habits and in the form of their mouth-parts. Even the simplest dipteran mouth-parts

Antennae of: **a.** *crane-fly;* **b.** *house-fly;* **c.** *horse-fly*

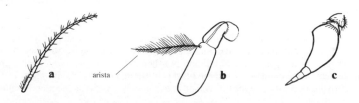

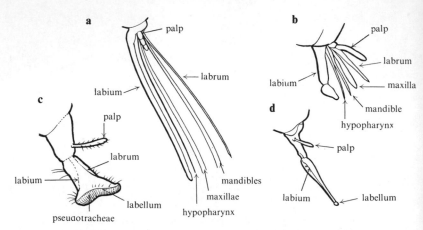

*Four kinds of sucking mouths found among the Diptera: **a.** mosquito; **b.** horse-fly; **c.** house-fly; **d.** stable-fly. In the mosquito the labium acts merely as a sheath for the needle-like mandibles and maxillae which all fit together to form a sharp piercing organ. The mandibles and maxillae of the horse-fly are more blade-like, and the labium also has a 'mop' at the tip for soaking up blood that oozes from the wound. The house-fly has a fleshy proboscis, formed mainly from the labium, and it can only mop up surface liquids through the little tubes, called pseudotracheae, in its sponge-like labellae. The proboscis of the stable-fly has been modified for blood-sucking in both sexes and it has numerous minute teeth on the labellum. These make a wound in the victim and the horny proboscis is then pushed in to suck out the blood*

are a far cry from the primitive biting mouth of the cockroach (fig. p. 14). The constant features of the dipteran feeding apparatus are the labrum, which forms the front wall or roof of the feeding channel; the hypopharynx, which carries the salivary duct and which forms the back wall or floor of the feeding channel; and the labium. Mandibles and maxillae are present only in some of the blood-sucking flies – the mosquitoes, horse-flies, and a few others – and they are sharp, piercing organs. Maxillary palps, however, are almost always present. The labium exhibits much variation, from being little more than a sheath for the stylets of the mosquito to being the main feeding organ of the non-blood-suckers. The tip of the labium carries two lobes or labella, small in most blood-suckers but large and spongy in the other flies, in which they are used to mop up the liquid food. In some blood-sucking species the labium, or proboscis as it is often called, is sharp and replaces the mandibles as the penetrating organ. Four of the main types of feeding apparatus are shown here and are more fully described under the relevant families. There are, however, a few groups of flies with poorly-developed mouth-parts or even none at all in the adult state.

Among the higher members of the order the head and thorax bear a number of distinct bristles, the arrangement of which is of great value in classifying and identifying the flies. Although relatively stout, these bristles are fragile and they break very easily – hence the advice to kill and pin flies as soon as they are caught. The arrangement of the main bristles of the head is illustrated on p. 171, although not all of the bristles necessarily appear together in any one fly. As far as the identification

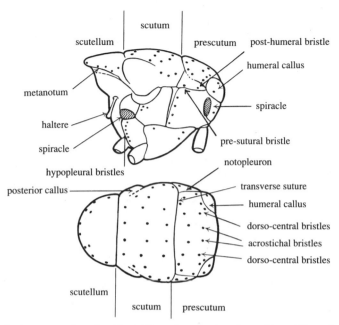

A fly thorax, seen from the side and from above to show the positions of the main thoracic bristles

of the families is concerned, the major head bristles are the post-verticals just behind the ocelli, the fronto-orbitals just in front of the eye, and the vibrissae. The latter are large, crossed bristles just above the mouth.

As would be expected, the thorax consists largely of the mesothorax, which is the wing-bearing segment. The prothorax and metathorax are reduced to little more than leg-bearing collars fore and aft. The upper surface of the mesothorax is clearly divided into scutum, prescutum, and scutellum, although the transverse suture dividing the prescutum and scutum is not always fully developed. There is often a post-scutellum as well, but this, together with the metathorax, is generally hidden beneath the scutellum. On each side of the prescutum, near the front outer edge, there is usually a swelling called the humeral callus. Similar swellings often occur on the hind outer margins of the scutum and these are known as the posterior calli. The notopleura are two somewhat triangular regions of the thorax, generally evident at the ends of the transverse suture.

The figure above shows the main groups of thoracic bristles as well as the principal divisions of the mesothorax. As far as identification of the insects is concerned, the main bristles to look for are the dorso-centrals and the hypopleural bristles. The latter, well seen in the blow-flies of the family Calliphoridae, stand on the hypopleuron – which is just above the coxae of the second and third legs – and form a backward-pointing arc.

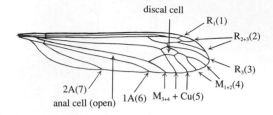

The venation of a crane-fly, showing the open anal cell characteristic of the sub-order Nematocera. The veins are labelled with their Needham-Comstock names and also with the simple numbering system

Wings are present in almost all flies, the main exceptions being some of the parasites such as the Sheep Ked. Some crane-flies are wingless, and others have very short, useless wings. The venation is fairly complete in the crane-flies and mosquitoes and also in the horse-flies and snipe-flies, but it is reduced in most other families, many of which can be recognised by the venation alone. The gall midges of the family Cecidomyiidae have virtually no veins in their flimsy wings.

Dipterists commonly use a simple numbering system when describing the wing veins. There are basically seven long veins and they are numbered from the front, starting with the radius (R_1 in the Comstock-Needham system). Numbers 6 and 7 are the two anal veins (veins 1A and 2A in the Comstock-Needham system). Some of the long veins branch before reaching the wing margin, but the branches still retain their basic numbers. The veins may also fuse with each other, and some disappear altogether, making it difficult to decide on their numbering, but the cross-veins provide valuable clues here. The anterior cross-vein, usually somewhere near the centre

Venation of Conops *(top) and* Musca *(bottom), showing the much-reduced venation in the sub-order Cyclorrhapha*

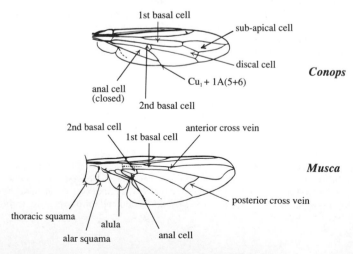

of the wing, always links veins 3 and 4, while the posterior cross-vein always links veins 4 and 5.

There are usually a number of roughly rectangular cells near the base of the wing. The anterior of these, usually terminated by the anterior cross-vein, is called the 1st basal cell. Just behind it lies the 2nd basal cell, and behind this there is generally a third cell known as the anal cell. The latter, lying between veins 5 and 6, is open in the crane-flies and other nematocerans but closed in most other flies. All three cells vary a great deal in length and are sometimes more than half as long as the wing. Somewhere near the centre of the wing there is often a discal cell. It varies in shape but at least part of its outer margin is formed by the posterior cross-vein.

The sub-costal vein is quite long in some nematocerans and brachycerans, but in other flies it is usually rather short. In many species it joins the radius or peters out entirely before reaching the wing margin. In many flies there is also a very short cross-vein, called the humeral vein, running between the costa and sub-costa close to the base of the wing. Among the smaller cyclorrhaphous flies the costal margin often has one or two 'breaks' in the basal half. They are not always easy to see, but the positions of these breaks are useful clues to the identity of the flies.

Along the hind edge of the wing, close to the body, the membrane usually forms three lobes. The outer one, known as the alula, is fairly conspicuous; the middle one, known as the alar aquama, is generally smaller; the inner lobe is attached to the thorax and is called the thoracic squama. This inner lobe is very small and quite inconspicuous in most flies, but it is well developed in the house-flies and bluebottles and their relatives in which is completely covers the haltere (fig. p. 174). The thoracic squamae are also known as calypters.

The halteres develop on the metathorax and are actually highly modified hind wings. Striking proof of this relationship has been obtained with the famous *Drosophila*, well known to all who study genetics. Certain mutations are known in which the halteres develop as stunted wings. Normally the haltere is a pin-like structure protruding from the thorax. It is clearly visible in crane-flies and other nematocerans (Pl.26) but needs to be looked for in many flies, particularly those with well-developed squamae. In flight, the halteres vibrate with the wings and, because of their relatively heavy heads, they continue to vibrate in the same plane even when the fly changes direction. This produces a strain on the cuticle at the bases of the halteres and the strain is detected by tiny sensory cells. Impulses sent to the brain inform the fly that it is deviating from straight and level flight and it can then make the necessary correction. The halteres thus act just like gyroscopic balancers or stabilisers.

The various spurs and bristles on the legs play some part in the classification of flies, but the feet are particularly important. There are normally two claws and most flies possess two pad-like pulvilli surrounding a central bristle or empodium. The major variations are the absence of the pulvilli in many nematocerans, and the pad-

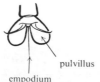

Feet of a horse-fly (left) and a house-fly, showing how the empodium may be pad-like or bristle-like

pulvillus

empodium   empodium

like nature of the empodium in the horse-flies and some other members of the Brachycera.

The abdomen varies a great deal in size and shape – compare the crane-fly and the bee-fly for two extremes of shape – and often gives some indication of the group to which a specimen belongs. Its anatomical details, however, are of practical concern only when dealing with the identification of individual species.

Most flies lay small, cigar-shaped eggs that hatch rapidly under favourable conditions to produce pale, legless larvae. There are a few exceptions to the egg-laying habit, however, mainly among the Pupipara (see p. 212).

There is an immense range of form and habit among dipteran larvae; in fact, no other insect order can approach it in this respect. There are a few straightforward phytophagous (plant-feeding) families, some of which are of great concern to the farmer. Some families have parasitic larvae, affecting both vertebrate and invertebrate hosts. The great majority of dipteran larvae, however, feed on decaying matter of one sort or another. A large number of them are aquatic. Even among the terrestrial species, the larvae usually live on quite different food from the adults and it is normally only one stage in the life history that is a nuisance to us. The mosquito larva, for example, lives harmlessly in stagnant water. Adult gall midges are tiny, insignificant insects that do no harm at all, but some of their larvae cause extensive crop damage by inducing galls and other deformities.

Fly larvae are always legless, although there may be some fleshy stumps not unlike the prolegs of caterpillars. The larvae simply wriggle about, aided by the false legs and various spines if they are present. The head capsule is generally well developed in the Nematocera – particularly so in the mosquitoes – and bears biting mouth-parts. The head capsule and mouth-parts are still present in the Brachycera, but there is a tendency towards the reduction of the head. This tendency is continued in the Cyclorrhapha, where the head capsule is much reduced and the mouth-parts are in the form of a tiny pair of hooks. The larvae of this latter group, typified by that of the House-fly, are carrot-shaped maggots, tapering towards the front and with few obvious external features.

There are generally four larval instars in the Nematocera, five to eight in the Brachycera, and only three in the Cyclorrhapha. In the first two sub-orders the last larval

A selection of fly larvae

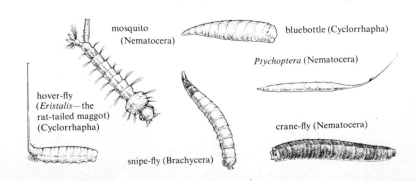

mosquito
(Nematocera)

bluebottle (Cyclorrhapha)

Ptychoptera (Nematocera)

hover-fly
(*Eristalis*—the
rat-tailed maggot)
(Cyclorrhapha)

crane-fly (Nematocera)

snipe-fly (Brachycera)

skin is cast off to reveal the obtect but quite mobile pupa. The mosquito pupa, for example, is very mobile, although its appendages are all firmly bonded to the body. The mobility of the pupa enables it to position itself suitably for the emergence of the adult. The pupae of the cyclorrhaphous flies are not free to move, for they are imprisoned in the last larval skin, which forms a hard, barrel-shaped puparium. Many nematocerans and brachycerans form some sort of cocoon or other shelter before pupating.

A few families of the Cyclorrhapha, including the hover-flies, have no special apparatus for escaping from the puparium. Most of them, however, have a balloon-like sac which they inflate to force off the end of the puparium. This sac is called the ptilinum and it lies within the head, its position marked by the ptilinal suture (fig. p. 171). When the time for emergence arrives, the ptilinum expands and pushes the front part of the face forwards and downwards, thus opening up the suture for further expansion of the balloon. This expansion breaks open the puparium and the fly escapes. Its function fulfilled, the ptilinum then deflates and the suture closes over it.

The life cycle may be extremely short – less than a week under favourable circumstances – but it depends on the species. House-flies, bluebottles, and others may have several generations in a year, even in cool climates, but many others are always single-brooded and their life cycles take a whole year.

As already mentioned, the flies are divided into three sub-orders: **Nematocera, Brachycera**, and **Cyclorrhapha**. The Nematocera contains the most primitive of the flies and these are easily recognised by their relatively long antennae which are composed of numerous distinct and similar segments. The Brachycera and Cyclorrhapha all have short antennae, often with no more than three short segments and a bristle at the end, and the principal difference between the two groups lies in the way in which the larval skin splits at each moult. In the Brachycera the split is straight or T-shaped and on the dorsal surface, but in the Cyclorrhapha it extends all the way round the body and cuts off a cap or lid. The same kinds of splits develop when the adult flies emerge from their pupae. Adult flies are not immediately attributable to one or other of these two sub-orders, but closer inspection reveals that most cyclorrhaphous flies have a dorsal bristle on the third antennal segment, while the brachycerous flies have a terminal bristle if they have one at all.

Left, Antenna of a soldier-fly, showing the terminal bristle typical of the Brachycera. Right, antenna of a blow-fly, showing the dorsal bristle or arista typical of the sub-order Cyclorrhapha

groove

Key to the Main Families of European Diptera

1.	Antennae usually long and slender, composed of at least 5 segments which are all more or less alike: veins 5 & 6, if present, usually diverge towards the wing margin and there is no closed anal cell [sub-order Nematocera]	2
	Antennae usually with less than 5 segments and never long and thread-like: if more than 5 segments they are not all alike: veins 5 & 6 converge and usually meet, forming a closed or almost closed anal cell [sub-orders Brachycera & Cyclorrhapha]	20
2.	Small and very hairy moth-like flies with 10 or 11 veins reaching wing margin and with no obvious cross veins	Psychodidae p. 189
	Flies not fitting this description	3
3.	2 anal veins reach the wing margin: top of thorax with a V-shaped suture	4
	1 anal vein at most reaches wing margin: no V-shaped suture on thorax, although there may be a U-shaped one (fig. p. 189)	5

4. Ocelli present: vein 7 very short and sharply bent   Trichoceridae p. 189

1A(6)

2A(7)

Ocelli absent: vein 7 longer and not sharply bent   Tipulidae p. 188

1A(6)

2A(7)

5.	Ocelli present	6
	Ocelli absent	13
6.	Very long-legged flies whose wings appear permanently creased	†Blephariceridae p. 192
	Insects not like this	7
7.	Tibiae clearly spurred at tip	8
	Tibiae without obvious spurs	12
8.	Discal cell usually present: vein 2 (Rs) forks at or near r-m cross-vein	Anisopodidae p. 189
	No discal cell: vein 2 (Rs) forks, if at all, well beyond r-m cross-vein	9

9.   Antennae short and inserted below   10
     eyes

     Antennae longer and more slender, with well-separated   11
         segments, and inserted near middle of eyes

10. Generally very dark flies with stout antennae and thick-   Bibionidae p. 194
         ened front veins: front tibiae with a large spur or circlet
         of spines

     Small brown or yellowish flies with weak spurs or none   Thaumaleidae p. 192
         at all on front tibiae: 1st & 2nd antennal segments
         stout, the rest slender

11. Eyes curve round to meet above antennae   Sciaridae p. 195

     Eyes do not meet above antennae   Mycetophilidae p. 194

12. Antennae short and stout: eyes   Scatopsidae p. 194
         generally meet above antennae:
         wings naked, with strong anterior
         veins

     Antennae longer, with distinct bead-like segments: wings Cecidomyiidae p. 195
         fringed and with greatly reduced venation

13. Wings very broad, with anterior veins much stronger than   Simuliidae p. 193
         the rest and no cross-vein in centre: antennae shorter
         than width of head

     Wings narrower, with all veins more or less equally promi-   14
         nent

14. 10 or more veins reach wing margin   15

     No more than 8 veins reach wing margin   18

15. Tibiae spurred: U-shaped suture on top of thorax   Ptychopteridae p. 189

     Tibiae without obvious spurs: no suture on top of thorax   16

16. Wing veins thickly scaled: mouth-parts long   Culicidae p. 190

     Scales confined to wing margins or absent: mouth-parts   17
         short

17. Scales on wing margins: wings no longer than abdomen: Chaoboridae p. 191
         male antennae strongly plumose

     Wings without scales and usually much longer than ab-   Dixidae p. 191
         domen: male antennae not plumose

18. No more than 4 veins reach wing margin: slender insects   Cecidomyiidae p. 195
     with slightly smoky and hairy wings

     At least 6 veins reach wing margin   19

19. Front legs often noticeably longer   Chironomidae p. 192
     than the rest: vein 4 (M_{1+2}) runs
     to wing-tip without forking but
     not always obvious: wings often
     shorter than abdomen and held
     roofwise over the body at rest

     Minute insects with front legs no   Ceratopogonidae p. 193
     longer than others: vein 4 (M_{1+2})
     clearly forked, although often
     faint: wings folded flat at rest

20. Very flat flies living ectoparasitically on other animals: 21
     generally with long legs and strong claws: often wing-
     less

     Normal flies without flattened bodies   23

21. Wingless flies <1.5mm long, parasitic on bees   Braulidae p. 207

     Larger flies, with or without wings   22

22. Head small and folded back on to small thorax: wingless   Nycteribiidae p. 212
     parasites of bats

     Head larger and not folded back on to thorax, although   Hippoboscidae p. 212
     often partly sunk into it: winged or wingless parasites
     of birds and mammals

23. Large flies with long antennae ending in an oval club: sev-   [†]Mydaidae p. 198
     eral veins parallel to rear margin of wing

     Antennae generally shorter than width of head, sometimes   24
     longer and with swollen tips, but then they always end
     in a point

24. Small bulbous flies with a tiny head much narrower than   Acroceridae p. 196
     thorax: very large squamae

     Flies not fitting this description   25

25. Wing-tips sharply pointed: no obvious cross-veins   Lonchopteridae p. 200

     Wing-tips not sharply pointed: at least one cross-vein near   26
     middle of wing

26. One or more veins running parallel to hind edge of wing   27
     and forming a false margin, with no veins reaching the
     true hind margin in outer region (fig. p. 201)

     No such false margin   28

27. A false vein (a pigmented fold) runs through 1st basal and   Syrphidae p. 201
    sub-apical cells

    No such false vein   [†]Nemestrinidae p. 198

28. Foot with 3 pads*   29

    Foot with 2 pads or with claws replacing pads   33

29. 3rd antennal segment stout and   30
    clearly composed of several fused
    parts: with or without a terminal
    bristle.

    3rd antennal segment without such traces of segmentation   Rhagionidae p. 196
    and ending in a slender bristle

30. Stoutly-built flies with veins forking to form a con-   Tabanidae p. 196
    spicuous Y across wing-tip, with lower branch meeting
    wing margin well below the apex: squamae large

    Generally more slender flies: if a prominent fork near   31
    wing-tip the lower branch meets margin at or above
    apex

31. Discal cell small and close to front of wing: all veins be-   Stratiomyidae p. 195
    hind it rather weak: costal vein stops at wing-tip: body
    often rather flattened

    Venation not like this: all veins equally strong   32

32. A closed cell behind discal cell (fig. p. 196)   Xylomyiidae p. 195

    No closed cell behind discal cell (fig. p. 196)   Xylophagidae p. 196

33. Head unusually large and spherical: sub-apical cell tapers   Pipunculidae p. 200
    or abruptly narrows towards wing-tip, becoming almost
    closed and beak-like

    Head not abnormally large   34

34. Hind tarsi usually broad and flat   Platypezidae p. 200

    Hind tarsi normal   35

35. Anal cell long and pointed and often reaching wing mar-   36
    gin (occasionally slightly open)

    Anal cell short and blunt or absent   40

36. Small black, naked flies   Scenopinidae p. 197

    Larger flies, often hairy or bristly   37

*   *A few Empididae and Dolichopodidae may have three pads*

37. More or less naked flies, often with stout, projecting anten-   Conopidae p. 201
     nae

     Hairy or bristly flies   38

38. A distinct groove between the eyes: usually bristly flies   Asilidae p. 197
     (except *Leptogaster*)

     No such groove between eyes   39

39. Hairy flies, often bee-like, with very slender legs: only 2   Bombyliidae p. 197
     or 3 veins reach wing margin between the apical fork
     and the (open) anal cell

     Legs stouter and bristly: 4 veins reach wing margin be-   Therevidae p. 197
     tween the apical fork and the (closed) anal cell

40. Frons with a ptilinal suture curving round the top of the   43
     antennae like an up-turned U

     Frons without a ptilinal suture   41

41. Anterior veins very prominent and joining costa well be-   Phoridae p. 200
     fore wing-tip: other veins faint and more or less paral-
     lel: mostly very small hump-backed flies

     Flies not fitting this description   42

42. 1st basal cell fairly long, with   1st basal cell   Empididae p. 198
     cross-vein r-m fairly obvious,
     although short, near centre of
     wing: head usually spherical,
     often with a long, rigid proboscis:
     flies never with metallic colours

     1st basal cell very short: only 1   1st basal cell   Dolichopodidae p. 199
     obvious cross- vein in wing: head
     rather long in profile: insects
     often with bright metallic colours

                                                                    2nd basal + discal cell

43. Thoracic squamae usually vestigial, if developed then posterior calli are not: eyes always well separated: 2nd antennal segment usually without a groove: transverse suture weak 44

no groove here

transverse suture weak

no posterior callus

Squamae usually well developed and concealing halteres from above: transverse suture strong and posterior calli well marked: male eyes often close together: 2nd antennal segment usually with a groove 81

groove

transverse suture

posterior callus

44. Mouth-parts vestigial: sturdy, furry flies up to 20mm long Gasterophilidae p. 208

Mouth-parts well developed: generally much smaller flies without much hair 45

45. Legs very long and thin: body usually very slender 46

Legs of normal proportions 48

46. Hind femora thickened and spiny below Megamerinidae p. 203

Hind femora slender and without spines 47

47. Anal cell closed by a straight vein Micropezidae p. 203

Anal cell closed by a curved vein Tanypezidae p. 203

48. Small, naked, ant-like flies, usually with rounded head and basally constricted abdomen: often with dark spot near wing-tip Sepsidae p. 205

Flies not fitting this description 49

49. 1st & 2nd basal, discal, and anal cells all present and closed 50

At least one of these cells open or absent altogether 74

50. Vein 6 (1Λ) projects only a short way or not at all beyond anal cell (fig. p. 204), although vein 2A may extend further 51

Vein 6 (1A) extends well beyond anal cell, reaching at least a quarter of the way to wing margin 56

51. Hind tibia carries a dorsal pre-apical bristle 52

Hind tibia without such a bristle 54

52. Post-vertical bristles diverge   Canacidae p. 206
     Post-vertical bristles converge and often cross   53

53. Costal wing margin complete   Lauxaniidae p. 204
     Costa broken near tip of vein 1   Diastatidae p. 206

54. Costal wing margin complete: sub-costal vein runs di-   Chamaemyiidae p. 204
       rectly to costal margin, more or less parallel to vein 1
       all the way
     Costal margin with at least one break: sub-costa joins vein   55
       1 or fades away before reaching costal margin

55. Costa broken twice – near humeral vein and near tip of   Milichiidae p. 205
       vein 1: 1st basal cell more or less rectangular
     Costa broken only once – near tip of vein 1: 1st basal cell   Tethinidae p. 206
       very narrow and tapering distally

56. Hind tibia carries dorsal pre-apical   57
       bristle

     Hind tibia has no such bristle   63

57. Post-vertical bristles converge or cross   58
     Post-vertical bristles are parallel or diverging   60

58. Costal margin spiny   Heleomyzidae p. 204
     Costal margin not spiny   59

59. Anal cell closed by a straight vein   Coelopidae p. 204
     Anal cell closed by a curved vein   Lauxaniidae p. 204

curved vein

60. Costal margin spiny   Helcomyzidae p. 203
     Costal margin not spiny   61

61. 2nd basal and anal cells short,   Sciomyzidae p. 203
       hardly reaching beyond alula

anal cell
2nd basal cell

     2nd basal and anal cells longer,   62
       reaching well beyond alula

anal cell
2nd basal cell

62. Costal margin entire: yellow or brownish flies   Dryomyzidae p. 203

     Costa clearly broken near vein Sc: generally shiny black   Lonchaeidae p. 205
     flies

63. 1st tarsal segment of hind leg short and thick   Sphaeroceridae p. 205

     1st tarsal segment of hind leg normal   64

64. Vibrissae present around the mouth   65

     No vibrissae   68

65. Sub-costa complete and joining costa well before vein 1   66

     Sub-costa fades away or merges with vein 1   67

66. Sides of thorax very bristly   Clusiidae p. 205

     Sides of thorax not bristly   Piophilidae p. 205

67. Post-vertical bristles diverge   Agromyzidae p. 207

     Post-vertical bristles converging or absent   Anthomyzidae p. 206

68. 1st two long veins converge strongly near wing-tip   Opomyzidae p. 205

     No such convergence of veins   69

69. Vein Sc is sharply bent, often forming a right angle, and Tephritidae p. 202
     then fades towards costal margin (fig. p. 202): wings
     generally strongly patterned

     Vein Sc not sharply bent, although often curved   70

70. Head concave at back: wings dark with clear spots: costa Platystomatidae p.202
     broken near humeral vein

     Flies not like this, although wings may be heavily pat-   71
     terned: costa entire, or if broken break is not near hum-
     eral vein

71. Costa entire: face deeply grooved (fig. p. 203)   Otitidae p. 202

     Costa broken: face not grooved   72

72. Post-verticals convergent: wings no more than lightly pat- Chyromyidae p. 204
     terned

     Post-verticals parallel, divergent or absent: if convergent,   73
     then wings are heavily patterned

73. Wings distinctly patterned   Pallopteridae p. 202

     Wings not patterned: a pale streak, not always easily seen,   Psilidae p. 203
     runs back from the costal break to outer edge of anal
     cell

74.   Minute flies (c.1.5mm) with only one or two closed cells: Carniidae p. 205
      vein 4, forming rear margin of 1st basal cell, does not
      extend much past that cell, leaving a wide open space
      in centre of wing

      Generally larger flies, with vein 4 reaching at least to   75
      centre of wing

75.   Anal cell present   76

anal cell

      Anal cell absent   77

76.   Costa broken once (near Sc & vein   Agromyzidae p. 207
      1): lower fronto-orbital bristles
      curve inwards from edge of eye

lower fronto-orbital
bristles

      Costa broken twice: antennae usually plumose and appar-   Drosophilidae p. 206
      ently forked at the tip (fig. p. 206)

77.   1st tarsal segment of hind leg short and thick   Sphaeroceridae p. 205
      1st tarsal segment of hind leg normal   78

78.   Posterior cross-vein well before middle of wing or absent   Asteiidae p. 206
      Posterior cross-vein at or beyond   79
      middle of wing

no anal cell

79.   Costa broken once: a large plate-like ocellar triangle   Chloropidae p. 207
      Costa broken twice   80

80.   Post-vertical bristles clearly crossed   Camillidae p. 206
      Post-vertical bristles absent   Ephydridae p. 206

81.   Mouth-parts small and functionless: flies generally softly   Oestridae p. 208
      hairy
      Mouth-parts well developed: flies usually more bristly   82

82.   An arc of hypopleural bristles stands just above coxa of   83
      3rd leg, just below and in front of posterior thoracic
      spiracle (fig. p. 173)
      No such arc of bristles   86

83. Post-scutellum strongly
     developed

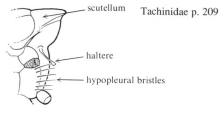

scutellum

haltere

hypopleural bristles

Tachinidae p. 209

Post-scutellum weak or absent   84

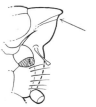

84. Thoracic squamae small, with inner margin diverging   Rhinophoridae p. 210
     from scutellum (fig. p. 210): vein 4 never sharply bent

     Thoracic squamae larger, with inner margin close to scutel-   85
     lum: vein 4 generally sharply bent

85. Post-humeral bristle level with or higher than pre-sutural   Sarcophagidae p. 210
     bristle when viewed from the side: greyish flies with
     chequered black abdominal pattern

     Post-humeral bristle lower than pre-sutural bristle when   Calliphoridae p. 209
     viewed from the side (fig. p. 173): flies often metallic,
     if with chequered abdominal pattern then thorax is
     clothed with golden hairs

86. Thoracic squamae as large as and generally much larger   87
     than alar squamae (fig. p. 174) : if reduced to a narrow
     strip then the back of the head is flattened

     Thoracic squamae reduced to narrow strips no more than   Scathophagidae p. 210
     half the length of alar squamae: back of head rounded

87. Vein 6 (from rear edge of anal cell)   Anthomyiidae p. 210
     reaches wing margin

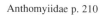

     Vein 6 does not reach wing margin   88

88. Veins 6 & 7 short and not converging   Muscidae p. 211
     Vein 7 generally longer than vein 6 and converging on it   Fanniidae p. 211

† denotes families not found in the British Isles

SUB-ORDER NEMATOCERA

Apart from their characteristically slender antennae, these insects are generally recognisable by their slender bodies. There are a few families in which both body and antennae are stouter than usual, but these can be recognised as nematocerans by the venation. The space between veins 5 and 6 (Cu and 1A) is open and always widens towards the wing margin. This space should strictly be called the cubital cell, but most dipterists retain the older system of naming the cells and continue to call it the anal cell. In the other two sub-orders, veins 5 and 6 converge and usually meet. The cell is therefore narrowed towards the wing margin and usually completely closed.

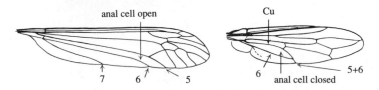

Left, a crane-fly wing showing the open anal cell typical of the Nematocera; Right, a conopid wing showing the anal cell closed by veins 5 and 6

Many nematocerans have the habit of swarming. Clouds of the insects can be seen, usually towards evening, dancing up and down a few feet above the ground. These are mating swarms, in which the females are relatively scarce. As in several other groups of insects, the swarm attracts the females, but as soon as they approach they are grabbed by males and whisked away.

The **Tipulidae** contains slender, long-legged flies popularly called crane-flies or daddy-long-legs. They can be recognised quite easily by the V-shaped suture on the thorax and by the two long anal veins which both reach the wing margin. The small discal cell in the outer third of the wing (fig. p. 174) is also a valuable guide: the only other families in the Nematocera with a discal cell are the Trichoceridae and the Anisopodidae, and neither of these has two long anal veins.

There are about 300 crane-fly species in the British Isles, ranging in size from *Tipula maxima* (Pl.26) which, with a wingspan of about 65mm, outstrips all other British flies, to small gnat-like flies with wingspans of only 15mm. Most *Tipula* species and some of the other large crane-flies rest with their wings outstretched, but most members of the family fold their wings over their bodies. Some *Tipula* females have vestigial wings and can be seen resting on walls in the autumn waiting for the males to find them. Swarming is common among the smaller species, many of which are known as bobbing gnats because of the way in which they bob up and down on their long legs. The legs in this family are weakly attached to the body and

head

Thorax of Tipula, *showing the v-shaped notch characteristic of the Tipulidae*

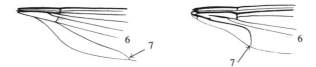

Wing bases of Tipulidae (left) and Trichoceridae, which differ markedly in the length of the second anal vein - vein 7

they readily break off, even in the living insect. Most of the crane-flies are nocturnal and many of the species are attracted to lights.

Larval crane-flies normally live in the soil, in decaying wood or leaf litter, or in the debris at the bottom of ponds and streams. Most of them are saprophagous or carnivorous, but the larger species are essentially vegetarians. Some of the soil-living species – the notorious leatherjackets – cause serious damage to crop roots. *Tipula paludosa* and the very similar *T. oleracea*, whose adults are the familiar grey or brown daddy-long-legs, are the commonest of these pests. The adults themselves do no harm. They can only lap up liquids with fleshy labella at the tip of a beak-like extension of the head.

The **Trichoceridae**, with nine British species, is closely related to the Tipulidae but easily distinguished from it by the short and strongly curved second anal vein. The legs are not deciduous. These insects, typified by *Trichocera annulata* (Pl.26), swarm throughout much of the year but are especially prominent in the winter months and are therefore called winter gnats. The larvae live in decaying matter.

Members of the **Ptychopteridae** resemble the crane-flies but the thoracic suture is U-shaped and there is only one anal vein (vein 6). There is no discal cell. The insects are generally black with yellow markings and they have spotted wings. *Ptychoptera contaminata* (Pl.26) is the commonest of the eight British species, being abundant in damp places throughout the summer. The larvae are aquatic and breathe through a slender, telescopic extension of the abdomen which carries a pair of terminal spiracles up to the surface (fig. p. 176).

The window midges of the **Anisopodidae** resemble both the winter gnats and the smaller crane-flies, but they have no thoracic suture and the second anal vein does not reach the wing margin. Four of the five British species possess a discal cell which, together with the lack of a thoracic suture, immediately identifies them. The family's common name refers especially to *Sylvicola fenestralis* (Pl.26), which often comes into houses. The larvae generally live in decaying matter, those of *S. fenestralis* being quite common in sewage beds.

One of the easiest families to recognise is the **Psychodidae**, which contains the moth-flies or owl-midges. There are about 80 British species, all minute insects with pointed, hairy wings which are mostly held roof wise over the body at rest. The lar-

head

Thorax of Ptychoptera, *showing its U-shaped suture*

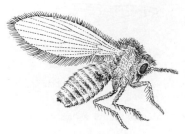

Psychoda - *one of the owl midges in the family Psychodidae. These insects are easily recognised by their hairy wings with numerous veins. Many species have patterned wings. The wings are usually held roofwise over the body at rest, but some rest with their wings partly spread*

vae feed on decaying matter, usually in water, and are often abundant in sewage filter beds. Adult flies often form huge swarms over such breeding sites. *Phlebotomus* species, known as sand-flies, are blood-suckers and carry a number of human and animal diseases in the warmer parts of the world, including some Mediterranean areas. The sand-flies, so-called because many of them breed in sandy soil, are now usually placed in a separate family – the **Phlebotomidae**. There are no British species.

As far as man is concerned, the most important of all the nematocerous families is the **Culicidae**, which contains the mosquitoes. These are nearly all blood-sucking insects and they are responsible for the spread of several serious diseases, including malaria, yellow fever, and elephantiasis. Mosquitoes are slender, long-legged flies in which the veins and the hind margins of the wings are covered with scales. A slender proboscis projects from the head in both sexes, although only the females use it for sucking blood. Males can be recognised by their bushy antennae, whose delicate hairs are sensitive to the flight tones of the females and thus enable the males to home in on mates. The males also have long and often ornately hairy palps. Female palps may be long or short, but they are always slender and sparsely haired.

The female mouth-parts are admirably suited to piercing and blood-sucking. The mandibles and maxillae are needle-like and these are the main piercing organs. The pointed labrum and hypopharynx also enter the wound. The labrum is grooved and, together with the hypopharynx, it forms the food canal through which the blood is taken (fig. p. 172).The hypopharynx, as usual, carries the salivary duct. All six structures are carried in a groove in the labium. The latter does not actually play any part in puncturing the victim's skin, although its sensitive labella may select a suitable site. Most female mosquitoes require a blood meal before they can lay fertile eggs, but some species can make do with nectar and other plant juices. These are the main foods of male mosquitoes, which lack the piercing mandibles and never take blood.

About 33 mosquito species occur in the British Isles. *Culex pipiens* (Pl.26) is one of the commonest, especially in and around buildings. It has two distinct sub-species: *C.p.pipiens*, which mainly attacks birds, and the less common *C.p.molestus* which readily bites man. *Culiseta annulata* (Pl.26), easily recognised by the black and white bands on its legs, is one of the largest mosquitoes. Its bite is quite painful and often results in blistering and severe inflammation, but it does not seem to carry any diseases.

Mosquitoes fall into two distinct groups – the anophelines and the culicines. The anophelines, represented in Europe by just a few species of *Anopheles*, rest with their bodies inclined at a steep angle to the surface and they have long palps in both sexes.

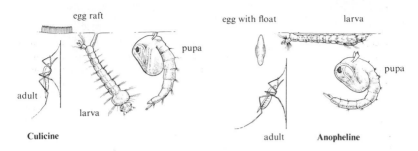

*The life cycles of culicine and anopheline mosquitoes. The resting attitudes of adults
and larvae are quite different in the two groups*

The culicines, which include all but five of the British mosquitoes, rest with the abdomen more or less parallel to the surface and they have very short palps in the female. Only the anophelines are able to transmit malaria. The malaria parasite has to
undergo a period of development in the mosquito and then reach the salivary glands
before it can infect another human, and the parasite is geared to do this only in anopheline mosquitoes. Although anophelines are quite common in Britain and most
other parts of Europe, malaria itself is now rare here.

Mosquito larvae live in water, although many species are very particular about
the kind of water in which they live. The eggs are usually laid on the water surface
and those of most *Culex* and *Culiseta* species are glued together to form tiny rafts.
The mosquito larva has a well-developed head and a very broad thoracic region. It
is well-supplied with hairs and it moves through the water with a jerky motion. It
feeds on protozoans and other minute organisms, which it wafts into its mouth with
tufts of hairs. Culicine larvae hang at an angle from the water surface, while anopheline larvae rest horizontally just below the surface film. This difference is associated with the positions of the spiracles – on a respiratory horn in the culicines and
on the dorsal body surface in the anophelines. The mosquito pupa is a very active,
comma-shaped creature, breathing through a pair of respiratory horns at the back of
the head.

Members of the **Chaoboridae** resemble the mosquitoes in many ways and used
to be placed with them in the Culicidae, but they have short, non-biting mouth-parts
and their wings have scales only around the rear margin. The wings are no longer
than the abdomen and in some species they are a good deal shorter, especially in the
males. These insects can easily be mistaken for chironomids (see p. 192), but the
chironomids have fewer veins in their wings and they have no scales. Chaoborid
larvae are aquatic and they prey on water fleas and other small creatures. That of
Chaoborus crystallinus is the phantom larva (p. 192), whose transparent body is almost invisible as it floats in the water and waits for its prey. The family contains six
British species.

The **Dixidae** is another family whose members were originally included in the
Culicidae, although they have no biting mouth-parts and the male antennae are not
plumed. The wings are generally broader than those of the mosquitoes and they have
no scales. They are often much longer than the body and the stem of vein 2 is strongly

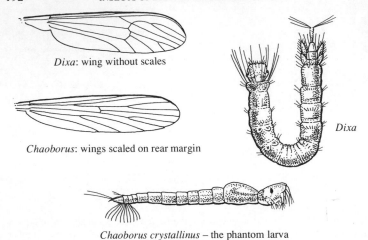

Dixa: wing without scales

Chaoborus: wings scaled on rear margin

Dixa

Chaoborus crystallinus – the phantom larva

Venation and larvae of Dixa *and* Chaoborus – *two mosquito-like genera of midges*

curved. There are 14 British species. The larvae are all aquatic and U-shaped, feeding on or just under the water surface.

Members of the **Blephariceridae** inhabit mountainous areas, where the larvae live in fast-moving streams. Adult emergence is a most unusual affair, with the pupa coming to the surface and exploding to catapult the adult into the air. The wings are already expanded in the pupa, although they are folded. They unfold as soon as the insect emerges, but they never lose their creases. *Liponeura cinerascens* (Pl.26) is typical of these long-legged and rather weak-flying insects, which rarely move far from the edges of their native streams.

The **Thaumaleidae** is a small family with only three British species. Its members are only 3-4mm long, but easily recognisable by the strong convergence of veins 2 and 3 and by the unusual form of the antennae, with the first two segments very much stouter than the rest. The larvae live in damp places, especially where water trickles gently over rocks.

The members of the **Chironomidae**, typified by *Chironomus annularis* (Pl.26), are generally small flies in which the thorax is conspicuously humped and often conceals the head from above. The front legs are noticeably elongated and the male antennae are very feathery. There are nearly 400 British species. The mouth-parts are poorly developed and the insects are not blood-feeders. Many do not feed at all as adults. They are known as non-biting midges to distinguish them from the blood-sucking ceratopogonids. It is not always easy to separate the smaller chironomids

Antenna and wing of Thaumalea *(family Thaumaleidae), a genus easily recognised by the apical convergence of veins 2 and 3*

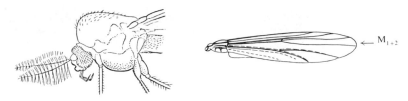

$\leftarrow M_{1+2}$

Chironomid midges can usually be recognised by the strongly humped thorax, largely overhanging the head, and the unforked vein 4 (M_{1+2}) in the centre of the wing

from these biting midges, although living insects can usually be identified by their resting positions: the chironomids rest with their wings apart – usually held more or less vertically along the sides of the body – while the ceratopogonids fold their wings flat over their backs. The wing venation also differs, but it is not easily detected because the posterior veins are very weak. Chironomid wings tend to be rather narrow and are often much shorter than the body. Chironomid larvae live in water or in decaying matter. The most familiar are the bloodworms (*Chironomus* spp), which are able to live in stagnant water because the haemoglobin in their bodies helps them to absorb what little oxygen is available.

The biting midges of the **Ceratopogonidae** rarely exceed 5mm in length, but their bite* is intensely irritating. The insects approach and bite almost unnoticed, but the irritation soon starts. In America they are appropriately known as 'no-see-ums'. Luckily, only a few of the 150 or so British species bite man, the commonest being *Culicoides obsoletus*. All *Culicoides* species feed on birds or mammals but the other British genera attack other insects. Male biting midges are unusual in retaining their mandibles, although they are not blood-feeders. Larval ceratopogonids live mainly in water, particularly in swamps and ditches with plenty of organic content.

The members of the **Simuliidae**, known as black-flies, are rather squat in all their features and can be recognised by their very broad wings. The veins at the front are noticeably thickened, but the rest are very faint. The antennae are hardly longer than

*   *It is conventional to talk about biting flies, but we should strictly talk of piercing flies, for none of them bites in the sense of closing two jaws together.*

forked vein M_{1+2}

Culicoides, a biting midge of the family Ceratopogonidae, showing the strongly humped thorax. Most of these insects are very small, and the venation is often indistinct, but they can be distinguished from chironomid midges by the forked vein 4 (M_{1+2}). The wings are usually held flat over the back at rest

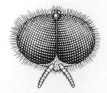

The head of Bibio, *viewed from the front to show the position of the antennae below the eyes*

the head. The females are blood-suckers and in some parts of the world they transmit a number of serious human and animal diseases. Immense populations build up in the Arctic during the summer, making travel almost impossible at times, and black-flies can also be a problem around the Danube delta and in other parts of south-east Europe. There are about 35 British species. *Simulium equinum* (Pl.26) sometimes plagues horses, and *S. posticatum*, commonly known as the Blandford-fly, sometimes torments people in parts of Dorset, but the black-flies are not otherwise very important in the British Isles. Black-fly larvae live in running water, attaching themselves to stones by means of hooks and sometimes silken webs.

Members of the **Bibionidae** are rather stouter than other nematocerous flies and their antennae, inserted below the eyes, are also unusually stout. They are hairy, black or brownish flies with characteristic spines on the front tibiae. The males have much larger heads than the females, composed almost entirely of their huge compound eyes. The adults are often abundant on grassland in the spring and are sometimes called March-flies. They probably play an important role in pollinating fruit trees and other plants. St. Mark's-fly (*Bibio marci*), so-named because it often appears around St. Mark's day (April 25th), is the most familiar of the 18 British species. The males drift slowly over the vegetation with their legs dangling loosely beneath them. *Dilophus febrilis* (Pl.26), commonly known as the Fever-fly, often occurs in gardens. It is smaller than St. Mark's-fly but is most easily distinguished from it by looking at the front tibiae: whereas all *Bibio* species have a prominent beak-like spine at the tip of each front tibia, *Dilophus* has a ring of short spines. Bibionid larvae live in the soil and in decaying matter, often causing some damage to plant roots.

The **Scatopsidae**, with about 35 small or minute British species, including *Anapausis soluta* (Pl. 26), is closely related to the Bibionidae but the tibiae are not spined and the body is not hairy. The larvae develop in decaying matter, especially animal droppings.

The **Mycetophilidae**, whose members are known as fungus gnats because of the dominance of fungi in the larval diet, contains nearly 300 British species. They are all very delicate flies with long, slender antennae and long legs, especially the back ones. The thorax is usually humped and it conceals the head from above. The eyes do not meet above the antennae. The larvae are pale, with dark heads and are often

A fungus gnat (Mycetophilidae), showing how the thorax completely overhangs the head in most species

abundant in fungi. They are easy to rear if the fungi are placed on bran or sawdust into which the larvae can crawl for pupation. Several species have carnivorous larvae, feeding on other insects living in the fungi.

The **Sciaridae** is closely related to the Mycetophilidae and has only recently been separated from it. The main difference lies in the eyes, which form a bridge over the bases of the antennae. There are about 85 British species. *Sciara thomae* (Pl.26) is a very common species which often damages mushroom crops. It breeds in all kinds of rotting matter as well as in fungi and the adults are not uncommon in houses. There are many similar species, all with a prominent fork in the middle of the wing. The larvae often damage crop roots, especially in soils that have been recently manured.

The **Cecidomyiidae** is one of the largest families of flies. Its members, which include over 600 British species, are commonly known as gall midges, although not all of them actually induce gall formation. They are very delicate insects, rarely over 5mm in length, with relatively long legs and wings which are rather hairy. The most characteristic features, however, are the very reduced venation, with a maximum of four veins reaching the wing margin, and the bead-like segments of the antennae, each separated from the next by a whorl of minute hairs. Common gall-causing species include *Taxomyia taxi* (Pl.26), which induces galls on the tips of yew shoots, and *Jaapiella veronicae* which causes fluffy white galls on the shoot tips of germander speedwell. Both galls consist of clusters of swollen and deformed leaves, among which live the flies' tiny orange larvae. Important non-gall-causing species include the Hessian-fly (*Mayetiola destructor*), which causes much damage to wheat in Europe and North America, although not to any great extent in the British Isles, and the Pear Midge (*Contarinia pyrivora*). Larvae of the latter feed inside young pears and prevent them from reaching maturity. A number of species have predatory larvae, feeding mainly on aphids and mites, and a few are actually parasitic.

SUB-ORDER BRACHYCERA

The members of this sub-order are generally well-built flies and most of them have a long, pointed anal cell. The antennae are short and stout. The third antennal segment is often ringed and may or may not carry a bristle or spur. In this respect the brachycerous flies are intermediate between the Nematocera and the Cyclorrhapha. The larvae also exhibit intermediate characteristics, their incompletely-developed heads linking the fully-developed heads of the Nematocera with the headless maggots of the Cyclorrhapha. The structure of the feet is important in the identification of these flies and, unless otherwise stated, each has two pads (fig. p. 175).

The family **Stratiomyidae** contains the soldier-flies – rather flattened insects with bright and often metallic colours. The discal cell is small and the veins beyond it are rather faint. The scutellum often bears spines on the rear margin. The feet have three pads. Soldier-flies are rather lazy insects and are most often seen sunning themselves on the ground or the herbage with their wings folded flat over their bodies. The larvae live mainly as scavengers in leaf litter and other rotting matter, but some are carnivorous. A number are aquatic. There are about 50 British species, varying a good deal in shape and size. *Oxycera rara* (Pl.27) is one of several similar species frequenting damp woods and hedgerows and breeding in moss and leaf litter.

The family **Xylomyiidae** is closely related to the soldier-flies but its members are immediately identified by the closed cell just behind the discal cell. The body is

Wings of xylophagid (left) and xylomyiid flies - two closely related families, but readily distinguished by the two closed cells in the middle of the xylomyiid wing

more or less cylindrical and the middle and hind tibiae bear prominent spurs. The foot has three pads. There are three British species, all breeding in decaying tree stumps and generally confined to ancient woodland. Members of the **Xylophagidae** also breed in rotting tree stumps. The adults are more slender than those of the previous family and the wing lacks a closed cell behind the discal cell. The foot has three pads. There are three British species.

The **Rhagionidae** contains slender, long-legged flies commonly known as snipe-flies. They are mostly brown and yellow and the feet have three pads. Vein 2 curves forward to enclose a lightly-pigmented stigma. The anal cell is sometimes open. Snipe-flies feed mainly on other insects, often darting from their perches to snatch them in mid-air. *Rhagio scolopacea* (Pl.27) is sometimes known as the down-looker-fly because, in common with some of its relatives, it often sits head-down on tree trunks and other vertical surfaces. Snipe-fly larvae (fig. p. 176) live in soil, leaf-litter, and rotting wood and feed on other insects. There are 17 British species.

The only brachycerous flies that harm man are the horse-flies and their relatives in the **Tabanidae** (Pl. 27). These are stoutly-built flies – known as stouts in some places – whose bulging eyes often show brilliant iridescent colours in life. The feet have three pads and the thoracic squamae are relatively large, but the flies are most easily recognised by the broad fork of vein 3 (R_4 and R_5) which encloses the wing-tip. Male horse-flies feed on nectar and other juices, but the females are voracious blood-suckers and inflict painful bites on man as well as on horses and other large mammals. Some species also attack reptiles and amphibians, but few seem to attack birds. The mouth-parts are basically similar to those of the mosquito (p. 190), although the stylets are broader and more blade-like. The labium has well-developed labella (fig. p. 172) which are used to mop up surface fluids in addition to the blood meals. Larval tabanids live mainly in damp soil and mud, where most of them eat assorted insects and other small creatures.

There are about 28 British species and many people will agree that the dull grey Cleg-fly (*Haematopota pluvialis*) is one of the most obnoxious. It flies with absolute silence, selects a suitable exposed area of skin, and sinks its mouth-parts into our flesh – the first indication we have of its presence. Most flies do at least make some sort of noise as they approach and we can take evasive action – but not so with the Cleg. *Tabanus bromius* is one of several similar large horse-flies found on pasture-land. Its colour ranges from yellowish grey to almost black. *Chrysops relictus* is one of a number of species with patterned wings and really brilliant eyes. It is usually found near water. *Chrysops* larvae feed on decaying vegetable matter.

Members of the **Acroceridae**, typified by *Ogcodes pallipes* (Pl.27), are easily recognised by the bulbous body and tiny head. The feet have three pads and the thoracic squamae are very large. The flies, which are not common, can sometimes be found sitting on flowers, although they do not feed. The larvae are internal parasites of spiders. There are three British species.

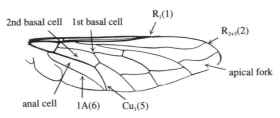

Venation of the bee-fly Bombylius, *in which the anal cell is not completely closed - thus readily distinguishing the bee-flies from superficially similar hover-flies (fig. p. 201)*

The members of the **Bombyliidae** (Pl. 27) well deserve their common name of bee-flies, for several of them are stout, furry insects with a strong superficial resemblance to bumble bees – although their long, spindly legs are very different from those of the bees. Several species have a long, rigid proboscis. The anal cell is never completely closed and only two or three veins reach the margin between this cell and the lower branch of the apical fork (vein 3). *Bombylius major* is the best known of the ten British species. It is commonly seen in spring, plunging its long proboscis into flowers. Its hovering and darting flight, accompanied by a high-pitched whine, is much more agile than that of a bumble bee. *Thyridanthrax fenestratus* has a similar flight. It lives mainly in sandy habitats and lacks a long proboscis. Bee-fly larvae are all parasitic on other insects. *Thyridanthrax* attacks caterpillars, but most bee-flies are parasites of solitary bees and wasps. The eggs are scattered near the host nests or laid on flowers, and the young larvae make their own way or are carried into the nests, where they attack both the food stores and the young bees and wasps.

The **Scenopinidae** contains small, black, bristleless flies which have a bullet-like appearance when resting with the wings tightly folded over the body. They are commonly known as window-flies, because they are most often seen resting on window panes. They are particularly common in stables and other out-buildings, where their worm-like larvae feed on the grubs of clothes moths and other debris-inhabiting insects. They also breed in birds' nests, where the larvae are quite partial to flea grubs. *Scenopinus fenestralis* (Pl.27) is the commonest and most domestic of the three British species, often breeding in household carpets.

Members of the **Therevidae** are rather elongate and very hairy flies, resembling some of the robber-flies but differing from them in having rather more slender legs and in lacking a groove between the eyes. Although these flies are sometimes stated to be predatory, the structure of the proboscis suggests that they probably do no more than lap nectar from flowers. The worm-like larvae live in soil and leaf litter and are at least partly predatory. *Thereva nobilitata* (Pl.27) is the commonest of the 13 British species.

The **Asilidae** contains the robber-flies – mostly sturdy insects with powerful, bristly legs. The feet normally have two pads. The most characteristic feature is the deep groove between the eyes. Robber-flies all feed on other insects of some kind or another, which they usually catch in mid-air. The horny proboscis is used to pierce the prey and suck its juices and the dense beard of bristles on the face serves to protect the eyes from the struggling prey. Despite the large size of many of these insects, they are quite harmless to man. *Asilus crabroniformis* (Pl.27) is one of the largest of the 27 British species. *Leptogaster* species are among the smallest: they

The head of a robber-fly (Asilidae), showing
the deep groove between the eyes

are slender, ichneumon-like flies that drift around in grassy places and pluck small insects and spiders from the leaves. These small robber-flies have virtually no bristles and lack pads on their feet. Robber-fly larvae feed mainly on dead vegetable matter, but at least some of the species appear to be partly predatory.

The **Nemestrinidae** contains a number of large-headed flies, many of which have numerous small cells at the tips of the wings. They do not fly a great deal and spend much of their time sitting on flowers. The bee-like *Fallenia fasciata* (Pl.27), which inhabits damp places in southern Europe, could be mistaken for a bee-fly, but the venation is very different and *Fallenia* has a downward-pointing proboscis. The larvae of this family are mostly endoparasites of beetle grubs.

The **Mydaidae** contains a number of large and more or less hairless flies with clubbed antennae. The family is centred in the tropics and contains the largest of all flies. Four species reach Europe. *Leptomydas corsicanus* (Pl.27) lives in Corsica, while two similar species occur in Spain and a fourth is found in Sardinia. The males are much smaller and darker than the females. Both adults and larvae are largely predatory.

The **Empididae** contains small and medium-sized flies which could be mistaken for small robber-flies were it not for the short, blunt anal cell. The head is more or less spherical and supported on a slender neck. There is a horny proboscis, often quite long, which is used for sucking the juices of other insects – usually other flies. The feet generally have only two pads, although *Clinocera* species have three. The most constant feature of the family, although not readily observed without at least a strong lens, is the 'eye-nick' – a small indentation in the inner edge of each eye. The larvae live in soil and decaying vegetation or in water and are at least partly predatory. The adults frequently congregate in dancing swarms, often over water, and are commonly called dance-flies. There are over 200 British species, one of the most

Left, The venation of an empidid fly, showing the long 1st basal cell. Right, the fly's
face, showing the characteristic eye-nick of this family

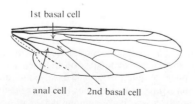

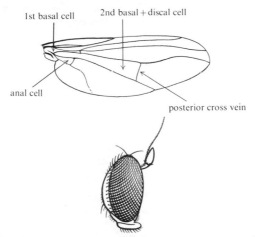

1st basal cell   2nd basal + discal cell

anal cell

posterior cross vein

Wing of a dolichopodid fly, showing the short 1st basal cell, the long cell formed by fusion of the second basal and discal cells, and the very prominent posterior cross-vein. The head profile shows the characteristically long shape of the head in the family

familiar being *Empis tessellata* (Pl.27). This rather drab, bristly fly often hunts its prey on hawthorn blossom and various umbellifer flowers. Like all members of its genus, it has a very short triangular cell at the wing-tip. *Hilara maura* (Pl.27) is one of many similar species, much less bristly than most other dance-flies and with a relatively long triangular apical cell. The flies are sometimes called balloon-flies because during courtship, which takes place in fast-moving swarms just above the surface of ponds and streams, the male presents the female with a small ball of silk – usually containing a small insect. The silk comes from the male's swollen front tarsi.

The family **Dolichopodidae** (Pl.28) contains small, bristly flies with long legs. The feet usually have only two pads, although a few species have three pads on each foot. Many of the species are metallic green or bronze. The posterior cross-vein is the only obvious cross-vein and this immediately distinguishes the dolichopids from most other flies. The male genitalia are usually very prominent and the male tarsi are commonly ornamented with swellings and tufts of hair. Dolichopids prey on other small insects, which are enveloped and crushed by the fleshy labella. The latter bear small teeth in some species. Several species, including *Dolichopus popularis*, hunt over water and often rest on floating vegetation with the front of the body raised on the long legs. *Sciapus platypterus* is one of several species in which vein 4 forks just beyond the cross-vein. There are over 250 British species.

SUB-ORDER CYCLORRHAPHA

These are the flies that pupate in barrel-shaped puparia and escape through more or less circular openings. The antennae have three segments, the third one being large and bearing a bristle. Venation is somewhat reduced in most families, especially towards the rear of the wing. There is great variation in the size of the insects in this group, but most are well-proportioned if not actually stout (fig. p. 170). The larvae of many species are known as maggots: they have no head and taper markedly towards the front (fig. p. 176).

There are two groups or series within the Cyclorrhapha: the **Aschiza**, in which there is no ptilinum, and the **Schizophora**, in which a ptilinum is used to escape from the puparium. Members of the Aschiza show affinities with both the Brachycera and the rest of the Cyclorrhapha and may be regarded as a transition group between the two. The Schizophora is itself divided into three groups: the **Acalyptratae**, in which the thoracic squamae (calypters) are not usually well developed; the **Calyptratae**, in which the squamae are generally large and conceal the halteres; and the **Pupipara** – parasitic flies whose larval development takes place entirely inside the female parent.

SERIES ASCHIZA

The anal cell, when present, is usually long and pointed in this group, as it is in most members of the Brachycera. In fact, virtually all flies with a long, pointed anal cell belong to one or other of these two groups.

The family **Lonchopteridae** can be recognised at once by the pointed wings. The venation differs slightly in the two sexes, but the only cross-veins are very close to the base. The 3rd antennal segment is more or less spherical and has a stout terminal bristle. *Lonchoptera lutea* (Pl.27) is typical of the seven British species. The larvae live in leaf litter and the vestigial head indicates their relationship with the Brachycera.

The **Phoridae** contains small hump-backed flies commonly known as scuttleflies. There are about 280 British species. Most are black, brown, or yellowish flies and they are easily recognised by the spiny front edge of the wing and the characteristic venation. The first three veins are short and thick – although vein 2 may be absent, as in *Phora aterrima* (Pl.27) – and they are crowded together at the base of the wing. The other veins are weak. Adult flies are abundant on vegetation, where they scurry about in the rather agitated fashion which gives them their common name. They often enter houses and swarm over window panes. Phorid larvae generally feed in decaying material, including the dead bodies of various animals. *Conicera tibialis* is known as the Coffin-fly because it regularly breeds in human corpses after burial. Some species are parasites of other insects, while others feed on fungi. *Megaselia halterata* is the Mushroom-fly, a common pest of cultivated mushrooms.

Members of the **Platypezidae** are small or medium-sized flies in which the hind tarsi are usually dilated. They are commonly known as flat-footed-flies. The wings are relatively large and the posterior cross-vein may be present, as in *Paraplatypeza atra* (Pl.28), or absent. There are 31 British species. The larvae are fungus-feeders.

The **Pipunculidae** contains small, dark flies with enormous heads composed almost entirely of the compound eyes. The wings are usually very much longer than the abdomen, with veins 3 and 4 converging strongly towards the wing-tip and forming a very characteristic beaked or pear-shaped sub-apical cell. These flies often hover low down in dense vegetation and they rival the syrphids in hovering ability. Verrall described them as the most exquisite fliers among flies. The larvae are internal parasites of homopteran bugs, especially plant-hoppers. There are about 75 British species, typified by *Pipunculus thomsoni* (Pl.28).

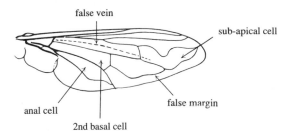

The wing of a hover-fly, showing the characteristic false vein and false margin. The sub-apical cell varies in shape, but is always closed

The hover-flies of the family **Syrphidae** (Pl.28) are among the most striking of the Diptera because of their generally bright colours and hovering ability. They are abundant on flowers for much of the year, feeding on both pollen and nectar. The insects vary a great deal in size and shape, but are easily recognised by the venation. There is a 'false margin' to the rear of the wing, formed by the outer margin of the discal cell and vein 4 (M_{1+2}), which bends forward and runs parallel to the wing margin and closes the sub-apical cell in the process. The true wing margin is often difficult to see. There is also a 'false vein' running between veins 3 and 4. It is really only a thickening of the wing membrane and it is not connected to any true vein, but it is usually quite conspicuous.

Mimicry (see p. 262) is well illustrated by the hover-flies, the main models being various species of bees and wasps. The Drone-fly (*Eristalis tenax*) is a good honey bee mimic, while *Volucella bombylans* exists in several forms and mimics several bumble bee species. Hover-fly larvae are extremely varied in both shape and habits. The best-known are the aphid-eating larvae of the sub-family Syrphinae, which includes the genera *Syrphus, Leucozona, Scaeva, Doros*, and *Baccha*. The larvae of *Brachypalpoides lenta* and *Milesia crabroniformis* live in rotting wood, while those of *Volucella* species live as scavengers in the nests of bees and wasps, feeding on dead and dying insects and other debris. Several species live in compost heaps and other rotting material, and some feed on organic matter in stagnant water. Best known in this last group is the larva of the Drone-fly, which has a telescopic breathing tube and is known as the rat-tailed maggot (fig. p. 176). A few species feed on living plants, including fungi. *Merodon equestris* is the Bulb-fly or Narcissus-fly, whose larvae feed in various kinds of bulbs and often damage garden daffodils. The adult is a bumble bee mimic and, like *Volucella bombylans*, it exists in several different forms. There are about 250 British hover-fly species.

The family **Conopidae** was formerly included in the Schizophora because its members have a ptilinum, but other features, including the possession of a pointed anal cell reaching almost or quite to the wing margin, suggest that it is closely related to the Syrphidae and belongs in the Aschiza. Several of the species, including *Conops quadrifasciata* (Pl. 29), are excellent wasp mimics. The head is as wide as or wider than the thorax and there is commonly a slender, forward-pointing proboscis. Some species also have long, forward-pointing, and clubbed antennae. The adult flies feed on nectar, but the larvae are internal parasites of bees and wasps.

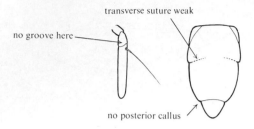

Antenna and thorax of a typical acalypterate fly

SERIES SCHIZOPHORA – ACALYPTRATAE

These are mostly very small flies and they rarely have much colour. The thoracic squamae or calypters are usually poorly developed and the transverse suture is generally weak or absent. The posterior calli are poorly developed or absent and there is no distinct groove on the second antennal segment. The eyes are always well separated in both sexes. The anal cell is generally short and blunt.

Several acalypterate families have wings which are heavily patterned with dark areas. Such wings are commonly described as 'pictured'. The **Tephritidae** is the largest of these families and can be recognised by the sharply-elbowed vein Sc, which fades away before it reaches the costal margin. The female abdomen is pointed and ends in a rigid, telescopic ovipositor. The larvae live in fruit and other parts of plants and often induce gall-formation. *Urophora cardui* (Pl.29) is a common species whose larvae live in the stems of creeping thistle and cause the development of hard, rounded galls. The Mediterranean Fruit-fly (*Ceratitis capitata*) attacks a wide range of fruit in southern Europe. *Euleia heracleii* is the Celery-fly, whose larvae mine the leaves of celery, parsnip, and other umbellifers. There are about 70 British species. Members of the **Otitidae** resemble the tephritids but vein Sc is never sharply angled and the face generally has deep grooves to accommodate the antennae. Most otitids move their wings slowly up and down at rest, although this wing-waving occurs in several other families as well. There are 21 British species, typified by *Melieria omissa* (Pl.29), although not all have pictured wings. The larvae live in decaying matter. The **Platystomatidae** is closely related to the Otitidae but differs in having a small break in the costa near the humeral vein. *Platystoma seminationis* (Pl.29) is the commoner of the two British species, but not all members of the family have such dark wings. Adults crawl slowly over vegetation in shady places, and the larvae develop in decaying vegetable matter. The **Pallopteridae** contains flies with long, lightly-

The wing of Urophora cardui, *showing how vein Sc curves sharply forward and dies away before reaching the costal margin. The dark pattern varies from species to species and the pointed extension of the anal cell is not present in all genera of the family*

Top, The face of Melieria omissa, *showing the pronounced grooves characteristic of the Otitidae. Bottom,* Micropeza *in its typical resting position, showing its very long legs and flat head*

pictured wings. They resemble some of the otitids, but lack the grooves on the face. The costa is broken close to vein Sc. There are 11 British species, most of which breed in vegetable debris, often under loose bark.

The **Micropezidae** contains slender flies with extremely long legs. Commonly called stilt-legged flies, they prey on other insects which they find as they walk rather hesitatingly over the vegetation – usually in damp, shady places. The larvae live in decaying matter. There are nine British species, including *Calobata petronella* (Pl.29). *Micropeza* species are even more slender, with very flat heads. The **Megamerinidae** is a closely related family, distinguished by the spines under the hind femur. There is just one British species. The **Tanypezidae** differs from the Micropezidae mainly in having a convex outer margin to the anal cell. There is just one rare species in the British Isles.

Members of the **Psilidae** are small and medium-sized flies, most easily recognised by a pale streak or fold running across the basal part of the wing – although this is not always immediately obvious. There is a clear break about a quarter of the way along the costal margin. The ocellar triangle is quite prominent. The larvae are plant-feeders. The Carrot-fly (*Psila rosae*) (Pl.29) is a widespread pest of carrots, its larvae tunnelling in the roots and often causing the leaves to take on a rusty appearance. It also attacks other umbelliferous crops.

The **Dryomyzidae** contains brownish flies with large wings, in which the second basal and anal cells are relatively large and reach well beyond the alula. *Dryomyza flaveola* (Pl.29) is one of only two British species. The larvae live in decaying fungi and other rotting vegetable matter. The **Helcomyzidae** is a closely related family, distinguished by the strong spines on the front edge of the wing. There are two British species, including the silvery-grey *Helcomyza ustulata* which breeds on the seashore. Some members of the **Sciomyzidae** could be confused with the dryomyzids, but the second basal and anal cells are much shorter and hardly reach beyond the alula. *Tetanocera elata* (Pl.29) frequents waterside vegetation where, like other members of

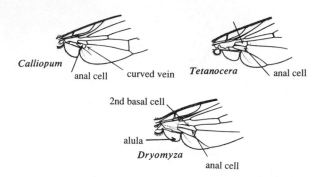

Wing bases of Calliopum, Tetanocera *and* Dryomyza, *showing the different lengths of the 2nd basal and anal cells. Those of* Dryomyza *extend well beyond the alula*

the family, the larvae feed on small snails. There are about 65 British species, some of them with stout, forward-pointing antennae and mottled wings. Members of the **Lauxaniidae** range from pale yellow to the greenish black of *Calliopum aeneum* (Pl.29). Some of them resemble some of the sciomyzids, but they are readily distinguished by the converging post-vertical bristles and by the short vein 6 which often ends just beyond the anal cell. The latter is closed by a curved vein. The larvae live mainly in decaying vegetation, although some attack living plants. The adults are found mainly in damp, shady places.

The **Chamaemyiidae** contains very small greyish and rather dusty-looking flies. Vein 1 is short, but fairly thick and expanded at its junction with the costa. Vein 6 is extremely faint, but vein 7 is stronger and usually at least as long as the anal cell. There are about 25 British species, typified by *Chamaemyia aridella* (Pl.29). The larvae feed mainly on aphids.

Members of the **Coelopidae**, known as kelp-flies because their larvae feed on stranded seaweeds, are rather flat, bristly flies of small or medium size and with relatively thick legs. They can be distinguished from members of the Lauxaniidae and other similar flies by the straight vein closing the anal cell. There are three British species, typified by *Coelopa frigida* (Pl.29), and they swarm on the seashore at almost any time of year.

The **Heleomyzidae** contains small or medium-sized yellow or brownish flies which are easily identified by the small spines scattered along the front edge of the wing. There are about 60 species, typified by *Suillia variegata* (Pl.30) – although not all have blotched wings. The larvae feed on fungi and various rotting materials, especially carrion. The **Chyromyidae** is a rather similar family, but the wings lack

Wing of Chamaemyia, *showing the prominent vein 1 and the very short vein 6*

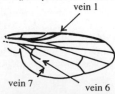

the costal spines and there is no dorsal pre-apical bristle on the hind tibia. There are six British species – all very small – and their larvae develop in bird droppings.

The **Sepsidae** contains small, dark flies many of which resemble ants because of the constriction of the base of the abdomen. The head is more or less spherical and the males' front legs are usually equipped with prominent spines or teeth which are used to grasp the females during mating. There is commonly a dark spot near the wing-tip. The flies frequently form dense swarms on low-growing vegetation and often blacken umbellifer heads as they jostle for nectar. Wing-waving is very common in these insects. The larvae feed in a wide range of decaying materials but are especially common in dung. Sewage sludge attracts several species. There are 25 British species, typified by *Sepsis punctum* (Pl.29). *Orygma luctuosum* is a rather aberrant species, confined to the seashore, in which the head is more or less triangular in profile.

The **Sphaeroceridae** contains minute or small dark flies with short, fat hind metatarsi. The hind tibia sometimes has a strong apical claw. The venation is very variable, but vein 5 commonly stops at the posterior cross-vein or continues to the margin only as a faint trace. Vein 4 sometimes behaves similarly. The second basal and discal cells are not always separated by a cross-vein. *Copromyza similis* (Pl.30) is one of about 100 British species. They nearly all breed in dung.

Members of the **Lonchaeidae** are small metallic flies, usually dark blue or green, with rather broad, clear wings. There is a prominent break in the costa near vein Sc. The larvae feed on a variety of living and dead vegetable matter. There are about 30 British species, typified by *Lonchaea chorea* (Pl.29).

The **Piophilidae** contains dark, shining flies in which the outer part of vein 6 bends slightly forward and then fades away. The costa is broken close to the tip of Sc. The head bears prominent vibrissae and the eyes are circular in profile. The larvae are scavengers and are particularly attracted by protein-rich foods such as carrion. *Piophila casei* (Pl.29) is the Cheese-skipper, whose larvae often infest stored cheese and bacon. There are ten British species. Members of the **Clusiidae** are very similar, but vein 6 does not bend and the sides of the thorax are rather bristly. There are ten British species, breeding mainly in fungi and rotting wood.

The members of the **Opomyzidae**, typified by *Opomyza germinationis* (Pl.30), are all small flies with spotted wings. They are readily distinguished from all similar flies by the apical convergence of veins 2 and 3 – these are the first two long veins, for vein 1 (Rs) is very short. The larvae live in the shoots of grasses, including cereals. There are 14 British species.

The family **Carniidae** (Pl.30) contains very tiny flies, rarely more than about 1.5mm long. The costa is broken near the tip of the very short vein 1 and vein 4 stops just beyond the anterior cross-vein. *Carnus hemapterus* has only one closed cell – the first basal cell. This minute fly is an ectoparasite of birds, sucking blood through its tiny proboscis. The larvae live on debris in the hosts' nests, and the emerging adults attach themselves to young birds. The flies then break off their wings and stay on their hosts for the rest of their lives. *Meonura obscurella* has two closed basal cells. It is not parasitic and often comes into houses. It breeds in various rotting materials. The family contains 13 British species.

The **Milichiidae** also contains minute, dark flies, but the venation is fuller than in the Carniidae and the costa is broken twice – once near the humeral vein and once near the tip of vein 1, although the first is not easy to make out. Both adults and larvae are scavengers and the adults are often known as jackal-flies because of their habit of hanging around larger predators to wait for scraps. *Desmometopa sordida* is known to lurk around robber-flies and wasps and even mantids and to nip in for a drink from the juices oozing from the prey. There are ten British species. The **Tethinidae** contains very similar flies but the costa is broken only near the tip of vein 1. The first basal cell is very narrow and tapers distally. There are ten British species, all living on the seashore. Members of the **Canacidae** also live on the shore. They are very small greyish flies with divergent post-vertical bristles and a dorsal pre-apical bristle on the hind tibia.

The **Anthomyzidae** contains slender flies, mostly under 3mm long and with relatively long, narrow wings. The long costal cilia and the rather central position of the posterior cross-vein should identify the family. There is also a stout spine underneath the front femur. The larvae develop in the leaf sheaths of reeds and other grasses and the adults are found mainly in wet places. *Anthomyza gracilis* (Pl.30) is one of 15 British species.

The **Asteiidae** contains very small flies which breed in vegetable debris. The costa is broken twice, although the breaks are very indistinct and the posterior cross-vein, when present, is well before the centre of the wing. There are six British species. The **Camillidae** is a rather similar family but the costal breaks are clearer and the posterior cross-vein is well beyond the centre of the wing. The post-vertical bristles are distinctly crossed. There are five British species, all breeding in fungi and decaying vegetation.

Members of the **Ephydridae** are all small or minute flies, commonly known as shore-flies because they are rarely found away from the seashore or the edges of lakes and ponds. The venation is characteristic, with two marked costal breaks and the second basal and discal cells joined to form one long cell. There is no anal cell. The wings are sometimes mottled and the antennae are frequently hairy. Some adults are predatory, but most feed on decaying matter. The larvae include leaf-miners and predators as well as detritus-feeders, on land as well as in the water. There are about 130 British species, typified by *Psilopa nigritella* (Pl.30).

The **Diastatidae** contains very small greyish flies, best recognised by the incomplete vein separating the second basal cell from the discal cell. The posterior cross-vein is well beyond the middle of the wing and the costa is clearly broken close to the tip of vein 1. Strong vibrissae are present and there is a prominent dorsal pre-apical bristle on the hind tibia. There are eight British species, breeding mainly in leaf litter.

The **Drosophilidae** contains minute and small flies – mostly brown, yellow, or grey with brightly-coloured eyes – the best known of which is the Vinegar-fly (*Drosophila melanogaster*). This species, usually referred to simply as *Drosophila*, has long been the geneticist's main aid because its large salivary gland chromosomes and its short life cycle make it ideal for genetical work. The whole family is attracted by fermenting materials and the insects are commonly called fruit-flies on account of their liking for rotting fruit. They can usually be recognised by the apparent forking of the antennal bristle and by the venation: the second basal and discal cells are normally joined but, unlike the Ephydridae and Chloropidae, there is an anal cell. There are two costal breaks. Most drosophilid larvae feed on rotting vegetable matter but some feed on fungi and a few are predatory or parasitic. There are about 50

Antenna of Drosophila

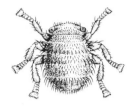

Braula coeca - *the Bee-louse*

British species. *D. funebris* (Pl.30) is one of a number of species that plague breweries, jam factories, and canneries. Like many other species, it is rather variable in colour.

The **Braulidae** contains just one European species – the minute Bee-louse (*Braula coeca*) which is an ectoparasite of bees. It is under 1.5mm long. The larvae consume wax and stored pollen in the bees' nests.

Members of the **Agromyzidae** are small, dark flies with the build of miniature House-flies. They can be recognised by the divergent post-vertical bristles together with inward-pointing lower-fronto-orbital bristles and a single costal break. The venation varies a good deal. The posterior cross-vein is absent in *Phytomyza ilicis* (Pl.30) but present in many other species. Vein Sc is distinct, although slender, and it either fades away before reaching the wing margin or runs into vein 1. There are over 300 British species and their larvae are mostly leaf or stem-miners. Each species has a more or less characteristic mine and tends to keep to one particular species or group of plants. *P. ilicis* is abundant on holly, making yellowish blotch mines in the leaves. A few species feed in roots and seeds.

Members of the **Chloropidae** (Pl.30) are easily recognised by the prominent, plate-like ocellar triangle that occupies most of the frons. The costa is broken once, near the tip of vein 1, and the second basal cell and discal cell are joined. There is no anal cell. All the species are small or minute and almost hairless. They are largely black, although often brightly marked with yellow or green. Some larvae are predatory, but most are plant-feeders and the family includes some important agricultural pests. The Frit-fly (*Oscinella frit*) is only about 1.5mm long, but its larvae cause heavy losses among cereal crops by burrowing into the stems and developing ears. Probably the most noticeable member of the family is the Small Cluster-fly (*Thaumatomyia notata*), huge numbers of which enter houses in the autumn in search of winter sleeping quarters. Its larvae feed on root aphids. *Lipara lucens* is one of the largest chloropids. Its larvae live in cigar-shaped galls on reed stems. There are about 150 British species.

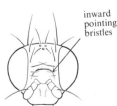

inward
pointing
bristles

Head of an agromyzid fly, showing the
inward-pointing lower fronto-orbital
bristles

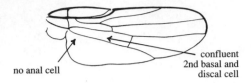

no anal cell

confluent
2nd basal and
discal cell

Wing of a chloropid fly, showing the absence of the anal cell in this family

SERIES SCHIZOPHORA – CALYPTRATAE

These are the flies in which the thoracic squamae are normally well developed and conceal the halteres. A few species have vestigial squamae, but they are usually easily distinguished from the acalypterates by the complete transverse suture on the thorax and the well-developed posterior calli. Most species are rather bristly.

On account of the vestigial squamae and incomplete transverse suture, the **Gasterophilidae** was for a long time included in the Acalyptratae, but it clearly resembles the Oestridae in several ways and is now placed firmly in the Calyptratae. Its members are known as bot-flies and their larvae are internal parasites of horses and other equines. Eggs are usually laid on the host's body and the larvae make their way to the mouth – often when the host licks itself – and then into the stomach, where they cling to the lining with their mouth-hooks. They feed there for about nine months and then pass out with the faeces to pupate on the ground. Heavy infestations of bot-fly larvae cause serious loss of condition in the host and may open the way for secondary infection of the stomach. The adult flies have vestigial mouth-parts and cannot bite, but they seem to worry their hosts much more than the biting horse-flies. *Gasterophilus intestinalis* (Pl.29) is the commonest of the four British species, all of which are large and hairy bee-like flies. The female ovipositor is always well developed. *G. pecorum* lays its eggs on vegetation and they hatch when they are eaten by the host.

The **Oestridae** (Pl.30) also contains stout, hairy flies whose larvae are internal parasites of mammals, but the adults are easily distinguished from the bot-flies by the large squamae and by the strong convergence of veins 3 and 4: these veins diverge strongly in the bot-flies. The adults have vestigial mouth-parts and a relatively short life. There are seven British species. The Warble-fly (*Hypoderma bovis*), one of several closely related species, lays its eggs on the legs of cattle and the larvae bore in through the skin. They gradually work their way through the body and end up just under the skin on the host's back. The larvae are then fat and spiny and each

Antenna and thorax of a typical calypterate fly

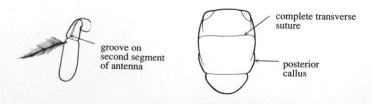

groove on
second segment
of antenna

complete transverse
suture

posterior
callus

one makes a small breathing pore in the host's skin. The tissues around the larvae become inflamed and produce the swellings known as warbles. The irritation causes the cattle to lose condition, and the damage to the skin also means that the hides are of little value. When fully grown, the larvae leave the warbles and drop to the ground for pupation. Some *Hypoderma* species attack deer. The very large and furry *Oedemagena tarandi* parasitises reindeer in the far north.

Oestrus ovis is the Sheep Nostril-fly, also known as the Sheep Bot. Much less hairy than other members of the family, it is easily identified by the warty texture of the top of the head and the thorax. The adult female deposits first-instar larvae in the nostrils of sheep and goats and the maggots complete their development in the nasal cavities and sinuses, causing giddiness in the hosts. Fully-grown larvae are sneezed out and they pupate on the ground. Species of *Cephenemyia* attack deer in the same way.

The **Tachinidae** (Pl. 31) is a large family, containing mostly medium-sized flies which can usually be recognised by the well-developed post-scutellum. As in the Calliphoridae and Rhinophoridae, there is a distinct arc of hypopleural bristles just below the haltere on each side. Vein 4 usually bends sharply towards vein 3 and sometimes joins with it just before the wing-tip – as in *Alophora hemiptera*. This fly varies a good deal in size and colour, but can usually be recognised by its very broad wings, especially in the male. Most of the tachinids are rather drab, greyish flies although there are some brightly coloured species, including *Tachina fera*, *Gymnocheta viridis*, and *Gonia divisa*. The larvae of this family are almost all internal parasites of other insects and their behaviour is very like that of ichneumon grubs (see p. 266) in that they attack the hosts' non-essential organs first and kill their hosts only when they themselves are fully grown and ready to pupate. The main hosts are butterfly and moth larvae, but all orders with sizeable members are liable to attack. Tachinid larvae get into their hosts by several routes: the female fly may pierce the host and lay her eggs inside it; eggs may be laid on or near the host, with the resulting larvae boring their way in after hatching; or eggs may be laid on the host's food-plant and hatch when they have been swallowed. There are about 240 British species in the family.

The **Calliphoridae** (Pl.31) contains some very familiar flies, including the bluebottles and greenbottles. Most are medium-sized flies, distinguished from most other calypterates by the fan of hypopleural bristles and the poorly-developed or non-exist-

Thorax of a calliphorid fly (left) and a tachinid fly, viewed from the side to show the hypopleural bristles. The tachinids also exhibit a well-developed post-scutellum

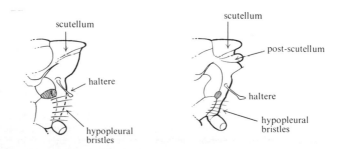

*The thorax of a typical rhinophorid fly,
showing how the thoracic squamae
diverge from the scutellum*

ent post-scutellum. Vein 4 usually bends sharply towards vein 3 in the outer part of the wing. The adults are surface feeders, with mouth-parts like those of the House-fly (see p. 172). Carrion and other decaying materials are the main larval foods. There are about 35 British species. *Calliphora vomitoria* is one of the commonest of the bluebottles or blow-flies that buzz around our houses in the summer in search of meat or fish in which to lay their eggs. It is usually only the females that come indoors. The males prefer to spend the day lapping nectar from flowers. The true greenbottles are species of *Lucilia*, but there are several other metallic green flies that might be mistaken for them. Most of these other species belong to the Muscidae and can be recognised as such by the absence of the hypopleural bristles. *Lucilia* does not often enter houses. Dead animals are the main egg-laying sites, but *Lucilia* can be a serious problem in sheep-rearing areas. The female lays her eggs in sores or cuts in the skin and the larvae develop there, eating the sheep's flesh away with alarming rapidity. The Cluster-fly (*Pollenia rudis*) may enter houses in large numbers in the autumn to seek out winter quarters in attics and roof-spaces. It can be recognised by the golden hair on the thorax. Cluster-fly larvae parasitise earthworms.

Members of the **Rhinophoridae** resemble the calliphorids but can be distinguished because the thoracic squamae are smaller and their inner margins diverge from the scutellum instead of curving around it. They are more slender than most of the calliphorids and are usually bristly grey or black flies. Almost all of their larvae are parasites of woodlice. There are ten British species.

The Sarcophagidae, typified by numerous species of *Sarcophaga* (Pl.31), differs from the Calliphoridae in the relative positions of two bristles on the prescutum. In the Calliphoridae the post-humeral bristle is lower on the thorax than the pre-sutural bristle (fig. p. 173), whereas in the Sarcophagidae the positions are reversed. *Sarcophaga* species and their relatives give birth to young larvae instead of laying eggs and they are commonly known as flesh-flies because most of them breed in carrion. A few are parasites and some utilise the food stored by bees and wasps. *Senotainia* species, commonly called satellite-flies, follow prey-carrying solitary wasps and nip in when they can to deposit their own larvae on the prey. Most of the sarcophagid flies are greyish with a chequered abdomen and unusually large feet. There are about 60 British species.

Members of the **Scathophagidae** differ from most other calypterates in having very small thoracic squamae – usually strap-shaped and never more than half the length of the alar squamae. The eyes are well separated in both sexes. The best-known species is the Yellow dung-fly (*Scathophaga stercoraria*) (Pl.31), which swarms on fresh cow-pats. In fact, only the males have the bright yellow hair: the females are greyish and much less furry – and also less common. The adults prey on other insects on the dung, while the larvae feed in the dung itself. There are more than 50 British species but not all are associated with dung: several species have herbivorous larvae, often living inside plant stems and roots.

The **Anthomyiidae** is a family of mainly slender, dark flies in which vein 6 always reaches the wing margin and vein 4 is almost straight. The thoracic squamae are generally as large as the alar squamae and often very much bigger, although in a few species

– recognised by the very flat rear of the head – the thoracic squamae are very small. Many of the larvae feed in decaying matter but many others are vegetarians and some are serious pests. One of the commonest of the 200 or so British species is the Cabbage root-fly (*Delia radicum*), which damages the roots of brassicas and occurs in immense numbers on rape fields. The adults are susceptible to fungal disease and their dead bodies festoon the vegetation around the fields in damp weather.

The **Muscidae** (Pl. 31) contains the Common House-fly (*Musca domestica*) and many other familiar flies. Some resemble small blow-flies, but there is no fan of hypopleural bristles on the thorax. Veins 6 and 7 are short and more or less parallel. Vein 4 bends sharply forward in some species, including the House-fly, but is usually no more than gently curved. There are about 180 British species. Although most of the adult flies mop up surface fluids, the family also includes blood-suckers and predatory species. The larvae feed mainly in dung and other decaying matter, either as primary scavengers or as predators of other insects. *Eudasyphora cyanella*, distinguished from *Lucilia* by the gently curving vein 4, is one of a number of viviparous species. It commonly over-winters in buildings with the Cluster-fly.

The Common House-fly is one of several species that occur regularly in houses, although it is even more common around farms. It has followed man to all parts of the world and is one of the most widely distributed of all animals. It does not bite but, as a result of its liking for almost any organic material, it carries numerous germs, many of which reach our food and our digestive and respiratory systems. It has been described as one of the world's most dangerous insects. The feeding apparatus consists largely of the labium, which forms a retractable proboscis. Its labella are large and fleshy and are traversed by numerous fine canals known as pseudotracheae (fig. p. 172). When the fly feeds it extends the proboscis and applies the labella to the food surface. Saliva then runs out through the canals and its enzymes begin to break up the food. The partly digested, liquefied food is then sucked up. The fly often regurgitates part of its previous meal when feeding and this is one of the main ways in which germs are carried to our food. The fly also defaecates frequently while feeding, and many germs are carried on its feet. House-fly eggs are laid in decaying material – rubbish dumps and manure heaps are favoured sites – and under warm conditions the whole life cycle may be completed in two weeks. Covering breeding sites with soil is one of the best ways to reduce the House-fly population.

The Stable-fly (*Stomoxys calcitrans*) often enters houses and is sometimes mistaken for a House-fly – until it bites! Horses and cattle are its usual victims, but it bites us when it gets the chance. The labium is a rigid, non-retractile proboscis which is able to pierce the skin and withdraw blood (fig. p. 172). Both sexes are blood-feeders in this and related species. The larvae feed in dung and stable litter. *Mesembrina meridiana*, one of the largest of the muscids, is fond of sun-bathing on walls and vegetation.

The **Fanniidae** is very similar to the Muscidae but veins 6 and 7 converge. Vein 7 is longer than vein 6, although often fainter. The family includes the Lesser house-

Wings of (from left to right) Anthomyiidae, Muscidae, and Fanniidae, showing how the families can be distinguished by the different arrangements of veins 6 and 7

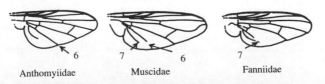

Anthomyiidae   Muscidae   Fanniidae

fly (*Fannia cancularis*), which in many areas is even more common in houses than the Common house-fly. It is the one that flies incessantly round lights and other objects. Smaller and more slender than *Musca*, it is best distinguished by the almost straight vein 4. It breeds in various kinds of dung.

SERIES SCHIZOPHORA – PUPIPARA

The flies in this group are all parasites of birds and mammals and are much modified for this way of life. They are commonly called louse-flies. The wings are often reduced or absent altogether and the insects have well-developed claws with which they cling to hair and feathers. The body is flattened and leathery and the head is partly retracted into the thorax. The mouth-parts are not unlike those of *Stomoxys*, but they are more slender and the bite of these flies – although they rarely bite man – is less painful. Both sexes take blood. The group name refers to the life history. The female periodically brings forth a single larva which is almost fully grown before it is born and which pupates almost immediately.

The **Hippoboscidae** (Pl.31) has about a dozen British species, although not all of them are native. *Hippobosca equina* is the Forest-fly, a winged species infesting horses, cattle, and deer. It occurs mainly in wooded areas and is particularly common on ponies in the New Forest. *Lipoptena cervi* is the Deer-fly, which attacks all kinds of deer. The fly is winged when it first emerges but it sheds its wings on finding a suitable host. The Sheep Ked (*Melophagus ovinus*) is completely wingless and often wrongly called a sheep tick. It does not do much direct harm to the sheep on which it lives, but the irritation causes the sheep to scratch themselves and open the way for *Lucilia* and other infections.

The **Nycteribiidae** are minute, wingless parasites of bats, distinguished from the hippoboscids by their relatively long legs and by the way in which the head folds back into a groove on the top of the thorax. There are just three British species, including *Phthiridium biarticulatum* (Pl. 30).

Collecting and preserving
The larger flies, such as horse-flies and hover-flies, can be stalked and netted individually, but sweeping is the best way to obtain the smaller species that do not fly much. Bear in mind the delicate bristles on which identification depends and make only one or two sweeps before examining the net, otherwise the specimens will be damaged. Specimens intended for the collection should be killed and pinned immediately to minimise the risk of broken bristles. Ethyl acetate is a good killing agent because it induces the flies to extrude their mouth-parts and genitalia – thus aiding identification. Do not allow the flies to get wet. Large flies can be pinned, usually through the thorax and to one side of the mid-line. Smaller species can be mounted on points, but those with long legs are best carded.

Order Lepidoptera – Butterflies and Moths (Plates 32-47)

Recognition features Minute to large insects usually with two pairs of membranous wings which, together with the body, are more or less covered with tiny scales. The mouth-parts, composed mainly of the maxillae, normally form a long sucking tube – the proboscis – which is coiled under the head when not in use. Mandibles are usually absent but may be vestigial or, rarely, functional.

Apart from a few wingless female moths and some of the clearwings, whose wings are nearly naked and which therefore resemble the Hymenoptera, the butterflies and moths are easily recognisable, even by the non-entomologist. The only likely confusion is between some of the smaller moths and the caddis flies but the scales and the proboscis will identify the moths upon closer examination.

The butterflies and moths form a very large order of insects with more than 150,000 known species. About 5,000 live in Europe and nearly half of these occur in the British Isles. Moths make up by far the greater part of the order. Only about 60 butterfly species regularly breed in the British Isles, although a few more make sporadic visits from the continent. Despite the size of the order, its members are very uniform in both appearance and habits. With the exception of the family Micropterigidae (p. 228), the adults, if they feed at all, are liquid-feeders, imbibing nectar and other juices through the proboscis. The larvae, on the other hand, all possess biting jaws and feed almost exclusively on plant material. The best-known exceptions to this are the clothes moths, whose larvae find sustenance in dry hair and other keratin-containing animal material.

The order is economically very important, mainly because of the damage caused by the larvae to our crops and other plants. On the credit side, a number of species provide us with silk and others are effective in keeping down weeds – the moth *Cactoblastis cactorum* was extremely successful in controlling prickly pear cactus in Australia, while the larvae of the Cinnabar moth help to control ragwort in some places. The aesthetic value of many butterflies should also be considered: although not making up for the damage caused by their larvae, they do at least brighten our fields and gardens. While pleasing our eyes, they also perform a useful service by pollinating the flowers.

'What's the difference between a butterfly and a moth?' is a common question but it does not have a straightforward answer. The division of the order into butterflies and moths is really an artificial division: there is the same degree of difference between hawkmoths and butterflies as between hawkmoths and geometer moths. The differences between butterflies and one group of moths may not hold true when we consider another group of moths. The popular idea of butterflies as all brightly

A butterfly in its typical resting position

coloured day-flying insects, and moths as dull night-fliers, is quickly dispelled by a look at the Dingy Skipper butterfly (Pl. 34) – admittedly day-flying, but very dull – and the brightly coloured, day-flying Speckled Yellow moth (Pl. 43). As far as the European Lepidoptera are concerned, however, there is a convenient way to distinguish the butterflies from the moths. All our butterflies have knobbed or clubbed antennae. Those of the moths are of various shapes, but only the burnet moths (Pl. 35) have clubbed antennae and here, if still in doubt, we can turn to another feature. The front and hind wings of the burnets, like those of many other moths, are coupled with a stout spine (the frenulum) projecting from the base of the hind wing (fig. p. 18). European butterflies never have such a device: in fact, only one butterfly in the world – an Australian skipper – is known to have a frenulum.

The head of a butterfly or moth is relatively large and much of its surface is occupied by the two compound eyes, each with several thousand facets. There are often two ocelli, but these are generally concealed among the scales and hairs of the head. The antennae vary enormously, ranging from the tiny points of the Swift moths (Hepialidae) to the huge feathery organs of some male Emperor moths (Saturniidae) which are capable of detecting females more than a mile away. The antennae are usually covered with scales.

The mouth-parts almost always take the form of a sucking tube called the proboscis. This is formed by the maxillae, which are grooved on the inner side and hooked together so that the grooves form a canal through which the insect draws nectar and other liquid food. When not in use, the proboscis is coiled neatly beneath the insect's head. Each half of the tube is hollow and composed of numerous horny rings separated by membranes. Muscles inside each half are attached to the rings, and there is also an elastic strip running along the top of each half. This strip is largely responsible for the coiling of the proboscis. When the insect wishes to feed – stimulated by the scent of food or by picking up its taste with the feet – the proboscis is extended, partly by blood pressure but mainly by the action of its muscles. When coiled, the upper surface of the proboscis is more or less flat, but when its muscles contract

A butterfly showing how the proboscis is uncurled and used to suck nectar from a flower. A flexible 'knee-joint' in the proboscis enables the butterfly to probe flowers at different angles without moving its whole body. The enlargement shows how the proboscis is formed from the two maxillae, which are joined together to form a canal

they cause the upper surface to become slightly domed – and this automatically causes the proboscis to uncoil.

The proboscis reaches a considerable length in some moths – 15cm or more in the Convolvulus Hawkmoth and even longer in some tropical species – and enables them to draw nectar from deep-throated flowers. But there are other species in which it is short or even absent. In the Vapourer moths, for example, the two maxillae do not link up, while in the Swift moths they are virtually absent altogether. Obviously these insects cannot feed as adults. Some species have even lost their mouths.

The rest of the mouth-parts are generally poorly developed and mandibles are completely absent in most species. Only in the pollen-feeding Micropterigidae (p. 228) are they at all functional. The labium is also small, although its palps are developed to some extent and held in front of the face.

The prothorax is clearly obvious in the more primitive members of the order, but in the higher groups it is reduced to a small collar-like ring behind the head. The mesothorax is always the largest of the thoracic segments and it carries a well-developed rounded scutellum. Overlying the base of each forewing and forming a sort of 'shoulder-pad' there is an arched, triangular sclerite called a tegula. Tegulae are found in many insects, but they are particularly large in this order, although often buried in the fur of the hairier species. The metathorax is always very much smaller than the mesothorax and is tucked in behind it, partially concealed. There is little to note about the legs other than a reduction of the front pair in certain butterfly families.

Among the more primitive groups the two pairs of wings are of similar size and shape, but in most other groups the forewings are noticeably longer. The name Lepidoptera means scale-wings (Greek *lepis* = scale) and refers to the tiny overlapping scales that clothe the wings. They are secreted by hypodermal cells and each fits into a minute socket in the wing membrane. Scales also cover most of the body. They are actually modified hairs, typically broad and flat, but often long and narrow and clearly showing their relationship to hairs. Unmodified hairs are also found to a greater or lesser extent, particularly on the thorax and the wing bases.

The scales are hollow and generally contain pigments responsible for the colours of the wings. The surface of the scale is generally delicately sculptured with longitudinal ridges, sometimes less than 1/1000mm apart. When they are as close as this the ridges interfere with light reflection and produce striking iridescent colours, which often change as you change the angle from which you view the wings. Special scent-discharging scales called androconia are found in some male butterflies. They are connected to scent glands in the wing membrane and the scent passes up through the hollow scales and into the air. Its dispersal is aided by minute plumes on the scales. Androconia may be scattered over the wing surface or grouped into prominent patches, as in some hairstreak and fritillary butterflies and many of the browns. Those of some skipper butterflies are held in a furrow near the front margin of the male forewing.

Wing venation is most fully developed in the Micropterigidae, where both pairs of wings are alike and retain most of the primitive pattern. The venation tends to be

The overlapping scales of a butterfly's wing

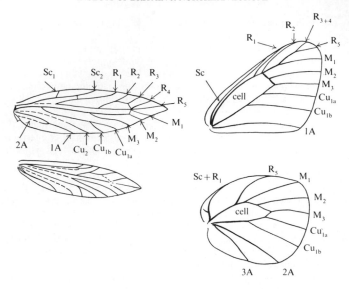

The venation of Micropterix *(left) and a butterfly (not to scale), showing the reduced venation in the higher families of the Lepidoptera. Notice the large cell in each butterfly wing*

reduced in other members of the order and cross-veins are always rare. One of the most noticeable features among the higher Lepidoptera is the large cell R+M, which comes into being through the disappearance of the basal part of the media. This large cell is often called the discal cell, but it does not correspond with cells of the same name in other orders. It is usually referred to simply as the cell. One of the key veins is Cu_2. This vein is usually present in both wings of the primitive families but it disappears, first from the forewing and then from the hind wing, as we move up the line to the more advanced insects.

The wing venation of butterflies and moths is not readily visible because of the covering of scales, but a few drops of alcohol or ether dropped on to the wings will show up the veins for a few seconds without damaging the specimen. The venation can be permanently displayed by removing the wings, wetting them in alcohol, and then immersing them in household bleach for a while to remove the colour. If the veins are particularly delicate they can be stained by immersing the wings in chlorazol black. After washing, the wings can be mounted on cards or on microscope slides. Euparal is a good mounting medium for use with microscope slides, but the wings must be thoroughly dehydrated in alcohol before being transferred to Euparal.

The wing-coupling apparatus in its simplest form consists of a small lobe – the fibula – at the base of the forewing and a few spines on the front edge of the hind wing. The fibula rests on top of the hind wing and is held in place by the spines. This arrangement is found in the Micropterigidae and some other primitive families. In the Swift moths the fibula is replaced by a longer lobe called the jugum (fig. p. 18). This also rests on top of the hind wing, but there are no spines to hold it in place.

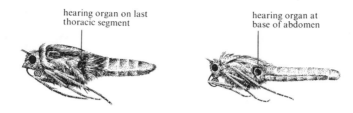

hearing organ on last
thoracic segment

hearing organ at
base of abdomen

The bodies of a noctuid moth (left) and a geometrid moth, showing the position of the
'ears'. The openings are in much the same place, but the membrane is on the thorax in
the noctuid moths and on the abdomen of the geometers

The most advanced form of wing-coupling in this order, found in most of the larger moths, involves an outgrowth from the 'shoulder' of the hind wing. This outgrowth is called the frenulum and in the male it consists of a single stout bristle. The female frenulum usually consists of several more slender bristles held loosely together, and in weak-flying species it may be considerably reduced. In both sexes the frenulum passes obliquely forward under the forewing, where it is held in place by the retinaculum. This is normally in the form of a hook on the underside of vein Sc in male insects (fig. p. 18), but in females it consists of a group of stiff hairs. Butterflies and some moth families exhibit a simpler form of wing coupling in which the frenulum is lost and the wings are held together simply by a large overlap.

Many moths carry hearing organs at the base of the abdomen. These organs are thin-walled chambers on each side of the insect. They are particularly well seen in the geometer moths, in which they are associated with the first abdominal spiracle. Some moths, however, bear their 'ears' on the metathorax.

Lepidoptera all pass through the normal four stages: egg, larva, pupa, and imago, although there is some variation in the length of the life cycle. The eggs may be laid singly or in groups ranging from two or three – as in the Puss moth and the Duke of Burgundy – to several hundred as in the Lackey moth. The total number of eggs laid by a female varies from about 50 to over 1,000, according to their size. The female uses taste receptors on her feet and elsewhere to make sure that she lays her eggs on the right plant. Without such parental 'planning' the tiny caterpillars would probably die before reaching suitable food. But some Swift moths, whose larvae feed on the roots of grasses and other plants, simply drop their eggs among the herbage, and so do some of the grass-feeding satyrid butterflies. Two or three weeks is the usual duration of the egg stage, except among those species that lay in late summer and pass the winter in the egg stage.

The larva eats its way out of its egg shell when ready, and often consumes the rest of the shell after hatching. It is typically an eruciform larva – a caterpillar – with a well-developed head, three pairs of true thoracic legs, and usually five pairs of fleshy prolegs on segments 3-6 and 10 of the abdomen. Each proleg bears an arc or ring of minute hooks at the end that enable the caterpillar to maintain a firm hold on its support. The power of these hooks is well known to anyone who has tried to remove an unwilling caterpillar from a twig.

All caterpillars possess a pair of silk glands which are highly modified salivary glands. Each gland is tubular and the total length of the coiled tube may be several times the length of the body in some of the silkmoth larvae. The ducts of the two

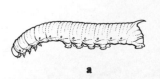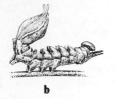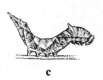

a

b   c

Some lepidopteran larvae: **a.** *a fairly typical caterpillar (hawkmoth), with the spiracles clearly visible on the side;* **b.** *Lobster Moth larva;* **c.** *hooktip moth larva*

glands join and open to the outside at the spinneret on the labium or lower lip. Each duct is also connected to an accessory gland. The silk is produced as a fluid material and is forced out through the spinneret. The secretions of the accessory gland are somewhat tacky, but quick-drying, and they help the silk thread to adhere to the surroundings and also to harden quickly. Caterpillars put their silk to several uses, including the formation of the protective tents and lifelines referred to below, but the major use is in the formation of the cocoons which surround the pupae of many moths.

Some caterpillars feed on the flowers or the developing fruits of their food-plants, and a few bore into stems and roots, but the vast majority feed on the leaves, using their strong jaws to carve each leaf methodically down to the tough midrib. A number of the smaller species, including many of the pigmy moths (Nepticulidae) which are the smallest of them all, actually live inside the leaves, tunnelling their way between the upper and lower surfaces. Insects living in this way – not all of them are Lepidoptera – are called leaf miners. One of the commonest is *Nepticula aurella*, whose whitish tunnels (fig. p. 230) can be found in bramble leaves nearly everywhere. Many of these leaf-mining caterpillars have no legs.

Feeding is an almost non-stop activity for caterpillars, apart from a day or two of rest at each moult, and growth is rapid. The number of moults varies between three and nine but most species undergo either four or five moults. Larval life may be as short as three weeks or, in those species hibernating as larvae, as long as nine months. In exceptional cases, such as the wood-feeding Goat and Leopard moths, larval life may exceed three years.

Caterpillars feeding exposed on the foliage of plants are naturally open to attack by birds and other enemies, and we therefore find many protective devices and behaviour patterns among caterpillars. Some species spin silken tents and hide in them, while others roll leaves or spin them together to form retreats. Several species escape from their enemies by attaching a silk thread to a leaf and simply falling off, paying out a life-line as they fall. When the danger has passed they merely climb back up the thread. Many caterpillars rely on camouflage: greens and browns are the dominant colours and the insects thus blend well with the leaves and twigs. Longitudinal and oblique stripes often add to the effect by resembling leaf veins or shadows. A number of caterpillars take this camouflage a stage further and not only merge with the background but actually resemble some part of it. The outstanding examples are the caterpillars of various geometer moths. These slender brown or green larvae bear a number of wart-like outgrowths that resemble buds, and when they sit motionless they are easily passed over as leafless twigs.

It might be thought that the brightly coloured caterpillars of the Cinnabar moth and the Large White butterfly are just asking to be eaten, but they are rarely taken by birds. Both have a very unpleasant taste and their bold colours and patterns serve to warn enemies of this fact. Young birds will try the caterpillars, but they soon learn to associate the colours with unpleasantness and they leave the caterpillars alone after that. Many other distasteful insects – ladybirds, wasps, and so on – have evolved similar warning coloration and a large number of 'tasty' insects have taken advantage of it through mimicry (see p. 262). The commonest warning coloration patterns in insects involve black with red or yellow.

Birds, lizards, and other predators rarely take very hairy caterpillars, and so the larvae of tiger and tussock moths can afford to show themselves. Many insect hairs have irritant properties which add to their repellent effect and it is as well to avoid handling hairy caterpillars if possible, although the effects vary from person to person.

These protective devices are often carried over into the adult state. The Cinnabar moth (Pl. 38) is brightly coloured, and the tiger moths (Pl. 38) are both colourful and hairy, while a great many other moths can sit undetected on tree trunks because they are beautifully camouflaged. A strange example of protective resemblance is afforded by the Chinese Character moth (Pl. 43), which spends the daytime sitting on leaves and looking very much like a bird dropping.

When fully grown and ready to pupate, the caterpillar stops feeding and looks for a suitable pupation site. It is at this time that many caterpillars are seen walking 'purposefully' across roads and pavements. Many species pupate in the soil or in moss or leaf litter, but others pupate on their food-plants without moving far from their feeding sites. The pupation site must be suitable for the caterpillar to change into the pupa, and also for the emergence of the adult insect. The soil, for example, must not be too heavy because, even if the larva could burrow into it, the newly-emerged, soft-bodied moth would not be able to get out. Wood-boring larvae make their way towards the outside before pupating just under the surface. The adults then have to break through only a paper-thin layer to reach the air.

It seems probable that the formation of a cocoon is a fairly primitive feature that has been or is being lost in several families, notably most of the butterflies. In its typical development, the cocoon is spun up among the leaves of the food-plant, in a bark crevice, or in leaf litter. Having found itself a suitable site, the caterpillar begins to extrude its silk and, by continuous movements of its head and body, it completely envelops itself with silk. The density and thickness of the cocoon vary enormously, reaching their greatest development in the cultivated silk moth (*Bombyx*

Some lepidopteran pupae. Left, 'Incomplete pupa' of burnet moth (Zygaenidae) protruding from its cocoon after emergence of the adult. Middle, Succinct pupa (Pieridae). Right, Suspended pupa (Nymphalidae)

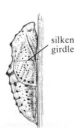

silken girdle

mori), whose cocoon contains more than half a mile of unbroken silk as well as the numerous shorter strands around the outside. The cocoon of the Puss moth (Pl. 38) is worth mentioning because of its extreme hardness. The caterpillar combines silk with saliva and particles of wood to make its cocoon on a tree trunk, and it is extremely difficult to spot – and equally difficult to squash. The caterpillar instinctively makes one end of the cocoon fairly thin and the moth, aided by a softening fluid, is able to escape without too much trouble.

Many moths pupate in the soil and these do not usually make much of a cocoon. The caterpillar hollows out a chamber for itself and binds the walls with saliva and perhaps a few strands of silk. The pupa lies freely in this chamber.

The only butterflies which make recogniseable cocoons are the skippers, which spin up among the grasses and other plants on which they feed. Some of the blues and browns surround their pupae with a few wisps of silk on the ground, but most butterflies pupate without any protection at all. Some pupae, including those of the tortoiseshells and most of the fritillaries, hang upside-down from the food-plant or other convenient support. The caterpillar spins a little silken pad before pupating and the suspended pupa – or chrysalis as the butterfly pupa is often called – grips this with its cremaster, which is a small hooked structure at the hind end. In the other method of pupating, used mainly by the white butterflies (Pieridae), the chrysalis remains upright. It is still attached to a pad of silk by the cremaster but it has an additional support in the form of a silk girdle or 'safety belt' slung from the twig or leaf on which it sits. Pupae of this kind are called succinct.

Having suitably concealed or attached itself, the caterpillar begins to change into the pupa. Internal changes have, of course, been going on for some time but visible changes now occur. The body gets shorter and fatter and the skin becomes rather wrinkled. The creature, now called the pre-pupa, looks rather dead, but then the skin splits and reveals the shining coat of the pupa. The pupa wriggles vigorously and the old larval skin is gradually shrugged off. In those species that pupate in a cocoon or earthen chamber the larval skin often remains loosely attached to the tail end of the pupa, but the butterfly chrysalis manages to free itself completely by deft manipulation of the cremaster hooks – quite a feat for a suspended pupa.

The eyes and proboscis and all the other appendages can be seen in outline in the pupa, although in most species they are all inside the main body of the pupa. This kind of pupa is called obtect (fig. p. 25). The pupae of the Micropterigidae and the Eriocraniidae are of the exarate type, with all their appendages free and mobile (fig. p. 25). They are equipped with jaws which they use to cut their way out of their cocoons. Burnet moths and several groups of 'micros' have an intermediate type of pupa which is often called an incomplete pupa. It has no jaws and the other appendages are only partly free from the body and not mobile, but the abdomen is more mobile than in the obtect pupa and, as the time for adult emergence approaches, the incomplete pupa can wriggle partly out of its tunnel or cocoon (fig. p. 219).

Most of our butterflies and moths pass the winter in the pupal stage, which may last as long as 10 months in single-brooded species. The Duke of Burgundy (Pl. 34), for example, emerges in May or June after pupating in August. On the other hand, double-brooded species and species that overwinter as eggs or larvae may have only a very short pupal stage in spring or summer. Many species have two broods in a year and a few, notably the Small Copper and the Small White may have three. Individuals of the third brood, which is often only a partial emergence, are usually noticeably smaller than their parents. In southern Europe it is possible for some species to have four broods in a year. Some butterflies and moths overwinter as adults, familiar examples being the Brimstone and Peacock butterflies which can be drawn from their sleeping quarters by warm sunshine as early as February.

The general uniformity of the Lepidoptera means that we must rely on quite small details to sub-divide the order. Details of the venation are particularly important in separating the families but, because such details are usually obscured by the scales, it is often quicker to identify a species by its general appearance (using illustrations or a reference collection) than to track down its family with a key. For this reason, no family keys are attempted here, but a simplified key to superfamilies is given below. Each superfamily is then described, together with its principal families, although taxonomists are continually moving families from one superfamily to another and the make-up of the superfamilies is not by any means agreed. It is hoped that the key, together with the descriptions and illustrations, will help to place most of our Lepidoptera in their correct families.

Key to the Superfamilies of Lepidoptera

1. Insects with clubbed antennae: hind wing without a frenulum (butterflies) — 2

   Insects with tapering antennae, or if clubbed a frenulum is present (moths) — 3

2. Antennae widely separated at the base and generally sharply bent or hooked at the tip: all veins unbranched in forewing: small brown or orange butterflies — Hesperioidea p. 224

   Antennae close together at base and never hooked at tip: usually a forked vein near tip of forewing — Papilionoidea p. 225

3. Very small moths with functional mandibles and no proboscis — Micropterigoidea p. 228

   Moths without functional mandibles: with or without a proboscis — 4

4. Fibula or jugum present, or else venation much reduced — 5

   No fibula or jugum: venation well developed — 8

5. Front and hind wings alike: fibula or jugum well developed: no frenulum — 6

   Venation reduced and different in the two wings: fibula present, but rudimentary in males, which have a strong frenulum — 7

   frenulum

6. Wingspan under 25mm: fibula and costal spines present — Eriocranioidea p. 229

   Wingspan over 25mm: long jugum present — Hepialoidea p. 229

7.   Wingspan rarely over 6mm: 1st   Nepticuloidea p. 229
       antennal segment expanded to
       form an 'eye-cap'

'eye-cap'

eye

       Wingspan at least 8mm: no 'eye-cap': antennae some-   Incurvarioidea p. 230
       times much longer than wings

8.   Wings split into a number of feather-like plumes   9
       Wings entire   10

9.   Each wing divided into 6 plumes   Alucitoidea p. 237
       Each wing divided into 2-4 plumes (although a few   Pterophoroidea p. 232
       species – see Pl. 36 – have undivided wings)

10.   Vein Cu_2 present in hind wing: mainly small moths – the   11
       'micros'* – but including some large species: wings
       often with conspicuous fringes

       Vein Cu_2 absent from hind wing: mostly large or medium-   17
       sized moths without conspicuous fringes

11.   Stem of vein M more or less fully   M   12
       developed in forewing, so there is
       no large cell

       Stem of vein M in forewing much   cell   14
       reduced or absent

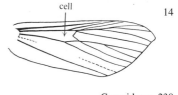

12.   Wingspan generally over 35mm   Cossoidea p. 230
       Wingspan generally under 35mm   13

13.   Antennae distinctly clubbed, or if not clubbed the wings   Zygaenoidea p. 231
       are usually metallic green: proboscis usually well de-
       veloped

*   *The early entomologists tended to divide moths into 'macros' and 'micros'
    mainly according to their size. Such a division is quite artificial and frequently
    cuts across true relationships. The separation of most of the smaller moths in
    this way has undoubtedly contributed to their neglect, but the division is still
    used as a matter of convenience. The 'macros' include the last four
    superfamilies in this key, together with the Hepialoidea, Cossoidea, and
    Zygaenoidea, although these last three groups are more closely related to the
    'micros' than to the other 'macros'.*

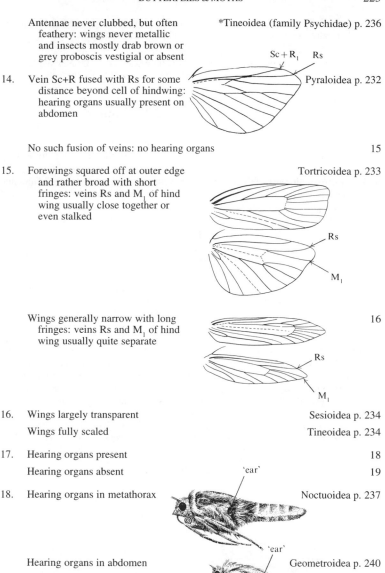

Antennae never clubbed, but often feathery: wings never metallic and insects mostly drab brown or grey proboscis vestigial or absent   *Tineoidea (family Psychidae) p. 236

14. Vein Sc+R fused with Rs for some distance beyond cell of hindwing: hearing organs usually present on abdomen   Pyraloidea p. 232

No such fusion of veins: no hearing organs   15

15. Forewings squared off at outer edge and rather broad with short fringes: veins Rs and M_1 of hind wing usually close together or even stalked   Tortricoidea p. 233

Wings generally narrow with long fringes: veins Rs and M_1 of hind wing usually quite separate   16

16. Wings largely transparent   Sesioidea p. 234

Wings fully scaled   Tineoidea p. 234

17. Hearing organs present   18

Hearing organs absent   19

18. Hearing organs in metathorax   Noctuoidea p. 237

Hearing organs in abdomen   Geometroidea p. 240

* *Members of the Limacodidae (Pl. 35) and a few members of the Zygaenoidea will also key out here.*

19. Frenulum present, although not always obvious: proboscis   Sphingoidea p. 241
     usually well developed: forewings usually narrow, with
     acute angle at apex: antennae usually thickest in middle

     Frenulum and proboscis absent: wings usually broad: an-   Bombycoidea p. 242
     tennae often feathery, especially in males

The Butterflies (Plates 32-34 and 44)

The main features of these insects are the clubbed antennae, lack of a frenulum, and the enlargement of the humeral lobe of the hind wing. Although these features may be found separately in various moths, in combination they are found only among the butterflies. As with most of the larger moths, vein Cu_2 is absent from both front and hind wings. Because of the clubbed antennae, the butterflies are sometimes referred to as the Rhopalocera – from the Greek *rhopalon* meaning a club and *keras* meaning a horn. The moths are often collectively known as the Heterocera, referring to the varied nature of their antennae.

Superfamily Hesperioidea

The only family in this group is the **Hesperiidae** (Pl. 34), which contains over 3,000 species of skippers. The main features by which these differ from other butterflies include the wide head and wide separation of the antennal bases, the gradual thickening of the antennal club, and the way in which all the wing veins spring directly from the wing base or from the cell and do not branch. The European skippers, which number about 38 species, are all fairly small brown, grey, or orange butterflies and they get their name from their bouncy, darting flight. Only eight species live in the British Isles, and of these only the Dingy Skipper (*Erynnis tages*) occurs in Ireland. Although most can hold their wings vertically over the body like other butterflies, the orange skippers of the sub-family Hesperiinae, represented by the Large Skipper (*Ochlodes venata*), have a characteristic basking attitude with the hind wings held

Left, The typical basking position of the orange skippers (sub-family Hesperiinae).
Right, the venation of a skipper butterfly, showing how all the veins arise from the cell
and do not branch

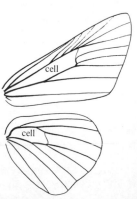

more or less flat and the forewings raised at an angle. Skipper larvae are more or less cylindrical, with a distinct neck, and they usually live in shelters made by binding leaves together with silk.

Superfamily Papilionoidea

This group contains all the other butterflies, with about 320 European species distributed in eight families. All of the families and many of the species can be recognised on sight, using simply the size and colour of the specimens as a guide.

The **Danaidae** is represented in the European fauna only by two very occasional immigrants – the Monarch or Milkweed (*Danaus plexippus*) (Pl. 32) from North America or the Canary Islands and the Plain Tiger (*D. chrysippus*) from Africa, although the Monarch has recently been breeding in southern Spain. The Monarch is a large and striking insect and quite unmistakable. Birds seldom attack it, for they know that the bold pattern warns of a tough body and an acrid taste. The front pair of legs is degenerate and useless for walking – a feature which is shared with the next two families and which leads some entomologists to treat the Danaidae and the Satyridae as sub-families of the Nymphalidae.

The **Satyridae** (Pl. 32) contains predominantly brown insects, known to lepidopterists simply as 'the browns'. Most of them are decorated to a greater or lesser extent with pale-centred eye-spots, but the most diagnostic feature of the family is the swelling of the bases of certain veins in the forewings. These swellings are hollow and among the suggestions for their function is the idea that they are concerned with sound detection. The antennae are not strongly clubbed and the front pair of legs are reduced to hairy 'brushes', indicating their relationship to the Nymphalidae. There are eleven British species.

The satyrids all live in grassy places. The Meadow Brown (*Maniola jurtina*) and the Small Heath (*Coenonympha pamphilus*) inhabit open grassland and are among our commonest butterflies. The Ringlet (*Aphantopus hyperantus*) and the Gatekeeper (*Pyronia tithonus*) frequent hedgerows and woodland borders, while the Speckled Wood (*Pararge aegeria*) prefers the shadier parts of the woods, as long as there is sufficient grass along the rides. The only non-brown members of the family are the Marbled White (*Melanargia galathea*) and its congeners which, as the name suggests, are white with dark markings. These butterflies, common in rough pasture, can be distinguished from the true whites of the Pieridae by the four walking legs and the swollen wing veins.

Most satyrid larvae are grass-feeders and they are mainly brown or green with smooth skins. They taper at both ends and there is always a short, forked 'tail' at

The forewing of a satyrid butterfly, showing the swollen basal veins, and the front leg of one of these butterflies. The brush-like front legs are alike in both sexes

The front legs of a male (top) and female nymphalid butterfly. The legs are brush-like only in the males, but still much less hairy than in satyrid butterflies

the rear (Pl. 44). Most pupae are suspended, although the graylings and some other species pupate in the soil.

The **Nymphalidae** contains the fritillaries, and tortoiseshells, together with the other colourful butterflies illustrated on Pl.33. All are strikingly marked and many of the fritillaries bear silvery spots on the undersides of the wings. As in the previous two families, the front legs are reduced, although brush-like only in the male. The structure of these legs is the only external clue to the sexes in some species. The antennae are clearly knobbed.

The family contains 16 British species, including the Red Admiral (*Vanessa atalanta*) and the Painted Lady (*Cynthia cardui*) which are both summer visitors. The Painted Lady is probably the greatest migrant of them all, and certainly one of the most widely distributed of the butterflies. It usually arrives in Britain and northern Europe in June, having grown up in North Africa or southern Europe. A summer generation is on the wing in August, but these insects cannot survive the northern winter. Many of them die where they grew up, but some travel south in the autumn and may get back to Africa where another generation is reared ready for the northward migration in the spring. A similar situation exists in North America, where the butterfly migrates between Mexico and Canada. Several nymphalids, including the tortoiseshells and the Peacock (*Inachis io*), hibernate as adults and all have very sombre undersides consistent with their habit of hiding in dark corners for the winter. The Camberwell Beauty (*Nymphalis antiopa*) (Pl. 34) is another well-known hibernator – and a migrant, although only occasional specimens turn up in Britain.

Both the larvae (Pl. 44) and the suspended pupae are rather spiny and the pupae are often adorned with metallic spots.

The family **Libytheidae** has only one European member – the Nettle-tree Butterfly (*Libythea celtis*) (Pl. 32). The family is related to the Nymphalidae, but can be recognised by the long palps – and by the prominent tooth on the outer margin of the forewing in our solitary species. The Nettle-tree Butterfly, found all over southern Europe, flies from June to September and then hibernates, waking to lay its eggs on the nettle tree in March and April.

The family **Nemeobiidae** also has only one European member – the Duke of Burgundy (*Hamearis lucina*) (Pl. 34). This little butterfly, found locally in woodland glades and scrub-covered pasture, differs from the nymphalids in that, although the male has only four walking legs, the female has all six in walking order. The young stages are also very different from those of the nymphalids: the caterpillar (Pl. 44) is flattened and resembles a hairy woodlouse, while the pupa is succinctly attached to the food-plant (cowslip). In these respects, the Duke of Burgundy resembles the members of the Lycaenidae. Most members of the Nemeobiidae live in South America.

The **Lycaenidae** (Pl. 34) contains the blues, coppers, and hairstreaks and is the largest of all the butterfly families. The butterflies are small or medium-sized and often brilliantly coloured, especially the males. There are over 6,000 known species, of which about 95 occur in Europe. Fifteen of them live in the British Isles. All six legs are functional in this family, although the male tarsi are not fully developed. The larvae of all the lycaenids are woodlouse-shaped (Pl. 44). The pupae are stout and are normally attached to the food-plant or to the surrounding leaf litter by means of their tail-hooks and a silken girdle. There may be a few other strands of silk as well.

The blues are generally easily recognised, or at least the males are, by their colour alone. Most of the females are dark brown but there are often a few blue scales, especially near the body. Otherwise, the attractively spotted underside will identify them. The Brown Argus (*Aricia agestis*) and a few other species are brown in both sexes, but their undersides immediately show that they are 'blues'. *Maculinea* species, which include the very rare Large Blue (*M.arion*), are of particular interest because their larvae enter into symbiotic relationships with ants. The first three instars feed on plants in the normal way, but then the larvae lose interest in the plants and begin to wander. By this time a honey gland called Newcomer's organ has become active on the abdomen and ants queue up to drink its sweet secretions. After a while the larvae allow themselves to be carried off by the ants – usually red ants of the genus *Myrmica* – and deposited in their nests, where they complete their development while feeding on the ant grubs. The larvae pupate in the ants' nests and the adults emerge there, unhindered and virtually ignored by the ants. Most other 'blue' caterpillars possess honey glands of some kind or another and they are nearly all attended by ants, but they are not usually taken into the ants' nests and, unlike the *Maculinea* species, they can survive without the ants. The Common Blue (*Polyommatus icarus*) is found in grassy places almost everywhere, but the Chalkhill Blue (*Lysandra coridon*) is confined to chalk and limestone grassland.

The coppers are named for their bright coppery colours, which are especially bright in some of the males. The Small Copper (*Lycaena phlaeas*) is very common in all kinds of rough habitats, but several others, including the rare Large Copper (*Lycaena dispar*), are restricted to damp habitats.

The hairstreaks get their common names from the narrow streak or row of dots on the underside of the hind wings. The upper surface is basically brown, although the Purple Hairstreak (*Quercusia quercus*) is tinged with iridescent purple. A dark, oval patch of scent scales is prominent near the front of the forewings of the males in some species.

Britain's sole representative of the **Papilionidae** is the Swallowtail (*Papilio machaon*) (Pl. 32), which maintains a slender hold on life in the Norfolk Broads. It is remarkable that the British race, *P.m.britannicus*, should be confined to the fens and broads, whereas the continental race, *P.m.gorganus*, which occasionally turns up in south-east England, occurs in a wide range of habitats. The front legs are fully developed in both sexes in this family and the inner margin of the hind wing is distinctly concave, with only one anal vein. The pupa is of the succinct type, supported on the food-plant by both cremaster and girdle. Several more members of the family occur on the continent, including the beautiful Apollo (*Parnassius apollo*) (Pl. 32) of the mountain slopes.

Our only really economically important butterflies – the cabbage whites – belong to the **Pieridae** (Pl. 34), a family in which white and yellow are the dominant colours.

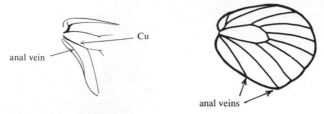

Left, The basal part of the hind wing of a swallowtail butterfly, showing its concave inner margin with just one anal vein. Right, the hind wing of a pierid butterfly, with its convex margin and two anal veins

All six legs are well developed and functional in both sexes and the inner margin of the hind wing is convex. The pupae are succinct and attached to the food-plant or other suitable support. Seven members of the family breed regularly in the British Isles, including the migratory Clouded Yellow (see below).

The Small White (*Pieris rapae*) is perhaps the most destructive of all butterflies, its pale green caterpillars (Pl. 44) destroying cabbages and other cruciferous crops nearly all over the world. The yellow and black caterpillar of the Large White (*P.brassicae*) is nearly as bad, although less widely distributed. The Green-veined White (*P.napi*), named for the greenish stripes on the underside of its hind wings, is not a pest, preferring cruciferous weeds to our cultivated brassicas. The Orange-tip (*Anthocharis cardamines*), in which only the male actually has an orange patch, also feeds on cruciferous plants in the caterpillar stage, although it is not interested in brassicas. The Black-veined White (*Aporia crataegi*) is common on the continent, where its larvae cause some damage to fruit trees, but it is no longer resident in Britain.

The Brimstone (*Gonepteryx rhamni*) is the only yellow butterfly permanently resident in Britain. The male is bright yellow but the female is a very pale greenish white and looks white in flight. This species over-winters as an adult and is one of the earliest butterflies to appear in the spring. The Clouded Yellow (*Colias croceus*) is resident in southern Europe and migrates northwards in the spring. A few individuals reach Britain each year, but every now and then there is a huge influx due to favourable winds following unusually favourable breeding conditions in the south. Several other clouded yellows live on the continent, with the Pale Clouded Yellow (*C. hyale*) and the very similar Berger's Clouded Yellow (*C. australis*) occasionally reaching Britain during the summer. Some of the clouded yellows live at high altitudes and in the far north.

The Moths (Plates 35-43 and 45-47)

Superfamily Micropterigoidea

This group, represented by the single family **Micropterigidae**, stands very much on its own among the Lepidoptera because of the functional mandibles of its members. It is often put into a sub-order of its own – the Zeugloptera – and some entomologists even suggest that these insects should have a whole order to themselves. They are certainly the most primitive of the Lepidoptera and they show a number of similarities with the caddis flies – with which the Lepidoptera undoubtedly share a common ancestor. There is no proboscis, the maxillae remaining short and separate and aiding the mandibles in the consumption of pollen. The insects rarely exceed 15mm in wingspan and they all fly by day. The narrow, pointed wings have a metallic sheen – bronze or golden in most species – and are coupled with a small fibula. Only five of the fifty or so European species occur in the British Isles. *Micropterix calthella* (Pl. 37) is one of the commonest species, being a frequent visitor to buttercups and similar flowers in May and June. Many of these small moths are also strongly attracted to the pollen-laden flowers of sedges. The larvae feed on leaf litter and fungal threads on the ground, and pupate there in tough silken cocoons.

Superfamily Eriocranioidea

This superfamily contains only one major family – the **Eriocraniidae** – represented in the British Isles by *Eriocrania purpurella* (Pl. 37) and eight other small species with a distinctive and somewhat metallic coloration. The wings are coupled with a small fibula. Mandibles are present, although much reduced and non-functional, and there is a short proboscis. The larvae are legless leaf-miners, living mainly on birch, oak, and hazel, but they pupate in tough cocoons in the soil. The pupae are exarate, that is with free appendages, and they have relatively huge curved mandibles. These are used to bite through the cocoon and to get to the surface, but they are left behind with the pupal skin when the adult emerges.

Superfamily Hepialoidea

This group of rather primitive moths is concentrated mainly in the Australian region and, to a lesser extent, in South Africa. The only family to extend beyond these areas is the **Hepialidae** (Pl. 35), represented in the British Isles by five species of Swift moths. These are medium and large-sized moths, but they can be distinguished from our other large moths by the jugum and the very short antennae and by the fact that all four wings are of the same shape. As to be expected from their common name, the moths are strong and fast fliers. The Common Swift (*Hepialus lupulina*) often comes to lighted windows at dusk, and so does the Gold Swift (*H.hecta*), but other species appear to be less attracted to light. The Ghost Swift (*H. humuli*) exhibits an interesting sexual dimorphism, with the upperside of the male typically pure white and the female pale brown. The ghostly appearance of the male as it dances over the vegetation at dusk apparently attracts the female – an unusual reversal of roles.

Swift moth larvae (Pl. 47) are generally subterranean and feed on the roots of various plants, including grasses, dandelions, and bracken. The pupa, although obtect (with appendages soldered down), is remarkably active and works its way to the surface of the soil before the adult moth emerges.

Superfamily Nepticuloidea (=Stigmelloidea)

The smallest of all the Lepidoptera belong to this group. The major family is the **Nepticulidae (=Stigmellidae)**, whose members rarely exceed 7mm in wingspan and are commonly called pigmy moths. The venation is greatly reduced, especially in the hind wing, and all the wings are fringed with long hairs. The colouring is often bright and metallic. A fibula is present, but it is weak in the males, in which sex there is a well-developed frenulum. The most characteristic feature is the 'eye-cap' formed by the swelling of the basal segment of the antenna. The larvae are legless

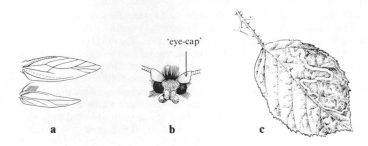

'eye-cap'

a   b   c

Some features of Nepticula *(family Nepticulidae):* **a.** *the much-reduced venation;* **b.** *the characteristic 'eye-cap', formed by the 1st antennal segment;* **c.** *the serpentine mine formed by the larva of* N. aurella *in a bramble leaf*

and most of them are leaf miners. Almost the only way to collect these tiny moths is by sleeving the mined leaves or by collecting the leaves when it is considered that the larvae are mature. The larvae leave their mines when they are mature and most of them pupate on the ground. Among the commonest of the hundred or so British species is *Nepticula aurella* (Pl. 37), whose serpentine mines decorate bramble leaves almost everywhere.

Superfamily Incurvarioidea

The members of this group resemble the pigmy moths of the last superfamily in having reduced venation and a fibula in the female and a frenulum in the male, but they are generally larger insects and they lack the 'eye-cap'. The dominant family – often split into several smaller ones – is the **Incurvariidae** (Pl. 37), whose members are generally of a metallic hue and are sometimes known as bright moths. There are 25 British species. Members of the sub-family **Adelinae** are sometimes called longhorn moths, for the males have extremely long antennae – six times as long as the body in *Nemophora degeerella*. There is a strong superficial resemblance between some of these longhorn moths and the silverhorn caddis flies (p. 252). Most of the moths fly by day and the males of several species, including *Adela viridella*, can often be seen dancing in large swarms around trees and bushes in the sunshine. The long, pale antennae are very conspicuous and the swarm attracts the females as it does among the mayflies.

The larvae of most species feed on leaf litter and make themselves portable cases with leaf fragments. Some larvae mine leaves when young, but they eventually leave their mines to live in the leaf litter. The larvae have no prolegs and they pupate in their larval cases.

Superfamily Cossoidea

This is a fairly primitive group of generally large moths, retaining a relatively full wing venation. In particular, the stem of the media is retained, so there is no large cell like that found in most other large moths. There is no proboscis, but the frenulum is well developed. There are only a few European species, all in the family **Cossidae** (Pl. 35), and only the following three species occur in the British Isles. The larvae of the rather rare Reed Leopard (*Phragmataecia castaneae*) live in reed stems, but

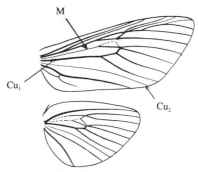

The venation of the Goat Moth, showing the lack of a large cell caused by the retention of the median vein (M)

the Leopard Moth (*Zeuzera pyrina*) and the Goat Moth (*Cossus cossus*), together with most other European species, are wood-borers. The Goat Moth, named for the strong smell emitted by its larva (Pl. 47), may take three or more years to mature. *Dyspessa ulula* is a fairly small grey and white moth whose larvae tunnel in onion bulbs.

Superfamily Zygaenoidea

These insects resemble the Cossoidea in retaining the basal part of the media, although it is often very faint. The major family is the **Zygaenidae**, which contains the brightly coloured, day-flying burnets and foresters (Pl. 35). The forewings of the burnets are black with a deep green or bluish sheen and are conspicuously marked with red – more red than black in a few species. The hind wings are red with black edges. Occasional specimens are found in which the red is replaced by yellow. The antennae of the burnets are clubbed, but there is a well-developed frenulum on the hind wing and this easily distinguishes the burnets from the butterflies. The forester moths have shiny green or bluish forewings and smoky, but translucent hindwings. Their antennae are lightly toothed or feathered, especially in the males. Both burnets and foresters are sluggish fliers and, although they beat their wings rapidly, they seem to drift through the air. Their larvae (Pl. 47) are short and plump and mainly pale with darker spots. Burnet larvae spin tough, yellowish cocoons, often quite high up on grass stems, but foresters pupate in flimsy cocoons on or close to the ground. The pupae are active and break through their cocoons before the adult moths emerge. Vacated cocoons are recognised at once by the empty pupal skins hanging from them (fig. p. 219). The family contains ten British species – seven burnets (genus *Zygaena*) and three foresters (genus *Procris*).

Several smaller families belong to the Zygaenoidea, although their members have little general resemblance to the burnets and foresters. Most of the European species are rather drab, brownish insects. Only the **Limacodidae** (=**Cochlididae**) occurs in Britain, where there are just two species – the Triangle (*Heterogenea asella*) and the Festoon (*Apoda avellana*), both illustrated on Pl. 35. There is little similarity between the adults, but their fleshy, slug-like larvae are clearly related.

Superfamily Pterophoroidea

This group, closely related to the Pyraloidea and sometimes included in it, contains the plume moths of the family **Pterophoridae** (Pl. 36). There are about 40 British species.The wings are slender and each is usually divided into two or three (occasionally four) feather-like plumes. At rest, the forewings are generally rolled around the hind wings and held at right angles to the body, giving the insect the shape of the letter T. *Pterophorus pentadactyla* is a common species, and very conspicuous because of its brilliant whiteness. It often comes to light at night. Its larvae feed on bindweed. *Agdistis* species have undivided wings, but the general outline and the characteristically long spiky legs clearly place the insects with the other plume moths.

Superfamily Pyraloidea

This superfamily contains upwards of 20,000 species of rather delicate moths, mostly from about 15mm to 30mm in wingspan. The forewings are generally narrow and the hind wings somewhat broader. Both pairs bear relatively short fringes. The insects are structurally much alike and may be conveniently treated as one large family – the **Pyralidae** (Pl. 36). The possession of abdominal tympanal organs distinguishes the pyralids from similar members of the Tortricoidea and Tineoidea, but the most characteristic feature of the Pyralidae is found in the hind wing: $Sc+R_1$ is fused with Rs for some distance beyond the cell.

Pyralid larvae have few distinguishing features, but one can often recognise a pyralid larva as such simply by its vigorous wriggling when it is disturbed. The larvae feed on a wide variety of materials, including grain and other stored products, and many of them live in silken tubes and tunnels.

There are about 200 British species, including a number of regular and casual migrants and various aliens which are established as pests in warehouses and other buildings. Major pests include the Meal Moth (*Pyralis farinalis*) and the Mediterranean Flour Moth (*Ephestia kuehniella*). The larvae of these and several other species feed on cereals and cereal products and they destroy or damage large quantities of food in granaries and flour mills. They also attack nuts and dried fruit. The European Corn Borer (*Ostrinia nubilalis*) is another important pest, although not common in Britain. A native of continental Europe, it was introduced into America

The venation of a typical pyralid moth, characterised by the fusion of $Sc+R_1$ with Rs in the hind wing

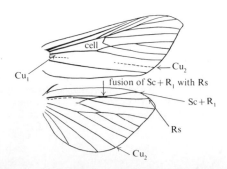

where its stem-boring larvae have done untold damage to maize. They also tunnel into a variety of other plants. The Wax Moth (*Galleria mellonella*) is a pest in bee hives, the larvae feeding on the combs and covering them with silken tunnels.

The china-mark moths, such as *Elophila nymphaeata*, are aquatic in their early stages. Young larvae mine the stems of various water plants, but older ones feed externally on the leaves and often spin leaves together to form shelters. The most familiar pyralids are probably the grass moths, also called grass veneers, of the sub-family Crambinae. These small moths are very common in grassy places and spend the daytime sitting vertically on the stems. The forewings are generally straw-coloured and they are wrapped tightly round the abdomen at rest. The moths do not fly far when disturbed, but they are not easy to find when they drop back into the grass. They often come to lights at night. The stout, forward-pointing palps, projecting horn-like from the head, and the characteristic folding of the wings distinguish the grass moths from most other pyralids. *Crambus pratella* and *Catoptria pinella* are typical examples.

Superfamily Tortricoidea

These are generally small moths, although some may exceed 25mm in wingspan, and their most noticeable feature is the almost rectangular shape of the forewings: the apical angle is very nearly 90° in many species. The wings are all relatively broad with short fringes. The frenulum and proboscis are well developed. The moths rest with the wings held roofwise over the body.

The major family is the **Tortricidae** (Pl. 36), with about 320 British species. Most of them are brownish or mottled grey but some, including *Cacoecimorpha pronubana* and *Croesia bergmanniana* are brightly coloured. A large proportion of tortricid larvae are leaf-rollers, living within rolled-up leaves or between leaves or flowers spun together with silk. Others bore into stems, flowers, or fruits and several are serious pests. The Codlin Moth (*Cydia pomonella*), whose larvae bore into apples, is a well-known example. *Tortrix viridana* is another very common species. This small green moth can be beaten from oak trees in immense numbers in some years. Its larvae live in rolled leaves, from which they fall on silken threads when disturbed, and they frequently defoliate the trees in the summer.

Agapeta hamana and *Aethes cnicana*, both pictured on Pl. 36, belong to the **Cochylidae**. This family is very similar to the Tortricidae, but may be distinguished by vein Cu_{1b} of the forewing arising in the distal part of the cell instead of near the centre.

Forewing venation of the Tortricidae (left) and the Cochylidae, showing the different origins of the vein Cu_{1b}

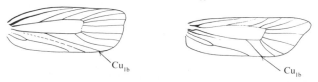

Superfamily Sesioidea

This group contains the clearwing moths of the family **Sesiidae** (Pl. 35). They are called clearwings because their wings are largely devoid of scales. The forewings are very narrow and readily distinguish these insects from the bee hawkmoths (Pl. 42). They are day-flying and many of them resemble wasps and other hymenopterans, providing excellent examples of mimicry (see p. 262). Some larvae, including those of the Fiery Clearwing (*Bembecia chrysidiformis*), feed on the roots of herbaceous plants, but most species are wood-borers, tunnelling in the roots, trunks, and branches of various broad-leaved trees. The Hornet Moth (*Sesia apiformis*) feeds in poplar trunks and roots. Some species cause considerable damage in fruit-growing areas, the Currant Clearwing (*Synanthedon tipuliformis*) being a common pest of red and black currants while the Red-belted Clearwing (*S.myopaeformis*) attacks apples and related trees. There are fifteen British species.

Superfamily Tineoidea

About one third of all the moths belong to this large and very varied superfamily, although many entomologists now split it into several smaller superfamilies. They are mostly small moths, including many tiny leaf-miners as well as the familiar clothes moths and many other pests. Many of the families are not easily distinguished from each other, but they can usually be recognised as a group by their narrow wings and broad fringes. Some families have broader wings and short fringes, but the forewings are never squared off as they are in the tortricids. The lack of tympanal organs distinguishes the Tineoidea from the pyralids. Larval foods and habits are extremely varied, but most of the larvae conceal themselves by boring or mining, or by constructing shelters of silk and leaves. Only the larger families or those with economically important members are described here.

The **Gelechiidae**, whose members are sometimes known as nebs and groundlings, can usually be distinguished by the wavy outline of the hind wing. Most of the larvae in this family feed within spun-up leaves or shoots, although many are seed-eaters and some species cause galls. The Angoumois Grain Moth (*Sitotroga cerealella*) (Pl. 37.) is an important pest whose larvae cause severe damage to wheat and maize grain, both in the field and in store. The Pink Bollworm (*Pectinophora gossypiella*),

The venation of a typical member of the Tineoidea

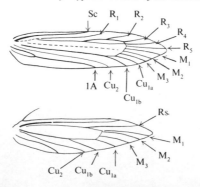

Left, the tuft of hair at the base of the antenna in the Oecophoridae. Right, the hind wing of a member of the Gelechiidae, showing the characteristically wavy outline

which destroys cotton crops in many parts of the world, also belongs to this family. There are about 150 British species.

The members of the closely related **Oecophoridae** (Pl. 37) are rather dull-coloured, flattened moths whose wings are rounded at the tips. There is usually a small tuft of hairs at the base of the antenna, although this feature is found in some other moths and is not diagnostic. There are about 80 British species. The larvae feed mainly on leaves and flower-heads, which they drape with silk to form shelters. *Depressaria pastinacella* spins up the flower heads of several umbelliferous plants and feeds on the developing seeds. The larvae of *Dasycera sulphurella* feed in dead wood, while those of the Brown House Moth (*Hofmannophila pseudospretella*) normally feed on plant and animal debris in birds' nests. They often find their way into houses and attack assorted fabrics and stored foods.

The **Elachistidae**, typified by *Elachista bisulcella* (Pl. 37), are all small moths with very narrow, pointed hind wings. Their larvae live as miners in grasses and other narrow-leaved plants. There are about 40 British species. The **Momphidae** is another family with very narrow and often heavily-fringed wings, but it can be distinguished from the Elachistidae because the scales on the head are relatively broad – generally broader than the thickness of the antennae. Many of these little moths, typified by *Glyphipteryx linneella* (Pl. 37), are brilliantly marked. The larvae are mostly leaf-miners. There are about 30 British species.

Members of the **Glyphipterigidae** are all small moths, often resembling the tortricids in general appearance although their hind wings are very much narrower than those of the tortricids. Most of the eight British species, typified by *Glyphipterix haworthana* (Pl. 37), are brown with silvery stripes on the forewings. They usually fly by day. Their larvae feed mainly on grasses, binding the leaves together with silk to form shelters.

The **Yponomeutidae** (Pl. 37) has few obvious family characteristics, but the hind wings are perhaps a little broader than those of other families in this group and the hind tibiae are smoothly scaled – not long-haired as in several other families of the Tineoidea. Vein R_5 in the forewing arises directly from the cell and does not share a common stalk with R_4. There are about 75 British species, of which the most familiar are the small ermines or ermels of the genus *Yponomeuta*, whose forewings are white with black spots. The larvae of the small ermines live in communal tents which they spin among the shoots of their food-plants. Hedges and small trees are often completely covered with these tents and may be completely defoliated. *Ethmia bipunctella*, easily identified by its wing pattern, is a rare moth associated with viper's bugloss. *Ypsolopha mucronella*, with a wingspan of nearly 30mm, is one of the larger members of the family. Like many of its relatives in the sub-family Plutellinae, it has pointed wings, and when at rest these are wrapped around the body to give it a rather twig-like appearance. The antennae are held forward at rest, whereas those of *Yponomeuta* are folded back along the body. *Plutella xylostella* is the Diamond-back

Moth, named for the pattern of small diamonds made by the folded wings. Its larvae are pests of cultivated brassicas.

Members of the **Coleophoridae** are small moths with very narrow, pointed wings and long fringes. They can usually be distinguished from the Elachistidae because they hold their antennae forward at rest. There are about 80 British species and all but three of them belong to the genus *Coleophora*. The larvae usually start life as leaf-miners, but soon emerge and spin portable cases of silk, sometimes strengthened with bits of leaf or a few small seeds. The moths are therefore commonly known as case moths. The cases are attached to leaves, stems, or seed capsules and the larvae are thus protected while they feed. Neat little holes are left when the larvae move away to other feeding sites. *C. alticollella* (Pl. 37) is a very common case moth and one of several whose larval cases are attached to the fruiting heads of rushes.

The family **Gracillariidae** (also called **Lithocolletidae**) (Pl. 37) contains small and minute moths with very narrow, long-fringed wings. Most of them can be recognised by their habit of resting with the body at an angle to the surface, propped up on the front legs. There are about 80 British species, most of them in the genus *Phyllonorycter* (=*Lithocolletis*). The larvae make blotch mines in the leaves of various trees and shrubs, although some other genera in the family make serpentine mines similar to those of the pigmy moths (p. 230).

Most of our household clothes moths belong to the **Tineidae** (Pl. 37). The members of this family, which has about 45 British species, are generally small insects, often with a golden or silvery sheen. The head is rather roughly haired and the proboscis is reduced or absent altogether. The adult insects therefore do not feed and it is their larvae that damage our fabrics. Clothes moths in general are dark-loving insects and, although males and spent females sometimes come to light, they are more likely to scuttle for cover than to fly into the open when disturbed. The larvae feed mainly on dried plant and animal material, the clothes moth larvae being among the few insects able to digest the keratin of hairs and feathers. The natural haunts of these insects are the nests of birds and small mammals, from where it is but a short step to human households in which carpets, clothing, and general debris provide abundant food. Pipe-lagging, because it is left undisturbed and is often warm, is a particularly favourable site for these moths, although modern plastic and fibre-glass materials are safe from attack.

The most important species, from the point of view of damage done, is the Common Clothes Moth (*Tineola bisselliella*). Its larvae feed on all keratin-containing materials – hair, wool, silk, feathers, and so on – and will also consume vegetable materials such as cotton and stored cereal products. The Case-bearing Clothes Moth (*Tinea pellionella*) plays a smaller role in fabric damage but is still a serious pest. Its common name stems from the larval habit of constructing a tubular case from silk and fragments of the surrounding materials. The larvae of the Tapestry Moth (*Trichophaga tapetzella*) also damage fabrics but they prefer coarser materials than the clothes moths. They are often found in owl pellets, which may be their natural food. Clothes moth damage has fallen off sharply in recent years as a result of more frequent dry-cleaning and the use of residual insecticides, but damage and the cost of controlling it are still considerable.

The **Psychidae** is a very specialised family, with only a few dozen species in Europe and only 18 British members. They are known as bagworms because the larvae make little portable cases for themselves. These cases are made from fragments of bark, bud scales, leaf fragments, sand grains, and so on bound together with

Cases of a clothes moth larva (left) and a bagworm larva. Some bagworm cases are smooth, but can always be distinguished from clothes moth cases because the front and rear ends are quite different: clothes moth cases are similar at both ends

silk. Each species has its own design and it is often possible to recognise a species from its case alone. The cases are carried about by the larvae and are enlarged as the insects grow. Most species are found on trees. When the larvae are ready to pupate the cases are firmly attached to leaves or twigs and pupation occurs inside them. The adult female is usually wingless and she often lacks legs and antennae as well. With few exceptions, she remains in her case throughout her life. The male, on the other hand, is fully winged and very active, seeking out the concealed female with the aid of his feathery antennae. Many species fly by day. The wings are sparsely covered with scales and hairs and have a dusky appearance – the moths are sometimes called smokes and sweeps – and there is a well-developed frenulum. There is no proboscis, so the moths cannot feed and their adult life is short. After mating, the females lay their eggs in or on their cases, and the first job of the young larvae is to begin their own cases. They do this before feeding, often using fragments of their mother's case or even of her dead body for the purpose. Several species have parthenogenetic females. *Sterrhopterix fusca* (Pl. 37) is one of the largest of the European species.

Superfamily Alucitoidea

This group contains just one European family – the **Alucitidae** – and very few species. The Many-plumed Moth (*Alucita hexadactyla*) (Pl. 36) is the only British species. Its wings, like those of other members of the family, are broken up into at least six feathery plumes, but these are not very obvious when the moths are at rest with their wings swept back along their bodies.

Superfamily Noctuoidea

This is a very large group, containing rather stout-bodied moths on the whole, characterised by the possession of tympanal organs on the metathorax. The various families are separated by relatively minor differences in the venation and the whole superfamily is quite uniform in appearance as far as the adults are concerned. Most of the species fly by night and, with a few notable exceptions, they are rather dull in colour.

The **Notodontidae** (Pl. 38) contains the Buff-tip (*Phalera bucephala*) and the Puss Moth (*Cerura vinula*) together with the prominents and kittens. The family can be distinguished from others in the group because vein M_2 in the forewing is more or less parallel to M_3 and not close to it at the base as it is in the other families. Most of the prominents can be recognised on sight by the tuft of scales on the hind edge of each forewing. When the moths are at rest the tufts come together to form the little humps that give the moths their common name. The Buff-tip and the Puss Moth

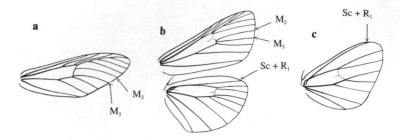

Venation in the Noctuoidea, showing the differences between the families: **a.**
Notodontidae (forewing only); **b.** *Arctiidae;* **c.** *Noctuidae (hind wing only)*

are also easily recognised, but it is the caterpillar of the latter (Pl. 45) that makes it
well known. The full-grown larva is green with a reddish-brown 'saddle' and it is
very well camouflaged among the sallow leaves on which it feeds, but when alarmed
it takes on a grotesque appearance by retracting the head into the front part of the
thorax and displaying two large eye-spots. At the same time a pair of whip-like filaments emerge from the highly modified last pair of prolegs – the claspers of other
caterpillars – and wave threateningly over the body. And, as if this weren't enough,
the caterpillar can also shoot a jet of irritating fluid from a gland on its thorax. Few
predators bother to press home an attack. Several other notodontid larvae are illustrated on Pl. 45. The family contains 25 British species, including the Lobster Moth
(*Stauropus fagi*), which is named for its weird caterpillar (fig. p. 218).

In many parts of southern and central Europe the pine trees are decorated with
large oval balls of silk. These are the tents or nests of the larvae of the Pine Processionary Moth (*Thaumetopoea pityocampa*), so called because the larvae move out
in single file to feed on the pine needles at night. There may be several hundred
larvae in a single tent, and they can defoliate whole trees in a few weeks. They hibernate in their nests and pupate in the ground in the spring. The Oak Processionary
Moth (*T. processionea*) (Pl. 38) is very similar, but a bit smaller and less common.
The larvae live in nests on oak trunks and travel in broader processions when going
out to feed. They pupate in the larval tents. The moths are closely related to the Notodontidae and are sometimes included in that family, but are now usually given a
family to themselves – the **Thaumetopoeidae**. There is no tuft on the hind margin
of the forewing, but the females all bear a conspicuous tuft of hair around the tip of
the abdomen.

The **Arctiidae** (Pl. 38) is characterised by the venation of the hind wing, where
vein Sc+R$_1$ is fused with the cell for about half the length of the cell (fig. above),
but most members of the family can be recognised as such without detailed examination. There are two fairly distinct groups or sub-families – the tigers and ermines
(sub-family Arctiinae) on the one hand and the footmen (sub-family Lithosiinae) on
the other. The tigers, typified by the Garden Tiger (*Arctia caja*), are stout, hairy
moths with broad wings and bright colours, while the ermines, typified by the Buff
Ermine (*Spilosoma lutea*), are cream or white with black spots. Tiger and ermine
larvae are stout and hairy (Pl. 46) and they feed on a variety of low-growing plants.
The Cinnabar Moth (*Tyria jacobaeae*) is included with the tiger moths, although it

Tent of Pine Processionary caterpillars.
These tents are packed with droppings as
well as with the caterpillars themselves. The
caterpillars' venomous hairs make the nests
hazardous to touch

is not typical of the sub-family. Its black and gold larva (Pl. 46) is a fine example of warning coloration. The footman moths are much more slender and their forewings are generally quite narrow. Most of them are drably coloured, like the Common Footman (*Eilema lurideola*), but the Rosy Footman (*Miltochrista miniata*) and a few others are a little more colourful. Footman larvae are hairy and they feed almost entirely on lichens. Like the tigers and ermines, they pupate in flimsy cocoons incorporating the larval hairs. The family contains 31 British species, including one sporadic visitor from the continent.

The **Ctenuchidae (=Syntomidae)** is related to the Arctiidae, although its members look more like burnets at first sight. They are day-flying insects, many of them being brightly coloured and mimicing wasps and bees. Only a few species occur in Europe and none lives in Britain, although *Syntomis phegea* (Pl. 38), which is the commonest of the continental species, has occasionally crossed the Channel.

The largest of all the families in the Lepidoptera is the **Noctuidae (=Agrotidae)** (Pl. 39), although it is sometimes split into several smaller families. The venation (fig. p. 238) is characterised by the fact that vein $Sc+R_1$ in the hind wing fuses with the cell only at the base (but see also Lymantriidae). A proboscis is almost always well developed. Browns and greys are the dominant colours, although the hind wings are sometimes brilliantly coloured, as in the red underwings and yellow underwings. The latter provide good examples of flash coloration. When disturbed, they fly erratically and flash the coloured hind wings. This confuses the attacker and makes the insects very hard to follow in flight, and then the moths drop down out of sight again. Similar flash coloration is exhibited by some of the grasshoppers (see p. 75). Noctuid larvae are generally without much hair, although there are some striking exceptions like that of the Sycamore Moth (*Acronicta aceris*) pictured on Pl. 46, and they usually pupate in the soil. A selection of noctuid larvae appears on Pls 46 and 47. That of the Large Yellow Underwing (*Noctua pronuba*) is one of a group known as cutworms and it can do a fair amount of damage to crops on the farm and in the garden by nibbling through the stems at ground level. There are just over 400 British species in the family.

The family **Lymantriidae** (Pl. 40), containing the tussock moths, is hard to distinguish from the Noctuidae as far as the venation is concerned, and the most obvious difference is the reduction or loss of the proboscis. Male tussock moths also have rather feathery antennae. Tussock moths in general are very hairy and their hairs are often barbed and irritating, thus making the moths unpleasant to handle. Many of the females have dense anal tufts on the abdomen. The larvae are also hairy, and equally unpleasant to handle, although, with their brightly coloured tufts, they are among the most attractive of all caterpillars. The pupae are found in loose cocoons, spun among the food-plants and incorporating the larval hairs. Common species include the Yellow-tail (*Euproctis similis*), whose larva is often a pest of fruit trees, the Pale Tussock (*Calliteara pudibunda*), and the Vapourer (*Orgyia antiqua*). All are pictured on Pl. 40. and their larvae appear on Pl. 45. The Vapourer is of special interest because the female has only vestigial wings. She rarely moves from her cocoon after emerging and she lays her eggs all over it. The Gipsy Moth (*Lymantria dispar*) also has a flightless female, although she is fully winged. She is much larger than the male (Pl. 40) and has creamy white wings with dark markings, not unlike those of the related Black Arches (*L.monacha*). There are eleven British species.

Superfamily Geometroidea

This is another very large group, whose members are mainly small or medium-sized moths. Although the wingspan may exceed 50mm in some species, the wings are mostly flimsy and the body is generally narrow. Most species therefore have a rather delicate appearance and few are strong fliers.

The family **Thyatiridae** (Pl. 43) differs somewhat from the rest of the Geometroidea because its members are rather stout. They hold their wings roofwise over the body like the noctuids, but they can be distinguished by their abdominal hearing organs and also by the venation of the hind wing. Vein $Sc+R_1$ is fused with the cell at the base in the noctuids (fig. p. 238), but in the present family it remains quite separate, although it may run close to the outer end of the cell. There are nine British species, of which the Buff Arches (*Habrosyne pyritoides*) is the commonest. Other species include the Peach Blossom (*Thyatira batis*) and the Frosted Green (*Polyploca ridens*).

Most of the members of the **Drepanidae** (Pl. 43) can be separated from the Geometridae by their hooked wing-tips, which give them their name of hooktip moths. The Scalloped Hooktip (*Drepana lacertinaria*) and the Pebble Hooktip (*D. falcataria*) are typical examples, but the Chinese Character (*Cilix glaucata*) is an exception in that it has rounded wing-tips. Hooktip larvae lack the last pair of prolegs – the claspers – and they rest with the tip of the abdomen turned up (Pl. 47). There are only six British species in the family.

The family **Geometridae** (Pl. 43) contains a large number of species, differing widely in size and shape but nearly all rather flimsy. Most of them rest with their wings spread flat on each side of the body and there is quite likely to be some confusion between these moths and some of the larger pyralids (p. 232). Both groups have abdominal hearing organs, but they can be separated by looking at the venation of the hind wing. Vein Cu_2 is present in the pyralid hind wing but never in the geometrid hind wing. In addition, the anterior veins of the geometrid hind wing fuse to form a small loop near the base.

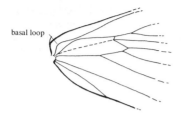

basal loop

The venation of a geometrid's hind wing, easily distinguished from the pyralid venation because $Sc+R_1$ is close to or fused with Rs only right at the base, forming a small basal loop

The name of the family means 'ground-measurer' and is derived from the behaviour of the caterpillars. These are generally long and slender and they have only two pairs of prolegs – on segments 6 and 10 of the abdomen. When walking they grip the substrate with the prolegs and then stretch out, as if measuring length, to find a hold with the thoracic legs. Having found a hold, they draw the prolegs up close to the thoracic ones and in doing so they throw the body up in a loop – leading to their common name of loopers. Many of the caterpillars feed on trees and shrubs and they are often remarkably twig-like. The pupae may be found in the soil or in flimsy cocoons among the herbage.

There are just over 300 British species. The Peppered Moth (*Biston betularia*) is of special interest because of the rapid increase of its melanic form (f. *carbonaria*) since it was first reported in 1848. This dark form is protectively coloured in the smoke-blackened industrial regions, but is now common in many rural areas as well and it must have some other advantage over the typical mottled form. It is believed that the larvae of the melanic form are hardier than those of the normal moths in the presence of slight air pollution – insufficient to blacken trees and walls. Industrial melanism occurs in many other moths, and in some other groups of insects as well, but in recent years there has been a noticeable drop in the numbers of melanic individuals as a result of the introduction of smokeless zones in many regions.

The females of several species, particularly those that emerge in the winter, have only vestigial wings. Examples include the Mottled Umber (*Erannis defoliaria*) and the Winter Moth (*Operophtera brumata*), both of which are troublesome pests in the caterpillar stage.

Superfamily Sphingoidea

The only family included in this group is the **Sphingidae**. Its members are the hawkmoths – swift-flying insects which are easily recognised by their large size, stout bodies, and narrow forewings with acute apical angles. There are 17 British species, although only nine of these are permanent residents. The rest are summer visitors, and of these only the Hummingbird Hawkmoth (*Macroglossum stellatarum*) is at all frequent. Most of the European species are illustrated on Pls 41 and 42. The proboscis is usually very long – that of the Convolvulus Hawkmoth (*Agrius convolvuli*) is so long that it has a special sheath to itself in the pupa – and the moths are able to take nectar from flowers while hovering in front of them, although some species have no proboscis and do not feed at all. Most hawkmoth larvae can be recognised as such on sight by the abdominal horn (fig. p. 218). The larvae of the Privet Hawkmoth (*Sphinx ligustri*) (Pl. 45) and many other species are green, with oblique stripes which aid concealment by breaking up the shape and by resembling leaf veins. One notable exception is the larva of the Elephant Hawkmoth (*Deilephila elpenor*) (Pl.

45), which is dark brown and bears two pairs of eye-spots on the front part of the abdomen. When alarmed, the caterpillar withdraws its head and thorax into the abdomen, causing the eye-spot region to swell and take on a threatening appearance. The larva of the Small Elephant Hawkmoth (*D. porcellus*) is similar but it lacks the abdominal horn. The larva of the Spurge Hawkmoth (*Hyles euphorbiae*) (Pl. 45) is one of the most colourful of all caterpillars, its boldly spotted coat warning predators of its poisonous nature. Like most caterpillars, it acquires its poisons from its foodplants. Pupation normally takes place in the soil below the food-plant.

Hawkmoths are generally nocturnal, although the Hummingbird Hawkmoth and the two bee hawkmoths fly by day. The bee hawkmoths are fully-scaled when they first emerge from their pupae, but most of the scales fall off during the first flight and leave the wings largely naked. The moths have some resemblance to bumble bees when in flight.

Superfamily Bombycoidea

The members of this group, with few exceptions, lack both proboscis and frenulum. They are generally large, hairy moths with broad wings. The major family is the **Lasiocampidae**(Pl. 40), whose members are all some shade of brown. There are eleven British species, including the Oak Eggar (*Lasiocampa quercus*), the Drinker (*Euthrix potatoria*), the Lappet (*Gastropacha quercifolia*), and the Lackey (*Malacosoma neustria*). The humeral region of the hind wing is enlarged and supported by two or more humeral veins. The moths are good fliers, often on the wing by day, and both sexes bear pectinate antennae, although this is much more marked in the males. The larvae of the Lackey Moth (Pl. 45) live gregariously for much of their life and can be pests in orchards. They often cover trees with silken tents. Pupation in this family takes place in a cocoon attached to the food-plant.

The **Saturniidae** contains some of the world's biggest moths, including the giant silkmoths of India. The Emperor Moth (*Saturnia pavonia*) (Pl. 40) is Britain's only representative, but there are several others on the continent, including the Giant Peacock Moth (*S. pyri*) which looks like a very large Emperor Moth. With a wingspan of about 15cm, it is Europe's largest moth. All the European species have some kind of eye-spot on each wing. The males are well known for their ability to pick up the females' scent from far away and home in on them with the aid of their large, scent-sensitive antennae. The larvae (Pl. 45) pupate in tough, fibrous cocoons attached to the food-plant.

The **Endromidae** contains only a single species – the easily recognised Kentish Glory (*Endromis versicolora*) (Pl. 40), whose larvae feed on birch in many parts of northern and central Europe. British populations are now confined to parts of Scotland. Europe has no native members of the **Bombycidae**, but this family includes the Cultivated Silkmoth (*Bombyx mori*) which is familiar to many people. The insect is not found in the wild state, even in its native China, but several races exist on silk farms. Centuries of breeding have increased the silk content of the cocoon and well over half a mile of unbroken silk thread is now yielded by one well-formed cocoon. During the process of domestication the moth has completely lost its power of flight.

Collecting and preserving
Most entomologists probably start by collecting butterflies and moths because these are the most obvious insects and because their distinctive patterns make them fairly easy to identify. Adult butterflies and day-flying moths are generally caught by chas-

ing them with a net, but night-flying moths must be brought to the collector with the aid of light or sugar.

Most moths are distracted by light and they spiral round and round a lamp until they crash into it. An ordinary bulb in a porch, or taken into the garden on a long lead well-protected from damp, will produce plenty of moths, especially if used in conjunction with a white sheet. The moths are easily picked off the sheet and surrounding vegetation, but specially constructed mercury-vapour moth traps are more efficient. The powerful light attracts moths from a considerable distance, and when they hit the lamp they fall down a funnel and into a closed box. This box is usually filled with egg-packing which provides plenty of nooks and crannies into which the moths can settle. Such a trap can be left unattended all night, and as far as we know it does no harm to the moths. The catch can be examined the next day and then released. There are, however, indications that traps used every night in one area lead to a decline in the number of moths. This is not a direct effect of the light, but results from birds' getting to know that good pickings can be had around the trap at daybreak. Care must be taken when releasing the night's catch: release the moths in the undergrowth where they will be relatively safe or, better still, keep them in the trap until the evening when the birds have gone to bed. Bats also find the pickings easy around the trap at night.

'Sugaring' for moths involves more work than light-trapping and usually produces fewer specimens, but it is certainly more instructive. The idea is to daub tree trunks, fence posts, and so on with sweet aromatic bait. A considerable mystique attaches to the brewing of the mixture and many collectors have their own peculiar and often exotic recipes, but brown ale (1/2 pint), black treacle (1lb), and rum (2 nips) make a highly effective – and palatable – mixture. Pear-drop flavouring (amyl acetate) can be added to increase the efficiency of the bait. A clean paint brush is used to put streaks of the mixture on tree trunks at about head height. Baiting inside a wood is not usually profitable: isolated trees and fences are best, but in the absence of these you can daub pieces of rag and tie them to shrubs and hedgerows. The weather is also important and, as with light-trapping, humid, overcast nights are usually far better than clear, moonlit nights. The sugaring should be completed before nightfall and the treated sites should not be too far apart. Each can then be visited at intervals during the night to collect the drunken moths. There is something quite exciting about finding a group of moths feeding at the bait, all sitting around the edge with their tongues reaching in to sample the brew.

Flowers are of interest to both butterflies and moths, and sweet-scented, nectar-rich varieties will attract many species. The entomologist's garden should always contain plants like buddleia, honeysuckle, lavender, michaelmas daisies, aubretia, and ice-plant.

The young stages of the Lepidoptera can be obtained by by beating and sweeping, or simply by searching: feeding damage and droppings often reveal the caterpillars' whereabouts. Most species are easy to rear in captivity, although those that hibernate as larvae may cause problems because they require constant attention to humidity. Rearing is the only way to get good adult specimens of leaf-miners and some of the other small moths. Mined leaves can usually be kept in good condition by placing them on damp peat in a closed container. The peat seems to restrict mould growth better than any other substrate.

Pupa-digging is a rather hit-and-miss business, involving careful sifting of soil and litter at the bases of trees and other food-plants, but it may be worthwhile when certain species are known to exist in a given area.

Adult insects destined for the collection should be killed as soon as possible after capture, otherwise they may batter their wings and lose their scales by trying to fly in confined spaces. The larger species are set in the normal way, with the hind edge of the forewings at right angles to the body as a rule. It is a good plan to set some butterflies in their resting positions in order to show the underside, for this is the position in which many of them will be seen in the wild. The smaller species are difficult to set neatly, but good results can be obtained with practice and then they can be staged on polyporus strips.

Order Trichoptera – Caddis Flies (Plates 48 and 49)

Recognition features Small, medium, and large insects with two pairs of wings
covered with tiny hairs. Wings have few cross-veins and are held roofwise over the
body at rest. Antennae very slender, often as long as and sometimes longer than the
wings. Normally found near water. Caddis flies are structurally very similar to certain moths and some of the smaller members of the two groups are easily confused,
but the hairy (not scaled) wings and the lack of a coiled proboscis will distinguish
the caddis flies. Caddis flies can be separated from the lacewings by the few cross-
veins, and from stoneflies and mayflies by the few cross-veins and the position of
the wings at rest.

*A typical caddis fly in its resting
position, with antennae held forward
and wings folded roofwise over the
body*

This is the only order of holometabolic insects in which the young stages are primarily aquatic. There are nearly 6,000 known species, of which over 400 occur in
Europe. About 190 of these are British. Only *Enoicyla* species do not have aquatic
larvae – they live in damp moss at the base of trees. Adult caddis flies are rather
dull brownish insects, usually flying at dusk. The smaller ones rarely travel far from
the ponds or streams in which they grew up, although the larger ones, with stronger
powers of flight, often turn up in light traps some distance from the water. During
the daytime most caddis flies hide in the waterside vegetation and are usually overlooked. The insects are of great importance in freshwater ecology, with both adults
and larvae being eaten in large numbers by fish and by various water birds. Caddis
flies are thus of great interest to the fisherman, who also knows them as sedge flies,
or, in Ireland, as rails.

The caddis antennae are slender and bristle-like. They are composed of many segments and are often as long as the wings or even longer. At rest they are held straight
forward in front of the head. The compound eyes are normally small and the ocelli,
if present, are three in number, although the central one is often right between the
antennae and difficult to detect. Caddis flies have simple biting mouths, but these
are poorly developed and often vestigial and, although some species feed on nectar,
most adults probably do not feed. The maxillary palps are long and often clearly
visible at the sides of the head or covering the face. These palps clearly distinguish
their owners from apparently similar micro-lepidopterans. All female caddis flies
have 5-segmented palps but the number varies in the males and is used in classification (see p. 250).

*The maxillary palps of three caddis fly
families:* **a.** *Phryganeidae;* **b.**
Rhyacophilidae; **c.** *Philopotamidae*

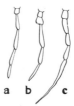

a   b   c

The wings of Hydropsyche, *showing the apical forks formed by the division of the veins. There are five forks in the forewing of* Hydropsyche, *but the 4th fork is absent from the hind wing*

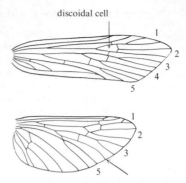

The prothorax is small and the mesothorax is the larger of the other two thoracic segments. Wings are fully developed in most caddis flies, although a few species, including *Enoicyla pusilla*, have wingless females. The name Trichoptera means hairy wings (Greek *trichos* = hair) and refers to the tiny hairs that clothe the veins and membranes of the wings. Unlike the scales of butterflies and moths, these hairs do not rub off easily. The forewings are relatively narrow and are rather more hairy and opaque than the broader hind wings. In most species there is an amplexiform type of wing coupling, the hind edge of the forewing being folded and engaging with the costa of the hind wing. Curved, interlocking hairs on the marginal veins also help to hold the wings together.

Caddis fly wings have few cross-veins but the main veins divide noticeably in the outer third of the wing to form the apical forks. Differences in venation lead to the disappearance of some of the forks, which are therefore useful identification guides. M_{3+4} does not divide in the hind wing, so apical fork 4 is never present. Another useful identification aid is the discoidal cell. Its shape varies considerably and it is absent from many species – in other words, there is no cross-vein between R_3 and R_4. One fairly constant feature is the thyridium – a small, pale, hairless spot near the centre of each wing. Its significance is not clear but it is possibly connected with some sort of sense organ.

The legs are long and the tibiae are spurred. The spurs are quite large and must not be confused with the smaller, darker spines that clothe much of the leg. The number of spurs on each tibia is used in classification and identification. When referring to the spurs it is usual to give just the numbers for the three legs: spurs 2,4,4 simply means that the front tibia has two spurs and the others have four each.

Caddis flies pair while resting on the vegetation, although pairing may begin in the air, and egg-laying follows in due course. Most species lay their eggs on the water surface or right in the water, but some lay on the waterside vegetation and even under stones on dried-up stream beds. The laying and spent flies are attractive

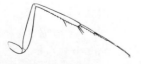

A caddis fly leg showing three spurs on the tibia

A caddis larva removed from its case, showing the tufts of simple gills on the lower border and the terminal hooks with which the larva grips its case

to fish and the angler uses a number of caddis species as models for his artificial lures.

The eggs are commonly laid in strings or masses which are covered with mucilage, although species with free-living larvae lay their eggs singly or in small groups. The jelly swells up when wetted, rather like frogspawn jelly, and protects the eggs. The latter hatch in two or three weeks and tiny, soft-bodied larvae appear. Those whose eggs were laid out of water make their way into it, simply by falling if they are on overhanging branches. Eggs laid on dried-up stream beds do not hatch until the water returns in the autumn.

The caddis larva has a well-sclerotised head and biting jaws. The thorax is partly sclerotised and bears well-developed legs, but the abdomen is soft and fleshy. Most caddis larvae surround themselves with protective cases, built with various materials gathered from their surroundings. A gland near the mouth produces a sticky silk thread which the larva spins around itself and to which it fixes the case-building materials. Each species uses its own particular materials – grains of sand, plant fragments, or even empty mollusc shells – and builds to a specific design. It is often possible to identify a species simply from its case. The sand grains and other materials are often very neatly cemented together to form a mosaic. As the larva grows, it adds fresh material to the front of the case. A variety of these cases can be seen on Pls 48 and 49.

The caddis case is always open at both ends, although the rear opening may be very narrow, and movements of the larva's body draw a stream of water through it. In this way the larva gets a constant supply of oxygen, which it extracts from the water with the feathery gills along the sides of its body. The head and legs protrude from the case, enabling the larva to move about in search of food. Two strong hooks at the tip of the abdomen grip the silken lining of the case and ensure that the caddis and its home do not part company. Caddis living in fast-flowing streams often add larger stones to their cases – presumably an instinctive action that serves to prevent their being swept away by the current. Trout and other fishes, as well as water birds, feed readily on caddis larvae and usually swallow them complete with their cases, although trout will often blow or suck the larvae from their homes. The larva of *Anabolia nervosa* (Pl. 48) has a neat defence against such predation. It attaches one or more twigs to its case so that it cannot be swallowed.

Not all caddis larvae make cases: a number of species live in non-movable silken nets which they spin among the aquatic vegetation. The nets afford a certain amount of protection, but their main function is to trap food particles. These net-spinners nearly all live in running water. *Rhyacophila* species (Pl. 49) make neither cases nor nets and live freely on the stream bed. The non-case-bearers have tougher bodies than those that do make cases. Most case-bearing caddis larvae are omnivorous, picking up whatever scraps they can find on the bottom of the pond or stream. The net-spinners must also eat whatever the current brings along, although many of them prefer animal food. *Rhyacophila* and other free-living species are largely predatory.

Pupation takes place in the case, which is previously cemented to some submerged object. Non-case-bearing larvae construct special pupal chambers with sand, and then spin their pupal cocoons inside them. The pupa is quite active and continues the ventilation movements of the larva. It also retains the larval gills for obtaining its oxygen. The pupa has free legs, antennae, and wings, and it also has a pair of large jaws. When the time arrives for the adult to emerge, the pupa becomes very active and bites its way out of its case. Adult emergence usually takes place on the water surface, although many pupae swim ashore for the transformation, using a pair of heavily-fringed legs as oars. The adults can fly almost immediately, although the wings need a period of hardening before the insects can fly well. Newly emerged caddis flies can be seen flying in large numbers over the water, often dancing vertically in little swarms like mayflies (see p. 53). Bats and birds take a heavy toll of them at such times. The whole life cycle takes a year, of which the greater part is usually taken up by the larval life. A few species overwinter as pupae but most of them pupate in the spring and emerge as adults in early summer.

Caddis flies are not easy to identify because the diagnostic features are small and often covered with hairs, but the European families may be separated with the following key. Use fresh or spirit-preserved material whenever possible as the legs and palps can then be manipulated more easily.

Key to the Families of European Trichoptera

1. Insects minute and hairy   Hydroptilidae p. 251

    Insects larger and with relatively short fringes   2

2. Maxillary palps 5-segmented   3

    Maxillary palps with less than 5 segments (males)   18

3. Last palpal segment much longer   4
       than all others together

    Last palpal segment not or only just longer than all others   7
       together

4. Ocelli present   Philopotamidae p. 251

    Ocelli absent   5

5. Anterior tibia 3-spurred   *Polycentropidae p. 251

    Anterior tibia with less than 3 spurs   6

6. First apical fork present   Hydropsychidae p. 251

    First apical fork absent   *Psychomyiidae p. 251

---

*   *But see Ecnomus tenellus, p. 251*

7.   Ocelli present   8
     Ocelli absent   11

8.   First two palpal segments short and   9
       thick: 3rd segment long and thin

     2nd palpal segment longer than first   10

9.   No discoidal cell   Rhyacophilidae p. 252

     Discoidal cell present   Glossosomatidae p. 252

10. Anterior tibia 2-spurred   Phryganeidae p. 250
     Anterior tibia with 1 spur or none   Limnephilidae p. 250

11. Discoidal cell present in forewing   12
     No discoidal cell   17

12. Antennae toothed   Odontoceridae p. 252

          Section of antenna

     Antennae not toothed   13

13. Antennae much longer than wings: hind tibia 2-spurred   Leptoceridae p. 252
     Antennae shorter than or only a little longer than wings: 14
       hind tibia generally 3 or 4-spurred, rarely only 2-spurred

14. Middle tibia 2-spurred   Sericostomatidae p. 250
     Middle tibia with 3 or 4 spurs   15

15. Hind tibia with 2 or 3 spurs   Brachycentridae p. 251
     Hind tibia 4-spurred: first antennal segment noticeably   16
       long

16. Hind wing with 2 conspicuously   Goeridae p. 251
       forked veins near middle of
       outer margin

     Hind wing with only 1 obvious fork   Lepidostomatidae p. 251

17. Spurs 2,4,4: insects generally over 12mm across   Molannidae p. 252
     Spurs 2,2,4: insects generally under 12mm across: first an-   Beraeidae p. 252
       tennal segment noticeably long

18. Palps 4-segmented   Phryganeidae p. 250

     Palps with less than 4 segments   19

19. Anterior tibia with 1 spur or none: palps 3-segmented and   Limnephilidae p. 250
     not very hairy

     Anterior tibia 2-spurred: palps with 1,2, or 3 segments and   20
     usually very hairy

20. Middle tibia 2-spurred: palps 1-segmented, very   Sericostomatidae p. 250
     broad and hairy

     Middle tibia with 3 or 4 spurs   21

21. Hind tibia with 2 or 3 spurs: palps 3-segmented   Brachycentridae p. 251

     Hind tibia 4-spurred: first antennal segment noticeably   22
     long

22. Hind wing with 2 conspicuously forked veins near middle   Goeridae p. 251
     of outer margin (see couplet 16): palps 3-segmented,
     3rd segment fairly long and bristly

     Hind wing with only 1 obvious fork: palps short   Lepidostomatidae p. 251
     and club-like, with 2 or 3 segments

Males of the families Phryganeidae, Limnephilidae, Sericostomatidae, Brachycentridae, Goeridae, and Lepidostomatidae have fewer segments to their maxillary palps
than the females. All the other European caddis flies have five palpal segments in
both sexes.

The **Phryganeidae** contains the largest of our caddis flies – *Phryganea grandis*
(Pl. 48), which has a wingspan of about 50mm. In this family the antennae are stout
and about as long as the forewings, and the male palps are 4-segmented. The discoidal cell is closed in both wings, being particularly long and narrow in the forewing, and the tibial spurs are 2,4,4. The larvae live in still or slow-moving water
and build their cases with plant material arranged in a spiral fashion. There are ten
British species.

The family **Limnephilidae** (Pl. 48) is a large one, containing species of widely
differing sizes. Most are pale brown with darker markings. The wings are never very
hairy and the forewings bear a number of clear patches. The hind wings are particularly clear. The discoidal cell is always closed and apical fork 4 is absent from both
wings. The antennae are usually about as long as the forewings and their basal joints
are bulbous. The male palps are 3-segmented. The anterior tibia never has more than
one spur. *Limnephilus lunatus* is a typical species, and the family also includes *Anabolia nervosa* and the very atypical *Enoicyla* (see p. 245). Members of this family
live mainly in slow-moving water and their larval cases, made from various materials, are often quite large. There are just over 50 British species.

In the **Sericostomatidae** (not illustrated) the antennae are moderately stout and
the large basal joint is very hairy. The maxillary palps of the male are 1-segmented
and very hairy and they are held in front of the face like a muff. The wings are usually
very hairy and the anterior tibia always has two spurs. The larvae live in running
water and build cases with various materials. There are only two British species.

Members of the **Brachycentridae** (Pl. 48) usually have three spurs on the hind tibia, and the male palps are 3-segmented and very hairy. The commonest species and the only British member of the family is the Grannom (*Brachycentrus subnubilus*), which has a spur count of 2,3,3. Very few other caddis flies (none of them British) have this arrangement. This species often forms huge swarms over slow-moving rivers in spring and early summer. The larva fixes its case to the vegetation and filters food from the water with its comb-like middle legs. Young larvae make their cases with plant debris, but older larvae live in cases made purely of silk. The **Goeridae** (not illustrated) has a spur count of 2,4,4 and the male palps are 3-segmented, with the third segment long and bristly. The basal segment of the antenna is large and hairy. There are two conspicuously forked veins near the middle of the outer margin of the hind wing (see couplet 16 of the key on p. 249). Larval cases are made of sand grains, with larger pebbles attached to the sides. There are three British species. The **Lepidostomatidae** (not illustrated) is similar to the Goeridae, but there is only one obvious fork in the hind wing. The male palps are short and club-like, with two or three segments. There are three British species. The last three families were until recently regarded as sub-families of the Sericostomatidae.

Members of the **Hydroptilidae** are very active insects and are quite unmistakable on account of their small size and the relatively long fringes on their hind wings. The fringes effectively double the width of the narrow wings. The antennae are relatively short and stout and there are no spurs on the front legs. The larvae feed on the juices of algae and make no case until the last instar, when they construct small silken chambers which are sometimes reinforced with sand grains or plant fragments. There are about 30 British species, typified by *Hydroptila sparsa* (Pl. 48).

In the **Philopotamidae** the antennae are short and stout-jointed, but the family is most easily recognised by the form of the palps – with a very long last segment (fig. p. 245) – and the possession of ocelli. The tibial spurs are 2,4,4. The wings are either smoky brown or patterned with brown and yellow and a discoidal cell is always present in both wings. The larvae are net-spinners and the family is found mainly in upland streams. There are five British species, typified by *Philopotamus montanus* (Pl. 48).

Members of the **Polycentropidae** have densely haired wings and the forewings are more rounded distally than in most other caddis flies. The insects are generally brown or grey with yellow markings. A discoidal cell is always present in the forewing but sometimes missing from the hind wing. The antennae are stout and the spurs are 3,4,4. The larvae are net-spinners and primarily carnivorous. *Polycentropus* species (Pl. 48) make pouch-shaped nets in which they lie waiting for anything that the current brings along. There are 13 British species.

In the **Hydropsychidae** the discoidal cell of the forewing is always broad and short and the spurs are 2,4,4. The basal joint of the antenna is swollen. *Hydropsyche* species (Pl. 48) are somewhat unusual in flying in bright sunshine. Like the two previous families, the Hydropsychidae is found mainly in streams and rivers, where the larvae spin net-traps among the stones. There are ten British species.

The members of the **Psychomyiidae** (Pl. 49) are all small insects – under 12mm in wingspan – with densely-haired wings which are usually of a fairly uniform, dark colour. The discoidal cell is very small in the forewing and usually absent from the hind wing. The latter is much shorter and narrower than the forewing and its front edge is usually cut away to some extent in the distal part. The spurs are 2,4,4 except in the rare *Ecnomus tenellus*, in which they are 3,4,4. This species also differs from

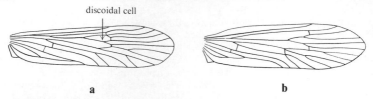

*Forewing of Glossosomatidae (**a**), showing the discoidal cell, which is absent from the closely related Rhyacophilidae (**b**)*

the rest of the family in retaining the first apical fork. The larval cases are usually in the form of long silken galleries, coated with mud and attached to submerged logs and stones. There are 13 British species, including *Tinodes waeneri*.

The **Rhyacophilidae** contains some of the more primitive caddis flies, in the genus *Rhyacophila*. The antennae are shorter than the forewings and rather slender. The forewing is quite pointed at the tip and contains no discoidal cell. The spurs are 3,4,4. The larvae of this genus are quite easily recognised by their bright green and brown bodies. They build neither case nor net and hunt among the stones on the beds of fast-flowing streams. There are four British species – all in the genus *Rhyacophila*. *R. obliterata* (Pl. 49) has bright yellow wings when freshly emerged.

The **Glossosomatidae** is related to the Rhyacophilidae, and often regarded as a sub-family of it, but is distinguished by the discoidal cell in the forewing and by the spur count of 2,4,4. The larvae are less carnivorous and feed mainly on algae. There are six British species. The genus *Agapetus* (Pl. 49), lives in fast-moving water and builds cases which are flattened on one side and domed on the other. Huge numbers of these cases, made of small stones, can be found on submerged boulders.

Odontocerum albicorne (Pl. 49), our only member of the **Odontoceridae**, is easily recognised by its greyish colour (fishermen call it the grey sedge) and by its toothed antennae (see couplet 12 of key on p. 249). It has a wingspan of over 25mm and is found near running water, where its larvae make curved cases of sand grains.

The family **Leptoceridae** is easily recognised by the antennae, which may be twice or even three times as long as the forewings. The antennae are often very pale and several species are known as silverhorns. There are only two spurs on the hind tibia. The insects are very hairy and generally dark in colour. There is a discoidal cell in the forewing but not in the hind wing. The latter is much shorter than the forewing and is joined to it by a row of tiny hooks. The larvae build slender, often curved, cases of sand or plant material. *Athripsodes aterrimus* (Pl. 49) is typical of the family, which has 31 British species.

The **Molannidae**, typified by *Molanna angustata* (Pl. 49), has very hairy palps and the antennae are stout and somewhat longer than the wings. The spur count is 2,4,4. The larvae live in still water and use sand grains to make very characteristic cases consisting of a central tube with a broad shield over it. There are only two British species.

Members of the **Beraeidae** are mainly black insects no more than about 12mm across. The maxillary palps are very hairy and held upright in front of the head. The antennae are about as long as the wings and quite stout. The first segment is noticeably long. The tibial spur count is 2,2,4. Shallow streams and marshes are the places for this family. *Ernodes articularis* (Pl. 49) is one of only four British species.

Collecting and preserving
You will find caddis flies in most places where you find stretches of water but, because most of them are nocturnal or crepuscular insects, you will have to search for them. Beating waterside vegetation and following up with a net will yield many specimens, but smaller numbers can also be found by searching tree trunks and walls near the water. A light will also attract plenty of caddis flies in the evening.

Several killing agents are suitable for caddis flies but it is vital to ensure that the insects do not get wet, for this spoils their hairy coats. Freshly-crushed cherry laurel is probably the best killing agent and it has the added advantage of keeping the insects in a relaxed condition. Caddis flies dry out very rapidly and they are not easy to relax once they have dried. The larger species can be pinned and set on boards but the smaller ones and any intended for detailed study should be preserved in spirit. Pinning damages the thoracic structures so important in critical study.

Caddis worms are easily collected from the water and most species can be kept alive in small aquaria as long as they are not overcrowded. Their case-building activities can be watched in this way and information obtained on feeding habits. This is also a convenient way of getting adult specimens for the collection. The cases can be dried when empty and kept with the adult specimens.

Order Hymenoptera – Bees, Wasps, Ants, and others
(Plates 50-60)

Recognition features Minute to large insects, usually with two pairs of membranous wings of which the front pair is the larger. The wings are coupled with a row of minute hooks on the front edge of the hind wing. Venation is often greatly reduced, with large cells. At first sight, many flies may be confused with the hymenopterans, but the flies have only two wings and are easily distinguished on closer examination. No other insect order has the large wing cells typical of many hymenopterans.

The Hymenoptera is second only to the Coleoptera in terms of numbers of species. It is an immense order containing over 120,000 known species and undoubtedly many thousands yet to be discovered. More than 40,000 species occur in Europe, and over 6,500 of these are found in the British Isles. They are extremely varied in size, appearance, and habits, but the order can be split into two well-defined sub-orders. These are the SYMPHYTA, in which there is no 'waist', and the APO-CRITA, in which there is a very narrow 'waist'. The first sub-order contains the sawflies, which are the most primitive members of the order. The Apocrita contains the bees, wasps, ants, ichneumons, and several other groups, many of which are highly advanced and specialised insects. Only in this order and among the termites (p. 86) do we find true social behaviour. A great many species are parasites of other insects and play a vital role in maintaining the balance of nature. Bees all feed on pollen and nectar and, while collecting it from flowers, they perform the vital function of pollination. Admittedly, many other insects help in pollination, but they visit flowers only for their own satisfaction and do not go relentlessly from flower to

A common wasp, one of the more advanced members of the order

flower as the bees do. Scores of different crops depend largely on bees for their pollination, and the honey bee is also the basis of an extensive honey industry.

The head is heavily sclerotised and quite hard. It is attached to the thorax by a slender neck and able to swivel freely. The compound eyes are almost always large and three ocelli are generally present. The antennae are often longer in males than in females and are rather variable, particularly among the lower families.

Hymenopteran mouth-parts are basically of the biting type and mandibles are always present, although they are not always used for feeding. The sawflies, especially the carnivorous species, have the most primitive mouth-parts in the order. There are toothed mandibles, fully developed maxillae, and a labium whose distal part is clearly divided into a glossa and two lateral paraglossae. The glossa may be used for lapping up nectar. The wasps and ants and the parasitic members of the Apocrita retain most of the sawfly features, although there is some reduction in the paraglossae and sometimes in the labial and maxillary palps as well. Particularly among the wasps and ants, there is an increase in the importance of the glossa, which becomes broad and tongue-like. It is used for lapping up sweet liquids. Some primitive bees retain the wasp-like mouth-parts, but most bees have much longer tongues than the wasps, in connection with their nectar-feeding habits. All stages of tongue development exist, from the wasp-like *Hylaeus* to the highly evolved honey bees and bumble bees in which the glossa is drawn out to form a long sucking tube sheathed by the labial palps. These bees can draw nectar from deep-throated flowers. Although possessing these elaborate sucking mouths, the bees still retain their mandibles, but they use them more for nest-building and other chores than for feeding.

Hymenopteran mouth-parts, partly dissected to show their components and drawn from below to show how the labial glossa or tongue has become broad in the wasps and long and slender in the bees: **a.** *sawfly;* **b.** *wasp;* **c.** *bee*

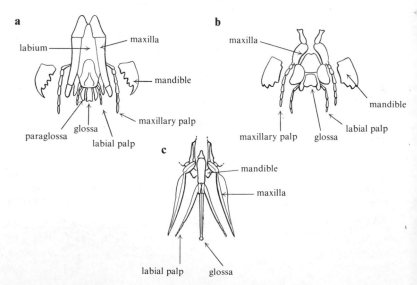

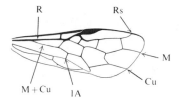

Forewing of the sawfly Diprion pini,
showing the large cells characteristic of the
Hymenoptera

The thorax is composed of the usual three segments, but among the Apocrita the first abdominal segment becomes fused with the thorax and is known as the propodeum. The characteristic 'wasp-waist' is therefore strictly between the first two abdominal segments and not between the abdomen and the thorax. The thorax and the propodeum together are sometimes called the alitrunk, but for practical purposes the whole unit can be called the thorax. The pronotum is usually small, although often extending back along the sides to reach the tegulae. The latter are always present, in the form of 'shoulder-pads' over the bases of the forewings, but they are occasionally very small and difficult to see. There is a distinct division of the mesonotum into scutum and scutellum but the smaller metanotum is tucked under the scutellum and not usually very obvious.

There are usually two pairs of membranous wings which give the order its name (Greek *hymen* = membrane), although several groups – notably the ants – produce wingless individuals. The hind wings are considerably smaller than the forewings and the two pairs are linked by a number of minute hooks, called hamuli, on the front edge of the hind wing (fig. p. 18). A pigmented pterostigma is often present in the forewing.

The main veins are reduced in this order, but there is some development of crossveins and branches so that the wings often have a reticulate pattern of large cells. This is characteristic of all the larger hymenopterans and these insects are not easily confused with any other order. The venation has deviated so much from the basic pattern that it is difficult to decide which vein is which and there is no widely accepted system of naming them. The sawflies have the most complete venation, in which there are four rather irregular major veins – Rs, M, Cu, and 1A. Both wings have a fairly distinct fold, known as the claval furrow, near vein 1A and this fold is a useful marker. In older books it is often called the vannal fold. There is a second fold, known as the jugal fold, near the hind margin. It is not very obvious in the forewing, but it marks off the jugal or anal lobe in the hind wing. There is usually a small notch where each fold meets the wing margin. The area between the two folds is the claval lobe. The jugal lobe is missing from the hind wings of many of the parasitic apocritans, in which the claval lobe may also be indistinct.

As already mentioned, the first abdominal segment becomes fused with the thorax in the Apocrita and is known as the propodeum. The rest of the abdomen, starting with the second segment, is known as the gaster and is greatly constricted at the front to form the 'waist'. The length of the constricted part, which is called the petiole, varies from group to group. It involves two complete segments in some ants, among which it is called the pedicel. The sawflies are without any such constriction.

A well-developed ovipositor is usually present in the female. The sawflies take their name from the saw-like nature of the ovipositor of most species, which is used to cut into plant tissues prior to egg-laying. Among the other hymenopterans the ovipositor is either used for drilling into plant or animal tissues during egg-laying or it

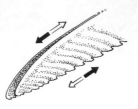

The ovipositor of a sawfly, used for cutting slits in plants prior to laying the eggs

is modified as a sting (p. 261) and no longer used for laying eggs. Because the sting is a modified egg-laying tool, only female insects can sting.

Hymenopteran eggs are generally white and sausage-shaped and they are usually laid singly. Parthenogenesis is common in several groups: male bees and wasps, for example, are produced from unfertilised eggs, while many gall wasp species (Cynipidae) exhibit an alternation of sexual and parthenogenetic generations. Males are extremely rare in some species and parthenogenesis is almost the only method of reproducing.

Hymenopterous larvae are of two distinct types. Most sawfly larvae are rather like caterpillars, with well-developed heads and thoracic legs, and often with fleshy abdominal legs as well, although those that tunnel in plants are usually legless. The larvae of the apocritans are always legless and their heads are generally greatly reduced. This is in connection with the fact that these larvae are always surrounded by food and do not have to search for it. The pupa has free appendages (exarate condition) and is usually enclosed in some sort of cocoon, although this may be so flimsy as to appear absent.

SUB-ORDER SYMPHYTA – THE SAWFLIES (Pl. 50)

These insects are readily separated from the rest of the Hymenoptera by the absence of a waist. The first abdominal segment, although modified to some extent, is not fused with the thorax and has no constriction behind it. This is the more primitive of the two sub-orders and its members do not exhibit the highly specialised social behaviour that we find in many of the apocritans. Very few of the sawflies are parasites.

Apart from the Cephidae, most sawflies bear two small knobs called cenchri on the metanotum. These raised areas are often pale in colour and they have rough surfaces. Each one engages with a similar roughened patch on the underside of the forewing when the wings are closed, thus holding the wings firmly in place. Sawflies can fly well, usually in the daytime, but many of them are more likely to scuttle away when disturbed. They spend much of their time just sitting on leaves and flowers. Umbellifers are particularly attractive to them, and so are the flowers of various trees. Pollen is the main food of adult sawflies, although some species are at least partly carnivorous.

The common name for these insects refers to the ovipositor, which is usually like a minute saw (fig. above). The pattern of the teeth varies from species to species. The females use their saws to cut slits in stems and leaves, and then they lay their

The larva of a sawfly can usually be distinguished from the caterpillar of a butterfly or a moth by its greater number of stumpy prolegs - usually at least six pairs

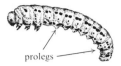

prolegs

eggs in the slits. Some species, however, have sharp, boring ovipositors that act more like drills. The Wood Wasp or Horntail (*Urocerus gigas*) (Pl. 50) has a long and powerful ovipositor that can drill into wood. Although the eggs are usually laid inside stems and leaves, most sawfly larvae feed freely on the outside. They resemble the caterpillars of butterflies and moths, but sawfly larvae can be distinguished because they always have at least six pairs of abdominal legs. The caterpillars of butterflies and moths never have more than five pairs of these prolegs. Those sawfly larvae that tunnel in leaves and stems have no abdominal legs and only vestigial thoracic legs. Pupation takes place in a cocoon, either in the soil or leaf litter or attached to the food-plant.

A Simplified Key to the Families of European Sawflies

1.	Antennae inserted below eyes: forewing without an obvious closed anal cell	Orussidae p. 258
	Antennae inserted between eyes: forewing has one or more clearly-marked, closed anal cells	2
2.	Antennae with 3 or 4 segments, the third being very long	3
	Antennae with more than 4 segments	4
3.	Antennae 4-segmented, the fourth being very short and hook-like: a cross-vein runs diagonally back from outer end of pterostigma	Blasticotomidae p. 260
	Antennae 3-segmented, the third often hairy and sometimes bifid: no cross-vein from pterostigma	Argidae p. 260
4.	Antennae with 3 segments of normal thickness, the third being very long and followed by a thread-like flagellum: insects under 5mm long	Xyelidae p. 258
	Antennae not like this: insects usually over 5mm long	5
5.	Cenchri present	6
	Cenchri absent: body usually very slender	Cephidae p. 259
6.	Antennae strongly clubbed	Cimbicidae p. 260
	Antennae not strongly clubbed	7
7.	Antennae feathery or lightly toothed or with small flaps on underside	8
	Antennae not branched or toothed, or if so only the basal segments are branched	9

8. Cross-vein (2r–rs) runs back from   Megalodontidae p. 259
    pterostigma of forewing

    No cross-vein below pterostigma   Diprionidae p. 260

9. Antennae with 11 or more segments: insects usually over   10
    10mm long

    Antennae usually with no more than 10 segments: if more   Tenthredinidae p. 259
    than 10 are present the insects are under 10mm long
    and pronotum does not have a straight hind margin

10. Abdomen strongly flattened   Pamphilidae p. 258

    Abdomen cylindrical   11

11. Vein Rs of forewing recurved at tip   Siricidae p. 259

    Vein Rs not recurved: insect with prominent 'neck'   Xiphydriidae p. 259

The **Orussidae** has only one European member – *Orussus abietinus*. The position
of the antennae distinguish this family from all other sawflies and some entomologists place it in a separate sub-order. The veins are poorly developed, especially in
the hind wing, and there is no closed anal cell in the forewing. The larva is a parasite
of timber beetles and the adult can be found running over tree trunks.

Members of the **Xyelidae** are generally under 5mm long and can be recognised
by the rather broad stigma and the characteristic antennae. *Xyela julii* is often found
around birch and pine trees in spring. The larvae live in male pine cones, while the
adults are attracted to birch catkins. These insects are weak fliers. There are two
British species.

Members of the **Pamphilidae** are very flat, broad-bodied insects between about
7 and 15mm long. They are generally fast-flying insects. Their larvae live on conifers
and other trees, spinning or rolling leaves together to make shelters. There are about
20 British species, typified by *Pamphilus sylvaticus* which breeds on hawthorn and
other rosaceous trees. Parthenogenesis is common in this family and the males of

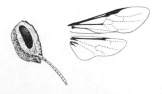

The head and venation of Orussus abietinus,
*a very rare sawfly which does not occur in
Britain. This sawfly is unusual in having its
antennae inserted below it eyes*

Two views of the antenna of Megalodontes, *showing how its overlapping flaps give it a toothed appearance on the underside*

several species are very rare. The **Megalodontidae** is a closely related family, distinguished by its flabellate antennae. *Megalodontes klugii* is typical of the European species, which all feed on herbaceous plants. None occurs in Britain. The larvae of both of these families lack prolegs.

The **Siricidae** contains the wood wasps or horntails – names which refer to their wood-boring habits and to the long, stout ovipositor. The insects are at least 14mm long and often much longer, and the family contains some of our most fearsome-looking species. The ovipositor is often mistaken for a sting, but the insects are quite harmless. Family characteristics also include the minute tegulae, slender antennae composed of 14-30 segments, and the deeply-curved rear margin of the pronotum. Our commonest species is the black and yellow *Urocerus gigas*. Females are often seen, but the males usually keep to the tree tops where they fly actively in sunshine. The females bore into pines and other conifers – usually selecting unhealthy trees – and lay their eggs in them. The larvae, which have vestigial legs, spend their time tunnelling through the timber. It is believed that they feed largely on the wood-destroying fungi that are always found in their tunnels. Adult females carry the fungi with them when they emerge from their tunnels and infect new trees when they lay their eggs. *Urocerus gigas* is probably the only species native to the British Isles, although several more have become established after importation with timber. *Sirex noctilio* and *S. juvencus* are smaller species. The males resemble those of *Urocerus* but the females have a dark metallic blue colour.

The **Xiphydriidae** resembles the Siricidae, but is easily distinguished by the prominent neck. The body is mainly black and the antennae normally have 13-19 segments. The larvae feed on birches and willows and related trees and, like the siricid larvae, they are completely dependent on symbiotic fungi. There are only two British species – *Xiphydria prolongata* with a red abdominal belt and *X.camelus* without a belt.

The **Cephidae** contains slow-flying sawflies with rather slender cylindrical or laterally compressed bodies up to about 20mm long. They can be separated from all other sawflies by the absence of cenchri. The antennae are usually long and thread-like, although some are lightly clubbed. The larvae of this family are stem-borers and several of them damage cereals and other crops. *Cephus pygmaeus* is important in this respect. There are about a dozen British species.

The **Tenthredinidae** is the major sawfly family, especially in the northern hemisphere. It contains about 900 European species, of which nearly 400 occur in the British Isles. They range from about 2.5mm to 15mm in length and most of them are either black or brownish yellow in colour. One of the commonest is the Gooseberry Sawfly (*Nematus ribesii*), whose larvae often defoliate gooseberry and currant bushes. Most of the larvae in this family feed openly on leaves, although some of the smaller species are leaf-miners. *Pontania proxima* is responsible for the little red bean galls (Pl. 50) found on willow leaves in the summer. Unlike most galls, this one starts to swell as soon as the insect lays its egg and it is almost fully developed before the egg hatches. The larva then eats the contents of the gall before leaving to pupate in the soil. Parthenogenesis is very common in this family and the males of some species are almost unknown.

Members of the **Argidae** range from 5mm to 12mm in length and are rather heavy, sluggish fliers. They are readily identified by the unusually large cenchri and the long, 3rd segment of the antenna. This segment is hairy in the male and in some species it is forked like a tuning fork. The larvae feed on the leaves of various shrubs. There are about 15 British species, typified by *Arge ustulata*.

The **Cimbicidae** contains stout sawflies with strongly clubbed antennae. They fly rapidly, often with a buzzing sound. They range from about 4mm to 30mm in length. The larvae feed on a variety of woody and herbaceous plants. There are about 15 British species, one of the commonest being the Hawthorn Sawfly (*Trichiosoma tibiale*) whose oval brown cocoons are common sights on hawthorn twigs in the winter. *Abia* species are mostly bright green metallic insects frequenting flower-rich grasslands.

Members of the **Diprionidae** can be recognised at once by their antennae – feathery in the males and toothed in the females. They are rather stout, slow-flying insects whose larvae feed on conifers. The adults range from 5mm to 10mm in length. There are about ten British species. The Pine Sawfly (*Diprion pini*) is a common and often serious forest pest. *Cladius* species, belonging to the Tenthredinidae, may possibly be confused with this family, but their antennae are toothed only near the base.

The **Blasticotomidae** has only one, rarely-found member – *Blasticotoma filiceti*, which may be recognised by the prominent pear-shaped cell in the middle of the forewing and by its unusual 4-segmented antennae. The third segment is very long and the fourth forms a small point at the tip. The insect occurs mainly in northern Europe, where its larvae tunnel in fern stems.

SUB-ORDER APOCRITA – BEES, WASPS, ANTS AND PARASITES
(Plates 51-60)

This is by far the larger of the two sub-orders and it contains some of the most advanced of all insects. They can be distinguished from the sawflies by their 'wasp-waists'.

There are two sections within the sub-order – the PARASITICA and the ACULEATA. The Parasitica are nearly all parasites and their ovipositors are adapted for piercing the host tissues. In some species the ovipositor is two or three times the length of the body (Pl. 52), enabling the insects to reach hosts that may be tunnelling inside plants. The Parasitica include the ichneumons and chalcids, most of which parasitise the young stages of other insects, and the section also contains the gall wasps, which feed on plant material and induce gall-formation in their hosts. Bees, wasps, and ants belong to the Aculeata, in which the ovipositor is usually modified as a sting. There is, however, no hard and fast division between the two sections. Not all the Parasitica are actually parasites, and quite a number of aculeate species are parasitic (see p. 270). The Aculeata, characterised by their stings, are probably a natural group, but it seems likely that the Parasitica are a heterogeneous group whose member families are not all closely related.

The larvae are always surrounded by food, provided by the host plant or animal or else by the parent insect, and are consequently rather immobile: they have no legs and their heads are much reduced.

True social behaviour, with insects living together in a colony and working together for the good of the whole community, is found only among the termites and the aculeate Hymenoptera. All the ants are social insects, but relatively few of the bees and wasps are social. Most of them are solitary insects and, apart from making some sort of nest and providing food for their offspring, they have much the same sort of life history as the rest of the insect world.

The social Hymenoptera live in colonies which are headed by one or more mated females known as queens. These queens do little more than lay eggs, the work of collecting food, rearing the young, and building and maintaining the nest being carried out by the workers. These are also female insects but they are not fully developed and only in exceptional circumstances can they lay eggs. They are generally smaller than the queens. Male insects, called drones among the bees, are less common and appear only at certain times of the year. They do no work in the colony and their sole function is to mate with new queens. Drones are produced parthenogenetically, when the queens lay unfertilised eggs.

Ant colonies and honey bee colonies last for several or many years, with new queens replacing old ones from time to time. Bumble bees and wasps, however, start afresh each year: only the newly-mated queens survive the winter and they start building new nests when they wake up in the spring. They must rear the first brood of workers themselves before they can hand over these duties and devote themselves to egg-laying.

Among the bees and wasps, and also some of the ants, the ovipositor has become the sting and is no longer concerned with egg-laying. The sting apparatus has been fully studied in the Honey Bee and the following brief account refers to that insect, although there are only slight variations in the other insects. The penetrating part of the sting is the shaft, consisting of three needle-like members – a stylet and two lancets. The stylet partially sheathes the lancets and the three together enclose the poison canal. The sting shaft, together with its muscles and the poison sac, is housed in the end of the abdomen when not in use. When the bee is about to sting, it arches its body and plunges the sting shaft perpendicularly into its victim. The lancets are barbed and, by moving them forward alternately, the bee sinks its sting deeper into

The bee's sting is housed in the tip of the abdomen and protruded when required. The shaft consists of two barbed lancets running on 'rails' on the pointed stylet. The lancets move forward alternately to penetrate the victim, and venom from the poison sac is then pumped along the central canal and into the wound

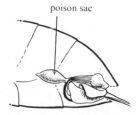

poison sac

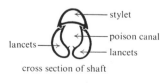

stylet
poison canal
lancets
lancets
cross section of shaft

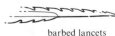

barbed lancets

the victim. This movement of the lancets also pumps venom down the canal and into the wound. The bee can withdraw its sting from the bodies of other insects but the barbs hold it tight in human skin: the bee has to tear herself away, leaving the sting behind and causing fatal damage to herself. Wasps and other bees, however, have smaller barbs and can easily withdraw their stings and use them again. The venom injected is a complicated mixture of proteins, enzymes, and other substances, its exact composition varying from species to species. No antidote is known at present. Formic acid is the main ingredient of ant stings. The sting is used mainly for repelling invaders at the nest and, among the wasps, for paralysing prey prior to taking it back to the nest.

As well as their stings, the bees and wasps have an acrid taste and/or a tough, hairy coat. All these features make the insects unpleasant eating for birds and other predators and many species advertise their unpleasantness with bold colour patterns. Black with yellow, orange, or red are the common combinations employed for this warning coloration. The theory of warning coloration, well supported by experimental evidence, is that a young predator tries the unpleasant insects, but rapidly learns to associate the bold colours with unpleasantness and then leaves the insects alone.

These brightly or boldly marked, unpleasant insects are imitated by a number of harmless, good-to-eat species, which benefit from the resemblance because predators mistake them for the unpleasant ones. This phenomenon is known as mimicry and is easily explained on the basis of natural selection. Any chance resemblance between a harmless insect and an unpleasant one with warning coloration will be increased as predators weed out the poorest imitators in each generation: only the best will survive and, over the course of many generations, the mimics will get more and more like the unpleasant insects that they resemble. The hover-fly *Volucella bombylans* (Pl. 28) exists in several different forms, each resembling a different kind of bumble bee.

The mimicry described so far should really be called Batesian mimicry – after H.W.Bates who first described it in 1862 – because there is another form of mimicry in which two or more species look alike and are all unpleasant. This is known as Mullerian mimicry – after Fritz Muller who described it in 1878. All the species sharing the common pattern benefit from the arrangement because a predator has to learn only one pattern before it avoids all the species involved. Unlike in Batesian mimicry, however, there is no deception by the Mullerian mimics: they all really are unpleasant.

There are many examples of Batesian mimicry in the European insect fauna. The bees and wasps are by far the commonest models, and their commonest mimics are the flies, especially the hover-flies. Mimics also occur among the moths, beetles, and other hymenopterans. Mullerian mimicry is particularly common among South American butterflies, where species from several different families share the same pattern. The best European examples involve the burnet moths (Pl. 35) and various other black and red insects such as the shield bug *Graphosoma italicum* (Pl.8) and the ladybirds, all of which have unpleasant tastes. The wasps can also be regarded as forming a Mullerian mimicry ring: although their shared black and yellow coloration stems from relationship and not from convergent evolution, it can be argued that they have *not* diverged from their common ancestral pattern because it has been advantageous to keep it.

The Apocrita is divided into a number of superfamilies, although entomologists are still far from agreed on the number of these superfamilies. The current trend is to reduce their numbers, especially among the aculeates. The following key can be used to place most winged adults in their superfamilies. Of the wingless forms in this sub-order – and there are many – the only ones likely to come to the notice of the non-specialist are the ants, which can be recognised by their elbowed antennae and the shape of the pedicel (fig. p. 270), and the velvet ants. The latter (Pl. 53) can be recognised by their hairy bodies.

A Simplified Key to the Superfamilies of the European Apocrita

Superfamilies marked with an asterisk belong to the Aculeata. The rest, which represent a rather heterogeneous mixture, are currently grouped in the Parasitica (see p. 260).

1.	Gaster attached near top of propodeum	Evanioidea p. 264
	Gaster attached near bottom of propodeum	2
2.	Antennae long and with more than 16 segments: forewing with stigma	3
	Antennae shorter, with les than 16 segments: stigma often absent	4
3.	Costal cell wide	Trigonalyoidea p. 265
	Costal cell almost or quite obliterated	Ichneumonoidea p. 265
4.	Jugal and claval lobes absent from hind wing, except in some Proctotrupoidea where the rest of the venation is characteristic (fig. p. 269): mainly small or minute insects	5
	Jugal and/or claval lobes usually present in hind wing, although sometimes indistinct: generally medium-sized or large insects, including bees and wasps: [male mutillids (Pl. 53) belong here, although hind wing lacks lobes in most species]	9
5.	First one or two gastral segments very narrow and sometimes scale-like (fig. p. 270)	*Formicoidea p. 270
	Gaster not so constructed	6
6.	Gaster laterally compressed: antennae never elbowed: forewing has no pterostigma, but radial cell at front of wing is usually clearly marked and strongly triangular	Cynipoidea p. 266
	Gaster rarely laterally compressed: antennae often elbowed: radial cell poorly defined or absent	7
7.	Pronotum extends back to tegulae	8
	Pronotum does not extend back to tegulae	Chalcidoidea p. 267

pronotum

tegula

8.   Front tibia with 2 spurs   Ceraphronoidea p. 269

     Front tibia with only 1 spur   Proctotrupoidea p. 268

9.   Hind wing with no closed cells   *Chrysidoidea p. 269

     Hind wing with at least 1 closed cell   10

10. Pronotum reaches back to tegulae   11

          pronotum
                                                    tegula

     Pronotum does not reach back to   13
     tegulae but forms a lobe over 1st
     thoracic spiracle
          pronotum
                                                     tegula
          lobe over 1st spiracle

11. Forewings folded lengthwise at rest: *Vespoidea p. 272
     eyes emarginate (Pl.42)

          wings folded
          lengthwise

     Forewings not so folded: eyes not usually emarginate   12

12. Legs long, especially hind femora   *Pompiloidea p. 275

     Legs usually short and stout   *Scolioidea p. 270

13. Hind tarsi broad and often very hairy   *Apoidea p. 277

     Hind tarsi not broadened   *Sphecoidea p. 276

Superfamily Evanioidea

The members of this group are medium-sized parasites, generally black or black with
a red abdomen. They are distinguished from all other hymenopterans by having the
gaster attached near the top of the propodeum. There are three families, best distinguished by the shape of the gaster. In the **Evaniidae** there is a long petiole, followed
by a small, laterally compressed rear section which is dwarfed by the huge thorax.
The insects are called ensign wasps in America, because the gaster sticks out behind
the thorax rather like a little flag. The insects parasitise the oothecae of cockroaches.
There are two British species. *Evania appendigaster* (Pl. 52) is a cosmopolitan insect
associated with large cockroaches of the genera *Periplaneta* and *Blatta* (Pl.7). In the
Aulacidae the gaster is pear-shaped, with a short stalk or petiole, and the female has
a long ovipositor. The larvae of this family parasitise the grubs of wood wasps and

Side view of Evania, *showing how the
small gaster is attached to the top of the
propodeum*

wood-boring beetles. *Aulacus striatus* (Pl. 52), the only British species, attacks the larvae of the wood wasp *Xiphydria camelus*. In the **Gasteruptiidae** the gaster is long and narrow and the forewings are folded lengthwise at rest. The female has a long ovipositor. The larvae develop in the nests of solitary bees and wasps, where they eat the eggs and grubs as well as the stored food. There are five British species, typified by *Gasteruption jaculator* (Pl. 52).

Superfamily Trigonalyoidea

The only European member of this group is the rare *Trigonalis hahnii* (Pl. 52), which belongs to the family **Trigonalyidae**. It can be distinguished from the superficially similar ichneumons by its clear costal cell. Its larva lives as a hyperparasite, attacking ichneumon and tachinid grubs living inside caterpillars. If one of these parasitised caterpillars is eaten by a wasp larva the *Trigonalis* grub can continue its development as a simple endoparasite of the wasp.

Superfamily Ichneumonoidea

This is a very large group of parasitic insects, accounting for about half of the known species of British Hymenoptera. Its members play an important role in controlling insect numbers and they are responsible for destroying huge numbers of insect pests. A few species attack spiders but the majority parasitise other insects, especially Lepidoptera. The group can be recognised by the long antennae, the stigma usually present in the forewing, and the almost or completely obliterated costal cell. There are just two families – the Ichneumonidae and the Braconidae – which differ mainly in their venation.

Members of the **Ichneumonidae** (Pl. 52) are mainly parasites of the larvae of butterflies and moths. Sawfly and beetle larvae are the other major hosts but many ichneumons are hyperparasites. There are over 2,000 British species, varying from very small to very large and including a number of wingless species.

The ichneumons are not usually confined to any one host species, although they generally keep to their own particular group of hosts. Adult ichneumons may often be seen on flowers or running about on the herbage as they search for hosts with their ever-moving antennae. Having found a suitable host, the female ichneumon prepares to lay her egg or eggs with the aid of her slender ovipositor. This arises from the underside of the abdomen, just in front of the tip, and is sometimes extremely long.

The ichneumon usually pierces the host with its ovipositor and lays its egg or eggs inside the host body, but some species merely lay their eggs on the outside of

The family Ichneumonidae (left) differs from the Braconidae (right) in possessing cross-vein 2m-cu in the forewing and in the much more distal position of cross-vein r-m in the hind wing

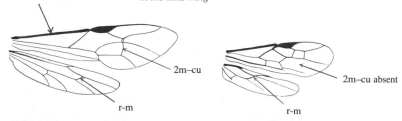

costal cell obliterated

2m–cu

r-m

2m–cu absent

r-m

the host. From there, the larvae may make their own way inside, or they may simply attach themselves to the host and feed from the outside. The ichneumon larvae concentrate on the non-essential organs of the host at first, draining its reserves but allowing it to go on living. Parasitised larvae are usually smaller than healthy ones and rather 'lazy': they often sit exposed on leaves, whereas healthy larvae usually conceal themselves. When the ichneumon grubs are nearly fully grown they turn their attention to the essential organs of the host and kill it. They then pupate in little silken cocoons. These may be formed inside or outside the host body, which by this time is little more than a shrivelled skin. The host may or may not pupate before the parasites are fully grown. The number of parasites to a host depends on the relative sizes of host and parasite and ranges from one to well over 100.

The ichneumons may overwinter as grubs in the host larvae or pupae, or else as pupae in their own cocoons. Some species overwinter as adults, but it is normally only mated females that do this: the males die in the autumn.

One of our commonest ichneumons is the yellowish brown *Netelia testacea*, which parasitises a number of noctuid moth larvae. Adults often come to lighted windows. *Ophion* species are superficially very similar, but their venation is slightly different. *Ichneumon* and *Amblyteles* species are often to be seen feeding on umbellifer flowers or scuttling over hedgerow vegetation in search of their host caterpillars. Certainly one of our most striking ichneumons is the female *Rhyssa persuasoria*, whose ovipositor is in the region of 40mm long. This insect parasitises the grubs of the wood wasp *Urocerus gigas* (p. 259) and is not uncommon in pine woods. *Rhyssa* is able to detect the host larvae tunnelling in the tree trunks and it then performs the seemingly impossible feat of driving its slender ovipositor into the wood. The two halves of the ovipositor rotate backwards and forwards very rapidly and they drill into the wood like a minute auger. One egg is laid next to each wood wasp larva and the larval *Rhyssa* feeds externally on its host. Some of the larger ichneumons can pierce human skin with their ovipositors and produce a slight stinging sensation, but they are unlikely to do this unless they are held.

The members of the **Braconidae** are essentially similar in habits and appearance to the ichneumons. *Apanteles glomeratus*, a parasite of the cabbage white butterflies, is one of the commonest species. A large *Pieris brassicae* larva may contain over 150 of these parasites, and their cocoons are often seen surrounding dead larvae and pupae in the autumn (Pl. 52). One group of the Braconidae attacks aphids. *Aphidius* species cement their host aphids down before pupating in them and the empty aphid skins remain on the plants long after the parasites have left through neat little holes. The family contains over 1,000 British species.

Superfamily Cynipoidea

The members of this group are small or minute insects with a rather characteristic wing venation, dominated by a triangular radial cell. The gaster is laterally compressed, more so in some species than in others, and the insects are generally dark in colour, although some are yellowish or reddish brown. The best known family is the **Cynipidae** (Pl. 51), whose members are of special interest because most of them induce gall formation on plants and many of them display a marked alternation between sexual and parthenogenetic generations. They are called gall wasps. Each species induces the formation of its own characteristic gall on its food-plant. Most of the European species occur on oaks, although some species attack roses and certain herbaceous plants. There are about 90 British species.

Neuroterus quercusbaccarum is a typical example, its reddish spangle galls (Pl. 51) being abundant on oak leaves in late summer. Inside each gall a tiny grub feeds on the gall tissue. The galls fall from the leaves in October but continue to grow for a while. The larval gall wasps complete their growth in the winter and pupate in the galls. The adults emerge in February and March and they are all asexual females. They lay their parthenogenetic eggs in oak buds and the resulting larvae induce the formation of spherical red or purplish galls on the leaves or male catkins (Pl. 51). These galls are known as currant galls and adult gall wasps emerge from them in May and June. There are both males and females in this summer generation and, after pairing, the females lay their eggs in the tissues of the leaves, leading to a new crop of spangle galls. Other familiar oak galls include the oak apple, caused by *Biorhiza pallida*, the marble gall of *Andricus kollari*, and the artichoke gall of *A. fecundator*.

Diplolepis rosae, the insect responsible for the familiar robin's pincushion or bedeguar galls on roses (Pl. 51), has no alternation of generations. Males are extremely rare and the species, like several of its relatives, reproduces almost entirely by parthenogenesis. *Diastrophus rubi* causes sausage-shaped galls on the soft young shoots of bramble (Pl. 51). The galls are green at first, but become brown and woody as they mature in the autumn. Males and females are more or less equally represented in this species, which has a perfectly normal life cycle.

The mechanisms of gall formation are not fully understood, but the essential factor as far as gall wasps are concerned seems to be that the presence of the larvae causes the plant tissues to react and grow in a particular way and provide abundant food for the larvae. Each species has its own special effect and even closely related gall wasps can produce very different galls.

Many other insects take advantage of the food and shelter to be found in plant galls. They include several species of gall wasp that induce no galls of their own but lay their eggs in the developing galls of other species. These inquiline species do no direct harm to the original larvae, although if there are too many inquilines to share the food the rightful occupants may starve. Parasites are also common in galls, attacking both the rightful inhabitants and the inquilines. The most frequent parasites are ichneumons and chalcids (see below), which use their long ovipositors to reach the host larvae inside the galls.

Superfamily Chalcidoidea

This superfamily rivals the Ichneumonoidea in size and may be the largest of all the insect superfamilies. There are over 1,500 known British species and, because of their small size, many more undoubtedly await discovery. They are common insects, rarely absent from the sweep net in the summer, but their small size deters many people from studying them. Most chalcids are less than 3mm long, but many are brilliantly coloured, often with metallic blues and greens, and they are extremely beautiful insects. Almost all are parasites or hyperparasites, attacking eggs, larvae, and pupae of a wide range of other insects. A few species feed on seeds or cause gall formation in other parts of plants. The parasitic species usually pupate inside their hosts.

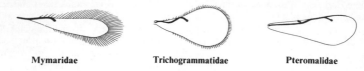

| Mymaridae | Trichogrammatidae | Pteromalidae |

Three types of chalcid wing, showing the greatly reduced venation in this group

As a group, the Chalcidoidea can usually be recognised by the elbowed antennae and (in the winged forms) the characteristic venation without any cells. The pronotum does not reach the tegulae. There are many families – 16 in the British fauna – but they are not all easy to separate. The **Mymaridae**, which can be recognised by the stalked, linear wings, are the fairy flies – minute insects which parasitise the eggs of various other insects. They include the smallest of all insects, some of them being under 0.25mm long. There are about 90 British species. The **Trichogrammatidae**, with about 30 British species, is another family of minute egg parasites, recognisable by their 3-segmented tarsi and distinct lines of hairs on their tiny wings. Several species in this and other families have been used in the biological control of injurious Lepidoptera. The **Pteromalidae** is one of the largest chalcid families and it has well over 500 British species, mostly shiny green or bronze insects with a triangular abdomen. *Pteromalus puparum* (Pl. 52) is a very common species which parasitises the pupae of many butterflies. Members of the **Torymidae**, typified by *Torymus nitens* (Pl. 52), resemble the pteromalids, but their hind coxae are noticeably larger than the rest and there is normally a very long ovipositor in the female. Many of the species parasitise gall-living insects and the long ovipositor enables the female to reach the host insects right inside their galls. There are about 75 British species.

The largest of the chalcids belong to the family **Leucospidae**. *Leucospis gigas* from southern Europe reaches 15mm in length and is a yellow and black wasp-like insect with enormous, toothed hind femora. The female has a long ovipositor which curves forward over her abdomen at rest. Males are known only from south eastern Europe and the species normally reproduces parthenogenetically. The larvae are ectoparasites on the grubs of solitary bees, especially those of *Chalicodoma parietina* (Pl. 58).

Superfamily Proctotrupoidea

The members of this and the two following superfamilies exhibit certain features that link the Parasitica and the Aculeata. The Proctotrupoidea contains a wide variety of small and minute parasites, but they have certain structural similarities with wasps.

The large chalcid Leucospis gigas, *showing the huge hind femur and the long ovipositor curved over the top of the abdomen*

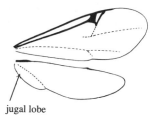

jugal lobe

Wings of Phaenoserphus *(family Proctotrupidae), showing the jugal lobe of the hind wing and the characteristic venation. The jugal lobe is missing in most proctotrupids*

They are nearly all slender, black or brown insects and they attack a variety of other insects, including the egg stages.

The wing venation is often very reduced and there are many wingless species. Several species exhibit polyembryony, with one egg being laid in the host but developing there into numerous larvae. Six families occur in Europe, distinguished by minor differences in the venation. Members of the **Platygasteridae** (Pl. 52) mainly attack gall midges (p. 195), the Hessian-fly – a serious pest of wheat – being kept in check by *Platygaster zosine.*

Superfamily Ceraphronoidea

This group is very closely related to the previous superfamily and has only recently been separated from it. There are just two families – the Ceraphronidae and the Megaspilidae – both containing small, dark parasites and hyperparasites, and they are best distinguished from the proctotrupoids by the possession of two spurs on the front tibia. No other apocritans have two such spurs. There are about 90 species in Britain, attacking a wide range of other insects but mainly associated with flies and neuropterans.

Superfamily Chrysidoidea

This and the following superfamilies all belong to the Aculeata. A sting is present, although not always functional. There are four families in Europe, of which the best known is the **Chrysididae** (Pl. 53). Members of this family, represented by *Chrysis ignita* and *Stilbum cyanurum*, generally have bright, metallic colours and they are commonly known as ruby-tailed wasps or jewel wasps. They are also called cuckoo wasps because of their habits. Females enter the nests of solitary bees and wasps and lay their eggs in them. The resulting grubs eat the host eggs or larvae and usually eat some of the stored food as well. The female's abdomen is modified at the tip to form a telescopic ovipositor. The sting is not usually functional in this family and most of the species lack poison. There are 31 British species. Other families in the Chrysidoidea contain small, dark insects. All are parasites and they have functional stings. The females are often wingless and remarkably ant-like.

Superfamily Scolioidea

Although included in the Aculeata, many members of this group are parasites and there are obvious affinities with the Chrysidoidea. Most of them have hard bodies and potent stings. The **Mutillidae** are commonly called velvet ants, although they are not ants at all. The name arose because most females – the sex most frequently met with – are wingless and the insects are more or less covered with soft hair. The males are fully winged but, unlike all other aculeates, most of them have neither jugal nor claval lobes in the hind wing. The larvae parasitise the grubs and pupae of bees and wasps. *Mutilla europaea* (Pl. 53) is the largest and commonest of the three British species, although none of these insects is really common. The **Tiphiidae** are more or less hairless insects in which the first and second gastral segments are separated by a deep groove. The males are always winged and have a large jugal lobe in the hind wing, although this is not clearly separated from the rest of the wing membrane. Females are winged or wingless. *Methocha ichneumonides* (Pl. 53) parasitises tiger beetle grubs and, with the male being very rare, reproduction is almost entirely parthenogenetic in this species. Other members of the family parasitise the larvae of scarab and chafer beetles. There are just three British species. Both sexes are winged in the **Sapygidae** and the hind wing has a small but prominent jugal lobe. There is no groove between the first and second gastral segments. The larvae develop in the nests of solitary bees, feeding on the stored food after destroying and eating the host eggs. There are only two British species, typified by *Sapyga quinque-punctatum* (Pl. 53).

The family **Scoliidae**, unrepresented in the British Isles, contains some of the largest of the Hymenoptera. They are hairy insects, often marked with red or yellow, and, unlike the velvet ants, both sexes are fully winged. The wings are generally dark and often have a metallic sheen. The larvae feed ectoparasitically on the grubs of various beetles, especially scarabs and chafers. *Scolia flavifrons* (Pl. 53) is the largest European member of the family.

Some recent classifications place the Scolioidea, along with the ants and all the other aculeates in which the pronotum reaches back to the tegulae, in the superfamily Vespoidea.

Superfamily Formicoidea – The Ants

This group contains just one very large family – the **Formicidae** (Pl. 53) – with something like 15,000 known species, 42 of which are native to the British Isles. All are social insects, living in colonies and usually having female (queen), male, and

Ants of the sub-family Myrmicinae (right) have a 2-segmented pedicel, often bearing bulges of various shapes. Other European ants, including Formica *species and the common black garden ants, have a 1-segmented pedicel (left) which is often scale-like*

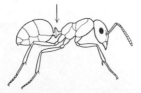 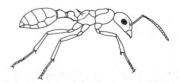

worker castes. A number of species are social parasites, however, and they rely on the workers of other species to do some or all of their work.

Ants, whether winged or not, can be distinguished from other insects by the structure of the pedicel at the front of the abdomen. This consists of one or two segments which usually bear little nodes or scales. The elbowed antennae of the ants will also help to separate them from other insects. Some sub-families possess well-developed stings but many ants have no sting, although they can often defend themselves by squirting formic acid at their attackers. The ants' jaws are tough and sharp and many of the larger species can inflict painful bites.

The majority of the ants in a colony are workers. These are all wingless females and, although they can sometimes lay eggs, they are not sexually fully developed. Some species have two or more worker castes. Large-headed workers mingle with smaller ones in colonies of *Messor barbara* and other harvester ants. These large-headed forms are often called soldiers, but this is misleading because the main function of their large jaws is to crack seeds. Very few ants have a true soldier caste whose main function is to defend the colony.

Male and fully-developed female ants are produced at certain times of the year. Both sexes are usually fully winged and they go off on their marriage flights. Every neighbourhood usually has one day each year on which all the black garden ants emerge and everyone is plagued by flying ants. Climatic conditions control the emergence of the ants, ensuring that all the nests in one area erupt at the same time. The males die soon after mating, which takes place in the air or on the ground according to the species, but the females break off their wings and seek suitable nesting sites, although only a small percentage of them escape the attentions of birds.

The mated females often enter existing nests, where they settle down to lay their eggs alongside the resident queen or queens. Alternatively, a young queen may find a place of her own, sealing herself up until the spring and surviving on the food reserves in her body and on the degenerating wing muscles that she no longer needs. Her eggs slowly mature and she lays them in the spring, feeding the first batch of grubs on her own saliva. As soon as these first young ants become adult they take over the building and running of the colony, leaving their mother to devote herself to egg-laying.

The nesting site varies from species to species and may be under the ground, in hollow trees or stumps, or in mounds of earth or other material built up by the ants themselves. The workers build the nest around the queen's chamber, making a number of rooms and a maze of tunnels. The queen remains in her chamber, laying eggs and being tended by the workers. Her eggs are taken away from the royal chamber and hatched elsewhere in the nest. They are very tiny, the 'ant eggs' sold for feeding to goldfish actually being ant cocoons. The larvae, which are reared on a variety of plant and animal material according to the species, are often transported from room to room in the nest as they grow. The pupae are usually kept near the surface of the nest, where the warmth of the sun helps them to mature more quickly. There is a remarkable co-operation between the workers in the colony, aided by an apparently continual exchange of information through mutual feeding and other contact. The colonies are remarkably stable and long-lasting. Individual worker ants come and go quite rapidly, but the queens live for several years and the 'community spirit' between the workers ensures that new queens are reared when necessary to maintain the colony.

Among the ants one can trace an evolution of feeding habits very similar to that seen in man. The most primitive ants, like the earliest men, are hunters. They are

272 INSECTS OF BRITAIN & NORTHERN EUROPE

mainly carnivorous and they raid their surroundings for food. Some of these hunters make no permanent nests and simply 'camp' from time to time to raise new broods. Those that do make permanent nests do not have very large colonies. The next stage is represented by the herders and harvesters – the ants that keep aphids for the honey-dew they provide and also collect nectar and other vegetable food. Several species of ants actually rear aphids in their nests, bringing them in and attaching them to roots growing through the underground chambers. Most European ants belong to the herding and harvesting group. The highest division is represented by the farmers, notably the leaf-cutter or parasol ants of tropical America. These ants are fungus eaters and they actually grow their own food on specially prepared beds of leaf frag-ments brought in from the surrounding vegetation.

The ants exhibit many degrees of social parasitism and slavery. A number of species practise temporary social parasitism, with the new queen entering the nest of some closely related species and laying her eggs there. The eggs are looked after and the grubs are reared by the host species. The host queen is usually killed at some stage and the host workers gradually die out, leaving the nest completely to the in-vading species. The latter is quite able to look after itself, but its early parasitic be-haviour enables it to get a nest without having to make one. *Anergates atratulus* is even more specialised and has no workers at all. The young queen enters the nest of *Tetramorium caespitum* and her young, which are all sexual forms, are raised entirely by the host species.

Formica sanguinea is one of the best known of the European slave-making ants. Workers of this species raid the nests of related species, such as *F. fusca*, and bring back pupae. These are tended in the *sanguinea* nest and the workers emerging from them begin work for their captors. *F. sanguinea* can manage without slaves, but there are several species that cannot. Among these species the first workers go out to col-lect slave pupae and no nest-building takes place until the slave ants emerge.

A great many other creatures find suitable food and shelter inside an ant nest and the study of these guests is a subject in itself. Three main groups of guests can be recognised: various predatory and scavenging beetles which are definitely not wel-comed by the ants, assorted small scavengers – including beetle and fly larvae, springtails, and the little white woodlouse *Platyarthrus hoffmannseggi* – which are more or less ignored by the ants, and welcome guests which are often deliberately brought in by the ants and which repay their hospitality by providing the ants with sweet secretions. The aphids are good examples, as are the larvae of the Large Blue butterfly (see p. 227).

Superfamily Vespoidea – the True Wasps

These insects are called true wasps in order to distinguish them from the 'digger wasps' of the other superfamilies (see p. 276). There are two families in northern Europe – the **Vespidae**, which contains all the social wasps, and the **Eumenidae** which contains solitary species.* These families are characterised by their deeply-notched, almost crescent-shaped eyes (see Pl. 56), three sub-marginal cells in the forewing (fig. p. 273), the lengthwise folding of the wings at rest, and the backward extension of the pronotum to reach the tegulae (fig. p. 264). A third small family –

* *Some recent classifications extend the Vespoidea to include the ants, the scolioids, and the spider-hunting wasps (see p. 275), in all of which the pronotum reaches back to the tegulae.*

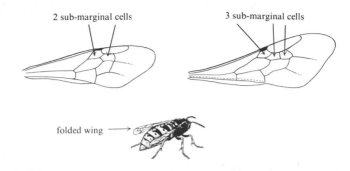

2 sub-marginal cells

3 sub-marginal cells

folded wing ⟶

Aculeate wings showing the sub-marginal cells which are so important in identification - especially in the separation of the numerous genera of bees. The large cells just behind the sub-marginals are the discoidal cells. The common wasp shows the longitudinal folding of the wings characteristic of the true wasps (Vespoidea)

the **Masaridae** – occurs in the south and can be distinguished from the others by its two sub-marginal cells. Most of the species also have clubbed antennae.

With the exception of the masarid wasps, which feed their young on pollen and nectar, the wasps all rear their offspring on meat – other insects, scraps of carrion, and so on. Adult vespid and eumenid wasps are fond of nectar and other sweet things, but instead of the nectar-sucking mouth-parts of the bees they have strong jaws and a short tongue (fig. p. 254). Wasps have no pollen-gathering apparatus and they are generally less hairy than the bees. Their colours are due mainly to the colours of their body plates or sclerites and not to the colours of the hairs as in bees.

The solitary wasps of the **Eumenidae** can be distinguished from the vespid wasps because they have only one spur on the middle tibia: vespids have two such spurs. The eumenids have no worker caste and they do not live in colonies, although the female does build a nest for her offspring. There are 22 British species. *Eumenes coarctatus* is the Potter Wasp of sandy heathland. Its nest is in the shape of a little flask, made of mud and attached to a plant (Pl. 55). The wasp lays an egg in the flask and then fills it with small caterpillars paralysed by her sting. She then seals the nest and flies off to build another one. Because the caterpillars are paralysed and not dead, they stay in good condition and the wasp larva feeds on them through the autumn. It pupates in the flask and emerges as a new adult in the following summer. *Delta unguiculata* (Pl. 55) is a closely related continental species whose nest is an irregular cluster of mud cells fixed to a rock or a wall. Like the *Eumenes* species, it has a bell-shaped first gastral segment.

The mason wasps, such as *Odynerus spinipes* (Pl. 55), have life histories like that of the potter wasp, although many of them are double-brooded. They nest in the ground or in various cavities such as hollow stems. Several species utilise holes in old walls and they often plaster neatly over their nests with mud. The nests usually contain several cells or chambers, each stocked with caterpillars or beetle larvae and containing a single egg. Although the cells are close together, the larvae lead independent lives and there is no co-operation or social activity. The parents never see their offspring.

The social wasps all belong to the family **Vespidae** and all live in fairly large colonies. With the exception of a few 'cuckoo' species (see p. 275), they all have a worker caste. Males and queens are much larger than the workers and the males can be identified by their longer antennae – 13 segments to the female's twelve. There are seven British species (all illustrated on Pl. 56), including the Hornet, and several others have recently become established in Britain. The Hornet is easily identified by its colour, but the other wasps are less easy to separate. Their faces are the best guides, although the pattern does vary slightly even within a species. The underside of the first antennal segment is usually yellow in males, but it is either yellow or black in the females according to the species. The species also differ in the length of the cheek or malar space – between the eye and the jaw. The number and arrangement of the yellow spots on the thorax will also help in the identification of these wasps.

Wasps never store food in their nests and in temperate climates they never swarm to increase the number of colonies. The latter are always annual affairs and only the newly mated queens survive the winter, tucked up in sheltered corners from which they emerge to search for nesting sites in the spring. The Common Wasp (*Vespula vulgaris*), the German Wasp (*V. germanica*), and the Red Wasp (*V. rufa*) generally nest under the ground, taking over and enlarging old mouseholes and similar cavities. The Tree Wasp (*Dolichovespula sylvestris*) and the Norwegian Wasp (*D. norvegica*) hang their nests from the branches of trees and bushes, and so does *D. media*, which is widely distributed on the continent and has recently established itself in the southeastern corner of England. The Hornet (*Vespa crabro*) prefers hollow trees, both upright and fallen.

Having selected their sites, the queens start to collect building material. Unlike bees, the wasps have no wax glands and they cannot build wax combs. They use paper, which they make from wood pulp. They use their powerful jaws to scrape the wood from trees and fences. They chew it up and mix it with saliva, and then spread it out to form the little sheets of paper of which the nest is composed. The first part of the nest to be made is a little umbrella-shaped dome, suspended from a branch or from the ceiling of the nest cavity. The cells are built on the underside of this and they open downwards. The queen fixes an egg in each cell and rears the resulting larvae on pulped insects. These larvae produce workers, which take over building work and food collection while the queen gets down to serious egg-laying. Further

Left, The nest of a common wasp with the covering removed to show the tiered arrangement of the horizontal combs. Right, The simple nest of Polistes

tiers of cells are formed below the first one, each attached to the one above by a number of slender paper stalks. The completed nest has about eight tiers and is ball-shaped. It is covered with thin sheets of wasp-paper, made up of shell-like lobes in some species. Each lobe is banded, each band being the work of one wasp and one load of wood pulp. The nest entrance is usually near the bottom.

A wasp nest may produce 20,000 individuals during a summer, although they are not all alive at the same time, and all of these will have been reared on insects – and as many of these insects are likely to be harmful species in the garden it is not such a good idea to destroy queen wasps in the spring. The adult wasps like sweet things and are certainly interested in our fruit and jam, but for most of the summer they are far too busy getting food for the grubs to bother us. They satisfy their craving for sweet things by occasional visits to flowers – although their short tongues do not allow them to get nectar from many flowers – and by taking saliva from the grubs in the nest. This saliva contains sugar over and above the needs of the sedentary larvae and provides energy-giving carbohydrates for the active adults.

At the end of the summer the wasps rear males and females in special large cells, and when these wasps reach maturity the colony begins to break up. The workers have no more larvae to feed and they can turn their attention to fruit and other sweet materials. It is at this time that the wasps make a nuisance of themselves, but they die as soon as the weather turns cold, leaving only the mated queens to carry on the race in the following year.

A few members of the family are cuckoo wasps – social parasites that lay their eggs in the nests of other wasps. They have no worker caste and rely entirely on the host workers to rear their young. *Vespula austriaca* is a parasite of the Red Wasp.

Polistes gallicus (Pl. 55) is one of a number of very similar continental species known as paper wasps. They can be distinguished from our other social wasps by the tapering front of the abdomen: in *Vespula* and *Dolichovespula* it is very square. Paper wasps make small, umbrella-shaped nests without any protective envelope (fig p. 274). They are usually hung in sheltered situations and are common on buildings in southern Europe. The nests rarely have more than about 100 cells and there are rarely more than about 20 wasps in the colony at any one time. *Sulcopolistes* species are social parasites or cuckoos in the nests of *Polistes*.

Superfamily Pompiloidea – The Spider-Hunting Wasps

This group, which is closely allied to the Vespoidea (see p. 272), contains a single large family – the **Pompilidae** (Pl. 54) – whose members are all solitary insects that provision their nests with spiders. Many of them are orange and black. The pronotum reaches back to the tegulae and the wings are laid flat over the body at rest. The forewings almost all have three sub-marginal cells (fig. p. 273). The legs, and especially the femora, are noticeably longer than those of the other wasp groups, giving the insects a good turn of speed over the ground. Most of them live in sandy areas and most make their nests in the ground. This habit is responsible for the name digger wasps, which is commonly applied to these insects and to the Sphecoidea (p. 276). There are about 40 British species.

After mating, the females set about looking for spiders, often chasing them rapidly over the ground and vegetation. *Cryptocheilus comparatus*, one of Europe's largest pompilids, hunts wolf spiders, including the infamous tarantula, and often chases them into their burrows. Having caught a spider, the wasp paralyses it with her sting and then drags it to a suitable spot in which to dig the nest burrow. Jaws and legs are used for digging and the front legs are commonly equipped with combs for sweeping away the sand. The spider is then dragged into the burrow, where the wasp lays an egg on it. She then seals up the burrow and goes off to repeat the process. The wasp larva feeds on the paralysed spider for weeks or even months. Most species overwinter as mature larvae and pupate in the spring, but in *Anoplius viaticus* it is the mated females that survive the winter. Male pompilids, which are usually smaller than the females, have no interest in spiders and they spend their days visiting flowers. As in the other groups of wasps, there are a number of cuckoo species that lay their eggs in the nests of others, or on the victims of other species before they are buried.

Superfamily Sphecoidea

This is by far the largest group of solitary wasps. They share with the spider-hunters the common name of digger wasps, although not all of them actually dig – some nest in hollow stems and similar cavities. There is only one family – the **Sphecidae** – but it is divided into many sub-families. There are about 115 British species.

The members of the sub-family **Sphecinae** are commonly called sand wasps because they excavate their burrows in sandy places. These insects, typified by *Ammophila sabulosa* and the closely related *Podalonia hirsuta*, are readily recognised by the shape of the abdomen, which is very slender in front and then ends in a 'club' (Pl. 54). The middle part of the abdomen is usually orange – always so in the British species. The rest of the family are more in line with the general idea of wasps, being either black or black and yellow in the main. They can be distinguished from the true wasps because the pronotum does not reach the tegulae and the wings are not folded lengthwise when at rest. The sphecid wasps are actually more closely related to the bees than to the other wasps, and some recent classifications place them with the bees in the superfamily Apoidea.

The prey of the sphecid wasps varies from group to group and includes aphids, flies, beetles, froghopper nymphs, and many other insects. *Sphex maxillosus* (Pl. 55) and its relatives catch bush-crickets and can often be seen dragging victims much larger than themselves. *Liris* species also catch crickets. *Philanthus triangulum* is the Bee-killer. It specialises in honey bees and is sometimes a real problem to bee-keepers on the continent. It is rare in Britain, although it appears to be increasing its range at present. *Cerceris arenaria* (Pl. 54) takes various weevils, while *Argogorytes mystaceus* (Pl. 54) plucks froghopper nymphs from their cuckoo-spit. *Mellinus, Ectemnius*, and *Crabro* species all collect flies for their larders. *Pemphredon lugubris* and its congeners collect aphids. A few sphecids, including *Sceliphron destillatorium* and *Pison atrum* (Pl. 55) catch spiders but, unlike the pompilids, they pack several small spiders into the nest instead of one large one.

Whereas the pompilids catch their victims before digging their burrows, almost all the sphecids do it the other way round and they are remarkably good at finding their way back to their burrows. Many fly back with their victims, but those that go in for larger prey have to drag it back to their burrows. Most burrows have just a single cell, but some species, notably those that nest in wood and hollow stems, build several cells in each burrow. Sphecids that collect large victims generally put just one in each cell, although most species fill their cells with several smaller victims. An egg is laid in each cell, the nest is sealed up, and the adult usually leaves the nest for good. There are, however, a number of species that take their parental care a bit further. Instead of mass-provisioning their nests and abandoning them, they start off with just a single victim and return from time to time to top up the larder with fresh supplies. *Ammophila pubescens* exhibits this progressive provisioning and can actually look after two or three nests at the same time. *Bembix rostrata* (Pl. 55), which stocks its nests with flies, actually lays its eggs in empty nests and does not bring the flies until the eggs hatch. As the larvae grow, the wasp brings progressively bigger flies for them. This progressive provisioning is a notable step towards social behaviour, for it establishes the all-important links between parent and offspring.

Like the other wasp groups, the sphecids include a number of cuckoo species that lay their eggs in the nests of their more industrious relatives.

Superfamily Apoidea – The Bees

All the bees, both social and solitary, are included in this superfamily. Until recently they were arranged in several families, but current opinion is that they should be placed in a single family – the **Apidae** (Pls. 57–60). There are about 30,000 known species, of which about 253 occur in the British Isles.

All bees, whether social or solitary, feed on pollen and nectar and they rear their young on the same diet. In this respect, they differ from almost all the wasps, whose young are fed on a meat diet. Visibly, the bees differ from the true wasps and the spider-hunting pompilids because the pronotum does not reach back to the tegulae (fig. p. 264), and they can be separated from the sphecid wasps by their broad and usually hairy back legs. The microscope also reveals that many of the bees' hairs are feathery – an adaptation for collecting pollen – whereas those of the wasps are unbranched.

The glossa or tongue is usually well developed, usually pointed and often very long, although bees of the genera *Hylaeus* and *Colletes* have very short, wasp-like tongues which are wider at the front than behind. *Andrena* and related genera have pointed tongues, but they are still relatively short and broad (fig. p. 282). These bees are important pollinators of many flowers, but they cannot reach nectar concealed in deep-throated flowers. Here, the important pollinators are the longed-tongued bees such as the Honey Bee, the bumble bees, and the flower bees (*Anthophora* species). Despite the great development of the glossa for sucking up nectar, the bees still retain their jaws, using them mainly for building their nests and often for cutting up wood and leaves in the process.

Pollen adheres to the bees' feathery hairs very well, and one often sees bees almost yellow with pollen as they wander over the flowers. Apart from the cuckoo bees, which rely on the pollen and nectar stored by other species, female and worker bees usually possess special pollen-carrying equipment, either on the back legs or on the underside of the abdomen. In its simplest form, this equipment is a brush of hairs to which the pollen is attached as it is periodically combed from the body. The pollen baskets formed on the hind tibiae of bumble bees and honey bees are rather more complex. The outer surface of the tibia is smooth and shiny, but it is bordered on both sides by stout, curved hairs which form a flexible cage or basket. Pollen is combed from the body with all the legs, moistened with regurgitated nectar, and then passed to the back legs to be packed into the pollen baskets. A good deal of pollen can be carried in this way – some bumble bees have been known to carry as much as 60 per cent of their own weight in pollen, although the average is probably about

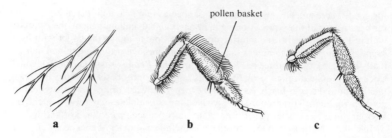

a. *The branched hairs from the body of a bee (highly magnified);* **b.** *the hind leg of a bumble bee* (Bombus) *showing the pollen basket on the tibia;* **c.** *the hind leg of a cuckoo bee* (Psithyrus), *with no pollen-collecting equipment*

20 per cent – and bulging yellow pollen baskets are a common sight on bees returning to their nests.

The various genera of bees are relatively easy to separate on the basis of shape, size, colour, and certain other reasonably visible features. The sub-marginal cells mentioned in the following key are the cells just behind and beyond the pterostigma of the forewing (fig. p. 273). The two closed cells just behind them are the discoidal cells. The radial cell, also known as the marginal cell and the apical cell, is the cell lying close to the front edge of the wing immediately beyond the pterostigma.

A Simplified Key to the Genera of European Bees, excluding a few rare genera found mainly in the Mediterranean region.

Parasitic or cuckoo genera are marked with an asterisk. Genera marked with ! do not normally occur in Britain.

1. Forewing with 3 sub-marginal cells   2

    Forewing with 2 sub-marginal cells   19

2. Radial cell (beyond pterostigma) very long and narrow: *Apis* p. 284
    hind tibia without spurs

    Radial cell shorter and broader: hind tibia spurred   3

3. Sub-marginal cells all about the same size: mostly large   4
    and very hairy bees

    Sub-marginal cells of different sizes   6

4. 1st sub-marginal partly divided by a   5
    very weak cross-vein: face black,
    with a clear cheek between eye
    and jaw   cheek

    1st sub-marginal without any such   *Anthophora* Pl. 59
    cross-vein: eye reaches upper
    edge of jaw, with no cheek

5. Hind tibia convex and covered with short hair: abdominal   *Psithyrus** p. 285
    hair sparse, with tergites shining through

    Outer surface of hind tibia more or   *Bombus* p. 284
    less flat, hairy in male but bare
    and shiny in female and with long   — pollen basket
    hairs along the edges: abdominal
    hair dense and concealing tergites

6. 3rd sub-marginal much bigger than 1st: large black bees   *!Xylocopa* p. 283
    with violet-tinged wings

    3rd sub-marginal equal to or smaller than 1st   7

7. 1st and 3rd sub-marginals more or less equal   8

    1st sub-marginal much bigger than 3rd   11

8. Abdomen black with white spots at the sides: 3rd sub-mar-   *Melecta** Pl. 59
    ginal about as broad at the front as at the rear

    Abdomen coloured differently: 3rd sub-marginal narrower   9
    at the front than at the rear

9. Body more or less clothed with long hair: antennae very   *!Tetralonia*
    long in male

    Abdomen largely hairless   10

10. Abdomen black or metallic blue   *Ceratina** Pl. 58

    Abdomen black and red or almost entirely red   *Sphecodes** p. 285

11. 2nd and 3rd sub-marginals more or less equal   12

    3rd sub-marginal much bigger than 2nd   15

12. Abdomen hairless and shiny, black or reddish brown and   *Nomada** p. 285
    usually marked with yellow

    Abdomen hairy or with pale felt-like patches on the sides   13

13. Abdomen hairy, often with pale bands: tongue very short   *Colletes* Pl. 57
    (fig. p. 282)

    Abdomen with pale, felt-like patches on the sides: tongue   14
    longer and pointed

14. Rear of scutellum smoothly rounded: 1st discoidal cell   *!Crocisa**
    very long

    Rear of scutellum drawn out into a triangular point at each   *Epeolus** Pl. 59
    side: 1st discoidal cell not unusually long

15. Basal vein almost straight (fig. p. 283)   16

    Basal vein strongly curved   17

16. Last tarsal segment noticeably enlarged: tip of antenna   *Melitta*
     truncated: jugal lobe of hind wing shorter than the cell
     in front of it: female lacks curly pollen brush at base of
     hind leg

     Last tarsal segment normal: antenna not truncated: jugal   *Andrena* p. 282
     lobe of hind wing as long as or longer than the cell in
     front of it: female has obvious curly pollen brush at
     base of hind leg

17. Abdomen almost hairless and largely black and red   *Sphecodes** p. 285

     Abdomen hairy and rarely with any red: female has hair-   18
     less furrow at tip of abdomen

18. Bands of hair on rear edge of each abdominal tergite   *Halictus* p. 283

     Bands of hair (if present) on front edge of abdominal ter-   *Lasioglossum* p. 283
     gites

19. Radial cell of forewing long and narrow, coming to a   20
     point on the wing margin quite close to wing-tip

     Radial cell not pointed, or if so the point is well removed   23
     from the wing margin

20. 1st discoidal cell reaches no further than junction between   21
     1st and 2nd sub-marginals

     1st discoidal cell extends beyond junction of 1st and 2nd   22
     sub-marginals, although sometimes only just

21. 1st sub-marginal larger than 2nd: very hairy bees with es-   *Dasypoda* Pl. 57
     pecially long hairs on hind legs

     1st and 2nd sub-marginals more or less equal   *Dufourea*

22. Abdomen rather rounded: smooth and shiny at front   *Macropis* Pl. 57

     Abdomen mainly dull black with clear bands of pale hair   *Rhophites*

23. Radial cell clearly truncated: abdomen shiny black: female   *Panurgus* Pl. 57
     with long hairs on hind legs

     Radial cell pointed or rounded at end   24

24. Hind legs with long, dense hair   *Dasypoda* Pl. 57

     Hind legs with only short hair   25

25. 2nd sub-marginal much bigger than 1st: male antennae   *Eucera* Pl. 58
     very long

     1st sub-marginal as big as or bigger than 2nd   26

26. 1st sub-marginal much bigger than 2nd: shiny black, hair-   *Hylaeus* p. 281
     less bees with pale faces: tongue short and broad (fig.
     p. 282)

     1st and 2nd sub-marginals about equal   27

27.	Abdomen boldly marked with yellow or orange spots on the sides	*Anthidium* Pl. 57
	Abdomen without such markings	28
28.	2nd discoidal cell extends as far as or beyond outer edge of 2nd sub-marginal: abdomen black with pale lines or spots at rear of segments: more or less hairless	*Stelis** Pl. 57
	2nd discoidal cell does not quite reach outer edge of 2nd sub-marginal	29
29.	Eyes hairy: abdomen black with white spots and almost hairless, almost triangular and sharply pointed in female but blunt and spiny in male	*Coelioxys** Pl. 57
	Eyes bare: abdomen differently marked	30
30.	Slender black bees with few hairs	31
	Broader and rather hairy bees, sometimes with metallic colouring	32
31.	1st gastral segment with a narrow ridge at the front	*Heriades*
	1st gastral segment without a ridge	*Chelostoma* p. 282
32.	Front of abdomen scooped out: dorsal surface relatively flat: male front legs often swollen	*Megachile* (incl. *Chalicodoma*) p. 283
	Front of abdomen not scooped out: dorsal surface rounded: feet with arolium between claws, although this shrinks after death	*Osmia* and *Hoplitis* p. 282

There is not room in this book for descriptions of all the bee genera, although most of those listed in the key are illustrated on Pls 57-60. The following paragraphs provide a brief survey of certain genera, illustrating the various degrees of social behaviour.

Bees of the genus *Hylaeus* (Pl. 57) are rather small, black and almost hairless insects with yellow faces – hence their common name of yellow-faced bees. In fact, they do not look much like bees at all, but they feed their grubs with pollen and nectar. They are all solitary insects and they make small nests – only half a dozen or so cells – in hollow stems and similar places. The cells are constructed with a secretion from the female's mouth. This secretion soon hardens into a transparent membrane which forms the walls of the cells. The short, blunt tongue – which distinguishes *Hylaeus* and *Colletes* from all other bees – plays a major part in the formation of the cells. *Hylaeus*, being almost hairless, cannot collect pollen in the usual way and the female fills her crop with both pollen and nectar. She provisions her nest cells with this mixture – the so-called bee-bread – and lays an egg in each. The cells are then closed and the parent bee dies. There is no contact between parent and offspring. *Hylaeus* has only one generation each year, the bees emerging in the summer and being particularly common at bramble flowers in July and August. The short, wasp-like tongue and the absence of any pollen-gathering equipment in *Hylaeus* lend support to the idea that bees evolved from wasp-like ancestors and grad-

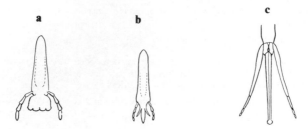

Tongues of bees: **a.** *the broad, wasp-like tongue of* Hylaeus *and* Colletes; **b.** *the short, ovate tongue of* Andrena; **c.** *the long, slender tongue of the Honey Bee*

ually evolved pollen-gathering equipment to go with their vegetarian habits. The bees have actually been described as sphecoid wasps that have turned vegetarian.

Members of the genus *Andrena*, with about 60 species in Britain, are rather variable in size and colour. They are generally quite hairy and are often mistaken for honey bees, although they can be distinguished quite easily by their short tongues (fig. above) and by the lack of pollen baskets on the hind tibiae. *Andrena* females carry their pollen home attached to curly brushes at the base of the hind legs. The abdomen is rather flat in most species. *Andrena* species are all solitary and they make their nests in the ground – usually selecting light, sandy soil. The rich brown *Andrena fulva* (Pl. 58) commonly nests in lawns, where she makes small volcano-like mounds with the excavated soil. *Andrena* species, together with *Halictus* species, are often called mining bees because of their burrowing habits. There may be many nests close together, giving the impression of communal life, but each female is working alone to excavate a small burrow with perhaps half a dozen earthen chambers. Each cell is lined with a waxy secretion from a gland in the female's abdomen. There is no contact between parent and offspring, the female showing no interest in her burrow after she has made and provisioned the cells. She is probably dead before her progeny emerge. Most of the species emerge from their nests in the spring and, after mating, the females set about making fresh burrows. Many species produce a second generation in the summer, but others take a whole year to complete their life cycles and adults are found for only a short period each year. *Andrena* bees are favourite hosts of stylopid parasites (see p. 162).

Osmia rufa (Pl. 58) and its relatives are commonly known as mason bees. They nest in all sorts of cavities, sometimes excavated by themselves, and construct their cells with sand grains and other particles glued together with saliva. They quite often nest in walls if the mortar is soft enough for them to tunnel in it. *Osmia bicolor* always builds her nest in an old snail shell, and after plastering over the entrance she covers the shell with grass. The genus *Hoplitis* is closely related to *Osmia* and has only recently been separated from it. The main difference concerns the thoracic ornamentation: *Osmia* has rounded punctures, while *Hoplitis* has rather elongate ones.

Chelostoma campanularum is a tiny, ant-like solitary bee that nests in old woodworm holes. Like the larger *C. florisomne* (Pl. 57), it confines its foraging to various kinds of campanula flowers. Pollen is collected on a dense orange pollen brush on the underside of the abdomen and the bee has to back into its burrow to off-load it.

Chelostoma is quite closely related to the leaf-cutter bees of the genus *Megachile* (Pl. 58), which are well known on account of their activities on our rose bushes. These solitary bees nest mainly in dead wood and their cells are constructed from pieces of leaf cut neatly from the plants with the bees' large mandibles. The leaf-cutters are not unlike honey bees in some ways, but they can always be distinguished because they have only two sub-marginal cells and the front part of the gaster is scooped out (Pl. 58). The pollen brushes, on the underside of the abdomen, are bright orange and very conspicuous. *Chalicodoma parietina* (Pl. 58) is another relative of *Megachile* and now commonly included in that genus, but it makes its nest cells with mud instead of with leaves. *Xylocopa* (Pl. 59) is a genus of large black bees which usually have a strong purple sheen on their dark wings. They tunnel in dead wood and are commonly known as carpenter bees.

Bees of the genus *Halictus* (Pl. 58) are hairy, although not markedly so, and generally rather small. They are often confused with *Andrena* species, but the two genera can usually be separated by looking at the basal vein near the middle of the forewing. That of *Halictus* is usually strongly curved, while that of *Andrena* is almost straight. Female *Halictus* bees also have a small, hairless furrow at the tip of the abdomen and the abdomen in general is less flattened than that of *Andrena*. Most species of *Halictus* are solitary bees with nesting habits like those of *Andrena*, but there are some sub-social and social species. Several species guard their nests after stocking them and laying their eggs, and the parent females often remain around long enough to make contact with their offspring. Progressive provisioning (see p. 277) is practised by some species, although there is not necessarily any co-operation between parent and offspring. *Lasioglossum malachurus* (Pl. 58), which is a close relative of the *Halictus* species and not uncommon in the southern half of Britain, has reached the stage of social co-operation, although it retains mass-provisioning of its cells. Mated females overwinter and begin nesting in the spring. As in *Andrena* – and many other solitary bees – the burrows are lined with waxy secretions, and then they are stocked with nectar and pollen in the normal way. The females – or queens as they can rightly be called – stay in and around the nest and guard it. So far, things are just as they are in some of the solitary species, but here comes the difference: the bees that emerge from the first cells are all worker females. They set to work building more cells and provisioning them ready for the queen to lay more eggs. This next batch of eggs gives rise to normal male and female bees, and after mating the females usually overwinter in their old nests. By producing a first brood of workers – although there are not more than a dozen or two – this species is able to raise a larger family than any of the solitary bees which have to rely on the efforts of a single female. The behaviour of *L. malachurus* is thus clearly intermediate between that of

The forewing of Andrena *shows the almost straight basal vein forming the inner margin of the 1st discoidal cell. In the superficially similar bees of the genus* Halictus *this vein is strongly curved - as it is in* Sphecodes *species.*

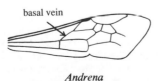

Andrena

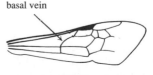

Sphecodes

the solitary bees, such as *Andrena*, and that of the fully social bumble bees and honey bees.

The large, hairy bumble bees familiar to everyone are usually species of *Bombus* (Pls 59 & 60). They are usually black with a greater or lesser amount of yellow banding and their common names – Red-tailed Bumble Bee, Buff-tailed Bumble Bee, and so on – often refer to their colouring. All of these bees are social insects and they usually make their nests under the ground, although some, often called carder bees, nest in dense vegetation and leaf litter at the bottoms of hedgerows and so on. The mated queens are the only ones to survive the winter and the bumble bee story is very much like that of the wasp. The queen wakes in the spring and looks for a suitable nesting site, such as a mousehole, but she is in no hurry to start her nest – perhaps she waits until there are sufficient flowers to provide for her offspring – and she spends much of her time at rest. Dried grass and moss are collected for the nest – these materials are often already present in the hole if it has been used by a mouse or a vole – and made into a light ball. Then the bee flies off for a load of pollen and nectar. On returning to the nest, the queen places a heap of pollen in the centre of the nesting material. She then lays about a dozen eggs on it and surrounds them with wax which she produces from special glands on her abdomen. She also builds a wax honey-pot, in which she stores nectar to keep her and her brood going in bad weather. She sits on her eggs to keep them warm. They hatch within about five days and the larvae grow rapidly on the pollen. The queen adds more pollen and nectar from time to time and, within a fortnight, the young bees have pupated and are ready to emerge. The new bees are, of course, all workers and they are a good deal smaller than the queen. The queen continues to build wax cells for her eggs, but the workers take over the job of feeding later batches of grubs. These later broods, with plenty of workers to feed them, yield progressively larger workers and towards the end of the summer they produce fully-fledged queens. Male bees appear at the same time and, after mating, the new queens take a few meals and then look for snug winter quarters.

The Honey Bee or Hive Bee (*Apis mellifera*) (Pl. 59) is probably the most widely and deeply studied insect in the world. Numerous lengthy books have been written on its social behaviour and on the wonderful ways in which the workers communicate with each other and pass on information about good sources of nectar. It is not really a native of Europe, although it has been here for some time. The perennial nature of its colonies suggest that it came from warmer parts – probably from south-east Asia.

The three castes – queen, drone, and worker – are more easily distinguished among the honey bees than among the other species. The queen does nothing in the way of household work or food collecting because she never founds a colony alone – she always comes into an existing colony or else takes some workers off to start a new one. She therefore has no pollen baskets and no wax glands for building cells, and she has a shorter tongue than the workers.

Honey bee cells are formed on large vertical sheets hung from the roof of the nesting cavity which, in the wild, is usually a hollow tree, although some bees actually nest in the open. Each cell is perfectly hexagonal and the cells are used for rearing the young and storing pollen and honey. Drone cells tend to be slightly larger than the normal brood cells and they occur mainly near the edges of the comb. Eggs are usually laid in them towards the end of the summer and the size of the cells somehow causes the queen to lay unfertilised, drone-producing eggs. Queen cells are irregular, cone-shaped chambers hanging downwards from the edges of the comb. They are produced when the colony is about to swarm or when the workers feel that the resident queen is failing. The eggs laid in the queen cells are just the same as those laid in worker cells and the future of the eggs is controlled by the workers. Larvae destined to become queens are fed entirely on 'royal jelly', which is a mixture of fatty and protein-rich secretions from the workers' salivary glands together with regurgitated sugars. Larvae destined to join the workforce receive the same food for the first two or three days, but then the fatty component is replaced by honey and pollen. Transferring eggs and young larvae from queen cells to worker cells and vice-versa clearly shows that it is the feeding and not the genetic make-up of the egg that controls queen-production. Bee-keepers actually transfer eggs from the comb to artificial queen cells in order to get more queens, and thus more colonies. Colonies that have lost their queens for some reason or other quickly set about increasing the size of some worker cells to produce 'emergency queens'. The loss of the original queen soon becomes very apparent in the colony because the workers miss her 'queen substance' – a mixture of pheromones which she gives out and which is spread through the worker population when they feed each other and communicate with each other.

The first new queen to emerge from her cell usually stings her rivals while they are still in their cells, and after a few days she goes off on her marriage flight. She normally returns to her own hive and the workers kill off the old queen if she is failing. Alternatively, before the new queens emerge, the old queen may take off with a swarm of workers to start another colony. Very occasionally a colony may swarm again a little later, but when this happens it is the new virgin queen that goes off with the swarm and not the established queen.

A well-established honey bee colony may contain more than 50,000 bees, almost all of them workers. The queen lives for several years but the drones and workers are short-lived, especially in the summer when there is much work to do. Summer workers rarely live for than a few weeks, although later-maturing ones will survive the winter. Drones are tolerated in the summer, but they do no work and they are thrown out in the autumn when the somewhat depleted colony settles down to rest, feeding on pollen and honey stored up during the summer months.

Mention has already been made of cuckoo bees, which grow up in the nests of other species. They do not usually feed on their hosts but merely take food which was intended for the host larvae. They are therefore social parasites, although some entomologists prefer to call them inquilines, retaining the word parasite for those animals that actually feed on their hosts. The genus *Nomada* (Pl. 58) contains many rather wasp-like bees with black and yellow or brown and yellow markings. Most of them grow up in the nests of *Andrena* and *Halictus* bees. Like other cuckoo bees, *Nomada* has no pollen-collecting equipment. Bees of the genus *Sphecodes* (Pl. 58), which also parasitise *Halictus*, are commonly black and brown and could be confused with some species of *Nomada*, but the basal vein of *Nomada* is almost straight whereas that of *Sphecodes* is strongly curved (fig. p. 283).

As a final example of bees, we will look at *Psithyrus* (Pl. 60), a genus of cuckoo bees associated with bumble bees. Each species sticks pretty well to one or two host species, which it resembles quite closely. *P. rupestris*, for example, is an inquiline in the nest of the very similar *Bombus lapidarius* (Pl. 60). *Psithyrus* females are quite easily distinguished from *Bombus* females by the lack of pollen baskets (fig. p. 278), but the males are not so easy. One of the best guides is the hairiness of the abdomen.

The abdominal tergites show through the coat of *Psithyrus* as shiny plates, but those of *Bombus* are almost always hidden by hairs.

The female *Psithyrus* overwinters just like the *Bombus* queen, but she does not wake until some weeks after *Bombus* has started work. By this time the nest has been made and a few small workers are in attendance. *Psithyrus* now makes her appearance and enters the host nest. She may be attacked by the workers, but there are not many of them and they are relatively small. Their stings are unable to penetrate the tough armour of the cuckoo bee. After the initial unrest, the *Psithyrus* is tolerated and she starts to lay her own eggs. These are reared by the *Bombus* workers but few, if any, *Bombus* grubs are reared from now on – the invader either kills the *Bombus* queen or eats her eggs as soon as they are laid.

Collecting and preserving
The larger species, including many of the bees and wasps, ichneumons, and sawflies, can be taken on the wing. It is often an easy matter to box them while they are feeding at flowers as well. The smaller insects can be obtained by beating and sweeping vegetation, and also by collecting the hosts of the parasitic species. Malaise traps are also ideal for collecting the smaller species.

All normal killing agents are suitable for the Hymenoptera. The method of display depends largely on the size of the insects. Large species can be pinned and set. Staging and pointing are both suitable for the smaller species, but a lot of practice is necessary before one can arrange the wings neatly. The smallest species, together with some of the soft-bodied ichneumons, are best preserved in spirit.

Glossary

Abdomen The hindmost of the three main body divisions of an insect

Acrostichal Bristles The two rows of hairs or bristles lying on either side of the mid-line of the thorax of a true fly (fig. p. 173)

Aculeate (Hymenoptera) Possessing a sting

Acuminate Tapering to a long point

Adeagus The part of the male genitalia which is inserted into the female during copulation and which carries the sperm into the female. Its shape is often important in separating   closely related species

Alar Squama The middle of three flap-like outgrowths at the base of the wing in various flies (fig. p. 174)

Alitrunk Name given to the thorax and propodeum of 'wasp-waisted' hymenopterans

Alula Outermost of the three flap-like outgrowths at the base of the wing in various flies: really a part of the wing membrane.

Annulate With ring-like markings

Antennae The pair of sensory organs on the head - the 'feelers'.

Antenodal Veins Small cross-veins at the front of the dragonfly or damselfly wing, between the wing base and the nodus (fig. p. 58)

Anterior Concerning or facing the front.

Apical At or concerning the tip or furthest part of any organ: apical cells, for example are at the wing-tip

Appendage Any limb or other organ, such as an antenna, which is attached to the body by a joint

Appendix A short vein, especially a short continuation after the main vein has changed direction.

Apterous Without wings

Apterygote Any member of the Apterygota - the primitive insects, such as the bristletails, which have never developed wings during their history.

Aquatic Living in water

Arista A bristle-like outgrowth from the antenna in various flies (fig. p. 171)

Aristate Bearing an arista or bristle

Arolium A small pad between the claws on an insect's foot. Usually very small, but well developed in grasshoppers and some other insects

Basal Concerning the base of a structure - that part nearest the body. Basal cells in Diptera are generally small cells near the base of the wing

Basitarsus The 1st segment of the tarsus - usually the largest

Bipectinate Feathery, with branches growing out on both sides of the main axis: applied mainly to antennae

Brachypterous With short wings

Bursa Copulatrix That part of the female genitalia which receives the adeagus and sperm during copulation. Its structure is often important in separating closely related species

Callus A rounded swelling: applied especially to swollen regions at the front or back of the thorax in various flies (fig. p. 173)

Calypter Innermost of the three flap-like outgrowths at the base of the wing in various flies. Also known as the thoracic squama, it generally conceals the haltere (fig. p. 174)

Campodeiform (applied to a larva) Flattened and elongated with well- developed legs and antennae. Many beetle larvae are of this type, and so are those of the lacewings (fig. p. 24)

Cardo The basal segment of the maxilla or secondary jaw

Carina A ridge or keel

Caste One of three or more distinct forms which make up the population among social insects. The usual three castes are queen, drone (male), and worker. The termites and some of the ants have one or more soldier castes as well.

Caudal Concerning the tail end

Cell An area of the wing bounded by a number of veins. A cell is closed if it is completely surrounded by veins and open if it is bounded partly by the wing margin.

Cerci The paired appendages, often very long, which spring from the tip of the abdomen in many insects (singular: cercus)

Cervical Concerning the neck region, just behind the head

Chaetae Stiff hairs or bristles (singular: chaeta)

Chaetotaxy The arrangement of the bristles or chaetae on an insect: especially important in the classification of true flies

Cheek (see **Gena**)

Chitin The tough horny material, chemically known as a nitrogenous polysaccharide, which makes up the bulk of the insect cuticle

Ciliated Bearing minute hairs (cilia)

Clavate Club-shaped, with the distal end swollen: most often applied to antennae

Clavus Posterior part of the forewing of of heteropteran bugs (fig. p. 100)

Clypeus Lowest part of the insect face, just above the labrum (fig. p. 14)

Coarctate (applied to pupae) Enclosed within the last larval skin, which therefore acts as a cocoon and protects the pupa. Such pupae are found in the flies of the sub-order Cyclorrhapha

Cocoon A case, made partly or completely of silk, which protects the pupa in many insects, especially the moths. The cocoon is made by the larva before it pupates

Contiguous Touching - usually applied to eyes (see also **Holoptic**)

Corbicula The pollen basket on the hind leg of many bees, formed by stout hairs on the borders of the tibia (fig. p. 278)

Corium The main part of the forewing of a heteropteran bug (fig. p. 100)

Cornicle One of the pair of small tubular outgrowths on the hind end of the aphid abdomen (Pl. 13)

Costa One of the major longitudinal veins, usually forming the front margin of the wing and usually abbreviated to C. The costal margin is the front edge of the wing (fig. p. 19)

Costal Cell The cell between the costa and the sub-costal vein

Coxa The basal segment of the insect leg, often immovably attached to the body (fig. p. 17)

Cremaster The cluster of minute hooks (sometimes just one larger hook) at the hind end of a lepidopterous pupa: used to grip the pupal support

Cross-vein A short vein joining any two neighbouring longitudinal veins

Cubitus One of the major longitudinal veins, situated in the rear half of the wing and usually with 2 or 3 branches: abbreviated to Cu (fig. p. 19)

Cuneus A more or less triangular region of the forewing of certain heteropteran bugs, separated from the corium by a groove or suture (fig. p. 100)

Cursorial Adapted for running

Dentate Toothed

Denticulate Bearing very small tooth-like projections

Diapause A period of suspended animation of regular occurrence in the lives of many insects, especially in the young stages

Discal Cell Name given to a prominent and often quite large cell near the middle of the wing. The discal cell of one insect group may not be bounded by the same veins as that of another group

Distal Concerning that part of an appendage furthest from the body

Dorsal On or concerning the back or upperside of an animal

Dorso-central Bristles The 2 rows of bristles running along the thorax of a fly on the outer side of the acrostichal bristles (fig. p. 173)

Dorso-lateral Towards the sides of the dorsal (upper) surface

Dorso-ventral Running from the dorsal (upper) to the ventral (lower) surface

Dorsum The upper surface or back of an animal

Ecdysis The moulting process, by which a young insect changes its outer coat

Ectoparasite A parasite which lives on the outside of its host: fleas and lice are the most familiar examples among the insects

Elbowed Antenna Antenna in which there is a distinct angle between two of the segments - usually between the 1st and 2nd segments, in which case the 1st segment is usually much longer than the others

Elytron The tough, horny forewing of a beetle or an earwig (plural elytra) (See also **Hemelytron**)

Emarginate With a distinct notch or indentation in the margin

Embolium A narrow region along the front margin of the forewing in certain heteropteran bugs: separated from the rest of the corium by a groove or suture (fig. p. 100)

Empodium An outgrowth between the claws of a fly's foot: it may be bristle-like or pad-like (fig. p. 175)

Endoparasite A parasite which lives inside its host's body. Most of the ichneumons (p. 265) are endoparasites

Endopterygote Any insect in which the wings develop inside the body of the early stages and in which there is a complete metamorphosis and pupal stage

Epimeron The posterior part of the side wall of any of the three thoracic segments

Epipharynx A component of many insect mouth-parts which is attached to the posterior surface of the labrum or upper lip. In chewing insects it is usually only a small lobe, but in the fleas it is greatly enlarged and used for sucking blood

Epiproct An appendage arising from the mid-line of the last abdominal segment, just above the anus. In the bristletails and some mayflies it is very long and forms the central 'tail'

Episternum The anterior part of the side wall of any of the three thoracic segments

Eruciform (applied to a larva) More or less cylindrical with stumpy legs at the rear as well as the true thoracic legs. The caterpillars of butterflies and moths are typical examples

Exarate Pupa A pupa in which all the appendages are free (fig. p. 25)

Excavate Hollowed out: applied to the coxae of many beetles, which are hollowed out to receive the femora when the legs are folded (fig. p. 135)

Exopterygote Any insect in which the wings develop gradually on the outside of the body. There is only a partial metamorphosis and no pupal stage

Exuvia The cast-off outer skin of an insect or other arthropod

Eye-cap Hood formed by the base of the antenna and partly covering the eye in certain small moths (fig. p. 230)

Facet The surface of an ommatidium - one of the units making up the compound eye

Femur The 3rd and often the largest segment of the insect leg (fig. p. 17)

Filament A thread-like structure, especially one at the end of an antenna

Filiform Thread-like or hair-like, applied especially to antennae

Flabellate With projecting flaps on one side, applied especially to antennae

Flagellum The distal part of the antenna, beyond the 2nd segment

Fossorial Adapted for digging

Frenulum The wing-coupling mechanism found in many moths (fig. p. 18)

Frons Upper part of the insect face, between and below the antennae and usually carrying the median ocellus or simple eye. In true flies (Diptera) it occupies almost all of the front surface of the head apart from the eyes

Frontal Bristles The two vertical rows of bristles running down the face of a fly from the ocelli to the antennae

Fronto-orbital Bristles The short row of bristles on each side of a fly's head between the eye and the frontal bristles (fig. p. 171)

Furcula The forked spring of a springtail

Galea the outer branch of the maxilla, the inner one being the lacinia

Gall An abnormal growth of a plant caused by the presence in its tissues of a young insect or some other organism. Aphids, gall wasps, and gall midges are among the major gall-causing insects

Gaster The hymenopteran abdomen - apart from the 1st segment (the **propodeum**) which is fused to the thorax. The front part of the gaster often forms a narrow waist

Gena The cheek - that part of the head below and behind the eye

Genal Comb A row of stout spines on the lower border of the cheek of certain fleas

Geniculate Abruptly bent or elbowed (see **Elbowed Antenna**)

Genitalia The copulatory organs of insects. The shape and arrangement of the genitalia are often used to distinguish closely related and otherwise very similar species

Genus A group of closely related species (plural: genera). The name of the genus is incorporated into the scientific names of all the member species: *Pieris napi* and *Pieris rapae*, for example, both belong to the genus *Pieris*

Gill Breathing organ possessed by many aquatic creatures, including numerous young insects. Insect gills are usually very fine outgrowths from the body and they contain numerous air-tubes or tracheae. Oxygen passes into the tubes from the water.

Glabrous Without hairs

Glossa One of a pair of lobes at the tip of the labium or lower lip: usually very small, but long in honey bees and bumble bees, in which the two glossae are used to suck up nectar

Gynandromorph An individual creature with a mixture of male and female characteristics. One half of the body may be male and the other half female. This is particularly noticeable when it occurs among the blue butterflies and others in which the sexes are differently coloured

Haltere One of the club-shaped 'balancers' found among the true flies (Diptera). The halteres are the much-modified hind wings.

Hamuli The minute hooks on the front edge of the hind wing of bees and other hymenopterans, used to link the front and hind wings together. The hook which holds the springtail's spring in place is also called the hamula

Haustellate Adapted for sucking liquids rather than biting solid food

Hemelytron The forewing of a heteropteran bug, differing from the beetle elytron in having a membranous tip (plural hemelytra)

Hemimetabolous Having an incomplete metamorphosis, with no pupal stage in the life history

Heteromerous (of beetles) Having unequal numbers of tarsal segments on the three pairs of legs

Holometabolous Having a complete metamorphosis, with larval and pupal stages in the life history

Holoptic With the eyes touching or almost touching on the top of the head: used mainly when describing flies (Diptera)

Holotype (See **Type**)

Homonym A scientific name which has been given to two different species. When such an instance comes to light one of the species must be given another name

Honeydew The sweet liquid emitted from the anus of aphids and some other sap-sucking bugs

Host The organism which is attacked by a parasite

Humeral Angle The front basal part of the wing, close to its attachment to the body

Humeral Vein A small cross-vein running from the costa to the sub-costa in the humeral (basal) region of the wing

Hyaline Clear and colourless, like the wings of most dragonflies

Hypermetamorphosis A type of life history which includes two or more different types of larvae (fig. p. 156)

Hyperparasite A parasitic organism which attacks another parasite

Hypognathous Having a vertical head and face with the mouth-parts at the bottom (fig. p. 14)

Hypopharynx A component of the insect mouth-parts arising behind the mouth and just in front of the labium or lower lip. Usually short and tongue-like in species with biting jaws, but often drawn out to form a tube for the salivary duct in those species with sucking mouths (fig. p. 172)

Hypopleural Bristles A curved row of bristles on the side of the thorax of certain true flies, just below and in front of the haltere and just above the base of the hind leg (fig. p. 173)

Imago The adult insect (plural imagines)

Inquiline A creature that shares the home of another species without having any obvious effect on that species

Instar The stage in an insect's life history between any two moults. A newly-hatched insect which has not yet moulted is said to be a first-instar nymph or larva. The adult (imago) is the final instar

Integument The insect's outer coat

Intercalary Vein An additional longitudinal vein, arising at the wing margin and running inwards but not directly connected to any of the major veins

Joint Strictly speaking, an articulation between neighbouring parts, such as the femur and tibia of the leg, but the word is commonly used as a synonym of segment - meaning any of the divisions of the body or its appendages

Jugum A narrow lobe projecting from the base of the forewing in certain moths and overlapping the hind wing, thereby coupling the two wings together (fig. p. 18)

Keel A narrow ridge: also called a carina

Labellum The expanded tip of the labium, used by many flies to mop up surface fluids (fig. p. 172)

Labial Concerning the labium

Labium The 'lower lip' of the insect mouth-parts, formed by the fusion of two maxilla-like appendages (fig. p. 14)

Labrum The 'upper lip' of the insect mouth-parts: not a true appendage but a movable sclerite on the front of the head

Lacinia The inner branch of the maxilla, the outer one being the galea

Lamella A thin, leaf-like flap or plate, the name being applied to the outgrowths of certain antennae (fig. p. 16)

Lamellate Possessing lamellae: applied especially to antennae (fig. p. 16)

Larva Name given to a young insect which is markedly different from the adult: caterpillars and fly maggots are good examples (fig. p. 24)

Lateral Concerning the sides

Ligulae Name given to the lobes at the tip of the labium: usually divided into glossae and paraglossae (fig. p. 14)

Mandible The jaw of an insect. It may be sharply toothed and used for biting, as in grasshoppers and wasps, or it may be drawn out to form a slender needle as in mosquitoes. Mandibles are completely absent in most flies and lepidopterans

Mandibulate Having mandibles suited for biting and chewing

Marginal Cell One of a number of cells bordering the front margin of the wing in the outer region

Maxilla One of the two components of the insect mouth-parts lying just behind the jaws. They assist with the detection and manipulation of food and are often drawn out into tubular structures for sucking up liquids (plural maxillae) (fig. p. 14)

Maxillary Concerning the maxillae

Media The longitudinal vein running through the central region of the wing in most insects: abbreviated to M (fig. p. 19)

Membranous Thin and delicate, often transparent

Mesonotum The dorsal surface of the 2nd thoracic segment - the mesothorax: usually the largest thoracic sclerite

Mesopleuron The sclerite or sclerites making up the side wall of the mesothorax

Mesoscutellum Hindmost of the three major divisions of the mesonotum, often more or less triangular or shield-shaped: usually abbreviated to scutellum (fig. p. 173)

Mesoscutum The middle and usually the largest division of the mesonotum (fig. p. 173)

Mesosternum The ventral surface or sclerite of the mesothorax

Mesothorax The 2nd segment of the thorax

Metamorphosis Name given to the changes that take place during an insect's life as it turns from a young animal to an adult. These changes may be gradual and not too large, as in the grasshopper, and metamorphosis is then said to be partial or incomplete. On the other hand, the changes may be much greater and they may take place in one big step - as in the butterflies and moths, which change from caterpillars to adults during the pupal stage. Metamorphosis of this kind is said to be complete.

Metanotum The dorsal surface of the metathorax. It is often very small and its subdivisions are usually obscured

Metapleuron The sclerite or sclerites making up the side wall of the metathorax

Metasternum The ventral surface or sclerite of the metathorax

Metatarsus The basal segment of the tarsus or foot: usually the largest segment

Metathorax The 3rd segment of the thorax

Moniliform (of antennae) Composed of bead-like segments, each well separated from the next (fig. p. 16)

Moult To moult is to shed the outer covering of the body - the exoskeleton

Nodus The kink or notch on the costal margin of the dragonfly wing. The name is also used for the strong, short cross-vein just behind the notch (fig. p. 58)

Notaulix One of a pair of longitudinal grooves on the mesonotum of certain hymenopterans, dividing the mesonotum into a central area and two lateral areas (plural notaulices)

Notopleuron A triangular area on the thorax of certain flies, just behind the humeral callus and occupying parts of both dorsal and lateral surfaces (fig. p. 173)

Notum The dorsal or upper surface of any thoracic segment: usually prefixed by pro-, meso-, or meta- to indicate the relevant segment

Nymph Name given to the young stages of those insects which undergo a partial metamorphosis. The nymph is usually quite similar to the adult except that its wings are not fully developed. It normally feeds on the same kind of food as the adult (fig. p. 24)

Obtect Pupa A pupa in which the legs and other appendages are firmly fastened down to the rest of the body - as in the butterfly chrysalis (fig. p. 25)

Occipital Suture A groove running round the posterior region of the head of some insects and separating the vertex from the occiput. On the sides of the head the same groove marks the posterior boundary of the cheeks or genae

Occiput Hindmost region of the top of the head, just in front of the neck membrane. In some insects it is separated from the vertex by the occipital suture, but it is not usually present as a distinct plate or sclerite

Ocellar Bristles Bristles arising around or between the ocelli in various flies

Ocellar Triangle A triangular area, usually quite distinct from the rest of the head, on which the ocelli of true flies are carried (Pl.30)

Ocellus One of the simple eyes of insects, usually occurring in a group of three on the top of the head, although absent from many insects

Ommatidium One of the units which make up the compound eye (fig. p. 16)

Ootheca An egg case, such as the purse-like structure carried around by cockroaches or the spongy mass in which mantids lay their eggs

Oral Vibrissae The pair of large bristles just above the mouth in certain flies: usually simply called vibrissae (fig. p. 171)

Oviparous Reproducing by laying eggs

Ovipositor The egg-laying apparatus of a female insect: concealed in many insects, but extremely large among the bush-crickets (Pl.5) and some parasitic hymenopterans (Pl. 52)

Palp A segmented leg-like structure arising on the maxilla or labium. Palps have a sensory function and play a major role in tasting food

Paraglossa One of a pair of lobes at the outer edges of the tip of the labium: with the central glossae, the paraglossae make up the ligula (fig. p. 14)

Paraproct One of the 2 lobes bordering the sides of the anus

Parasite An organism that spends all or part of its life in close association with another species, taking food from it but giving nothing in return. Ectoparasites live on the outside of their hosts, while endoparasites live inside the host's body

Parthenogenesis A form of reproduction in which eggs develop normally without being fertilised. This is the usual method of reproduction among some stick insect species and among some generations of gall wasps and aphids

Pecten A comb-like structure found at the base of the antenna in some insects (fig. p. 235)

Pectinate Having branches which arise from the main axis like the teeth of a comb: usually applied to antennae

Pedicel The 2nd antennal segment: the name is also given to the narrow waist of an ant

Petiolate Attached by a narrow stalk

Petiole The narrow waist of bees and wasps and some other hymenopterans: often known as the pedicel when referring to ants

Pictured A term used to describe wings, especially among the Diptera, which have dark mottling on them (Pl. 29)

Pilose Densely clothed with hair

Pleural Concerning the side walls of the body

Pleural Suture A vertical or diagonal groove on each of the thoracic pleura, separating the episternum at the front from the epimeron at the back

Pleuron The side wall of a thoracic segment

Plumose With numerous feathery branches: applied especially to antennae (fig. p. 16)

Pollen Basket The pollen-carrying region on the hind leg of a bee: also known as the corbicula (fig. p. 278)

Porrect Extending horizontally forward: applied especially to antennae

Posterior Concerning or facing the rear

Postmentum The basal region of the labium

Postscutellum A small division of the mesonotum just behind the scutellum: usually very small or absent, but well developed in certain flies (fig. p. 209)

Post-vertical Bristles A pair of bristles - divergent, parallel, or crossing - on the back of the head of various flies, some way behind the ocelli (fig. p. 171)

Pre-apical Arising just before the tip: many flies, for example, have pre-apical bristles just before the tip of the tibia (fig. p. 184)

Prementum The distal region of the labium, from which spring the labial palps and the ligula (fig. p. 14)

Prepupa A resting stage through which many larvae pass before pupating. The larvae are usually rather shrunken at this stage and often look dead

Proboscis Name given to various kinds of sucking mouths in which some of the mouth-parts are drawn out to form tubes (fig. p. 15)

Prognathous Having a more or less horizontal head, with the mouth-parts at the front

Proleg One of the fleshy, stumpy legs on the hind region of a caterpillar

Pronotal Comb A row of stout spines on the hind margin of the pronotum of certain fleas (fig. p. 165)

Pronotum The dorsal surface or sclerite of the 1st thoracic segment

Propodeum The 1st abdominal segment in the hymenopteran group known as the Apocrita: it is completely fused with the thorax (see p. 255)

Prosternum Ventral surface of the 1st thoracic segment

Prothorax The 1st thoracic segment

Proximal Concerning the basal part of an appendage - the part nearest to the body

Pruinose Covered with a powdery deposit, usually white or pale blue: especially applied to Odonata (see p. 58)

Pterostigma A small coloured area near the wing-tip of dragonflies, bees, and various other clear-winged insects: also called the stigma (fig. p. 58)

Pterygote Any member of the sub-class Pterygota, which includes all winged insects

Ptilinum A tiny balloon-like structure seen in certain flies as they emerge from their puparia. It erupts from the front of the head and, as it is inflated, it pushes off the lid of the puparium. Having done its job, it is deflated and withdrawn, its position being marked by the ptilinal suture (fig. p. 171)

Pubescent Covered with short, soft hair

Pulvillus The little pad beneath each claw on the foot of a fly (fig. p. 175)

Punctate Covered with tiny pits or depressions, like the elytra of many beetles and the thoraxes of many hymenopterans

Pupa The 3rd stage in the life history of butterflies and other insects undergoing a complete metamorphosis. It is during the pupal stage, which does not feed and does not usually move about, that the larval body is rebuilt into that of the adult insect (fig. p. 25)

Puparium The barrel-shaped case which conceals the pupa of the house-fly and many other true flies. It is formed from the last larval skin and, unlike the actual pupa, it carries no indication of the positions of the wings or other appendages

Pupate To pupate is to turn into a pupa

Pupiparous Insects which give birth to fully-grown larvae which pupate almost immediately are said to be pupiparous. The main examples are various blood-sucking flies

Quadrilateral A cell near the base of the damselfly wing, whose shape is important in separating the families (fig. p. 58)

Radial Sector The posterior of the two main branches of the radius, usually abbreviated to Rs. It usually has several branches of its own

Radius One of the main longitudinal veins, running near the front of the wing and usually abbreviated to R. It gives off a posterior branch - the radial sector - and the smaller branches of these veins are numbered R_1, R_2, and so on (fig. p. 19)

Raptorial Adapted for seizing and grasping prey, like the front legs of a mantis (Pl. 7)

Reticulate Covered with a network pattern

Rostrum A beak or snout, applied especially to the piercing mouth-parts of bugs and the elongated snouts of weevils (fig. p. 99)

Rudimentary Poorly developed

Scape The 1st antennal segment, especially if it is longer than the other segments

Scarabaeiform (applied to a larva) Having a thick, soft body with a well-developed head and strong thoracic legs but with no legs on the hind region: often permanently curved into a C. The larvae of the lamellicorn beetles are of this type (fig. p. 24)

Sclerite Any of the individual hardened plates which make up the exoskeleton

Scopa The pollen-collecting apparatus of a bee, whether it be the pollen basket on the leg or a brush of hairs on the abdomen

Scopula A small tuft of hairs

Scutellum The 3rd of the major divisions of the dorsal surface of a thoracic segment: usually obvious only in the mesothorax and very large in some bugs

Scutum The middle of the three main divisions of the dorsal surface of a thoracic segment (fig. p. 173)

Segment One of the rings or divisions of the body, or one of the sections of a jointed limb between two joints

Serrate Toothed like a saw

Sessile Attached to one place and unable to move, like many female scale insects

Seta A bristle

Setaceous Bristle-like, applied especially to antennae

Species The basic unit of living things, consisting of a group of individuals which all look more or less alike and which can all breed with each other to produce another generation of similar creatures.

Spinose Spiny

Spiracle One of the breathing pores - openings of the tracheal system - through which insects get their air supplies. They occur on most segments of the body but are most clearly seen in certain non-hairy caterpillars (Pl. 60)

Spur A large and usually movable spine, normally found on the legs

Spurious Vein A false vein formed by a thickening of the wing membrane and usually unconnected with any of the true veins

Squama Any of the membranous flaps that arise near the base of the wing in many true flies (plural: squamae) (fig. p. 174)

Stadium The time interval between successive moults in an insect's life

Sternite The plate or sclerite on the underside of a body segment

Stigma See **Pterostigma**

Striae Grooves running across or along the body: applied especially to the grooves on beetle elytra

Stridulation The production of sounds by rubbing two parts of the body together: best known in grasshoppers and other orthopterans

Style A slender bristle arising at the apex of the antenna

Stylet A needle-like object: applied to the various components of piercing mouth-parts and also to a part of the sting of a bee or other hymenopteran

Sub-apical Situated just before the tip or apex

Subcosta Usually the first of the longitudinal veins behind the front edge of the wing, although it is often missing or very faint: abbreviated to Sc

Sub-imago Found only among the mayflies, the sub-imago or dun is the winged insect which emerges from the nymphal skin. It is rather dull in colour, but very soon moults again - the only example of a winged insect undergoing a moult - to reveal the imago

Sub-marginal Cells Cells lying just behind the stigma in the hymenopteran fore-wing: important in the identification of bees and sphecid wasps (fig. p. 273)

Sub-species A sub-division of a species, usually inhabiting a particular area: visibly different from other populations of the same species but still able to interbreed with them

Suture A groove on the body surface which usually divides one plate or sclerite from the next: also the junction between the elytra of a beetle

Synonym One of two or more names which have been given to a single species. The earliest name usually takes precedence

Tarsus The insect's foot: primitively a single segment but consisting of several segments in most living insects

Tegmen Name given to the leathery forewing of a grasshopper or similar insect, such as a cockroach (plural tegmina)

Tegula A small lobe or scale overlying the base of the forewing like a 'shoulder-pad' (fig. p. 264)

Tergite The primary plate or sclerite forming the dorsal surface of any body segment

Tergum The dorsal surface of any body segment

Thorax The middle of the three major divisions of the insect body. The legs and wings (if present) are always attached to the thorax

Tibia The leg segment between the femur and the tarsus (fig. p. 17)

Trachea One of the minute tubes which permeate the insect body and carry air to all parts. The tracheae open to the air at the spiracles

Transverse Suture A suture running across the thorax of many flies and dividing the mesonotum into a scutum and a prescutum

Triangle A triangular region near the base of the dragonfly wing, often divided into smaller cells (fig. p. 58)

Triungulin Name given to the active 1st- instar larva of oil beetles and some of their relatives: it appears to have 3 claws on each foot (fig. p. 156)

Trochanter A segment of the leg between the coxa and the femur: often very small and easily overlooked (fig. p. 17)

Truncate Ending abruptly: squared off

Tymbal The sound-producing 'drum-skin' of a cicada

Tympanum The auditory membrane or ear-drum of various insects

Type The type specimen of a species is the actual insect from which the original description of that species was produced. If several specimens were used for this purpose, one of them should have been designated as the type. Because the type can be of only one sex, it is usual to designate a certain individual of the opposite sex as the allotype. The original type specimen is then called the holotype. These type specimens are very important and are usually carefully preserved in museum collections

Ventral Concerning the lower side of the body
Vertex The top of the head, between and behind the eyes (fig. p. 14)
Vestigial Poorly developed
Vibrissae See **Oral Vibrissae**
Viviparous Bringing forth living or active young instead of laying eggs

Entomological Suppliers

* Suppliers of living material as well as equipment

L.Christie,
129 Franciscan Road,
Tooting,
LONDON,
SW17 8DZ
Also supplies entomological books

The Living World,*
Seven Sisters Country Park,
Near SEAFORD,
E. Sussex,
BN25 4AD

Marris House Nets,
54 Richmond Park Avenue,
Queen's Park,
BOURNEMOUTH,
BH8 9DR
Malaise traps and all kinds of
  nets and rearing cages

Watkins & Doncaster,
Four Throws,
HAWKHURST,
Kent

Wilford Manufacturing Co.Ltd,
Grange Works,
Great Northern Road,
DUNSTABLE,
Bedfordshire
Suppliers of Plastazote

Worldwide Butterflies Ltd,*
Over Compton,
SHERBORNE,
Dorset

A wide range of entomological books may be obtained from:

E. W. Classey Ltd,
PO Box 93,
FARINGDON
Oxon,
SN7 7DR

Natural History Book Service,
2 Wills Road,
Totnes,
Devon,
TQ9 5XN

Selected Bibliography

Works dealing with the Biology and Identification of Insects

The works listed here are mainly in English and they deal mainly with British insects. Many of them contain further references.

The *Handbooks for the Identification of British Insects*, hereafter abbreviated to *HIBI*, are published by the Royal Entomological Society of London and are technical books providing keys for the identification of all British insects, although not all parts in the series have yet been published. Volume XI in this series is a complete revision of Kloet and Hincks *Check List of British Insects*, providing a full list of the scientific names of all the British insects. It is published in five parts. Part 1 covers all the exopterygote insects, together with the lacewings, scorpion flies, and caddis flies; Part 2 covers the butterflies and moths; Part 3 covers the beetles; Part 4 covers the bees and wasps and all the other members of the Hymenoptera; and part 5 covers the flies and fleas.

Insects occurring in France may be identified with the aid of *Atlas d'Entomologie* – a series of pocket books by various authors and published by Boubée - and various volumes in the *Faune de France* series.

General Entomology
Askew, R.R. 1971 *Parasitic Insects* Heinemann
Borror D.J., Triplehorn, C.A., & Johnson, N.F. 1989 *An Introduction to the Study of Insects* Saunders College Publishing (6th Edition)
Chinery, M. 1986 *Collins Guide to the Insects of Britain and Western Europe* Collins
Imms, A.D. 1971 *Insect Natural History (3rd Edition)* Collins
Oldroyd, H. 1958 *Collecting, Preserving, and Studying Insects* Hutchinson
O'Toole, C. 1986 *The Encyclopaedia of Insects* George Allen & Unwin
Redfern, M. & Askew, R.R. 1992 *Plant Galls* Richmond
Richards, O.W. & Davies, R.G. 1977 *Imms' General Textbook of Entomology (10th Edition)* Chapman & Hall
Tweedie, M.W.F. 1968 *Pleasure from Insects* David & Charles
Zahradnik, J. & Chvala, M. 1989 *Insects: a Comprehensive Guide to Insects of Britain and Europe* Hamlyn

Apterygote Insects
Delany, M.J. 1954 *HIBI Vol.1, Part 2: Thysanura & Diplura*

Mayflies
Goddard, J. 1966 *Trout Fly Recognition* Black
Goddard, J. 1970 *Trout Flies of Still Water* Black
Harker, J. 1989 *Mayflies* Richmond
Harris, J.R. 1956 *An Angler's Entomology* (2nd Edition) Collins
Kimmins, D.E. 1950 *HIBI Vol.1, Part 9: Ephemeroptera*
Kimmins, D.E. 1972 Freshwater Biological Association Scientific Publication 15: *A Revised Key to the Adults of the British Species of Ephemeroptera*
Mellanby, H. 1975 *Animal Life in Fresh Water* (6th Edition) Chapman & Hall

Dragonflies

Aguilar, J.d', Dommanget, J-L. & Prechac, R. 1986 *A Field Guide to the Dragonflies of Britain, Europe, and North Africa* Collins

Askew, R.R. 1988 *The Dragonflies of Europe* Harley

Corbet, P.S. 1962 *A Biology of Dragonflies* Witherby

Corbet, P.S., Longfield, C., & Moore, N.W. 1960 *Dragonflies* Collins

Fraser, F.C. 1956 *HIBI Vol.I,Part 10: Odonata*

Gibbons, B. 1986 *Dragonflies and Damselflies of Britain and Northern Europe* Country Life

Hammond, C.O. 1983 *The Dragonflies of Great Britain and Ireland (2nd Edition, revised by R. Merritt) Harley*

McGeeney, A. 1986 *A Complete Guide to British Dragonflies* Cape

Miller, P.L. 1987 *Dragonflies* Richmond

Stoneflies

Goddard, J. 1966 *Trout Fly Recognition* Black

Harris, J.R. 1956 *An Angler's Entomology (2nd Edition)* Collins

Hynes, H.B.N.1977 Freshwater Biological Association Scientific Publication 17: *A Key to the Adults & Nymphs of British Stoneflies (Plecoptera) (3rd Edition)*

Kimmins, D.E. 1950 *HIBI Vol.I,Part 6: Plecoptera*

Grasshoppers and Crickets

Bellman, H. 1988 *A Field Guide to the Grasshoppers and Crickets of Britain and Northern Europe Collins*

Brown, V.K. 1983 *Grasshoppers* Richmond [includes crickets]

Harz, K. 1969 *The Orthoptera of Europe: Vol.I [Crickets & Bush- crickets] W.Junk, The Hague [in German & English]*

Harz, K. 1975 *The Orthoptera of Europe: Vol.II [Grasshoppers & Groundhoppers] W.Junk, The Hague [in German & English]*

Marshall, J.A. & Haes, E.C.M. 1988 *Grasshoppers and Allied Insects of Great Britain and Ireland* Harley [a tape recording of the insects' songs is available to accompany this book]

Ragge, D.R. 1965 *Grasshoppers, Crickets, and Cockroaches of the British Isles* Warne

Stick Insects

Harz, K. & Kaltenbach, A. 1976 *The Orthoptera of Europe Vol.III* W.Junk, The Hague [in German & English]

Marshall, J.A. & Haes, E.C.M. 1988 *Grasshoppers and Allied Insects of Great Britain and Ireland* Harley

Ragge, D.R. 1965 *Grasshoppers, Crickets and Cockroaches of the* British Isles *Warne*

Earwigs

Harz, K. & Kaltenbach, A. 1976 *The Orthoptera of Europe Vol.III* W.Junk, The Hague [in German & English]

Marshall, J.A. & Haes, E.C.M. 1988 *Grasshoppers and Allied Insects of Great Britain and Ireland* Harley

Web-spinners
Chopard, L. 1951 Faune de France Vol.56:*Orthopteroides*
Ross, E.S. 1966 Bulletin of the British Museum (Natural History) Entomology
Vol.17, No.7: *The Embioptera of Europe and the Mediterranean Region*

Cockroaches and Mantids
Harz, K. & Kaltenbach, A. 1976 *The Orthoptera of Europe Vol.III* W.Junk, The
Hague [in German & English]
Marshall, J.A. & Haes, E.C.M. 1988 *Grasshoppers and Allied Insects of Great Britain and Ireland* Harley
Ragge, D.R. 1965 *Grasshoppers, Crickets, and Cockroaches of the British Isles*
Warne

Termites
Harz, K. & Kaltenbach, A. 1976 *The Orthoptera of Europe Vol.III* W.Junk, The
Hague [in German & English]

Psocids (Booklice, etc)
New, T.R. 1974 *HIBI Vol.I, Part 7: Psocoptera*

Lice
Askew, R.R. 1971 *Parasitic Insects* Heinemann [biology, but no identification]
Baer, J.G. 1971 *Animal Parasites* Weidenfeld & Nicolson [biology, but no identification]

Bugs
Blackman, R. 1974 *Aphids* Ginn
Dixon, A.F.G. 1973 *Biology of Aphids* Arnold
Dolling, W.R. 1991 *The Hemiptera* Brit. Mus. (Nat. Hist.)/OUP
Hodkinson, I.D. & White, I.M. 1979 *HIBI Vol.II, Part 5(a): Homoptera Psylloidea*
Le Quesne, W.J. 1965 *HIBI Vol.II, Part 2(a): Hemiptera Cicadomorpha (excluding Deltocephalinae & Typhlocybinae)*
Le Quesne, W.J. 1969 *HIBI Vol.II, Part 2(b): Hemiptera Cicadomorpha Deltocephalinae*
Le Quesne, W.J. & Payne, K.R. 1981 *HIBI Vol.II, Part 2(c): Cicadellidae (Typhlocybinae)* (contains a full check list of British Auchenorrhyncha)
Le Quesne, W.J. 1960 *HIBI Vol.II, Part 3: Hemiptera Fulgoromorpha* [covers the superfamily Fulgoroidea]
Savage, A.A., 1989 Freshwater Biological Association Scientific Publication 50:
Adults of the British Aquatic Hemiptera Heteroptera
Southwood, T.R.E. & Leston, D. 1959 *Land and Water Bugs of the British Isles*
Warne
Stroyan, H.L.G. 1977 *HIBI Vol.II, Part 4(a): Aphidoidea – Chaitophoridae and Callaphididae*
Stroyan, H.L.G. 1984 *HIBI Vol. II, Part 6: Aphids –Pterocommatinae and Aphidinae (Aphidini)*
White, I.M. & Hodkinson, I.D. 1982 *HIBI Vol.II, Part 5(b): Psylloidea (Nymphal Stages)*

Thrips

Mound, L.A., Morison, G.D., Pitkin, B.R., & Palmer, J.M. 1976 *HIBI Vol.I, Part 11:Thysanoptera*

Lacewings and other Neuroptera

Aspock, H., Aspock, U., & Holzel, H. 1980 *Die Neuropteren Europas* Goecke & Evers (2 Vols.) [in German]

Fraser, F.C. 1959 *HIBI Vol.I, Parts 12&13: Mecoptera, Megaloptera, Neuroptera*

Killington, F.J. 1936-37 *Monograph of the British Neuroptera* Ray Society [2 vols]

Beetles

Balfour-Browne, F. 1940-50 *British Water Beetles* Ray Society [2 Vols]

Balfour-Browne,F. 1953 *HIBI Vol.IV, Part 3: Coleoptera: Hydradephaga*

Brendell, M.J.D. 1975 *HIBI Vol. V, Part 10: Coleoptera: Tenebrionidae*

Buck, F.D. 1954 *HIBI Vol.V, Part 9: Coleoptera: Lagriidae to Meloidae*

Clarke, R.O.S. 1973 *HIBI Vol.V, Part 2(c): Coleoptera: Heteroceridae*

Crowson, R.A. 1956 *HIBI Vol.IV, Part 1: Coleoptera: Introduction and Key to Families*

Duffy, E.A.J. 1952 *HIBI Vol.V, Part 12: Coleoptera: Cerambycidae*

Duffy, E.A.J. 1953 *HIBI Vol. V, Part 15: Coleoptera: Scolytidae and Platypodidae*

Evans, G. 1975 *The Life of Beetles* Allen & Unwin

Forsythe, T.G. 1987 *Common Ground Beetles* Richmond

Halstead, D.G.H. 1963 *HIBI Vol.IV, Part 10: Coleoptera: Histeroidea*

Harde, K.W. 1984 *A Field Guide in Colour to Beetles* Octopus

Jessop, L. 1986 *HIBI Vol.V, Part 11: Coleoptera: Scarabaeoidea*

Johnson, C. 1966 *HIBI Vol.IV, Part 6(a): Coleoptera: Clambidae*

Levy, B. 1977 *HIBI Vol.V, Part 1(b): Coleoptera: Buprestidae*

Lindroth, C.H. 1974 *HIBI Vol.IV, Part 2: Coleoptera: Carabidae*

Linssen, E.F. 1959 *Beetles of the British Isles* Warne [2 Vols]

Majerus, M. & Kearns, P. 1989 *Ladybirds* Richmond

Morris, M.G. 1990 *HIBI Vol.V, Part 16: Coleoptera: Curculionoidea (part)* [excludes Curculionidae]

Morris, M.G. 1991 *Weevils* Richmond

Peacock, E.R. 1977 *HIBI Vol.V, Part 5(a): Coleoptera: Rhizophagidae*

Pearce, E.J. 1957 *HIBI Vol.IV, Part 9: Coleoptera: Pselaphidae*

Pope, R.D. 1953 *HIBI Vol.V, Part 7: Coleoptera: Coccinellidae and Sphindidae*

Thompson, R.T. 1958 *HIBI Vol.V, Part 5(b): Coleoptera: Phalacridae*

Tottenham, C.E. 1954 *HIBI Vol.IV, Part 8(a): Coleoptera: Staphylinidae (part)*

Walsh, G.B. & Dibb, J.R. 1975 *A Coleopterist's Handbook* Amateur Entomologists' Society

Zahradnik, J. 1985 *Käfer Mittel- und Nordwesteuropas* Parey [in German]

Stylopids

Linssen, E.F. 1959 *Beetles of the British Isles* (Vol.II) Warne

Scorpion Flies

Fraser, F.C. 1959 *HIBI Vol.I, Parts 12&13: Mecoptera, Megaloptera, Neuroptera*

Fleas

Askew, R.R. 1971 *Parasitic Insects* Heinemann
Rothschild, M. & Clay, T. 1952 *Fleas, Flukes, and Cuckoos* Collins
Smit, F.G.A.M. 1957 *HIBI Vol.I, Part 16: Siphonaptera*

True Flies (Diptera)

Askew, R.R. 1971 *Parasitic Insects* Heinemann
Coe, R.L. 1953 *HIBI Vol.X, Part 1: Diptera: Syrphidae*
Coe, R.L. 1966 *HIBI Vol.X, Part 2(c): Diptera: Pipunculidae*
Coe, R.L., Freeman, P. & Mattingly, P.F. 1950 *HIBI Vol.IX, Part 2: Diptera: Nematocera (part)*
Colyer, C.N. & Hammond, C.O. 1968 *Flies of the British Isles* Warne
Disney, R.H.L. 1983 *HIBI Vol.X, Part 6: Diptera: Phoridae (except Megaselia)*
Disney, R.H.L. 1989 *HIBI Vol.X, Part 8: Diptera: Phoridae (genus Megaselia)*
Edwards, F.W., Oldroyd, H. & Smart, J. 1939 *British Blood-sucking Flies* British Museum (Nat. Hist)
Emden, F.I.van 1954 *HIBI Vol.X,Part 4(a): Diptera: Cyclorrhapha* (Tachinidae, Calliphoridae)
Fonseca, E.C.M. d'Assis 1968 *HIBI Vol.X, Part 4(b): Diptera: Cyclorrhapha (Muscidae)*
Fonseca, E.C.M. d'Assis 1978 *HIBI Vol.IX, Part 5: Diptera: Dolichopodidae*
Freeman, P. 1983 *HIBI Vol.IX, Part 6: Diptera: Sciaridae*
Freeman, P. & Lane, R.P. 1985 *HIBI Vol.IX, Part 7: Diptera: Bibionidae and Scatopsidae*
Gilbert, F.S. 1986 *Hoverflies* Richmond
Hutson, A.M. 1984 *HIBI Vol.X, Part 7: Diptera: Hippoboscidae and Nycteribiidae*
Hutson, A.M., Ackland, D.M. & Kidd, L.N. 1980 *HIBI Vol.IX, Part 3: Diptera: Mycetophilidae*
Marshall, J.F. 1938 *The British Mosquitoes* British Museum (Nat. Hist.)
Oldroyd, H. 1964 *The Natural History of Flies* Weidenfeld & Nicolson
Oldroyd, H. 1969 *HIBI Vol.IX, Part 4: Diptera: Tabanoidea and Asiloidea*
Oldroyd, H. 1970 *HIBI Vol.IX, Part 1: Diptera: Introduction and Key to Families*
Pitkin, B.R. 1988 *HIBI Vol.X, Part 5(e): Diptera: Sphaeroceridae*
Pont, A.C. 1979 *HIBI Vol.X, Part 5(c): Diptera: Sepsidae*
Smith, K.G.V. 1969 *HIBI Vol.X,Part 2(ai): Diptera: Lonchopteridae*
Smith, K.G.V. 1969 *HIBI Vol.X, Part 3(a): Diptera: Conopidae*
Smith, K.G.V. 1989 *HIBI Vol.X, Part 14: Diptera: An Introduction to the Immature Stages*
Snow, K.R. 1989 *Mosquitoes* Richmond
Spencer, K.A. 1972 *HIBI Vol.X, Part 5(g): Diptera: Agromyzidae*
Stubbs, A.E. & Chandler, P. 1978 *A Dipterist's Handbook* Amateur Entomologists' Society [contains keys to larvae]
Stubbs, A.E. & Falk, S.J. 1983 *British Hoverflies* British Entomological and Natural History Society
White, I.M. 1988 *HIBI Vol.X, Part 5(a): Diptera: Tephritidae*

Butterflies and Moths

Beirne, B.P. 1954 *British Pyralid and Plume Moths* Warne

Bradley, J.D., Tremewan, W.G., & Smith, A. 1973 and 1979 *British Tortricoid Moths* Ray Society [2 vols]

Carter, D.J. & Hargreaves, B. 1986 *A Field Guide to Caterpillars of Butterflies and Moths in Britain and Europe* Collins

Chinery, M. 1989 *The New Generation Guide to the Butterflies and Day-Flying Moths of Britain and Europe* Collins

Emmet, A.M. & Heath, J. *The Moths and Butterflies of Great Britain and Ireland Vol.7, Part 1: The Butterflies* Harley

Ford, E.B. 1957 *Butterflies* Collins

Ford, E.B. 1972 *Moths* Collins

Friedrich, E. 1986 *Breeding Butterflies and Moths - a Practical Handbook for British and European Species* Harley

Goater, B. 1986 *British Pyralid Moths - a Guide to their Identification* Harley

Heath, J. 1976 *The Moths and Butterflies of Great Britain and Ireland Vol.I (Micropterigidae - Heliozelidae)* Curwen Press

Heath, J. & Emmet, A.M. 1985 *The Moths and Butterflies of Great Britain and Ireland Vol.2 (Cossidae - Heliodinidae)* [includes burnets and clearwings] Harley

Heath, J. & Emmet, A.M. 1979 *The Moths and Butterflies of Great Britain and Ireland Vol.9 (Sphingidae - Noctuidae (part 1))* Curwen

Heath, J. & Emmet. A.M. 1983 *The Moths and Butterflies of Great Britain and Ireland Vol.10 (Noctuidae (part 2) and Agaristidae)* Harley

Higgins, L.G. & Hargreaves, B. 1983 *The Butterflies of Britain and Europe* Collins

Higgins. L.G. & Riley, N.D. 1983 *A Field Guide to the Butterflies of Britain and Europe* Collins

Howarth, T.G. 1984 *Colour Identification Guide to Butterflies of the British Isles* Viking

Novak, I. 1980 *A Field Guide in Colour to Butterflies and Moths* Octopus

Scoble, M.J. 1992 *The Lepidoptera: Form, Function and Diversity* Brit. Mus. (Nat. Hist.)/OUP

Skinner, B. 1984 *Colour Identification Guide to Moths of the British Isles* Viking

Thomas. J.A. 1986 *Butterflies of the British Isles* Country Life

Thomas, J.A. & Lewington, R. 1991 *The Butterflies of Britain and Ireland* Dorling Kindersley

Whalley, P. 1979 *Butterflies of Britain and Europe* Hamlyn

Whalley, P. 1980 *Butterfly Watching* Severn House

Whalley, P. 1981 *Pocket Guide to Butterflies* Mitchell Beazley

Caddis Flies

Goddard, J. 1966 *Trout Fly Recognition* Black

Hickin, N.E. 1967 *Caddis Larvae* Hutchinson

Macan, T.T. 1973 Freshwater Biological Association Scientific Publication No. 28: *A Key to the Adults of the British Trichoptera*

Marshall, J.E. 1978 *HIBI Vol.I, Part 14(a): Trichoptera Hydroptilidae*

Mellanby, H. 1975 *Animal Life in Fresh Water* (6th Edition) Chapman & Hall

Bees, Wasps, Ants, and other Hymenoptera

Alford, D.V. 1975 *Bumblebees* Davis-Poynter

Andrewes, C. 1969 *The Lives of Bees and Wasps* Chatto & Windus

Askew, R.R. 1968 *HIBI Vol.VIII, Part 2(b): Hymenoptera: Chalcidoidea (part)*

Askew, R.R. 1971 *Parasitic Insects* Heinemann

Benson, R.B. 1952 *HIBI Vol.VI, Part 2(b): Hymenoptera: Symphyta* [covers only family Tenthredinidae]

Benson, R.B. 1958 *HIBI Vol.Vi, Part 2(c): Hymenoptera: Symphyta* [covers only sub-family Nematinae of family Tenthredinidae]

Betts, C. & Laffoley, D. 1986 *The Hymenopterist's Handbook* Amateur Entomologists' Society (2nd Edition)

Bolton, B. & Collingwood, C.A. 1975 *HIBIVol.VI, Part 3(c): Hymenoptera: Formicidae*

Darlington, A. 1968 *The Pocket Encyclopaedia of Plant Galls in Colour* Blandford

Day, M.C. 1988 *HIBI Vol. VI, Part 4: Hymenoptera: Pompilidae*

Donisthorpe, H.St J. K. 1927 *British Ants, their Life History and Classification* Routledge

Donisthorpe, H.St J. K. 1927 *The Guests of British Ants, their Habits and Life Histories* Routledge

Eady, R.D. & Quinlan, J. 1963 *HIBI Vol.VIII, Part 1(a): Hymenoptera:Cynipoidea (part)* [includes the gall wasps]

Fergusson, N.D.M. 1986 *HIBI Vol.VIII, Part 1(c): Hymenoptera: Cynipoidea (part)*

Ferriere, C. & Kerrich, G.J. 1958 *HIBI Vol.VIII, Part 2(a): Hymenoptera: Chalcidoidea (part)*

Fitton, M.G., Shaw, M.R. & Gauld, I.D. 1988 *HIBI Vol.VII, Part 1: Hymenoptera: Ichneumonidae (Pimplinae)*

Free, J.B. & Butler, C.G. 1959 *Bumblebees* Collins

Gauld, I.D.& Bolton, B. 1988 *The Hymenoptera* British Museum (Nat. Hist.)/OUP

Gauld, I.D. & Mitchell, P.A. 1977 *HIBI Vol.VII, Part 2(b): Hymenoptera: Ichneumonidae (part)*

Morgan, D. 1984 *HIBI Vol.VI, Part 5: Hymenoptera: Chrysididae*

Nixon, G.E.J. 1980 *HIBI Vol.VIII, Part 3(di): Hymenoptera: Proctotrupoidea - Diapriidae (Diapriinae)*

Nixon, G.E.J. 1957 *HIBI Vol.VIII, Part 3(dii): Hymenoptera: Proctotrupoidea - Diapriidae (Belytinae)*

Perkins, J.F. 1959 *HIBI Vol.VII, Part 2(ai): Hymenoptera: Ichneumonidae (part)* [includes key to sub-families]

Perkins, J.F. 1960 *HIBI Vol.VII, Part 2(aii): Hymenoptera: Ichneumonidae (part)*

Perkins, J.F. 1976 *HIBI Vol.VI, Part 3(a): Hymenoptera: Bethyloidea* [covers families Embolemidae, Bethylidae, and Dryinidae - all now in Chrysidoidea]

Prys-Jones, O.E. & Corbet, S.A. 1987 *Bumblebees* Richmond

Quinlan, J. 1978 *HIBI Vol.VIII, Part 1(b): Hymenoptera: Cynipoidea - Eucoilidae*

Quinlan, J. & Gauld, I.D. 1981 *HIBI Vol.VI, Part 2(a): Hymenoptera: Symphyta (except Tenthredinidae)*

Richards, O.W. 1953 *The Social Insects* MacDonald

Richards, O.W. 1956 *HIBI Vol.VI, Part 1: Hymenoptera: Introduction and Key to Families*

Richards, O.W. 1980 *HIBI Vol.VI, Part 3(b): Hymenoptera: Scolioidea, Vespoidea and Sphecoidea*

Spradberry, J.P. 1973 *Wasps* Sidgwick & Jackson
Westrich, P. 1989 *Die Wildbienen Baden-Wurtembergs* Eugen Ulmer [in German:
    covers all British species. 2 Vols]
Yeo, P.F. & Corbet, S.A. 1983 *Solitary Wasps* Richmond

Index

Figures in bold type refer to colour plates